AGRICULTURE, ECONOMICS, AND RESOURCE MANAGEMENT

AGRICULTURE,
ECONOMICS, AND
RESOURCE MANAGEMENT

MILTON M. SNODGRASS

New Mexico State University

L. T. WALLACE

University of California, Berkeley

PRENTICE-HALL, INC.

Englewood Cliffs, New Jersey

Library of Congress Cataloging in Publication Data

SNODGRASS, MILTON MOORE
    Agriculture, economics, and resource management.

    Published in 1964 and 1970 under title: Agriculture, economics, and growth.
    Includes bibliographical references and index.
    1. Agriculture—Economic aspects—United States.
I. Wallace, Luther T., joint author.   II. Title.
HD1761.S58   1975   338.1′0973   74-23959
ISBN   0-13-018812-3

© 1975 by Prentice-Hall, Inc., Englewood Cliffs, New Jersey

Ed. 3

Printed in the United States of America

10   9   8   7   6   5   4   3   2   1

Prentice-Hall International, Inc., *London*
Prentice-Hall of Australia, Pty. Ltd., *Sydney*
Prentice-Hall of Canada, Ltd., *Toronto*
Prentice-Hall of India Private Limited, *New Delhi*
Prentice-Hall of Japan, Inc., *Tokyo*

Contents

v

PART FOUR

PART FIVE

Preface

Agriculture, Economics, and Resource Management, formerly published under the title *Agriculture, Economics, and Growth,* has several objectives: (1) to combine descriptive material into a meaningful context of resource use management in agriculture; (2) to provide a brief, easy-to-read exposition of the more important microeconomic principles and other business management tools used in decision making; (3) to give an analytical presentation of some of the physical and human resource adjustment problems resulting from our economy's development; and (4) to provide relevant data for interpretation and analysis. This book is intended for use as a beginning text in agricultural economics, but it should also be useful in rural economics, resource economics, agricultural business management, and other introductory courses in which an applied problem-solving approach is normally used. The material is directed more toward the beginner in economics and related courses than the intermediate or advanced student. It is designed for easy reading and understanding. No attempt is made to take a sophisticated approach to economics by using highly technical presentations. Appendices are used to entice the more advanced student to delve deeper into the subject. Everyday language has been used in the text because we feel that this approach is more likely to stimulate the beginning student's interest in economics.

The focus of this book is on agriculture and resource use and the adjustment situations people face with their productive resources. We have tried to impress the student with the dynamics of economics, the breadth and scope of the subject, and the excitement, stimulation, and personal satisfaction that come from its study. For these reasons we frequently refer to the interrelationships evident in the economy, such as those between the agricultural and industrial sectors, population and food supply, government policies and their effects on agriculture and the household, and legislative policies and the physical environment.

We have divided our book into seven parts. Such a division allows us to place the elements, description, theory, management, and policies of economics in proper perspective. Part One provides the setting for resource use management and decision making. It deals with the substance of economics and the interrelationships of agricultural and non-agricultural economic life.

Part Two includes descriptive chapters on the physical environment and the sometimes competitive public and private interests in resource use. Waste management, energy resources, and resource use policy are also discussed. Separate chapters on population and labor force, technology, and capital integrate these resources into the decision making process.

Part Three describes the characteristics of U.S. farms and food production. It also has chapters on the systems for marketing food and fiber. Food consumption, nutrition, and dietary levels around the world are presented.

Part Four describes the basic micro principles and tools of economic analysis. No attempt has been made to include all of them, leaving the teacher with the task of carrying the student through whatever refinements of the basic principles are considered desirable. Concepts of a production function and simple input-output analysis, including factor-factor, factor-product, and product-product relationships, are explained. The notion of supply and cost curves is derived from a discussion of production, while the idea of demand is developed from a discussion of consumption. Price discovery and determination in perfect and imperfect market situations are presented along with a study of the principles of consumption, elasticity, and profit maximization.

Part Five focuses on the role of management in decision making. The functions of observing, analyzing, taking action, assuming responsibility, and evaluating are carried through three kinds of management situations: production, finance, and marketing. In addition to the many examples used in the text, a case problem is set out for interested students.

Part Six provides an overview of the world agricultural situation.

One chapter examines world food needs; the other discusses the potential for increasing world food supplies. Resource availability, the "package of technology" concept, infrastructure, and research and education are topics which are woven together with the material covered in preceding chapters.

Part Seven provides an introduction to the problem-solving approach in policy formulation. It draws on material from the previous sections to discuss relevant policy issues of resource development, farm price and income policy, and international trade. A brief discussion of other persisting problems, including the future of family farms and some of the issues involved in regulation, taxation, and land use, concludes the book.

To summarize, this book emphasizes resource management for both public and private gain, rather than economic growth. It also expands the treatment of applied business management, and integrates farm and nonfarm agricultural enterprises with a focus on the total food system. These new directions have resulted in a substantial change in direction from our first book.

We are indebted to all who helped us in writing and revising this book. Their help has been, and continues to be, invaluable to us. We would also like to express our gratitude to our many colleagues who have used the book and made valuable suggestions for increasing its classroom effectiveness. Particular thanks go to Ellie Rotondo, who typed and assembled the necessary materials, to Marion O'Regan, who updated the statistical information presented, and to Frances Balcomb, who compiled the index.

Milton M. Snodgrass

L. T. Wallace

AGRICULTURE, ECONOMICS, AND RESOURCE MANAGEMENT

PART ONE

1

An Introduction to Economics, Agricultural Economics, and Resource Management

THE WHY AND WHAT OF ECONOMICS

Why Study Economics?

There are many reasons why people study economics. Perhaps the most important reason is that everyone makes economic decisions throughout his entire life whether he knows it or not. Although everyone is a practicing economist, the old adage, "practice makes perfect," is not usually true unless economic decisions are accompanied by an awareness and understanding of the fundamentals of the social science of economics. From the day one gets his first penny to spend or save, he is involved in making economic decisions. Studying economics helps a person make better decisions about spending and saving money, about using his time, and about making a living for himself and his family. In fact, the functioning and well-being of our entire democratic and capitalistic society depend to a large extent upon the degree to which the citizenry is well-informed and economically literate. These are some of the reasons people study economics.

3

What Is Economics?

All social sciences concern human behavior. Whereas the physical scientist deals with inanimate objects and the biological scientist is concerned with living plants and animals, the social scientist is interested in people and their reactions to different situations. Social sciences include psychology, for example, which is concerned primarily with individual behavior, and sociology, which is devoted more to group activities. Economics is the social science concerned with how individuals and society choose to allocate their scarce resources (means) among different ends over time.

Becoming proficient in the use of economics is an art that draws heavily on personal insight, training, and judgment. An exceptional economist is one who can combine an excellence in identifying relevant economic questions, an excellence in the understanding of economic theory, and a proficiency in solving problems and interpreting the results.

Any definition of economics includes certain basic notions:

1. The idea of *allocation*—of putting resources (synonymous with inputs, raw materials, and factors of production) or products (synonymous with output or goods) to some use.
2. The idea of *scarcity*—that there simply are not enough inputs to make enough goods to satisfy the nearly insatiable wants of all the individuals and groups in the world.
3. The idea of establishing *goals* or *ends* or *objectives*. Human wants (desires) are unlimited for us as individuals and groups. This necessarily means that *wants compete* for the scarce resources. Because of this competition, we must decide on a priority among our competing wants, and do our best to get the most satisfaction from those chosen.
4. Finally, we must include some reference to *time*. This permits flexibility between short and long time periods and allows for changes in the entire system of goals over time.

The following incorporates these ideas into a definition of economics: *Economics is the allocation of scarce resources between competing ends for the maximization of those chosen ends over time, with provision for maintaining and modifying the system of choice.* (Figure 1-1 illustrates the general subject matter underlying the study of economics.)

The Nature of Human Wants

Everyone can think of something that he would like to have more of. Little children want "just one more" drink of water before they go to bed at night. The head of the family wants more money than he now makes so he can give his family more. A housewife wants a little more

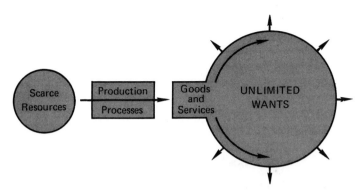

FIGURE 1-1
Scarce Resources Attempt to Satisfy Unlimited
Wants via Production

time to make her house clean and neat. We all want just a little more time to enjoy life and not to be so rushed. All of us, as individuals and as parts of groups of people within society, want things we do not have. Church groups want more churches. Civic groups say we need more schools, better roads, and more of the "right kind" of local government. State governments have long lists of things they need. National governments are the same way. Congress is always considering legislation that the entire society or special-interest groups want. Remember any election platform you can think of, and check off all the items for which improvements were promised.

Unlimited or insatiable wants are not restricted to only economic, material things. You may want to be a better artist or piano player just for your own personal enjoyment. Or you may want to help out at Sunday school or in a volunteer children's group. These things bring satisfaction to you, and in making you aware of this satisfaction, they make you want more.

There are at least five broad groupings of human wants. A desire for the essentials of life (food, clothing, and shelter) commands first priority on man's productive efforts. All people in all societies and countries are alike in this respect. When a family has only a bare minimum of these essentials, it can be said to exist at a subsistence level.

The relative importance of the remaining four groupings of human wants varies among individuals and societies. These groupings are a desire for self-expression and development, a desire for recognition and approval by others, a desire for power, and a desire for the welfare of others. By attending college, one develops his own mental capacities and communicative skills. Perhaps you have already won public recog-

nition and approval by winning a scholarship. Everyone yearns for social acceptance; some seek it from the masses, others seek discriminating
praise from a select few. Economic wealth can bring you a degree of
power over other people. Being captain of a winning team may also
satisfy this desire. You can observe a desire for the welfare of others
most easily within the family group. Some parents willingly make financial and other sacrifices so their children can attend college. Other people devote their lives to missionary and social work. Our local, state, and
federal governments give aid to the needy.

The Economizing Process

The economizing process helps solve the conflict between unlimited
wants and scarce resources. The best way to understand this process is in
terms of a resource–product or input–output relationship. This relationship simply describes the amount of product produced from a certain
set of resources. Essentially, the economizing process is used to improve
on this input–output relationship. Improvement can be made in one
of three ways:

1. Getting more from the same amount of resources by holding inputs
   constant and increasing output. Example: A greater amount of corn
   may be obtained from sowing the same amount of seed by using an
   improved hybrid variety.
2. Getting the same amount of product but using less resources by decreasing inputs while holding output constant. Example: Fewer total
   dollars may be required to produce an automobile if certain pieces of
   automatic equipment are used.
3. Getting more product by using relatively less resources by increasing
   input while increasing output relatively more. Example: A department-
   store manager may more than double sales by doubling his sales force.[1]

The economizing process is useful in analyzing many questions
found in everyday living. Automation is an effort to implement the
economizing process, as is the situation in which a farmer buys a self-
propelled combine and no longer needs a hired man.

The Basic Questions Every Society Must Answer

Every society the world over has been confronted with four basic
questions: *What* should be produced? *When* should it be produced?
How should it be produced and distributed? *Who* should receive the

---

[1] Point 3 is really a matter of selecting the correct point on a production surface
at which to operate.

income from its sale? We as individuals must also answer these questions. By answering them again and again, we continually go back to the basic conflict that gives rise to economics—limited resources and unlimited wants. The answers we find also point out the role each person plays in the economy: producer, consumer, citizen, or planner.

What goods and services shall be produced?   Limited resources keep a society from having all the goods and services the people want. So a society needs some mechanism to guide the use of limited resources into the production of goods and services that will satisfy as many of the people's wants as possible. In our private-enterprise economy, we rely on our commodity pricing system and the buying habits of all individuals taken together to be the mechanism that determines the amount and the kinds of goods that will be produced. Every time a person purchases a candy bar, he is essentially voting for the use of some resources in the production of candy bars. Historically, when people began to use more automobiles than horses for transportation, fewer buggy whips and carriages were bought. Society discontinued its votes for whips and carriages and, accordingly, fewer resources were allocated for their production.

Some goods and services in our economy, such as national highways and defense protection, are consumed collectively by all the citizenry. The decisions of how much and what kind of goods are to be consumed collectively, and the amount of resources that are to be used in their production, are made by elected and appointed officials of county, municipal, state, and federal governments. This is often referred to as the public sector of the economy. By voting for representatives to state and national legislatures (the state senate, state house of representatives, or Congress), we essentially have a voice in what goods will be produced by the public sector. One may also vote on local issues, such as whether or not to build a new school. In these ways, each individual in society helps decide what use, public or private, will be made of the limited resources at hand.

When shall goods and services be produced?   The question of *when* to produce a good or service is important because society's output must satisfy both immediate wants and wants that exist over a long period of time. Decisions made now must be based partially on what we want for the present and what we expect in the future. A decision facing a newly married couple is *when* to build a house. Even though they will not build the house themselves, they help make the decisions as to when houses are built by deciding when they can afford to buy a house.

Another example of the *when* question is, Should there be a crash program to produce a commodity quickly (such as a cancer cure), should there be a gradual program of orderly research, or should there be no program at all? In this instance, as before, the spending habits of people (market voting), commodity prices, and policies of chosen and appointed government officials guide the decision as to when goods will be produced.

How shall goods and services be produced and distributed? We have already said that it requires scarce resources to produce any good or service. Common sense tells us to attempt to economize on these scarce inputs, since they cost money. A producer must decide *how* to produce his product. He will try to utilize the latest technology possible. He will try to combine the proper amounts of each of the inputs necessary for production so that he can produce at as low a cost as possible. The *how* question is thus solved or decided upon by entrepreneurs (producers) as they attempt to find the least-cost way (minimum use of resources) in making the product. They search for the best way because other competitors are after their markets and they want to realize as much return as possible from their efforts.

Once the product is made, the manager must decide how to get it into the hands of the people who want to use it. Should he send it by truck, rail, air, or water? Should he store it in warehouses in various parts of the country? What should be his inventory policy based on his probable production and the anticipated desire for the product? These are the kinds of production and marketing questions each business manager, each farmer, and every government agency must ask and answer.

Who should receive the income from the sale of the goods and services produced? This question could be illustrated in the following way: When a homemaker buys a loaf of bread for 55 cents, how many of the 55 pennies should go to the farmer who produced the wheat, how many to the grain elevator that stored the wheat, how many to the railroad or truck agency that transported the wheat to the milling company, how many to the milling company, how many to the bakery, and how many to the retailer who sold the bread? This is a difficult question. In our relatively free-enterprise economy, where individuals are able, for the most part, to own the factors of production, we believe that each scarce resource should bring a "fair" return to its owner.

However, when viewing the total economy, we realize that not all people in our society are able to contribute inputs to the production processes. Should any of the income generated in the economy go to those who do not participate in production? Certainly, family breadwinners use their income to care for the members of their family who are not producers in the same sense. But above that, the humanitarian drive in most of us says that people sometimes deserve income even though they supply little or no inputs. For example, many people give money to charities. Those suffering from flood or fire disaster, or those unemployed for long periods of time, are given aid. The question of *who* essentially revolves around how the total income pie will be cut; how big a piece of money income should each member of society receive?

Micro- and Macroeconomics

In a capitalistic economic system such as we have in the United States, private ownership of productive resources predominates. The question of *what* is produced, *how,* and *when* get answered in market-places. For example, references to the auto market, the labor market, the food market, and the money market are common. *Microeconomics* is the study of individual business firms and markets and the relationships among them. Prices established in various markets through the forces of supply and demand act to answer the *why, how,* and *when* questions. Prices allocate resources into the production of goods and services and then move them into consumption. *Microeconomics,* then, concerns itself with individual producers, consumers, and markets. The economic principles discussed later in the book will be *micro* in their orientation.

However, when attention is given to large groups in the economy and we are involved in economic studies and policies directed toward broad aggregates such as the level of employment, the subject is referred to as *macroeconomics.* Forces that determine the total output of goods and services, the total level of spending by consumers, the total investments made by businessmen, or the total effects of government taxation —these are some of the items of interest in *macroeconomics.*

Both are equally important. An understanding of *microeconomic* principles may be relatively more important in helping a businessman make his everyday operational decisions. However, an understanding of *macroeconomics* is helpful also, because it explains part of the economic environment within which the businessman works. For example, macro-economic policies may determine interest rates in general, and business-men must adjust their firms' operating and credit policies to make profits accordingly. In this case, the micro adjusts to the macro.

Nonmarket Resource Allocation

Nonmarket allocations of resources refers to the production of goods and services that are not generally demanded in any consumer market but that exert an increasingly large impact on our economy. Nonmarket allocations most usually result from government decisions to do something that is in the public interest. The creation of national and state parks is an example. No one goes out to buy or sell a park; there are no markets for parks as there are for shoes or cars. However, the government decision to create parks, urged by many private groups and individuals, has led to much employment and income generation associated with their "production." It has led to much debate about *where* the park site ought to be (should land be bought here or there?), and to many satisfied "consumers" (park visitors).

Another example of nonmarket allocations of resources is dams for power, irrigation, conservation, and recreation. The continued subsidy for the postal service is the result of a decision to partially finance mail service for all of America. Certain types of public-health funding and educational programs would also be instances. Perhaps the most dramatic example of nonmarket resource allocations is activities associated with war and defense. Certainly, no one ever went out and bought and sold wars, but just as certainly, a large proportion of the economic activity in this country today is associated with defense industries.

ECONOMIC GOALS OF SOCIETY

Economic Progress

Stop and think for a moment what you want the economic system to provide for you. A good job that will allow you to earn money so that you can provide for yourself and a family probably rates very high. But how good a job? How much money or how many goods and services will you be happy with? Will you be satisfied with the job as a job? You would probably like to see your income grow over time, so that a larger quantity of goods and services can be yours. In short, you want economic *growth* or *progress*. This is one of the goals of individuals and of the whole nation.

Economic Stability

You also want the dollar you earn to have a stable purchasing power. Inflation, which means a rise in price levels without more goods and services, reduces your purchasing power. So another goal you have is economic *stability*. Closely allied to price stability is output stability. Output decreases result in unemployment, which is a severe blow to the families involved. In the early 1970s, the U.S. economy was plagued with both unemployment and inflation at undesirable levels at the same time, a situation of great economic instability.

Economic Justice

A third goal is economic *justice*. What is the "best" distribution of the national income pie? How many rich people are enough? What about those who cannot work, or seemingly do not want to work? Our tax system is progressive, meaning that as one's income level increases, his relative burden of tax increases. Charities are a popular and acceptable way to redistribute income from the rich to the poor. Virtually all ancient civilizations exhibited a high degree of inequality. How do you feel about the present situation in the United States?

Economic Security

Fourth, citizens want some degree of economic *security*, for themselves and their families, against old age, death, disability, and unemployment. In many civilizations past and present, this type of security has been provided by the person's family, his religious order, or his tribe. The life insurance industry thrives because people wish to provide, after their death, economic security for their families. In order to cover those who do not carry life insurance with private companies, and to provide them some income after active employment, a Social Security system is imposed by law for nearly all workers, regardless of their involvement with private pension plans.

Economic Freedom

Finally, everyone wants economic *freedom*. This means freedom to compete in the production of goods and services at a job of one's choosing. It also means freedom to spend one's income without interference and consume whatever goods and services one chooses.

However, all citizens accept some constraints on freedom. No one wants a person qualified only as a truck driver to perform brain surgery. Neither are citizens free to purchase (consume) the services of a professional gunman. Thus, one boundary to freedom is legal constraints. Another constraint is physical limitations. You are not free to purchase and consume a meal in a restaurant if all the tables are occupied.

Interrelationships among Economic Goals

It should be apparent already that certain of the economic goals compete with one another. Economists continually debate whether eco-

nomic growth can occur over time without generating economic instability. The Social Security system, which requires every worker to put
aside some of his current income, directly restricts his economic freedom.
So does the law that limits the acreage of a crop a farmer can produce.
The progressive income tax system restricts the freedom of some, but
contributes to increased economic opportunities for others.

However, there are also complementarities among the goals. Economic growth tends to improve a person's economic security. For the
poor, more economic justice contributes to their economic security and
freedom.

The important idea to remember is that neither the individual nor
society as a whole can have all these goals in an unlimited amount. It is
vital, however, that each citizen understand them and exercise his privilege of communicating his feelings about them to others and to his
government representatives. It will become evident in later chapters that
compromise and trade-offs among these goals are the foundations and
essence of economic policy determinations.

ECONOMIC METHOD AND METHODOLOGY

How and why do economists think in the ways they do? What do
they do? Some economists work to describe actual situations in the
economy; others consider theoretical situations, which might explain
observed or potential economic behavior of individuals, groups, and nations. Other economists concern themselves with applied studies directed
to helping solve the here-and-now kinds of economic problems of firms
and communities. All three general economic interests are woven together in the making of economic policy.

But first, let's establish the difference between method and
methodology. *Methodology* concerns itself with the philosophy of economics that is pursued by an economist, that school of economic thought
he deems pertinent to the problem on which he is working. It covers the
broad theoretical bases of economics, from capitalism to communism,
from the "invisible hand" to international cartels, from institutionalists
to laissez-faire to pure government control.

Method, on the other hand, is simply a tool of analysis. Method
covers many analytical techniques—regression, cross-tabular analysis,
simulation, input–output, and so on. But in each case, the method is
governed by the methodology—by the framework in which the economic
analyst chooses to display his tool kit. *Method* embraces all the statistics
and mathematics devised and devisable. *Methodology* decides how and
where and why these tools should be used.

Descriptive Studies

Descriptive economic studies are concerned with gathering the facts relevant to a particular economic problem or part of the economy. Gathering facts on the behavior of individuals as they produce, exchange, and consume goods and services is not easy. The real world is cluttered with a myriad of facts. Careful sorting and arranging for relevancy is an important task for economists.

Theoretical Studies

An economic theory is a valid generalization or principle concerning economic behavior, derived by observation and logical reasoning. An economic theory of consumption, for instance, is that people will buy more steak if the price is lowered. Theory or principle formulation is one of the most practical things man has. You do things a particular way because you know what will happen if another way is chosen instead. You eat meals pretty much on schedule because if you do not, you might go hungry or you might have to cook your own. Again, look around you and observe how many things you do consciously or unconsciously that are based on theory, and how often you think, "If I do not do this or act in this way, then these will be the consequences." Theory is a practical guide in almost every phase of our human existence.

Economic-Policy Formulation

A policy is a specific plan of action, by a legislative body or a firm's management, designed to attain a specified goal within a designated span of time. All policies control and influence economic behavior or its consequences. All policies internalize value judgments about economic growth, stability, justice, security, and freedom. Whether you as an individual are in favor of a particular policy depends on the relative importance of each of these economic goals in your own value system. Thus, two reputable economists can disagree over what the policy ought to be, even though they use the same body of theoretical economics. Their different points of view are a reflection of their own personal value systems with regard to the five economic goals and their particular methodological views, and not the result of "bad economics." An economist who works in the policy area of economics often wears two hats— one as an economist and the other as a policy maker. Test yourself. Can you distinguish among economic facts, economic principles, statements of value judgments, and economic policy?

Using Economics to Solve Problems

Economics utilizes the problem-solving approach in situations now found in real life or in possible future situations. By understanding economic theory, we are better able to identify problems that are occurring within our economy now and might occur as our country grows. After a problem is identified, theory is used to choose the most meaningful alternative ways of solving it. Policy makers then choose the alternative they feel will best solve the problem. This procedure has been called the "alternative-consequence" approach to problem solving through economics. This approach is equally applicable to an individual or a group.

The dynamics (changing nature) of the economic growth process enable us to see how one part of our economy is related to another. For example, one can trace the consequences of people's moving out of farming into manufacturing and service jobs. One can predict and test what the economic results of a particular course of action will be by identifying and describing the problem situation in meaningful terms, and analyzing it with the problem-solving "alternative-consequences" approach.

The economist is placed in a unique position by being trained to be aware of the various roles played by business firms, government agencies, and consumers in our interrelated economy. Because of his training to seek cause and effect, to discover the "why" of decision making, he can help formulate courses of action, or policies, that society deems desirable. He can also help in the adjustment of resources and people in a dynamic economy.

POSSIBLE OBSTACLES IN STUDYING ECONOMICS

Many people think economics is so complicated that they will never master the subject. Perhaps some of the following points will help you find economics easier than others have found it.

Economic Terminology

All sciences use words that pertain specifically to the subject matter of their disciplines. Economics is no different. Some words—for example, the words "capital" and "investment"—have meanings different from those commonly used "on the street." Also, several words are sometimes used to describe essentially the same thing. For instance, the words *law, principle, theory,* and *economic model* have essentially the same meaning, and so do *input, resource,* and *factor of production.*

"Other Things Equal" Assumption

Since social scientists deal with people, and people cannot be locked up and isolated as plants, animals, and atoms can, the economist must use certain specialized techniques. For example, in analyzing the relationship of the price of steak to the amount consumers buy, he assumes "other things to be equal"; that is, he assumes that other factors are not influencing the situation. He uses the term *ceteris paribus* to describe this assumption. This assumption does not invalidate economic experiments, but it does require careful interpretation of results.

Expressing Ideas

There are four ways in which economic ideas can be expressed. These are narrative, tabular expression, graphic expression, or mathematical formula. All but the last are used extensively in this book. Students should attempt to understand each as presented but will no doubt prefer one over the other.

Fallacy of Composition

Many people hold false preconceptions about economics because of the *fallacy of composition.* This is the fallacy of contending that what is true for the individual, or part, is necessarily true for the group as a whole. For example, every farmer strives to produce a larger crop, which will surely give him a larger income. But if a majority of farmers have bumper crops, income to each of the farmers may fall.

Remember the distinction made earlier between *macroeconomics* and *microeconomics.* The former is concerned with the overall aggregates or groups, while the latter is concerned with specific individuals or units. The fallacy of composition reminds us that what is valid at the macro level may or may not be true at the micro level.

Preconceived Biases

Unlike the student of physics or microbiology, each student enters the study of economics with an idea that he already knows something about the subject. After all, he has no doubt earned some money and spent it; he has already experienced economics as a consumer. As a result, he has preconceptions about the operation of the economy, the farm problem, the national debt, and other issues. These ideas, some of which are based on inaccurate or incomplete information, are detrimental to effective study and learning in economics. You are urged, then, to keep an open mind as you pursue economic knowledge and understanding.

Cause and Effect

In any science, it is difficult to ascertain cause–effect relationships. Because of the absence of controlled experiments in the social sciences, even more caution should be used in drawing conclusions. Of particular importance is avoiding the conclusion that just because event A preceded event B or is associated with it, event A caused event B to happen. In economics, cause-and-effect relationships are rarely self-evident.

AGRICULTURE AND AGRICULTURAL ECONOMICS

The word *agriculture* has long been associated with the industry of basic food production, known as farming. Agriculture and farming were synonymous before farmers began selling their products in a commercial market. However, today, producing food and fiber (farming) is only one part of scientific agriculture. Modern agriculture also includes the farm-supply industries (feed, seed, machinery, pharmaceuticals, etc.) as well as the product-processing and distribution industries, which convert the raw food into the form consumers want and move it to them (Figure 1-2). Often, these are referred to as agriculturally related industries, or agribusinesses.

Farming (On-Farm) Sector of Agriculture

Farming is a big and expanding business, requiring continually increasing amounts of capital, technology, and management. However, as the efficiency of scientific farming increases, fewer and fewer operators and workers are needed each year to feed our growing population, a fact that has caused farming to be referred to by some people as a declining industry.

Productivity per farm worker is currently at an all-time high; this is one of the factors that has allowed a doubling of our national population and large increases in per capita disposable income since 1910. Continued increases in the productivity of farm workers in the 1970s will result in more food raised on less land with less labor.

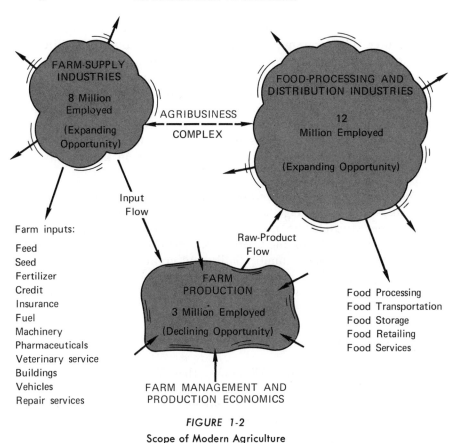

FIGURE 1-2
Scope of Modern Agriculture

Modern farming is dynamic and requires men and women with scientific knowledge, skill, and ambition. Knowledge of engineering, chemistry, pathology, entomology, genetics, nutrition, and economics is necessary to successful farming. Farmers are key men in the nation's economy, and their opportunity for outdoor living and self-employment is a privilege few others enjoy. Because of the ever-increasing efficiency in farm production, however, fewer and fewer job opportunities will be available on the farm.

Agribusiness (Off-Farm) Sector of Agriculture

Farm-supply industries.   Farmers purchase a greater share of their inputs today than ever before. As a common example, the farmer once grew oats as fuel for horses, which he had also raised. Today, the farmer

buys gas and oil to fuel a tractor purchased from a farm-equipment manufacturer. The farm-supply industries include feed, seed, fertilizer, agricultural pharmaceuticals, machinery, pesticides, and lime—for which
farmers spend over $40 billion a year. Government-related farm credit
institutions and commercial banks lend money capital. Credit is an essential input for food production and hence could also be classified as
a part of the farm-supply industry. Farm-supply industries employ more
than twice as many people as are employed on farms. While job opportunities are decreasing on the farm, employment in farm-supply industries is expanding.

Food-processing and distribution industries.   Specialized agricultural industries process, package, and move the food and fiber products to the
consumer. Included in these industries are dairy plants, food-freezing
firms, drying and canning operations, meat-packing plants, fats and oil
manufacturing plants, lumber mills, and grain mills. Every type of industry that processes and transports the raw food produced on the farm
is included in this category. These industries are expanding and already
employ more than 12 million people, or four times the number in farming.

Other Service Industries Related to Agriculture

Education.   More than 2,000 new teachers each year go into positions
in high schools, agricultural-college staffs, adult teaching with the agricultural extension service, and vocational agriculture. In addition, agricultural education for foreign students is an area that has recently
expanded and promises much for the future. Both public and private
agencies are increasing staffs of qualified people to teach up-to-date agricultural technology in other countries. The need for teachers in vocational agriculture will probably decline, because fewer and fewer
students are going back to the farms. The role of extension educators has
expanded from demonstrating techniques to showing new agricultural
technologies (new seeds, the use of fertilizer, different methods of field
cultivation), to issues of farm price and income policy, foreign trade,
and urban-industrial development.

Communications.   The service industry of agricultural communications
is expanding. Widespread dissemination of information concerning
agricultural technology, prices, and cost of production is essential to the
continued productivity of our agricultural sector. Interviewing farmers,
scientists, and industrialists, attending conventions, demonstrations, and
legislative sessions, and reporting new research developments are all part
of agricultural communications. Colleges, extension services, market reporting agencies, newspapers, farm publications, and television and radio

stations all report on agricultural services to farmers and to the general public. These agencies need writers, broadcasters, television and motion-picture producers, and photographers.

Research.   Research in agricultural industries needs at least 1,500 college graduates each year. Agriculture looks to researchers for new ideas in farm equipment, nutrition of livestock, genetics, disease control, processing, marketing, and economics. There are some 8,000 research scientists in the agricultural experiment stations, 8,000 more in agricultural industries, and 6,000 in the U.S. Department of Agriculture. Research work usually requires people with advanced college degrees.

Government services.   Government agencies on a national, state, and local basis serve agriculture through many service agencies. Communications and research have already been mentioned. Regulatory agencies act to protect farmers in their purchases of inputs, in regard to quality and quantity. Public health is safeguarded through food inspection and grading. Nursery inspection requires particular specialists in entomology, pathology, botany, and horticulture. Local activities of community-planning and recreation agencies are other examples. Foreign-service opportunities with the federal government are expanding.

Agriculture employs about 30 percent of the labor force in the United States and, at its present rate of growth, needs 15,000 new college graduates each year. Employment needs of the agribusinesses of agriculture are expanding, while those of the farm segment are declining. The three segments of agriculture (farm production, farm-supply industries, and food-processing and distribution industries) are interdependent, and their combined scope is of vital importance in the total economy.

Agricultural Economics

Agricultural economics is an applied phase of the social science of economics in which attention is given to all aspects of problems related to agriculture. The development of agricultural economics as an applied social science in the United States extends back to about 1900, when the discipline began as a study of farm management, which in turn had its roots primarily in agronomy and horticulture.

At the beginning of the twentieth century, interest in economic issues related to agriculture erupted in several educational centers. The depression of the 1890s had hurt agriculture severely, and organized farm groups, particularly the Farmers' Alliance, had stirred considerable interest in farm problems. This new field of agricultural interest, later to be designated as agricultural economics, attracted professors of agriculture who had formerly labored only in such technical areas as agricultural chemistry, agronomy, and horticulture, as well as general economists and business leaders.

By 1910, about twenty men were identified as agricultural economists. Thomas F. Hunt is recognized as a pioneer in agricultural-college and agricultural experiment-station work. He was an agriculturist who recognized the physical, biological, and economic aspects of farming and their interdependence in promoting good farm-management practices. Courses in agricultural economy, rural economy, farm management, and agricultural history grew rapidly in the early 1900s. Work in farm management in the U.S. Department of Agriculture was started by William J. Spillman in 1902. In the early years, farm-management work was directed toward such questions as how to choose a farm, how to choose the proper enterprises for a farm, how intensive the cultivation should be on farms, and how large farms should be.

After World War I, interest in the marketing of farm products was spurred by the expansion of commercialized farming, surplus farm production, and the subsequent farm depression. Orderly marketing was the objective, and considerable attention was given to the importance of marketing cooperatives in marketing farm products more successfully. Staff members of the National Bureau of Agricultural Economics and the agricultural colleges studied general marketing problems, prices, foreign competition, transportation, city produce markets, and market statistics. More than fifty commodities received their attention.

Since the 1920s, farm price and income policy have received much attention by agricultural economists as a natural outgrowth of surplus farm production, marketing problems, and depressed farm incomes. Agricultural policy is a course of action decided upon and followed in the field of agriculture. Most people associate it with debates about parity prices, agricultural price supports, production allotments, or the merits or faults of some national agricultural act. However, it has grown much broader. Agricultural-policy analysis is also directed toward such topics as the reasons for the creation and development of the land-grant colleges, the issues in public reclamation and development of irrigated lands, the basis of conflict between persons advocating free trade and those supporting protections in international trade, the merits of the family farm, soil-conservation issues, tax issues, education, planning and zoning, and economic development.

Agricultural economists. Professional agricultural economists are typically classified as working in production economics, farm management, agricultural marketing, and agricultural policy. Specialists in farm finance, farm-work simplification, and land economics are more closely allied with farm management. In marketing, agricultural economists may be specialists in any of the commodity areas, such as grain, dairy, poultry, livestock, fruits and vegetables. In the policy area, agricultural economists may concentrate on price and income policy, land policy, marketing policy, and local government. Recently, there has been increased attention given to international agricultural-policy questions, including the Common Market in Europe, the economic development of less-developed nations, and the commodity and price implications of domestic farm policies. Agricultural price analysts contribute to all phases of agricultural economics. With the recent emphasis on management problems in the agribusiness segment of agriculture, business-management specialists are appearing within the scope of agricultural economics. These men may work principally in finance, production, marketing, or policy in the agricultural-supply, food-processing, or distribution industries.

FORMS OF BUSINESS ORGANIZATION

Having described several kinds of business activities in the preceding pages, we should now explore some of the legal business forms controlling and marshalling the production and marketing of the nation.

Proprietorships

Proprietorships comprise about 75 percent of the total number of businesses in the United States. About one-third are in the agriculture, forestry, and fisheries sector. In the sole proprietorship, the owner is the operator. It is simple in legal structure, with the owner in direct control. He provides the working capital and most of the labor and the management. Some of the disadvantages, however, include unlimited liability (the debts of the business are also the debts of the individual owner) and limited expansion potential because of difficulties in raising operating and investment money. In economic efficiency, proprietorships may compare favorably with large corporate firms.

Partnerships

Several individuals can pool their resources and jointly own a business organized legally as a partnership. About 8 percent of U.S. businesses were organized this way in the early 1970s. The liability of each partner is extended to the partnership, making each partner liable for his partners' actions. Some of the advantages are low start-up costs, a broader management base than proprietorships, and limited outside regulation. Of nearly one million partnerships active in the United States, about 12 percent are in the agriculture, forestry, and fisheries sector.

Corporations

Corporations comprise some 13 percent by number of business concerns but account for about 80 percent of total business receipts. Advantages of the corporate form of business include limited liability for individual owners (stockholders), a continuous existence, ease in raising money, and potential use of specialized management. However, corporations are more closely scrutinized and regulated by government, are more expensive to organize, and are more complicated in function. Corporate profits are taxed by the federal and state governments, and stockholders are taxed again on income received as dividends.

A modification of the corporate form of business organization commonly used in family-farm businesses is the "Subchapter S Corporation," approved by law in 1958. Double taxation is avoided, as corporate income can be legally divided among the shareholders, according to their ownership interest or other agreements, and included in their individual tax returns. The corporation itself does not pay a corporate profits tax. For a farm to qualify, however, specified requirements must be met.

Cooperatives

Cooperatives are a special form of corporations organized to serve their members with needed goods or services. Cooperative owners participate in management, usually on a one-member, one-vote basis. The general public is served in a more limited capacity. Special laws establish certain limitations as to the nature of the operation, prescribe the maximum return owners may earn on their money invested, and stipulate the distribution of net earnings on a patronage basis. Cooperatives are an important form of business organization in agriculture and are discussed further in Chapter 9.

FORMS OF SOCIAL ORGANIZATION
AFFECTING BUSINESS AND ECONOMICS

Certain forms of social organization go along with and help implement the business forms. These social forms, sometimes called institutions, can be defined as a persistent or continuing group control over individual behavior. Partial financing of the government budget through personal income taxes, the notion and rigors of public education, marriage, inheritance, court procedures, and the concept of Social Security—all are types of institutions that control our economic and business behavior. In all cases, institutions demand the use of inputs (labor, capital, and management), there is a definite sort of outcome or product evident, and there is a consumer or beneficiary of the pressure or control.

RESOLVING ENVIRONMENTAL CONCERNS, BUSINESS, AND ECONOMIC GROWTH

Despite all the growing and legitimate concern about the degradation of our physical environment, there is still reason to be equally concerned about the provision of jobs and income for our present and future population. Economic growth does not have to be thought of in an either-or context: "Preserve the environment *or* have growth." Instead, we must turn our minds to creating the best possible place for all the peoples of our nation and the world to live—physically, economically, and socially. This longed-for goal will not be achieved in a vacuum. Economic growth is meaningless if it kills the countryside around it and poisons the people who live and work in its polluted air. On the other hand, natural open spaces and wilderness hold little promise of permanence and public support when economic depression becomes widespread. There must be some middle road, some policy compromise. Some of the tools for that policy compromise are found in this book. But first, let's look at what economic growth *is*.

Definition of Economic Growth

Defining economic growth or measuring a rate of growth is a difficult task. By far the most common approach is to measure the total output of goods and services produced by the economy, and divide the output by the number of people.

$$\frac{Physical\ output\ of\ goods\ and\ services\ (national\ product)}{Population} = \frac{National\ product}{per\ capita}$$

National product can be expressed in dollars by multiplying the total amount of each good or service produced in the economy by its average retail market price. National product in money value becomes national income, and our growth measure is converted from physical goods and services to dollars, a more appropriate measure:

$$\frac{National\ income\ (dollars)}{Population} = National\ income\ per\ capita$$

Two problems arise. First, an increase in the price level (inflation) can be mistaken for a change in the rate of growth. To avoid this problem, any misleading influence of a price change can be removed by adjusting the national income for given years to a rise or fall in the general level of prices. For example, in 1929 the money national product was $96 billion, and in 1933 it was $48 billion. However, during this period, the price level dropped by 25 percent, from an index of 100 down to an index of 75, based on 1929 prices. As a result, when priced using the 1929 price level, the real national product fell from $96 billion to only $64 billion ($48 ÷ 75 × 100 = $64).

Second, part of the production of goods in any economy must be allocated for replacing worn-out equipment, buildings, and other capital goods. Otherwise the capital stock or wealth of an economy at the end of the year would be less than at the beginning. In national-income statistics, capital consumption or depreciation allowances for depletion of capital stock accounts for the difference between gross national product and net national product. In computing national product (income) per capita for use in measuring growth and growth rates, the net national product should be used. In order for an economy to show growth, the increase in net national product must be greater than the increase in population.

Factors Affecting the Rate of Economic Growth

There is no one theory that fully explains the process of economic development. Certainly, a country's growth rate is influenced by social, political, institutional, and economic factors. To isolate the influence of any one of these is most difficult. And the importance of a particular factor in the economic growth rate of the United States may have little or no bearing on the situation in some other country.

Much attention is now being focused on "underdeveloped" nations. In the sense of utilizing all its resources to gain the largest national product possible, however, no country can ever be fully developed except in theory. The measure of national product in determining a country's state of development relegates social or political development to a minor role. Perhaps the ancient Roman or Greek empires were more highly developed in a cultural sense than many of today's "developed" nations.

What are the economic factors conducive to a country's achieving a high growth rate? First, there are natural resources. A country that is fortunate enough to be endowed with a large supply of natural resources will find its growth potential aided materially. A high-quality soil resource and basic raw materials, such as iron ore, natural gas, bauxite, coal, and oil, are conducive to economic development.

Second, there is the human resource—people—which provides the inputs of labor and management. The larger a country's population, the more mouths there are to feed. On the other hand, the larger the population, the greater is the potential labor and management supply and, hence, a greater growth potential exists in the economy.

Third, a country's capital vitally affects its growth potential. Capital includes all business structures and producers' durable equipment, farm and nonfarm residential structures, inventories of raw and finished goods, and assets abroad owned by a country's populace.

Fourth is the resource of technology—the accumulation of knowledge about production that helps increase output per unit of input and lowers costs of production. In this context, technology improves the productivity of land, of labor, of capital, and of management.

That a lack of any one of these resources can be restricting is apparent in the world situation today. Brazil, for example, has many natural resources but lacks capital and skilled labor. China has lots of labor but little capital. Egypt has little fertile land and other natural resources. Economic growth in some countries of Europe was relatively slow until outmoded capital destroyed by war was rebuilt with new technologies. It is true that, to some extent, one group of factors may be substituted for another. This is most true for labor and capital. Producers are always searching to find the least-cost combination of factors that will produce a unit of output. But substitution can go only so far before other problems are encountered. For example, witness the immense social and economic problems created as automated technology and machines replace workers in coal mines.

The next chapter traces some of the history of economic life. It discusses the evolution of commercial agriculture, and the role that some of our institutions and business forms played in the development of that economic part of our nation.

2

Agriculture and the Development of Economic Life

As we trace, in this chapter, the development of economic life from a subsistence agricultural economy to a complex industrial society in the Western world, the reader will note the importance in the economic growth process of specialization and trade, with the resulting increase in interdependence among sectors of the economy. Throughout the world, one can find countries that exhibit great variations in kind and amount of economic and social development.

We live in an exciting age, surrounded by a rapidly changing environment. Some scientists believe that more technological developments have taken place since 1900 than in all previous time in man's known history. Yet if all of man's past were represented by a 24-hour day, the twentieth century would represent only 1/1000th of a second.

PRINCIPLE STAGES OF ECONOMIC DEVELOPMENT IN HISTORY

Man's advancement in his control over nature closely follows his progress in developing tools. As man slowly came to the realization that he was different from other forms of animal life, he also became aware that he was in competition with them for nature's limited food supply. Anthropologists study the physical characteristics that link man to animals, man's social organization, and his skills. Economists are interested in man's ability to organize and increase production in order to satisfy his wants.

The Hunting or Collectional Economy

In the collectional economy, man was essentially a parasite and lived from the gifts of nature. This period accounts for 98 percent of man's known history.

As man's intelligence gradually increased, he changed from a wielder of randomly acquired weapons to a crude toolmaker. Increased efficiency in hunting and collecting allowed time for other activities, such as transmitting knowledge through language. Man's natural sociability, together with his language development, provided the means for cultural progress.

The development of the human brain gave man the ability to meet many challenges and bring him safely through the Ice Age, which began some 700,000 years ago and lasted about 200,000 years. Although hundreds of animal species, many physically stronger than man, perished during this time, stamina and development of physical and communications skills enabled man to survive on the hunting grounds of Europe and Asia.

After migrating with the animals across natural land bridges formed by the glaciers, man continued as a hunter throughout the entire Old Stone Age, from 500,000 B.C. to 8000 B.C. His progress in technology over this period was limited to slow changes in basic stone instruments. With the vast nuclear power of the twentieth century, one easily forgets that during nine-tenths of man's existence, his only tools were chipped stones and simple shafts of wood. Man had learned to make most of his fundamental tools by the end of the Old Stone Age. He still had only one form of power—his muscles—and he knew nothing of farming.

It is not clear when man learned to harness fire for his own good. It most likely took a longer time for him to learn to make fire than to use it to provide warmth in his cave shelters and for crude cooking. Fire also aided man as a hunter. Since animals were afraid of fire, it could be used to guide them into traps and over mountain precipices. Bones of an estimated 100,000 horses found in France give evidence of cooperative hunting where, with the aid of fire, the horses were driven up a slope to a cliff from which they fell to their deaths. As the Stone

Age closed, man had learned to provide himself with shelter and clothing, which, together with his more finely wrought weapons and aggressive
intelligence, made him better equipped to find food.

The Pastoral Stage

The Middle Stone Age, which began about 8000 B.C., found man
beginning to use the bow and arrow. He trapped fish, dried them, and
stored them for future use. He also learned to store other seasonal foods,
such as seeds, nuts, and fruits.

In the New Stone Age, estimated as beginning between 6000 and
7000 B.C., man discovered the secret of the relation between seed and
plant, and farming and the pastoral stage were born. He also began to
domesticate cattle, sheep, goats, and pigs as animal sources of food.
These two developments were decisive factors in agricultural evolution
during the pastoral stage. Improved stabilization in his food supply
enabled man to gain the necessary leisure time to engage in wars,
religion, and the arts.

The dog was trained both as a working companion and a pet.
Polished stone implements, particularly the stone axe, were developed,
although unpolished stone implements were still used. The women spun
and wove fibers into cloth. Progress in cooking methods prompted pottery utensils. Although man was still nomadic, he tended to settle in a
more fixed abode and to spend more time on farming and less on
hunting.

The Agricultural or Settled-Village Economy

With the disappearance of the nomadic life, villages began to grow.
Economic life in these local communities centered around the daily tasks
of farming. Relatively speaking, growth in this period was rapid. The
first urban civilization dawned only 3,500 years after farmers began
sowing seeds and reaping their own harvests. It arose in the Middle
East region called Mesopotamia, and in northern Africa.

The first village people were probably united by bonds of kinship.
The concept of property was born through individual family settlements
on specific plots of ground. In the process, social intercourse was en-
riched, group religious observances took form, economic trade was
initiated, and a crude form of government evolved as a logical consequence. Thus began the evolution of man's social institutions.

Life in the early villages was full and active and quickly resulted
in a higher standard of living. Labor specialization contributed to a
longer life-span.

The transition of man from a food collector to a food producer was one of the longest steps toward a stable society that mankind has ever taken. The climate throughout Asia Minor was warm and dry; rainfall was adequate to irrigate the natural meadows of wild wheat and barley, and the area was also well adapted to man's first domesticated animals.

Grain cultivation may have begun when discarded seeds in the garbage dump sprang into growth. Man might have experimented by sowing seeds in the soil and watched to see what the next year would bring forth. Over time, rough fields of man-cultivated grain wove patterns across the land. The art of cultivation spread swiftly throughout the Fertile Crescent, an area bending north from Egypt through Palestine and Syria and turning south again through the Tigris and Euphrates river valleys.

Although some food problems were solved, some conservation problems were created. By altering the natural environment through soil tillage and forest clearance, man set processes in motion that wasted the soil and created deserts and wastelands. To overcome these problems, dikes were built to hold the swollen rivers, and ditches were dug to carry water to fields for irrigation. Cattle were trained to pull the newly invented plow. The substitution of animal power for human labor constituted a revolution in food-production methods. With the use of sail and oar, man turned the broad rivers into highways, and a great upsurge in trade and commerce was possible. Towns developed along the river banks where farmers could trade their goods.

The stage was set for the development of the great civilizations of Europe and Asia. The elements of a civilized society usually include pursuit of knowledge and the arts, a high level of political organization, a complex social and economic order, true specialization in crafts and skills, and the adherence of individuals to the impersonal requirements of the state. The ability to write, record, and convey information is a necessary skill in such a society.

Three important civilizations in the history of the world were Greece, Rome, and Britain. Unlike the situation in Egypt, soil conditions in Greece were not favorable to farming. There was no river Nile to provide water and aid in maintaining soil fertility by depositing silt during flood periods. Thus, the Greeks were obliged to either fertilize or resort to letting their land lie idle every other year.

Population pressures and wars encouraged the Greeks to establish colonies. Olive oil and wine were the principal agricultural exports. Slave labor dominated the situation both in agriculture and in the rest of the early village economies.

The Romans' genius lay primarily in the political realm. They were the greatest organizers and administrators of all antiquity, providing stability to the world for the years between 200 B.C. and 200 A.D. As the population of Rome, the city that grew into an empire, increased to unparalleled proportions, immense imports of food became necessary. The burdens of paying for grain imports (money raised by taxation) fell heavily, curiously enough, on those in agriculture. The government felt itself politically obliged to sell grain to the city population at less than cost, or to actually give it away. Ironically, the Roman cultivator found himself heavily taxed to pay for grain that competed in this unfair way with his own production.

The ruling class was not blind to the dangers involved in depending so heavily on imported grain. The situation got so serious that Roman citizens were attached to the soil, becoming serfs but not quite slaves. By the end of the fourth century, practically no one in the empire was legally free to move from his place of origin. The growth of large estates and government interference were notable features of Rome's rural decline.

Lessons learned in the early years of Roman rule resulted in some striking changes in the Roman administration of Spain, France, and England. The strong central government of Rome maintained military order but allowed these provinces to make limited economic progress. In order to control outlying areas, Roman armies provided protection for trade and communication over improved roads.

The decline in Roman power began in the third century, when the empire lacked the power to repress internal revolts, to repel the inroads of barbarians from the North, and to maintain communications with outlying provinces. Motives for commerce grew weaker, culture diminished, and obstacles to trade were compounded. The "Fall of Rome" occurred in 476 A.D., and the last remnants of Roman progress disappeared as the European world passed into the Dark Ages.

One must understand the methods employed in Roman governmental organization in order to understand why feudalism developed. Cities in the provinces were linked to Rome by a communicative network of roads and highways. Taxes collected by provincial officials and reports of all kinds streamed to Rome, while official orders and instructions flowed in the opposite direction. This system became increasingly difficult to use as Roman power fell. Roads were destroyed and travelers robbed. As a result, few taxes reached Rome, and the government no longer had the means to pay its bills. Finally the time came when Rome had to recognize the change in conditions and adopt quite different methods. Basically, the man who had previously been a salaried official found that he had to support himself from land revenues that formerly went to Rome for taxes. In reality, however, the state split into little self-regulating units, and the central government in Rome lost all control over its provinces.

The provincial official became a little king or lord, who enclosed the land he supervised into a self-sufficient community known as the feudal manor or villa. It is estimated that perhaps 100,000 or more of these communities were established. Although the peasants or serfs were certainly not free, they did gain a degree of protection by living in the manor.

The economic life of these small village groups, sometimes consisting of less than 100 people, was highlighted in their self-sufficiency. A majority of the people in each manor were farmers. Crude farming methods were used. The livestock was so poor that a grown ox was little larger than a present-day calf. Stock were few in number, but even so it was sometimes necessary to kill some at the beginning of winter from lack of fodder to feed them. Intensive cultivation on limited land without sufficient fertilizer exhausted the land's productive capacity quickly. A yield of six bushels of wheat per acre, of which two bushels had to be retained for seed, was probably normal.

Houses were constructed of forest materials, clothes were made from flax and wool, and furniture and implements were likewise fashioned within the manor. Nearly every villa had a mill run by water, some had a carpenter, but few special artisans were to be found.

Such a self-sufficient system with little commerce resulted in alternate periods of waste and want. There was no market for any surplus grain harvested in a good year, and it was not possible to import any in a bad year. Little economic growth could come about as long as everything had to be produced on the spot and used by the manor people themselves.

The Town Economy

The decline of the manor system began about 1000 A.D. in northern Italy. As chaotic conditions lessened, towns began to spring up; they have been aptly described as "isles of freedom in a sea of serfdom." A town was a group of people who settled closely together and maintained themselves chiefly by manufacture and trade. Probably they were the younger, more aggressive, and braver people who tired of manor living and risked escape. For a while, they continued to pay some taxes to nearby manor lords for appeasement and protection. Town population grew as the custom was established that a serf who escaped from his manor lord and lived a year and a day in a town was free. Consequently, manor lords were forced to lighten their requirements to discourage people from leaving. The Black Death, or Plague, which was to ravish the European countries for several centuries to come, also contributed to the decline of the manor system.

Towns brought a new era in commercial production, and manufacturing became a profession. The result was specialization of labor, bringing increased production income and a higher standard of living. The country people could devote themselves entirely to farming and could exchange their surplus for a profitable exchange with town artisans.

The revival of trade took place first between towns in the same country, and eventually between countries. The town was the unit for regulating trade. Each town had its custom tariffs, and national regulation was subordinated by municipal laws. The economic life of the town was closely regulated by the *guild,* the forerunner of today's labor unions. All merchants and craftsmen (manufacturers) were organized in guilds. Trading merchants banded together for protection in their journeys to other towns and had to follow guild rules or pay a fine. Often guild members were obliged to carry armor and fight for mutual protection. Craftsmen also had guilds, which established regulations designed to prevent fraud and maintain quality of workmanship.

Trade flourished, and the period centering about the year 1500 was marked by many rapid changes. These changes affected not only the intellectual life of Europe (the Renaissance) and its religious life (the Reformation), but they also caused a revolution in the world of politics, industry, and commerce.

The Industrial Economy

The industrial economy began with the Industrial Revolution, which can be simply defined as the emerging of the factory system in the production of goods. It originated in England in the last third of the eighteenth century.

The primary object of industry is the production and distribution of goods desired by people. The factory system concentrated and multiplied the means of production so that output could be both accelerated and increased. Machinery was developed that with remarkable precision and rapidity performed the most complicated and the heaviest tasks.

Once manufactured, goods must be sold. The immense stimulus given to production by the factory system immediately affected the distribution system for the goods. An increased quantity of goods on local markets meant lower prices, which put the nearby consumer in a more favorable position. As transportation methods improved, the effects of increased production extended from individuals to regions and to nations.

Two fundamental facts, closely interwoven, infinitely varied in their consequences but always the same in principle, govern the evolution of economic life. These are the exchange of commodities and the division of labor. Every extension or multiplication in the exchange of goods makes use of an ever more elaborate and effective division of labor by throwing open more channels to production. The division of labor also implies cooperation between interdependent specialized jobs that necessarily involve large numbers of people.

The woolen industry in England was probably the most characteristic and complete example of an early system of manufacture. The first instance of extreme specialization in agriculture was in the sheep industry in England. As the feudal system collapsed, small fields were combined into larger acreages for pasturing sheep. There was a good market for wool across the English Channel in Belgium and France. After the Norman conquest, Flemish artisans crossed to England and taught the English how to use some of this wealth themselves, and textiles became the predominant type of manufacture.

The domestic system. Before we proceed any further, let us take a look at the nature of the cloth-manufacturing industry that immediately preceded the factory system. The Domestic System, as it was called, was so named because the manufacturing of cloth took place in the homes of the workers.

The necessary apparatus for weaving was simply a loom, hand cards, and a spinning wheel, all inexpensive machinery. If a weaver had a large family, some specialization and division of labor was possible, with the family handling all the necessary operations. Many times, however, a weaver distributed wool for spinning into other homes to keep enough thread available for looms. It was in this way that specialization first came about outside the family circle. There were houses where only spinning was done. In others, several weaving looms were gathered together and the weaver, while still remaining an artisan working with his hands, had a small number of hired laborers under his supervision. In this system, the weaver, in his cottage that was both a dwelling place and a workshop, controlled production. He was not dependent upon outside capital, since he owned both the tools and the raw materials.

The same weaver who managed the production phase also marketed the cloth, usually in the nearest town. At Leeds in England, the market was held in the High Street, with long counters on each side. The market opened at a specified time, and cloth merchants would walk up and down among the tables making purchases.

However, domestic industry of such a nature could continue to exist only as long as local consumption absorbed local production. When production increased beyond this point, the manufacturer was forced to come to some agreement with the cloth merchant or trader, who bought goods for resale either in another home market or abroad. The trader now became an indispensable middleman. This new market element soon reacted on the production phase of the industry.

As it was common for the weaver to deliver the cloth in unfinished form, the merchant had to employ workmen to dress and dye the cloth. This was the first stage in the gradual transformation of commercial capital to industrial capital. In fact, it became quite common for the merchant to buy the raw wool and have it carded, spun, woven, fulled, and dressed at his own expense.[1] The workmen thus became employees performing tasks for remuneration by an employer.

The workmen in the domestic industry were much different from those employed in a modern factory of today. Most lived in the country and earned some of their income from farming. For most, spinning and weaving were additional occupations for supplementary income. As a result, the workers produced more goods in the winter, when there was less farm work to do, and very little goods at planting or harvest time.

The advantage to the merchant capitalist was that he needed no building in which to house equipment. The disadvantages were that he could exercise no supervisory control over his employees in their private home "factories"; that distribution of raw materials and the collection of small amounts of widely scattered manufactured cloth were costly; and that the merchant manufacturer was plagued by pilferage and other problems.

To some people, the early domestic-type industry was "the golden age," and the craftsman, either in country or small town, lived a simpler and healthier life than workmen in today's modern industrial centers. He worked at home, cultivated a few acres, and produced according to his own time, needs, and strength. His moral fibers was thought to be enhanced by good family life, and he was considered a respectable member of society.

But as capital was separated from labor and the workman became only a wage earner, he was more at the mercy of his employer. Spinning, usually done by women and children, commanded the lowest pay, and as the industry passed from simple to more complicated production processes, labor specialization grew at a fast pace. As the domestic system was replaced by the factory system and the Industrial Revolution continued, the lot of the laboring classes was not necessarily improved.

The factory system. These problems associated with the domestic-type industry confronting the capitalist played a major role in the estab-

---

[1] *Report on the State of the Woolen Manufacturer,* p. 8, Parliamentary Debates, II, 668

lishment of factories. In factories the workers could all be kept under the eye of a supervisor, and specialization of labor could more easily be accomplished.

Complaints of today's factory workers are litle different from those of English workers of the eighteenth century. Low wages, unemployment, long working hours, and poor working conditions were a few of their grievances. As a result, workers of various kinds banded together, and a renewal of the town guilds, now more appropriately named *labor unions,* had their birth. Wool combers were among the first to succeed in organizing themselves. Their work was done by hand, requiring considerable skill, and there were few of them. These characteristics create favorable conditions in organizing an effective labor union.

The progress of industry and the development of commerce are closely interwoven and mutually influence each other. For example, England found herself needing additional markets for her goods. The mercantilists who pushed for expanding exports and few imports were interested in building the gold supply; to them, this was the most important source and indication of wealth. The realization that trading among various countries has many advantages to all was slow to develop. Exchange of goods among countries stimulates competition and search for new efficiencies in production. Freer trade does not require that commercial development precede industrial progress. Development in transport enables the producer to increase the extent of his market beyond the known wants of a localized market.

COLONIAL AMERICA—1607 TO 1776

After peace was established between England and Spain around 1600, England was able to turn more attention to developing new colonies. Although an earlier attempt had failed, the king of England granted a charter in 1606 that created two joint-stock companies, known as the London Company and the Plymouth Company, whose main purpose was to make profits by exploiting the new lands. A second aim was to carry Christianity to the Indians, and this, it was hoped, would induce people to buy stock in the company out of a sense of Christian duty. Stockholders were of two kinds: the "adventurer," who bought shares and remained in England, and the "planter," who ventured to the new land and received stock for agreeing to "adventure his person." Later, a grant of fifty acres was given to each immigrant who paid his way across the Atlantic. This procedure became the basis of the Virginia land system known as the "headright" system.

The first pioneers built a settlement on the James River and named it Jamestown. The area appeared lush with good land and wild berries, but extreme difficulties were faced as winter came and food supplies were low, because the settlers were not adept in the cultural practices necessary to grow food in the new land. Despite food shortages and sickness, Jamestown grew and prospered, with the result that Virginia became the first of the royal colonies.

Soon after the establishment of Jamestown, a group of discontented Protestants, called "Puritans," were granted rights to sail to the New World and settle in the Virginia colony. On the voyage, the famous *Mayflower* ran off course and landed her passengers on the shores of Cape Cod late in 1620. With winter at hand, the Pilgrims were forced to stay. The native population had been destroyed by the plague, and there was a satisfactory harbor, good water, and much cleared land. Since they were far from the Virginia colony, the men drew up the Mayflower Compact, forming a "civil body politic" in which each man pledged to submit to the will of the majority. Thus, the Plymouth colony became a little republic with a remarkable democratic spirit. To pay their debts to the English capitalists who had financed their trip, they established fishing stations and posts for trading with Indians on the New England coast. Although half the settlers did not survive the first winter, the Plymouth colony survived and gradually increased in stature.

The Massachusetts Bay colony was founded a decade after the Pilgrims landed. It was successful and influential enough in its early development for Massachusetts to be considered the mother colony. Connecticut soon followed, and the seventeenth century found the establishment of colonies at virtually all points on the eastern coast of what is now the United States.

Colonial Agriculture

The two most important characteristics of colonial agriculture were its self-sufficiency and the extensive nature of food production. Most of the original "planters" were to continue the pursuit of agriculture in the New World, from both experience and necessity. The occupation of farming offered the best prospect for a self-sufficing economy. However, to retire English debts and pay English taxes, it was also necessary to diversify production into those lines that would permit exports. New England possessed great advantages for the export of furs, fish, and lumber, and tobacco was a chief export item for the southern colonies.

Continuing in the European tradition, farmers lived in hamlets surrounded by arable fields. Few plows were used in the seventeenth century, and tillage systems were crude. Most often the seed was poked into hills along with a herring for fertilizer, a trick the American Indians also used, and cultivation was done with handmade tools. Stock raising was as unscientific as crop growing. The limited supply of arable land, the necessity to provide exports, and the proximity of the sea led to the rapid growth of the fishing industry.

The creation of one industry fostered the growth of others. Fishing prompted an industry of shipbuilding. The use of horse power in early agriculture spurred the trade of blacksmithing. Woodworking, spinning and weaving, and shoemaking trades grew to satisfy domestic requirements. Commercial development originated in much the same fashion as it did in Europe.

In the southern colonies of Virginia, Maryland, and the Carolinas, natural resources promoted a different type of economic activity. The tobacco industry fulfilled both domestic and export market needs. The supply of labor was even less adequate than in the New England colonies, and indentured servants were also more numerous. It was not until the eighteenth century that Negro slavery eclipsed indentured white servitude on the plantations. Large plantations owned by rich men were not characteristic of seventeenth-century Virginia.

Eighteenth-Century Development

Little westward expansion had taken place by 1700. However, inroads were beginning, particularly along the rivers. To the frontiersman, most land was abundant and cheap, and people could reap a harvest from all they could till without sharing with any landlord.

Natural resources were inherently productive, and as farmers employed improved crop production practices, output of the native Indian crops increased. Even today, about half the food produced in the United States comes from crops native to the land that had been cultivated by the American Indian in a crude, inefficient manner.

A one-story house of logs was typical in this self-sufficient agriculture. It was unpainted and unheated except for a fireplace in the room that served as kitchen, dining, and living room, and in cold weather as a bedroom. Homespun garments were the rule; books probably included only the Bible and an almanac; and infrequent trips to town served as a social event as well as for trade.

The eighteenth century was also a period of rapid industrial development. Continued immigration from Europe brought many talented and skilled people to live in the colonies. Among the non-English inhabitants were many mechanics who established small-scale manufacture of stoves, ironwork, glass, paper, and other products. In contrast to the commerce of the northern and middle colonies (fishing, lumber, and shipbuilding), the chief trade of the southern colonies was in tobacco, indigo, and rice and was carried on primarily with England.

The life of the interior frontiersmen contrasted sharply with that of those living on the coast. The coastal inhabitants welcomed the westward settlement of lands as a protection against Indians, but those in political power took care to keep the interior communities subordinate to the minority on the seaboard. The men of the back country did not meekly accept their position of inferiority and soon pushed to get more liberal and representative government.

During the first half of the eighteenth century, France continued her explorations south from Canada into the vast interior along the Mississippi River. The fur trade was one of the principal incentives, and the English watched French progress with jealous eyes. Rivalry between the French and English from Quebec to New Orleans was revealed in undercutting of fur prices, minor skirmishes, and finally in war. By the Treaty of Paris in 1763, France yielded Canada and all claims to territory east of the Mississippi River to Great Britain, retaining only two small islands, of importance to fishermen, in the St. Lawrence River.

The original goals held by British mercantilists in promoting the colonization of the New World were not realized. The American colonies were never able to provide the kind and quantity of goods that would free England from dependence on other countries. However, in the attempt to exploit the American colonies, greater and greater controls were imposed that soon drove the colonists to rebellion. A minor incident in April 1775 in Lexington and Concord precipitated the Revolutionary War.

THE TRANSITION PERIOD—1776 TO 1865

The change from self-sufficient agriculture (Colonial period) to commercial agriculture (typical after the Civil War) took approximately one century, called the Transition Period. As the United States was ushered into the company of nations upon victory over the British, Europeans looked cynically upon the new country, and few believed that the feeble bonds of union would hold the states together.

It was a demanding task to set up an economic and political structure independent of the British crown. Economic self-sufficiency was necessary in the readjustment period, since commerce with Europe was interrupted and trade boycotts were employed. In 1783, an act of Parliament renewed trade with the United States, and the preference for British over French goods soon brought the United States and England into close trade relationships. By 1793, one-fifth of all British exports found their way to American shores.

Land Policies

Notwithstanding all the political discontent and physical hardships, America was stirred to increase its population and expand into new areas at the close of the Revolution. Cessation of rights by states to land west of the Appalachians paved the way for an organized and planned settlement of the interior. The Ordinance of 1784 divided the whole region extending between these mountains and the Mississippi into eighteen regions, each of which was to become a state when its population equalled that of the smallest of the original states. The Land Ordinance of 1785 delineated the method for a system of surveys, which became known as the "rectangular" system. By this method, a "base line" was first laid out running due east and west. North and south across the base line, meridians were marked off at intervals of six miles. Similar lines at six-mile intervals were laid off parallel to the east-west base line, creating blocks of 36 square miles known as "townships." Each township was subdivided into square-mile sections.

Besides the survey system, the ordinance laid down the terms regarding land sales. Following an old New England practice, section 16 in each township was set aside for supporting schools, and the remainder was to be sold at auction to the highest bidder in the minimum quantity of one section and at the minimum price of one dollar per acre. The Treasury Department needed funds and urged Congress to deal with the public lands as a source of revenue. However, $640 was a considerable fortune for the poor frontiersmen who became the first settlers. Although Congress expected groups to purchase large plots of land, speculators were often the chief buyers at the auctions. Land sold slowly under the ordinance, and eventually the government was compelled to forego revenue in order to get the land settled.

Private land ownership was the dominant aim of congressional land policy. After a series of plans offering liberalized credit had failed to promote private settlement, the historic Homestead Act was signed by Lincoln in 1862. Under the Homestead Act, a man would be given ownership of a tract of 160 acres (quarter section) if he would establish a home on it, attempt to improve its productivity, and stay five years. The penniless settler now had an incentive to settle the free land, and thousands quickly took advantage of the opportunity. Although there were some who gained land titles illegally by not meeting the requirements, the Homestead Act stands as a historic landmark in national land policy. One need only look at other countries where private land ownership by the masses is not encouraged, to see the problems that arise.

A census map of 1830 shows a population of 13 million, with all but 3 percent east of the Mississippi. With the purchase of the Louisiana Territory in 1803 and of Florida in 1819, the annexation of Texas in 1845, the Northwest Treaty of 1846, and the acquisition of Mexican territory (California, Nevada, Utah, Arizona, and part of New Mexico) in 1848, present-day boundaries of the United States were almost complete. Each succeeding decade saw waves of population move westward.

State of agriculture. The relative abundance of land contributed to wasteful use of land in the extensive agriculture. An observer said in Missouri in 1849, "Farming is here conducted on the regular skinning system . . . most of the farmers in this country *scratch* over a great deal of ground but *cultivate* none."[2] Handicapped by a lack of markets, the frontier farmer could easily support his family with food but had little incentive to produce commercially. The attempt to profit through land speculation and rising land values was often more dominant than doing so through agricultural production.

In the South, where tobacco was the principal crop in the eighteenth century, a new competitor, cotton, had a meteoric rise in importance in the early 1800s. Mechanical inventions in cotton manufacture, culminating with Eli Whitney's cotton gin in 1793, revolutionized the industry and opened vast new markets for raw cotton at home and abroad. The increasing importance of cotton also helped to open up the Southwest as prospective growers expanded westward in search of new rich soils, pushing Indians, Spaniards, and cattle ranchers ahead of them. By the period between 1850 and 1860, New Orleans had displaced Charleston and Savannah as the commercial center for cotton. Rice, sugar cane, and hemp were additional commercial crops produced in the southern states.

Further north, different problems were encountered as settlers pushed west. The tough prairie soil of the Midwest was first mistakenly thought not to be very rich, and trees to provide lumber for buildings were relatively scarce. Soon, however, it was learned that the soil and climate were adaptable to cereal-grain production and to raising livestock.

Effect of Industrial Revolution

After the turn of the century, the effects of the Industrial Revolution transformed New England into a manufacturing center. The urban population, constituting about a third of the total in New

---

2 *Cultivator*, New Series VI, 1849, p. 302.

England by 1860, became dependent on the farmer and thus provided a market for food products.

In the early 1800s, cities (New York, the largest, had 200,000 people) had no practical water systems, gas, electric lights, well-paved streets, paid fire departments, or effective police forces. Hardly two dozen miles of railroad had been constructed; it took 36 hours to go from Boston to New York by stage and steamboat. Coal stoves were a rarity, and virtually no furnaces existed. However, by 1850, railroads were rapidly being built, gold had been discovered in California, and farming was on its way to becoming a scientific industry.

An improved plow in 1819, a mowing machine in 1831, and McCormick's reaper in 1834 were additional boosts in improving the productivity of the farming industry. Improved breeds of cattle were imported, and knowledge of these superior breeds, new inventions, and improved tillage methods were disseminated by agricultural societies, fairs, schools, and farm periodicals.

Education. Agricultural education started with specialized instruction in existing schools. The first institution of a distinctively agricultural character was established at Gardner, Maine, in 1822. The state of Michigan appropriated money for a state school of agriculture in 1850, and was followed by Maryland and Pennsylvania two years later. In 1862, Congress passed the Morrill Act, which founded the land-grant college system, resulting in the establishment of at least one state-supported college in each state, to be devoted to the development of the agricultural and mechanical arts. In the same year, the U.S. Department of Agriculture was established, although national aid to agriculture had begun in 1839, when a Patent Department was initiated to collect statistics and make investigations for the promotion of agriculture.

COMMERCIAL AGRICULTURE SINCE 1860

Volumes have been written on the significant industrial advances made in the last half of the nineteenth century, which almost obscured agricultural developments of equal magnitude. Certainly, the industrial and agricultural revolutions reinforced each other, and it is impossible to separate many of the cause-and-effect relationships. The half-century after 1860 saw the rapid adoption of newly invented agricultural machinery and scientific tillage methods. The number of farms increased from 2 to 6 million, and over 500 million new acres of land were brought under cultivation. Even though expansion was great, this period was characterized by farmer discontent and uncertainty. The Civil War had caused inflated prices, and when these collapsed, the farmer in a debtor position was hurt.

The businesses engaged in the processing and distributing of food products were growing. Virtual monopolies in the meat-packing and milling industries were often able to hold farm prices artificially low on the buying side while profiting also by charging high prices to consumers. In addition, holders of patent monopolies were often able to overcharge the farmer for farm supplies. "There are three great crops raised in Nebraska," said one of the farmers' papers in 1890. "One is a crop of corn, one is a crop of freight rates, and one is a crop of interest. One is produced by the farmers who by sweating and toil farm the land. The other two are produced by men who sit in their offices and behind their bank counters and farm the farmers."[3]

The feeling of bitterness over exploitation speeded the organization of farmers' societies to unify farmer effort in alleviating this situation. The first of these groups, organized in 1867, was called the National Grange. The Grange promoted the development of cooperative buying and selling organizations and farmers' insurance companies. In 1887, Congress created the Interstate Commerce Commission to regulate trade among states, and in 1890 passed the Sherman Antitrust Act to prevent business from exercising monopoly powers on the public. The Pure Food and Drug Act in 1906 was another milestone in protecting the consuming public from unethical business practices.

In 1887, the passage of the Hatch Act established the Agricultural Experiment Stations in conjunction with the land-grant college system and provided funds for research on agricultural problems. However, it was not until 1914 and 1916 that the Smith-Lever and Smith-Hughes acts were passed, the first establishing the Agricultural Extension Service and the second providing vocational agricultural training in high schools.

In general, the history of American agriculture was chiefly the opening of new lands to food production. Farming was still extensive in nature until just before World War I. With the turn of the century, rural population and acreage of productive farmland began to decrease.

The 25-year period before World War I has sometimes been called the Golden Era. Total production increased some 30 percent, and strong domestic and foreign demands made for the most prosperous quarter-century for farmers in our history. The period from World War I to the present day is incorporated in the various sections of this book dealing with farm-policy formulation, international trade, and rural development. It is in these chapters that the federal government's participation in agriculture is discussed from a policy viewpoint.

---

[3] *Farmers' Alliance*, August 23, 1890.

PART
TWO

3

Environment,
Natural-Resource Use,
and Energy

No discussion of natural-resource use is complete without mention of overall environmental conditions. In this country, it had long been thought that the allocation and use of resources were the sole domain of the individual private firm, and that society could solve any differences it might have about resource use in the marketplace. However, there is a growing realization that maintaining the natural state of one's environment involves some cost that cannot be left entirely to the play of supply and demand in the marketplace.

In addition, there is an increasing awareness that if we are to keep producing adequate supplies of food and fiber for the world's rapidly expanding population, there must also be more attention paid to the disposal of agricultural, municipal, and industrial wastes. Further, inventories of energy resources such as fossil fuels have been compared with present usage rates, and the startling conclusion is now evident that we are using up many of our irreplaceable natural resources at increasingly exploitative rates. This chapter discusses some of the uses and the inventories of the more important resources.

ENVIRONMENT AND ENVIRONMENTAL ECONOMICS

Environment is a combination of physical and institutional conditions. The physical conditions involve all the natural resources—land, water, sun's energy, air, minerals, and the flora and fauna that grow on the land and in the sea. The institutional part of the environment is created by people, and includes the psychological and value-oriented decisions of how the physical environment is used. The institutional environment depicts the things that people value highly about their natural resources, and the organizations, procedures, and regulations set up to use or legitimize those natural resources in the production of the goods and services necessary or desirable for a growing society. Environmental management, then, becomes both a technological and a social problem. Man learns that certain kinds of technology or forms of organization will not handle satisfactorily some of the problems posed by the economy, and therefore he designs either new technologies or new social organizations to implement the change in the system, based on his new learning and better understanding of the situation.

Environmental economics has been defined as *the study of the unintended, or unknown, consequences of choice*.[1] The key to this statement, and the challenge to economic analysts, is that it implies a range of choice for decision makers. Not only is there the ability to choose, there is the possibility and challenge of increasingly better environmental management than now exists.

An undercurrent maintains itself through this range of choice, however, and that is the eternal necessity to provide for the food needs of the world's people. But only providing for basic food needs and material acquisitions has proved to be inadequate to satisfy mankind once minimal levels are attained. There is in addition a need to preserve, maintain, or create a certain quality of life without which mere material acquisition is a sham. However, until the basic needs of food, housing, health care, and education are met, there is a trade-off between resource use—waste management and environmental degradation—and maintaining the "pure" state of the natural environment. This suggests that a point is reached where one might consider substituting well-paid labor for capital in the production and marketing processes instead of the conventional substitution of capital for labor.

But what kinds of questions arise for the economic analysts and ordinary citizens to consider? We know that waste production and therefore the necessity for waste management are direct products of the economic production of goods and services. Furthermore, they are directly connected with the economic-growth processes, and the more economic growth that is encouraged, the more wastes of all kinds that

---

[1] Some of the ideas in the following section are more fully discussed in P. W. Barkley and D. W. Seckler, *Economic Growth and Environmental Decay—The Solution Becomes the Problem* (New York: Harcourt Brace Jovanovich, 1972).

occur. With inadequate waste management, a situation will lead to pollution and inevitable environmental degradation.

The depletion of resources can occur not only in the quantity but in the quality of the resources themselves. For example, redwood forests may be logged and reseeded, but young redwood timber does not have the rot and insect resistance that old-growth redwood timber has. Therefor, even the same amount of redwood boards may, in fact, be two different commodities with entirely different properties—the one of considerably less performance quality than the other.

Referring back to the fact that society and individuals have choices about resource use (not only in the allocation of resources to various types of production, but also in the rate of resource use), it is relevant to ask the questions, How much economic growth? What kind of growth? For whom is the production, and to whom is it distributed? Where does it occur? When does it take place? and Who pays the cost? An explicit part of the choice mechanism should be the awareness that some resources are irreplaceable. Once the resource is used up, there is no replenishment. Examples of irreplaceable resources include oil fields, trapped-water basins, fossil-fuel beds, mineral deposits, and selected species of animals and plants.

Resource-Use Choice Model

Let's look at a simplification of the choice model. We are all on a planet of fixed size with relatively fixed rates of natural waste absorption. When man starts technological processes and cities, industries, and farms begin to throw off wastes as by-products of the production and living processes, there is great pressure put on the natural self-cleansing functions of the physical environment. The ecological balance is disrupted, and the equilibrium that was exists no more.

Emptying our planet of wastes is then both a function of human technology and of nature. Here it is useful to note that our natural ecological system relies almost entirely on recycling, whereas man-made waste-disposal systems have rarely if ever incorporated recycling. Part of the reason for man's not considering recycling systems is that until recent years, and then only in the world's more advanced industrial countries, industrial, municipal, and farm wastes have been disposed of as though the surrounding environment were a costless disposal plant capable of infinite "filling up." Thus, the costs of keeping the environment in a somewhat natural state have been left to the general public rather than to the producer of the wastes.

Political decision-making groups all over the nation and world are beginning to reassess society's needs in terms of the public interest in the collective good we call our environment. The politicians, urged on by private groups and individuals, are addressing themselves to issues concerning the quality of life and the identification of costs necessary to maintain or improve that quality. There is increasing realization that keeping up the environment costs someone something, and that, to date, that someone has generally not been the person producing the wastes. In economic terms, this situation is called one of *cost externalities,* where the cost is borne by someone other than the person causing the cost to occur. Major wastes that farmers and processors might cause others to pay to clean up include sediment, animal waste, food-processing-plant effluent, plant nutrients, forest and crop residues, pesticides, and smoke.

It is evident that many decisions about resource use are clouded with uncertainty and risk. For example, a new drug or insecticide may well be marketed and widely used with the expectancy of many positive results, but then be banned from the market when disastrous side effects are observed. A prime example of this situation is Thalidomide. Another one seems to be DDT, although the debate on that chemical still rages.

There are ways to reduce the consequences of irreversible resource use. One is to try to make no decisions that result in such an irreversible process. This attempt, however, is hampered by a lack of knowledge concerning the outcomes of resource use—the technological aspects and the effects they may have on human values and perception. Not using as many resources is another control method, and includes recycling of materials rather than continued exploitation of new resources. A third method is keeping as many options of resource use open as possible. If a particular decision is seen to be unfavorable, then there are still alternative choices of resource use open. In all cases, it should be noted that the maintenance of quality of life and resource use necessitate consideration of (1) the resources that are actually used in the production processes and the wastes that evolve from the processes, (2) the performance of the resource in the production process and the product it makes, and (3) a reasonable balance to be achieved over time so that the environmental equilibrium is not put off center too far.

Future Use of Rural Resources

The future use of resources is directly related to what is called "population–resource" balance. When the population exerts too great a pressure on the available resources, problems occur. There are two main groups of forces bearing on rural resources: forces causing increased extractive-resource production (food, fiber, lumber, and minerals), and those forces for increased production of nonextractive uses such as open space, recreation, and clean air. To give some idea of the rapidly increasing people pressure on resource use since 1950, our population has increased about 35 percent but our electric-energy consumption has increased over 300 percent, our natural-gas usage has risen over 250 percent, and crude-petroleum usage and the number of cars and trucks has more than doubled. It appears that our standard of living lets us consume more resources at a faster rate than ever before.

The information above leads us to ask again, Consumption for what ends—without end? Can we slow our economic growth, our resource use, and maintain our standard of living? What are the relationships between our economic goals of growth and stability as they relate to consumption and equity?

The solution necessarily involves changes in present resource-use policies. With an increased awareness of the worsening physical condition of our world space, the goals of environmental policy are not to go down with a sinking ship, but to save captain, crew, ship, and the sea on which they sail.

There are several reasons for anticipating a rather slow adjustment by society in finding the solutions to the problems posed by the questions above. One of the reasons is that in a society originally based on the notion of private property and a free-market system, the concept of a collective good called environment as a common property shared by all people is a difficult thing to accept. The attempt to force society to accept responsibility for cleaning up its own wastes and not pass them on to "external parties" is an about-face from the way many cities and industries now perform.

Another reason for a slow adjustment is that we do not know what the various communities really want. Demands have not been made clear or explicit, and for those communities that *have* articulated specific demands, few studies have been made of the consequences of their implementation. We also know little about the technology for producing certain types of rural services. For example, in the field of health, there is little specific knowledge about which health services rural communities need most and how these services can be produced well and cheaply for both the rural and the urban consumer. Further, even though we talk about multipurpose use of resources, there is an inherent conflict between intensive recreational use of a given area and its being designated as a wilderness spot.

A fourth reason for a slow adjustment is that, to date, total costs of production of goods and services have often been obscured, because the producer has not had to pay the full costs, owing to the externalities noted. There are also institutional blocks to human mobility, so that people may choose not to adjust too quickly. Some of these obstacles include the fixity of capital investments such as housing, water and sewer systems, and utility contracts. Another restraint is simply that if one moved, one might not be able to gain employment in the new area.

A fifth adjustment constraint is that there are policy unknowns that put a brake on the production possibilities concerning the environment and resource use. For example, revenue sharing is still a concept that has many bugs to be ironed out in the identification and implementation of federal-state-local program initiation and funding responsibilities.

Growing concern about the environment should have been visible to all citizens in the country since 1969, when the federal and state governments were required to file environmental-impact statements under the National Environmental Policy Act. This act has been extended to states for land use and transportation planning, accompanying air- and water-quality plans, and now land use and development plans. The *Friends of Mammoth* v. *Mono County Board of Supervisors* case was decided by the California Supreme Court on September 21, 1972. This critical case originated as a citizen's response through the vehicle of the California Environmental Quality Act of 1970, which requires the filing of environmental-impact reports on development projects that may have a "significant effect on the environment." The act was upheld.

The difference between compliance under the federal act and under the California court decision is that the *Mammoth* decision made mandatory the publication of an environmental-impact report by a local agency on a private project. No longer are private developers exempt from environmental-impact responsibility. The next few years will see an increased need to develop adequate and relevant guidelines for these statements.

Planning Conflicts

Increasing awareness of the environment inevitably imposes land-use planning conflicts. One is that the number of options available to the owners of privately held land is reduced. No longer can the individual act without consideration of the public at large.

A second conflict area arises from the diversity of social goals concerning land use, and the fragmenting opinions of people in the affected community about what is "best." There may be conflicts about the size of ownership, related to land parcels, such as the controversy that now exists about the 160-acre limitation on federally developed irrigation water.

Another area of conflict must be resolved concerning the delegation of land-use planning authority. Who has the final say about land use—

the state, region, county, or city? And finally, what might be the "correct balance" between public and private ownership of land? For example, how many parks and wilderness areas can a geographic region afford before its tax base is eroded and private lands bear too heavy a burden?

The institutional pressures helping to bring about these conflicts include rising property taxes and the economic squeeze this puts on individual incomes and business expenses. Income tax write-offs for depreciation and depletion allowances are also evident unresolved issues of the future. And finally, the new requirements for environmental-impact statements, which in some cases call for performance bonds on the part of developers, are adding to the pressures of conflict.

NATURAL RESOURCES

Rich natural-resource endowments have been a necessary condition for most countries if they are to enter the take-off stages of productivity that enable farm people to grow enough food so that they can migrate to other employments. A sufficient condition for continued production of food and fiber, and the promise of economic and social betterment, is that there are enough capital and other resources to combine with labor to provide jobs and markets for the migrants. One of the paradoxes of our natural environment is that the natural resources in it are distributed throughout the world in an uneven fashion. Chile, North America, and Zambia hold the bulk of the world's discovered copper, and Malaysia produces one-third of the world's tin. Thus it is that the economic systems of the world combine to produce, market, and redistribute these unevenly allocated resources.

LAND

Including the states of Hawaii and Alaska, the land area of the United States is 2,271 million acres. Fortunately, however, the productivity of land depends not on its area but on man's ability to apply his labor, management, capital, and technology to it. More productive techniques are rapidly being developed and there is every prospect that more will be forthcoming. This challenge is not easy, however. Adapting the use of our land to a dynamic civilization and to the increasing demands of a growing population will continue to tax the resourcefulness of man for all time.

Land is a resource base for virtually all kinds of production. Besides producing food, lumber, and other products from cropland, grasslands, and forests, land also provides space for the things man builds, such as cities, highways, airports, recreation areas, and schools. Although no two pieces of land are exactly alike, many differences are small and can be changed by man. Air conditioning, heating, and electricity can alter the temperature or hours of light, bulldozers can alter topography, drainage and irrigation projects can modify water availability, and highway construction can change spatial relationships by reducing the time needed to get from one location to another.

The potential uses of land and the resulting output of goods and services from it change with the passage of time, and even though its physical location remains always the same, its location in an economic sense can change. As distances shrink because of newer and faster modes of transportation, land areas expand in potentials. Today, nearly all physically productive land in the United States can contribute products to an international market. As a result, land uses shift and the number of uses increases accordingly. The mobility of people with money to spend for travel now makes the land area of Yellowstone National Park accessible to many thousands of people and thus much more productive in terms of fees charged and output measured in recreation satisfaction. Its spatial relationship from an economic viewpoint has changed, as has its economic potential.

The United States encompasses 6 percent of the world's land area, which lies almost wholly in the temperate zone, an area with climate favorable to most animals and plants. This land area has different population densities, which range from 67,808 per square mile on Manhattan Island to 750 in Rhode Island, to less than 2 in Nevada and about .05 in Alaska, as of 1970. The average is 100 persons per square mile. Our concern will be principally with land use, however, since there is no necessary relationship between population density and the rate of economic growth experienced in an area.

Land Use for Food and Fiber Production

Land for food production is a key resource in feeding future populations. Nearly three-fifths of our land area is used for crops and livestock production; more than one-fifth is ungrazed forest land; and about 3 percent is devoted to urban and transportation uses. It might be added that when Alaska and Hawaii became states, total land area of the United States increased by one-fifth.

Even though the percentages of acreage in cropland, grassland pasture, and range have not changed much, there have been marked changes in land use. A particular stride forward is the improvement of land for crops and grassland pastures by means of drainage systems, flood control, irrigation, and brush clearing. Substantial shifts have oc-

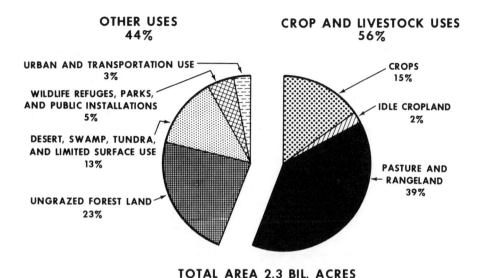

OTHER USES
44%

URBAN AND TRANSPORTATION USE
3%

WILDLIFE REFUGES, PARKS,
AND PUBLIC INSTALLATIONS
5%

DESERT, SWAMP, TUNDRA,
AND LIMITED SURFACE USE
13%

UNGRAZED FOREST LAND
23%

CROP AND LIVESTOCK USES
56%

CROPS
15%

IDLE CROPLAND
2%

PASTURE AND
RANGELAND
39%

TOTAL AREA 2.3 BIL. ACRES

U.S. DEPARTMENT OF AGRICULTURE   NEG ERS 8847-73 (10)   ECONOMIC RESEARCH SERVICE

FIGURE 3-1
Land Use in the Fifty States, 1969

curred among regions. Cropland is concentrated on fertile, more level areas, while grass and trees are generally planted on hilly land subject to erosion.

Virtually all the cropland is in private ownership. Of the total land area in the 50 states, 58.3 percent was privately owned in 1969, 5.8 percent was owned by state and municipal governments, and 33.7 percent by the federal government. Most of the public domain land is in Alaska. About one-half the forest land and about one-third the grassland pasture and range is owned by the federal government.

Cropland used for crops. The physical acreage from which crops were harvested was nearly the same in 1970 as in 1900. But since the average acre yield was two-thirds greater than in 1900, the equivalent increase in the land supply for crops was nearly 250 million acres. In addition, over the same period, the substitution of machine power for animal power on farms released some 80 million acres for nonfeed uses. By 1970, less than 2 percent of the cropland used for crops was needed to provide feed for horses and mules, as compared to 25 percent needed in 1920.

Cropland harvested in 1971 was just under 310 million acres, a decline of 11 percent since 1949. Acreage in irrigated crops increased 10 million acres during the same period. There is considerable regional variation in land use within the United States. The Corn Belt, Mountain, and Pacific states show increasing acreages in cropland while all the others have declined. Over one-half the total land area in the Corn Belt states is in cropland; the Mountain states contain only 8 percent. In the Southeast, 63 percent of the land area is in forest and woodland, as opposed to only 3 percent in the Northern Plain states.

TABLE 3-1

Distribution of Cropland Use in the United States
By Major Crops, 1950 to 1959, 1960, and
Projections for 1980 and 2000

Use	1950-59	1960	1980	2000
		(Percent)		
Feed grains	29.6	28.4	23.6	26.3
Wheat	11.9	9.8	7.2	8.4
Cotton	4.0	3.4	3.4	4.2
Soybeans	3.8	5.1	7.7	9.2
Hay	15.7	14.8	20.9	24.8
All other crops	6.0	5.1	5.8	6.5
Total crops harvested	71.0	66.6	68.6	79.4
Cropland pasture	14.9	16.8	16.0	12.2
Total crops and pasture	85.9	83.4	84.6	91.6
Fallow, idle, failure	12.8	11.7	9.6	8.4
Excess cropland acreage	1.3	4.9	5.8	—
Total cropland	100.0	100.0	100.0	100.0

SOURCE: Hans H. Landsberg, et al., *Resources in America's Future* (Baltimore: The Johns Hopkins Press, 1963). Adapted from Table A 18-8, p. 987. Published for Resources for the Future, Inc.

Use of cropland by individual crops.   Feed grains were raised on about 30 percent of the cropland in 1971. Wheat acreage accounted for almost one acre in six, and hay one acre in five. Soybeans has increased rapidly during recent years and output is expected to double by the year 2000. Acreages of wheat, feed grains, and cotton are expected to decline relatively to 1980, then increase at the expense of cropland pasture (Table 3-1).

Pasture and Range (Grazing Land)

Grazing takes place on many kinds of land. In the majority of cases, there is little incentive for the individual to increase the productivity of grazing land, particularly if the land grazed is owned by someone else. Therefore, even though range acreage is large, it produces only about one-third of the livestock feed. Most of the grazing lands are in the Mountain and Pacific states, where federal range is a vital element in livestock production. For purposes of comparison, 160 million acres of average western land provide approximately the same number of feed units per acre per year as 8 million cropland pasture acres or only 3 million acres of corn.

Permanent farm pasture land is of greater importance for the future, because this category holds the greatest hope of increasing yields per acre. The 540 million acres of privately owned grassland pasture and range were equivalent to about 80 feed units produced per acre. If yields were doubled, which is considered a definite possibility, the equivalent of 80 million acres of cropland pasture would be added to the farm economy.

Projections of Farming Uses for Land

By the year 2000, total cropland needed by the United States will be 418 million acres (Table 3-2). This projection assumes that sources of plant foods from yeast cultures or the ocean will not be important contributors to total output, although the success of new technologies is difficult to predict. After consideration is given for roughage needs and yield increases, medium projections indicate that cropland available may be about 6 million acres short of combined pasture and crop requirements by the year 2000.

Land Used for Forestry

The North American continent has a much greater and richer variety of forest species and types than has any other part of the temperate world regions. There are over 100 native conifer and hardwood species, compared to less than a dozen in Europe. The virgin forests were a natural resource estimated to have contained 7,500 billion board feet of timber. Only about one-fourth of this timber remained in 1960.[2]

Commercial forestry.   Two-thirds of the total forest land in the United States was considered commercial in 1970. Commercial forest lands

---

[2] Marion Clawson, et al., *Land for the Future* (Baltimore: The Johns Hopkins Press, 1960), p. 281. Published for Resources for the Future, Inc.

TABLE 3-2

Projected Needs in the United States for Land Use
in Future Selected Years Compared to 1960

	Land Required (Millions of Acres)[a]				
	1960	1970	1980	1990	2000
Feed grains	133.6	102.6	109.6	118.4	124.6
Wheat	45.8	35.1	34.3	36.4	39.5
Cotton	15.7	15.4	16.4	17.8	19.9
Soybeans	24.3	30.2	36.3	41.2	44.0
Hay	67.6	82.5	97.8	110.4	118.3
Total for crops above	287.0	266.0	294.4	324.2	346.3
Total cropland harvested[b]	313.0	290.0	323.0	353.0	378.0
Crop failure, idle, fallow	55.0	50.0	45.0	43.0	40.0
Total cropland required	368.0	340.0	368.0	396.0	418.0
Acreage in excess of requirements based on 470 million acres of cropland	102.0	130.0	102.0	74.0	52.0

a Based on medium assumptions for both demand and yields. See Chapter 18 of reference below for explanation.

b Equivalent to 109% of 5-crop total, based upon historical records.

SOURCE: Hans H. Landsberg, et al., *Resources in America's Future* (Baltimore: The Johns Hopkins Press, 1963), pp. 979, 980, 982. Published for Resources for the Future, Inc.

amounted to 525,500 acres in 1900, increasing to 500 million acres in 1970. Thirty-six percent of the land is in the North, 39 percent in the South, and 25 percent in the West. Virtually all timber in the Mountain and Pacific states and Alaska is softwood, while hardwoods comprise 80 percent of the total in the northern states. The South has about half hardwood and half softwood. Nearly three-fifths of the commercial forest land is privately held.

The amount of land devoted to commercial forestry in the future is expected to remain relatively stable, at slightly under 500 million acres. Whether there will be sufficient timber to meet the country's needs will depend upon its productivity per acre. To date, the productivity status of much forest land is far below its potential, but management practices of farmers and commercial loggers have materially improved since 1950.

Use of noncommercial forest land. About one-third of the forest lands are used for noncommercial purposes, principally recreation and wildlife enhancement. Approximately 27 million acres of forest land in the 50 states (2 million acres are in Hawaii and Alaska) are in parks, wildlife refuges, and wilderness areas.

Urban Uses of Land

For those living in Los Angeles or New York City, it may seem as though cities are rapidly eating up the land area in the United States. With 70 percent of the population living on 1 percent of the land area, the United States is now essentially an urban economy.[3] This situation has an important effect on land-use patterns.

A city uses land directly for its physical occupancy area and indirectly for transport and water supply, and usually demands some land area for recreational purposes. The urban population was estimated to occupy some 3 percent of the land in 1970, but total land reported by incorporated cities of populations over 2,500 includes over 13 million acres. Total area withdrawn for urban and transportation uses is estimated at about one million acres annually. By 1980 and 2000, a medium projection estimates land withdrawn for urban use to climb to 30 and 41 million total acres respectively. As a nation we remove about 2 million acres per year from rural lands. About half this land goes into parks and recreation areas.

Special Uses of Land

Recreation. Recreation is a rapidly expanding industry in the United States, where per capita incomes are rising and working hours per week are declining. There is no evidence that the trend will be reversed.

Of the land area in national forests, over 14 million acres are estimated to be primarily used for recreation purposes. In addition, all the land in the national park system (28.9 million acres) is set aside for recreation; there are an additional 8.5 million acres in state parks and 900 thousand acres in municipal parks. TVA reservoirs add an additional 200 thousand acres, and Corps of Engineer reservoirs contribute another 3.3 million acres to recreation-oriented land areas. Hunting and fishing pursuits occur on many additional lands.

Transportation. Although requiring only a small total volume of land, transportation uses are highly specialized and can easily preempt other uses of land. Railroad rights-of-way now use about 8 million acres, and

---

[3] Marion Clawson, et al., *Land for the Future*, p. 95. Their estimates show that perhaps one-third of the land within city boundaries is idle, particularly in the smaller cities. This land is held for expansion purposes and is often used quite uneconomically. From a land-use viewpoint, the total land withdrawn from alternative uses is the more important criterion.

although freight volume may increase, improved efficiencies will probably allow the increase to be carried on existing trackage. Highways for automobiles now occupy over 16 million acres. This amount of land is estimated to increase by an additional 3 million acres by the end of the century. Airports and landing strips occupy nearly 1.5 million acres, a figure that may double by the year 2000. Total land needed for transportation uses will be in the neighborhood of 30 million acres by 2000.

Wildlife refuges.   Although man shares all his land with birds and animals, certain areas are set aside strictly for wildlife refuges. About 15 million acres are now given over for wildlife uses, and an additional 5 million acres may be added by the year 2000. The latter will be principally wetlands used for the benefit of waterfowl.

Water reservoirs.   Some 12 million acres in the United States have been inundated by dam-created storage reservoirs or artificial lakes. With increased demand for water for consumer and industrial uses, almost another 8 million acres will be covered by the end of the century.

Other miscellaneous uses.   The remainder of the land area not covered in the preceding discussion is in mineral production, sand dunes, bare rock, deserts, mountain tops, and swamps. These uses comprise about 6 percent of the total land area, but will decline as land is reclaimed or adapted to other, more productive uses in the future.

Multiple Uses of Land

Throughout the preceding discussion, land has been classified and discussed with reference to its primary use. Some land serves two purposes well, such as wildlife and recreation, forestry and recreation, or farmland and hunting. Urban land serves the varied interests of its residents.

WATER

Water is a vital element to virtually all production processes. Too little or too much water in the soil severely limits plant life. Other water uses on farms include stock watering, sanitation, spraying, drinking, and fire protection. Industry is increasing its demands for water each year, and the human-consumption demand for water will be intensified by the continuing rise in population, outdoor recreation, and growth of cities.

Approximately 350 billion gallons of fresh water were used daily in homes, factories, steam generating plants, or on irrigated farm land in

1972. Other large quantities are utilized without being withdrawn from their natural habitat, for such purposes as boating, swimming, supporting inland navigation, turning generators of hydroelectric plants, carrying wastes, and providing scenery. Total use is expected to rise to about 443 billion gallons daily by 1980.

The water from rainfall and that which already exists in oceans, lakes, rivers, and streams constitutes the natural resource of water. Using water in various ways to improve the efficiency of production processes converts water from a free good to an economic good.

Two characteristics of water demand present unique problems. The first is a quality problem. Some uses of water affect the acceptability of water for other uses. Stream pollution from toxic home and industry waste products drastically reduces the demand for the resulting polluted water. Continued high demand for fresh water, however, has led to many technical refinements in overcoming water pollution in streams and lakes.

A second unique characteristic of water is the significance of its regional distribution. The commercial value of water is relatively low, because its physical characteristics make transport costly over long distances except in times of emergency. One region of the country may experience severe limitations of economic activity because of a water shortage while other regions may have large quantities of fresh water flowing into the ocean. Therefore, to think in terms of a national market for water, or of supply and demand for water on a national basis, is of limited significance.

The Overall Water Picture in the United States

Water supply originates with rain and snow. If the quantity falling on the United States in an average year were spread evenly, it would stand about 30 inches deep. Seventy percent (21 inches) returns to the atmosphere via evapotranspiration—a part of which supports cultivated crops, forests, and native grasses. The remaining nine inches constitute the manageable water supply. In the 1950s, three inches of the manageable supply was withdrawn for use, one inch of which returned to the atmosphere and two inches of which returned to the stream network. The other six inches of manageable supply simply flowed into the ocean via the streams and rivers.[4] Annual precipitation varies widely within the United States. Arizona, Nevada, and New Mexico receive an average

---

[4] U.S. Senate Select Committee on National Water Resources, 86th Cong., 2nd sess., Committee Print No. 3, "National Water Resources and Problems" (Washington, D.C.: U.S. Government Printing Office), pp. 3–4.

of less than 10 inches per year, while Alabama, Louisiana, and Alaska receive over 50 inches.

The use made of water is related to both population density and kind of use. For example, more water is used in the heavily populated Ohio River region than in the less-populated Missouri River region, even though the latter has four times as much land area. Some uses consume more water than others. Boating, for example, consumes no water during use, but irrigation may cause evaporation of 60 percent of the water used. Industry, on the other hand, requires huge volumes of water, but evaporation claims about only 2 percent of it. Water is used primarily for irrigation in the West and for industry in the East.

For purposes of discussing the various kinds of demands for water, three classes of demands will be considered: (1) withdrawal uses, in which water is actually removed from sources of supply; (2) flow uses, such as hydropower generation, recreation, and waste carrying; and (3) on-site uses, such as maintenance of wetlands for wildlife habitat and land-treatment measures for soil conservation.

Withdrawal Uses of Water

There are four principal categories of withdrawal uses of water: municipal, industrial, thermoelectric power, and irrigation uses. Of minor importance in terms of volume is the water withdrawn by rural household supplies, livestock watering, and mining operations. Withdrawal amounts to three inches (10 percent) of average annual precipitation in the United States, of which less than one-half is actually consumed or used up. The remainder is returned to streams.

Municipal use.   Only 5 percent of total water withdrawn is for municipal uses. This includes water used by urban residents for washing, cooking, drinking, lawn watering, and air cooling. These uses averaged about 60 gallons per capita per day in 1960 and by 1971 had risen to about 75 gallons per capita.

Residential use is influenced mostly by income levels, climate, and use of household devices. Pronounced regional differences occur resulting from differences in climate, size of city, degree of industrialization, and many other factors. States having high temperatures with relatively low rainfall show higher per capita usages, owing to such factors as air conditioning and lawn watering.

Commercial and industrial uses accounted for 65 gallons per capita per day in 1960, of which 26 gallons were supplied to commercial establishments connected to public supply systems. Another 25 gallons per capita per day go for purely municipal public uses like street cleaning and fire protection. The same proportions are likely to hold in the 1970s.

Total municipal needs in the future are difficult to estimate. Excluding industrial use of municipal supplies, some evidence suggests that per capita requirements may diminish, owing to the increasing prevalence of apartment living and other multifamily dwellings. On the other hand, further increases in the use of automatic appliances, air-conditioning units, and swimming pools suggest much higher per capita uses. Assuming a population of 330 million by 2000 and current per capita usage rates, the total municipal requirement by 1980 and by 2000 could be 29 and 43 billion gallons per day, respectively.

Industrial use.   Since 94 percent of the industrial use of water is for cooling, industry is largely a nonconsumptive user of water. In addition, saline water can be used for about one-sixth of the cooling processes in industry. Most cooling water is discarded after one using, but some industries, such as petroleum, recirculate water an average of four times.

In 1972, industrial and certain kinds of commercial establishments were using about 59 billion gallons of water per day. The primary effect of industry use of water is the degradation of quality as effluents are discharged with the water, giving rise to waste carriage and other disposal problems. Five major groups use over 90 percent of the total water used by industry. These include, in order of importance, chemicals, primary metals, petroleum and coal products, paper and allied products, and food products.

Thermoelectric power use.   Thermoelectric power generation was using water at a rate of 128 billion gallons per day in 1971. This use was second only to irrigation. Virtually all water used for steam-electricity generation is for condenser cooling, and although more electric power is developed with steam than with hydropower, the latter requires more water. Both have little effect on water supply, since the temperature of the water is all that is changed. About one-fifth of the water used for thermoelectric cooling is recirculated. The main factors determining whether or not water is recirculated are the relative costs of water and of additional equipment. Saline water is used as a substitute for fresh water for cooling purposes, particularly in coastal regions, but high-priced noncorrosive equipment is needed.

Irrigation use.   Irrigation is the largest use of fresh water (122 billion gallons per day in 1972). Irrigated land in farms increased from some 14 million acres in 1930 to nearly 40 million acres by 1971. Irrigated land is concentrated heavily in the 17 western states (Figure 3-2).

Irrigated acreage in the East (using a medium projection) is expected to increase to 6.2 million acres by 1980 and to 9.6 million acres

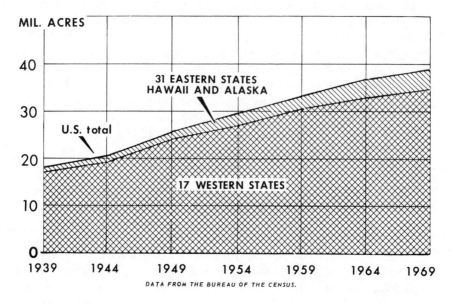

DATA FROM THE BUREAU OF THE CENSUS.

U.S. DEPARTMENT OF AGRICULTURE   NEG. ERS 8436 – 72 (8)   ECONOMIC RESEARCH SERVICE

FIGURE 3-2
Irrigated Land in Farms

by 2000. Projections for the West are 34.2 and 43.2 million acres, respectively, for 1980 and 2000. Total water requirements would advance to 135 and 170 billion gallons per day for 1980 and 2000.

Flow Uses of Water

Quantitative analysis of flow uses is exceedingly more difficult than analysis of withdrawal uses, since a stream or lake often has a multipurpose use. The principal flow uses include hydroelectric power, navigation, provision of habitat for aquatic life and fishing, swimming, and boating, and waste carriage and disposal.

Hydroelectric power.   Flowing water has been used as a source of power for many centuries. The share that hydropower contributes to total power will probably decline in the future, from about 18 percent in 1960 to approximately 8 percent in 2000, even though capacity and output generated will continue to rise.

Navigation use. Inland waterways are important arteries of commerce and communication. They were developed early in the nation's history and then declined in relative importance owing to the advent of railroads and the telephone. Since World War II, waterway navigation has experienced a major comeback. Ton miles doubled, 1950 to 1970, to 318,560 million. The Mississippi River system carries more than 2.5 times the freight of the Great Lakes system. All in all, there are about 21,000 miles of commercial inland waterways.

Aquatic-life habitats and water recreation. Principal flow uses of water in lakes and streams are the maintenance of aquatic life and the provision of recreation in the form of boating, swimming, and fishing. Present water-recreation facilities are generally overcrowded, and national-park visits are expected to increase by the years 1980 and 2000 three times and over six times, respectively, above the 1959 level of 63 million. With one-third of all households having one or more members who engage in hunting and fishing, and with family incomes higher and more leisure time available, the demand for water for wildlife and recreation will increase rapidly. The demand for total outdoor recreation is estimated to increase ten times between the years 1960 and 2000.

Waste-disposal use. Water is needed for waste disposal primarily to dilute the waste material so that its harmful effects are diminished. Waste disposal is an extremely complex problem. Many kinds of pollutants get into water courses. Sediment from soil erosion, agricultural pesticides washed off fields, chlorides for ice control washed off highways, salt leached from the soil by irrigation water, organic wastes from households, and both organic and inorganic compounds from industry are some of the more important examples. Warm water returned to streams after its use for cooling purposes may speed up the metabolism of microbes and facilitate more rapid breakdown of organic wastes, but it may also have harmful effects on fish as the oxygen saturation level is lowered.

The ability of a stream to handle waste materials depends on the quantity of flow, rate of flow, temperature, and chemical content. Another important variable is the extent to which waste is treated before being discharged into the streams. A measure used for the organic pollution load is Biochemical Oxygen Demand (BOD), which indicates the rate at which dissolved oxygen is used up in waste-receiving water. The U.S. Public Health Service estimates that waste loads from municipalities and industries prior to any treatment will increase about 3 times by the year 2000. Laws vary widely with regard to the discharge of wastes into streams, but regulation of stream flow to provide more water during low

flow periods is considered to be the least costly means of supplementing
waste-treatment measures to maintain water quality for most areas.

On-Site Uses of Water

On-site uses are of two principal kinds: the provision of wetlands
and swamps for wildlife habitat, and the provision of farm ponds and
other soil-conservation measures. Swamps and wetlands deplete water
supplies through evapotranspiration. Farm ponds slow water runoff.

Waterfowl require wet and marshy lands with many small ponds
to maintain their populations. Future needs of these lands will increase
as the population of hunters increases. Most waterfowl are migratory.
This means that satisfactory environmental conditions are required at
both ends of their migration. The United States has several major flyways (East Coast, Mississippi Valley, and West Coast) that run from
Canada to Mexico and the Caribbean. There have been major efforts to
protect winter and summer nesting and feeding areas in these countries
and along the flyways.

Soil-conservation practices have been a major federal program since
the 1930s. With federal assistance, the number of farm ponds has increased rapidly to aid in watering stock, in retarding erosion, and for
recreation purposes. Ponds deplete only modest quantities of water and
do not constitute a major use of fresh water.

A Summary of the Water-Demand Outlook

Demand on fresh water will continue to increase simply from increases in population and economic activity. However, the demand is intensified because of the boom in outdoor recreation and by the need to
dilute an increasing amount of organic wastes. The latter use constitutes
a relatively new problem, since only fairly recently has the concentration
of people and industry pushed pollution beyond the point of tolerance
for most communities. Although irrigation will continue as the major
source of water depletion, municipal and industrial uses will rise.

ENERGY AND MINERAL RESOURCES

Minerals and the energy forces derived from them differ from land
and water as natural resources in that they are not only exhaustible, but
also mostly not reproducible. Man can rejuvenate worn-out soil and
develop reservoirs to capture water, but he participates primarily only
in the exhaustion of minerals. Mere existence of huge mineral deposits

does not in itself assure a high rate of economic development. The key is technical knowledge in utilizing minerals, which lays the foundation for progress. For example, the Indians who originally occupied the United States received relatively little benefit from the minerals deposited in the area.

Mineral resources can be classified in several ways: for instance, metallic and nonmetallic, or basic and contributory.[5] The fertilizer minerals (potash, phosphate, and nitrate) form another group. The precious metals are in a class by themselves because they are valued chiefly as one basis of currencies. The two major classes considered here will be mineral fuels and nonmetallic nonfuel minerals.

Mineral Fuels

Energy. Energy is the arena for many debates about current resource use, because of the fact that we are faced with aspects of an energy-fuel crisis in this country over the next few years. One source of evidence is the heating-energy shortage, mostly fuel oils and natural gas, in the winter of 1972–73 in the population centers of the northeastern part of the nation. Low supplies were temporarily relieved by the political response of allowing more foreign oil imports to enter. However, by alleviating the immediate shortage problem, the government helped exaggerate our balance-of-payment problems abroad.

The fuel-energy crisis of 1973–74 exploded on an unprepared world. Oil-producing Arab nations reduced production and export of crude oil. Gasoline and diesel fuels used in transport doubled in price within a few weeks. Gas rationing appeared a distinct possibility. A nationwide truck strike highlighted the need for rational fuel allocations among the states and among commercial and other uses. Products from petroleum derivatives skyrocketed in price. Farmers in the spring of 1974 paid fertilizer bills 125–150 percent greater than those of 1973 for the same amount of material. Costs of most farm inputs rose as a result of fuel shortages.

Perhaps the most critical problem was the increasing food gap between the "have" and the "have not" nations. Drought and famine persisted in parts of Africa, but worldwide food shortages and high-priced energy inputs made the task of aiding these countries much more costly than a year previous. The upsurge in the price of food and feed grains, meats, milk products, and most vegetables was one of the prime causes

---

[5] Metallic minerals include aluminum, antimony, chromite, copper, iron, lead, manganese, mercury, nickel, tin, tungsten, and zinc. Nonmetallic minerals include asbestos, barite, china clay, coal, fluorspar, graphite, gypsum, magnesite, mica, nitrates, petroleum, phosphate, potash, pyrites, sulphur, talc, and soapstone.

of inflation both at home and abroad. The surplus trade balances of most countries were threatened or drastically reduced, and the less richly endowed countries of the world faced drastic domestic economic situations. One question became how eager were the food and energy producing nations of the world to take on the task of feeding the nations who could not adequately provide for themselves.

But let's look at some of the dimensions of the energy situation, consumption trends, and resource-use projections for the United States.

Who uses our fuel resources?[6] In 1971, household and commercial sources consumed about 25 percent (17.4 quadrillion BTUs) of the total energy consumed in the United States. Transportation and electrical utility generation plants each used about one-quarter of this amount, and industrial consumers and conversion losses absorbed the rest.

As a nation, we doubled out total energy consumption, 1950 to 1971, from 34.1 quadrillion BTUs to 68.8 quadrillion BTUs. During this time, our population increased by only a third, while our GNP more than doubled.

These figures illustrate the resource-use problem. They show the close connection between economic growth and energy consumption for an expanding and industrially sophisticated population. The conclusion and trend holds for all industrially advanced nations. Japan, other parts of Asia, and Europe are just as "guilty" of extravagant use of energy resources as we are. Environmental degradation is just as evident abroad as it is here. This does not lessen the challenge to reverse the situation, but it does put it in a more realistic perspective than that in which it is sometimes cast.

Materials from the U.S. Bureau of Mines—*Minerals Yearbooks* and other releases—show that in 1972, as prime sources of energy, coal contributed only 23 percent of the total energy consumed, down from over 50 percent even as late as 1940. Natural gas was the source for 40 percent of the total energy consumed in 1972 (three times what it was in 1940), and petroleum as a source controlled about 31 percent. Electricity accounted for only 5.5 percent of the total energy used in 1972, up from only 3.9 percent in 1960.

In absolute terms, however, the BTUs of coal used were about the same in 1930, 1950, and 1970. Natural-gas use increased from almost 2.0 quadrillion BTUs in 1930 to 22.5 quadrillion BTUs in 1970. Petroleum usage increased five times from 1930 to 1970 (29.6 quadrillion BTUs), and hydro and nuclear sources three times more (2.8 quadrillion BTUs) in 1970 than in 1940.

---

[6] For an excellent discussion with many supplementary data, see S. H. Schurr, *Energy, Economic Growth, and the Environment* (Baltimore: Johns Hopkins Press, 1972).

If we look at consumption of energy resources by source and by major consuming sector, another kind of picture unfolds. From 1950 to 1970, coal fell to one-ninth its energy contribution in households, electricity use rose about 5.5 times, natural-gas usage increased five times, and petroleum uses doubled.

During that same 20-year period, the industrial sector used almost the same BTUs of coal, but three times the BTUs of natural gas, twice the petroleum BTUs, and four times those of electricity. The transportation sector virtually stopped using coal, increased its use of natural-gas BTUs 4.5 times, upped its petroleum BTU usage 2.5 times, and dropped its use of electricity (already small) by a fourth. The electric utilities used four times more BTUs from coal in 1970 than they did in 1950, six times more BTUs from natural gas, 3.5 times more BTUs from petroleum, and almost five times more from electricity itself.

There is no doubt about the positive relationships among technology, realized consumer preferences, and resource use. Sixteen percent of the increase in kilowatt hours (from 196 billion kwh to 402 billion kwh) produced in the United States from 1960 to 1969 was attributable to the increased use of household air conditioning, and 12 percent of the increase was due to more space heating. If current trends continue, overall per capita use of electric energy is estimated to increase to about three times the 1970 rate of 7,573 kwh by 1990.

World consumption of energy. World consumption of energy is estimated to have doubled per capita from 1948 to 1968 (Table 3-3). Although there is a worldwide shift away from coal as a share of total energy resources consumed, there is an increase in the proportion of oil and gas resources used.

Fossil fuels will continue to account for the major share of energy consumed in the United States and the world through the year 2000. The lack of feasible hydropower and dam sites will curtail the expansion of water-powered sources of energy. Nuclear-powered energy will increase to perhaps 50 percent of the total by the year 2000.

With increasing use of resources for energy, there will be increased awareness of other problems. The use of nuclear fuels will cause fears of radioactive contamination. Certain aspects of coal and oil production will still cause personal and environmental concern. Mining is a hazardous, accident-filled occuption. Surface mining poses erosion problems and unesthetic slag heaps. Underground mining presents problems of surface subsidence and rising production costs. Increased oil exploration and drilling cause increased possibilities of oil contamination, such as the Santa Barbara offshore oil leak and the San Francisco Bay tanker collision of the early 1970s. Globs of oil are increasingly found covering the waters of the world.

TABLE 3-3
World Energy Consumption and Population by
Major World Region, 1950 and 1968
(in percent)

Region	1950		1968	
	Energy Consumption	Population	Energy Consumption	Population
North America	48.0	6.6	36.2	6.4
United States	44.5	6.1	32.9	5.8
Western Europe	22.8	12.1	21.9	10.1
Oceania	1.2	0.5	1.2	0.5
Latin America	3.1	6.5	4.2	7.7
Asia (excl. Communist)	5.0	32.2	8.8	33.9
Japan	2.3	3.3	4.6	2.9
Communist Asia	1.6	22.8	4.9	22.0
Africa	1.7	8.7	1.8	9.7
USSR and Communist Eastern Europe	16.7	10.8	21.0	9.8

SOURCE: S. H. Schurr, *Energy, Economic Growth, and the Environment* (Baltimore: Johns Hopkins Press, 1972), p. 180.

Where will the future energy resources come from? Domestic consumption of oil is currently about 15 million barrels per day, or about 31 percent of the total worldwide needs. We import about 2.5 million of the 15 million barrels. By 1980, it is estimated, we might use about 25 million barrels of oil daily in this country, and we might have to import about half that amount. World demand for oil will most likely rise to 80 million barrels daily by 1980. Where will it come from? Possibly from as yet undiscovered oil fields. In addition, the new North Sea oil fields, the fields off the coasts of Indonesia, and those in other areas will be increasingly exploited.

Coal. Coal resources of the United States are on the order of 1.7 trillion tons.[7] With the projected demand to 2000 at 25 to 35 billion tons, it is

[7] See U.S. Geological Survey Bulletin 1136 and Department of Interior Report to Joint Committee on Atomic Energy, Vol. 4, of *Review of the International Atomic Policies and Programs of the United States* (2 McKinney Report), Joint Committee Print, 86th Cong., 2nd sess., October 1960.

clear that coal reserves are more than adequate, providing a cushion capable of absorbing large chunks of industrial energy demand should gas and oil use become limited. However, the bulkiness of coal makes transport costly, increasing total cost an average of 70 percent over the value at the mine. This transport-cost factor encourages electric generating plants using coal to be located near the mining area, although the construction of pipelines to carry a slurry of coal and water over relatively long distances permits generating plants to be located several hundred miles away from their sources of fuel.

Oil. Throughout the 1950s, annual crude-oil production in the United States was between 2.0 and 2.5 billion barrels. Oil reserves are established mainly by inference, and the commonly used quantitative measure is "proved reserves," which have averaged about twelve times ordinary annual production for some time.[8] The figure of twelve years is about the average life expectancy of a new well, and companies tend to gear their exploration activities to maintain about twelve years of reserves. Therefore, the figure is erroneous if used to indicate the potential supply of oil remaining as a natural resource. Estimates of oil awaiting future recovery or potential availability range up to 500 billion barrels. The percentage of this amount that will be recoverable is largely dependent upon advances in technology, but a recovery figure of between 50 and 60 percent is not unreasonable to expect in the future, even though current recovery is nearer one-third.

Natural gas and natural-gas liquids. The commonly used measure of "proved reserves" is also used for natural gas, the energy source for manufacturing fertilizer nitrogen. Seventy-five to 80 percent of gas supplies are economically recoverable, and estimates of potential supplies are based on ultimate oil reserves and a gas/oil ratio. In 1960, 13.3 trillion cubic feet of natural gas were withdrawn for use, and proved reserves at the end of the year were 263.8 trillion cubic feet, or about 20 times the amount withdrawn.[9] Assuming that only one-third of the 500 billion barrels of oil potential is recoverable and that a gas/oil ratio of 7,000 cubic feet of gas per barrel exists,[10] gas reserves would be in the neighborhood of 1.2 quadrillion cubic feet, or about 100 years' supply at

---

[8] From Committee on Petroleum Reserves, *1961 Report to the American Petroleum Institute,* March 10, 1961.

[9] *Report* of the Committee on National Gas Reserves of the American Gas Association, for year ending December 31, 1961.

[10] The ratio is not a true relationship of the occurrence of gas and oil in nature. It is a factor based upon different types of experience and is conditioned by assumptions made in the commercial evaluation of the occurrences. It should be noted that increasing the recovery rate of oil will not necessarily increase the recoverable gas supply.

1960 use rates. However, a medium projection of use in 2000 is estimated at about 35 trillion cubic feet, and the maintenance of proved reserves at 20 times production would require a recoverable supply of 1.7 quadrillion cubic feet in the year 2000, which is the upper limit of current estimates.

Hydropower.   The limits of hydropower were discussed to some extent in the previous section on water. Hydroelectric capacity is determined by the average flow of streams and the vertical descent of the water. Potential for the United States has been estimated to be no less than 230 and no more than 390 million kw.[11] Much of this potential cannot be developed from an economic viewpoint. The Federal Power Commission recently set the potential hydro capacity at 127 million kw.[12] Installed capacity in 1972 was 57 million kw, and it is unlikely that additional capacity will be developed to exceed about twice this amount.

Nuclear energy.   Nuclear power used for generating electricity is expected to gain rapidly in importance after 1970. Supplies of fissionable material (uranium and thorium) are adequate to provide energy equal to the 1960 total requirement at the current level of technology. With a more highly developed technology, energy potential of up to 100 times the 1960 requirements has been estimated. It seems clear that the use of nuclear energy will be determined more by the state of reactor technology than by the reserves of fissionable materials.

Nonmetallic Nonfuel Minerals

Although the metallic and fuel minerals account for the major value of our mineral supply, another group is also important. Three of these minerals (lime, phosphate, and potash) are of vital use in agriculture. Others, such as salt, sand, stone, and quartz, are in sufficient abundance so that concern over reserves is unwarranted. For example, between 15 and 20 percent of the surface of the United States is underlaid by limestone, and there is no indication that this resource will be depleted. Sulphur deposits are less than the foreseeable demand, but discoveries in the past have tended to keep up with demand. New technology has permitted sulphur to be recovered from gas and oil deposits, and this will help considerably.

Phosphate.   Total apparent phosphate domestic consumption was about 28 million short tons in 1970. Half the consumption went into commer-

11 Sam H. Schurr, et al., *Energy in the American Economy* (Baltimore: Johns Hopkins Press, 1960), p. 476. Published for Resources for the Future, Inc.

12 Federal Power Commission, *Hydroelectric Power Resources of the United States, Developed and Undeveloped, 1960* (Washington, D.C.: undated).

cial fertilizer for farm production, with a large amount of the remainder used in the chemical industry. The growth rate for demand for phosphate is estimated at 2.5 percent per year. World reserves are adequate, with 25 percent of them in the United States, particularly in Florida. The sea provides another source, which may be commercially feasible in the near future.

Potash.   Potash demand increases faster than that for phosphate in agricultural use; an annual 3.7 percent growth rate would require 200 million tons for the years from 1960 to 2000. Crops currently remove some 5 million tons of potash from the soil annually, and if crop output doubles, requirements would be closer to 300 million tons for the 40-year period. Ninety percent of deposits in the United States come from New Mexico. Even if these deposits become depleted, reserves in Canada and Germany are huge.

SUMMARY

Natural resources contribute greatly to a nation's economic growth if the state of technology permits their extraction and use in an increasing number of production processes. Concern over the adequacy of natural resources and their conservation is legitimate. Concern, too, about their negative effects on the environment is equally socially legitimate.

The degree of scarcity of a natural resource in economic terms varies not only with the size of demand but with the technology used in its extraction and processing. As a result, physical existence cannot be equated with economic availability. The limitation is the cost of developing the resource so that it can be used in desired production processes.

In the past century, the "real cost" of natural-resource products, measured by their prices in comparison with the general price level, has shown no marked change except in isolated cases. For example, the minimum grade of copper ore mined in 1940 was about 3 percent, whereas in 1960, ore with 0.7 percent copper was being profitably mined without any relative price increase in refined copper. Clearly, technology made a major cost-reducing contribution.

It is increasingly clear that with accelerated resource-use rates and expanding populations, more considered and long-range policies concerning resources must be adopted. Will we take up the long-run challenge? Can we afford not to?

4

Population and Labor Force

In Chapter 3, physical resources from an energy- and materials-production point of view were discussed. The perennial question of a balance between population and resources is equally important from the viewpoint of food production, and in this chapter the subject of population is discussed as it relates to the labor force and farming.[1]

History is replete with stories of famine, even in the last few years. Today, obtaining enough food is of prime concern for many of the world's people. We shall relate the population pressures on food production to the people working within farming and to the other working people and their families who are dependent upon an ever-decreasing proportion of the total labor force for their food and natural-fiber production.

---

[1] For the more interested student we recommend the following sources of information about population: U.S. Bureau of the Census, Washington, D.C., population reports; the many materials put out by the Population Reference Bureau, 1755 Massachusetts Avenue N.W., Washington, D.C.; the materials and studies of the Population Council, 245 Park Avenue, New York, N.Y.; and Paul R. Ehrlich and Anne H. Ehrlich, *Population, Resources, Environment—Issues in Human Ecology,* 2nd ed. (San Francisco: W. H. Freeman, 1972).

POPULATION–RESOURCE BALANCE
AND TECHNOLOGY

Why discuss population and resources here? Because an increasing number of people are having to share a limited amount of resources, and economics is one of the sciences concerned with managing the world's resources in such a way that the real level of living for all people is improved.

Everyone should recognize the resource-use implications of the fact that our finite world must cope (at present rates) with population increases equal to a New York City every 40 days. Why? Because these people need to have food, and because their simply "being here" will also add to the already-compounded social and environmental problems of housing, health, education, and transportation. Understanding the "human arithmetic," the limitations of technology[2] to handle certain types of questions, and the importance of personal and group choice in the decision-making process will prepare us to make choices more intelligently than if we did not have a knowledge of population dynamics.

Worldwide, the "population explosion" can be traced primarily to the importation of Western industrialized technology into agrarian nations. By and large, these countries were not yet equipped with the managerial and institutional know-how and resolve necessary to handle the complex social and economic conditions associated with the goal of economic and social betterment in an industrialized situation.

As the West absorbed the Industrial Revolution during the eighteenth and nineteenth centuries and changed from a rural farming society to a predominantly urban service-employment-oriented one, the people had time to evolve lower rates of population growth. In many agrarian countries of the world, massive doses of Western technology have been injected during the last fifty years. There has not been time for people to fully understand and reflect on their changing economic and social conditions, and to reconcile them with their value structures related to population growth. Increased agricultural productivity (for example, the Green Revolution in the Far East, in which rice and wheat yields were greatly enhanced) has permitted increased urbanization. However, in many cases, large segments of the population are still on the borderline of starvation, and most have not shared proportionately in the economic and social progress of their nations.

Perhaps the most significant type of technology causing upward

---

[2] Technology is more fully discussed in Chapter 6.

population pressures stems from medical public-health programs. In the last 100 years, it is estimated, death rates were about halved for the developed nations; in the underdeveloped countries, this phenomenon has occurred only since around 1950![3] Health and life-promoting programs were found and used for diseases such as the plague, yellow fever, cholera, typhus, dysentery, tuberculosis, and malaria. Infant mortality rates plunged. The net result was that increasing numbers of people were being born and kept alive the world over, and the governments and economies of these countries quite suddenly had to cope with immense problems, larger in sum than any nation had ever tackled before. This situation will be more fully discussed in Chapters 20 and 21.

WORLD AND U.S. POPULATION

There are many ways to classify population for purposes of description and analysis. The most common ways are by sex, age, and race. Although these three classification systems are closely interrelated, each class can be analyzed separately for different purposes.

Other classifications include geographic distribution, population density, place of residence, nationality, language, religion, occupation, income, health, and marital status. Two populations (country, state, county, town, etc.) may be compared and the differences noted, using any of these classifications. These differences will provide insights into their respective rates of growth and their economic and cultural well-being. They will also offer an indication of possible future problem areas. For example, differences in urban and rural population growth may lead to problems related to taxation, political representation, schools, education, and health.

World population has been estimated by many different people. Some countries conduct incomplete censuses of population or do not take any at all. Thus, any estimate of the number of people living in these countries is necessarily an educated guess. World population approximated 3.8 billion in 1972, with an annual rate of increase approaching 2 percent (Table 4-1). Although it has taken the human race approximately 200,000 years to achieve its present population level, if current growth trends continue, the number of people in the world will almost double within the next 30 years.

Population in the United States reached 204 million in 1970 (Table 4-2). Population data on the United States are fairly reliable, because a census has been taken systematically every ten years since the birth of the

---

[3] *The World Population Dilemma,* Population Reference Bureau, Washington, D.C., 1972, pp. 20–21.

TABLE 4-1
Estimated World Population by Major Region or
Area, 1960–2000
(in millions)

	1960	1970	1980	1990	2000
World total	2,986	3,632	4,457	5,438	6,494
East Asia	785	930	1,095	1,265	1,424
South Asia	865	1,126	1,486	1,912	2,354
Europe	425	462	497	533	568
Soviet Union	214	243	271	302	330
Africa	270	344	457	616	818
Northern America	199	228	261	299	333
Latin America	213	283	377	500	652
Oceania	15.8	19.4	24.0	29.6	35.2

SOURCE: United Nations, *World Population Situation in 1970*, Department of Economic and Social Affairs, Population Studies No. 49 (New York, 1971), p. 46.

nation. The projected population for the year 2000 is 262 million, which represents an annual increase of less than 1 percent per year.

If U.S. population is described by place of residence, in 1790 about 95 percent of our 3.9 million people lived in rural areas. By 1920, a third of the population lived on farms, half lived in urban areas, and about one out of five people lived in a rural nonfarm setting. In 1972, almost three out of four people were classified as urban dwellers, and farm population was just over 4 percent of the total.

THEORIES OF POPULATION GROWTH

There are two main schools of thought about population growth, each of which generates its own theories. One school is based on a naturalistic, almost mechanistic, approach. Factors considered by this school as limiting population include the biological capacity of women to produce children (fecundity), the actual number of children born to each woman in the population (fertility), the inability to reproduce (sterility), natural ecological conditions affecting food and physical resources, economic goods and standard of living, and the geographical density of population. The other school of thought is based on a sociological approach. This school believes that reproductive behavior is de-

TABLE 4-2
U.S. Population, 1960 to 2000
(in thousands)

Year	Total Population	Increase
1960	180,671	
1970	204,879	24,198
1980	224,132	19,253
1990	246,639	22,507
2000	262,756	16,117

NOTE: Projections assumed 2.1 birth per woman.
SOURCE: U.S. Department of Commerce, Bureau of the Census, *Current Population Reports*, Series P-25, No. 493, December 1972.

rived from a pattern of human custom based on institutions devised by human beings. Population growth is considered a social rather than an environmental phenomenon. This latter school attempts to explain population growth in terms of the influences of cultural patterns and social behavior.

In the late eighteenth century, an Englishman named Malthus formulated a "natural" theory of population growth. His principal contention was that nature is limited in its capacity to produce plant life and meat, whereas mankind's prolificacy is not bounded by anything but himself. Malthus observed that food production increased in an arithmetic ratio (1, 2, 3, 4, . . .), but population increased in geometric ratio (1, 2, 4, 8, . . .). He concluded that human population growth is ultimately limited by the amount of food the world can produce, and that if population grows faster than food production, natural checks of famine and pestilence will soon bring the population level into balance with food production (Figure 4-1).

Criticism of Malthus centers around two main points: that he neglected the influence of man's inventive abilities to produce more food on less land, and that man might devise culturally acceptable ways to control the birthrate.

In the "social" school of population growth, theorists point to the decisions man has already made concerning himself and population growth. Some of these decisions stem from overt institutional influences, such as religion, law, and medicine. Other decisions stem more from a sociocultural background. Theories in this school involve such factors as the place of the children in family life goals, the influence of women

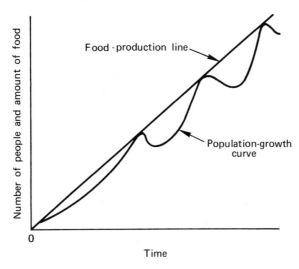

FIGURE 4-1
Diagram of Malthus' Theory of Population Growth

working outside the home, and parental motivation concerning child-bearing. Explicit decisions to use birth-control devices and undergo abortions to prevent actual births are other examples of man's own control of population.

Malthus differentiated between two types of checks on population growth. One type was composed of "natural" checks such as famine, disease, violence, vice, and misery. The other type included "preventive" checks of late marriage, abstinence, and celibacy. The natural check was attributed to population's outrunning available food supply; the second comprised socially acceptable modes of population restriction imposed by individuals. Other restrictive methods of population control include infanticide, cultural taboos of various kinds, "mercy killing," and colonization.

Public goals relative to population may be designed to (1) slow up or prevent an increase in population numbers, (2) encourage an increase in numbers, (3) increase the "quality" of the population (eugenic selections) or (4) secure a "better" distribution of people relative to the resources devoted to their support. In addition, sterilization of those judged medically to be permanently insane is legally practiced in several countries, including the United States. One of the reasons governments established colonies throughout the world was to attain a better ratio of people and resources. For many years, the western frontier in the United States acted as a continual colonization area, capable of absorbing easily the population increase associated with the transitional growth stage.

Zero Population Growth

With world population taking only about 33 years to double, many people are searching for a "no-growth" population policy. They see continued growth at the current annual rate of 2 percent leading to famine, increased pollution, wars, and social chaos in the beginning of the next century unless something is done soon. They also recognize that any population creates its own momentum based on the factors we have previously discussed. In fact, it may not be realistic because of this momentum to consider a "steady state" of world population at any less than double its present size. For example, if worldwide fertility rates could be reduced by 1985 to the point where man and wife were simply replacing themselves, population would still have increased to an equilibrium of about 7 billion people. The longer it takes to reduce the fertility rate, the greater will be the static number of people living on earth.

Some scientists are skeptical about how many people can be provided for by the present world-resource support systems. One study estimated what drain might be exerted on resources if 5 billion people were brought to the U.S. average 1970 standard of living. It concluded that a worldwide level of resource consumption of ten times the present level would be required. Clearly, this is beyond the currently known level of identified resources and of foreseeable technology. A trade-off is due, and that within the next thirty years.

FACTORS AFFECTING POPULATION GROWTH

The total number of people living in a geographical area at any one time is the net result of the number of people born there, the number of people who die, the number of people moving out of the area (emigration), and the number of people moving into the area (immigration). Population growth for the world is simply the excess of births over deaths. Population growth for an area is the excess of births over deaths *plus* the difference between people moving into and out of the area.

Let us work through an example in order to more clearly show the relationship between birthrate, death rate, and annual rate of population increase (often called the natural rate of increase). The birthrate is simply the number of babies born per 1,000 population in a year's time. The death rate is the number of people who die per 1,000 population in a year's time. The difference between the two rates divided by 1,000 and expressed as a percentage gives the annual rate of increase excluding immigration and emigration. For example:

Birthrate   24
Death rate   10

Difference   14
Annual rate of increase 1.4%

Factors Influencing Birth and Death Rates

Currently, the world birthrate is approximately 33, ranging from a low of 15 in Western Europe to a high of 44–50 in Africa and Asia. Although the relative importance of factors influencing birthrates varies between countries as well as regions within a country, the following list of factors is generally applicable:

Number of marriages
Age at which females marry
Divorce rate
Diseases affecting reproductive capacity
Use of contraceptives and abortion
General business conditions
Cultural and religious influences
Education
Government policies

The world death rate currently averages about 13, ranging from a low of about 7 to a high of about 25 in some parts of Asia and Africa. Although death rates are primarily influenced by the level of medical technology, the acceptance and practice of that technology is also crucial. In many countries, the causes of death lie largely in areas in which present medical knowledge is relatively inexpensive and adequate to reduce mortality substantially (malaria, typhoid, tuberculosis, respiratory and intestinal infections, measles and whooping cough).

The infant mortality rate (deaths under one year of age per thousand live births) is considered one of the most sensitive indicators of death rates. In some of the more underdeveloped areas of the world, deaths of infants account for over 50 percent of the total deaths. This is particularly true in a high-birthrate nation. Infant mortality ranges from a low of about 12 in Sweden, the Netherlands, and Iceland, to nearly 200 in parts of Africa. The United States rate is 19.2.

Longer average life-span is due to lowered infant and child mortality and reduced mortality of the older population. Mortality-rate reductions are in turn due primarily to the innovation and adoption of medical technology, sanitation, and nutrition. Life expectancy at birth appears to have been about 20 years in Rome at the height of the Roman

Empire. Average life expectancy in some countries may soon be four times that figure.

Population Pyramid

An easily applied tool of population analysis is the population pyramid. It relates age structure to population growth. A pyramid can be constructed for the world, nation, state, or community. Beginning with zero age and rising up the graph in five-year intervals, the number of males and females in each five-year age bracket can be represented by a horizontal bar. The number of males will not equal that of females, so you can actually see the different age groups by sex for any area. By comparing two or more pyramids for an area, you can see what proportion of the population is growing or declining; what pressures the needs of the older people might exert on an area relative to the needs of the young, and vice versa; and the proportion of actively employed people compared to the young and the elderly.

POPULATION AND ECONOMIC GROWTH

Countries can be classified into three groups according to population growth and economic development (Figure 4-2). The high growth-potential countries have a high birthrate and a high death rate. Countries in this category—Africa, much of Latin America and the Caribbean nations, and all of Asia except Japan—contain approximately three-fifths of the world's people. The standard of living is extremely low in these countries, and man is constantly forced to fight for physical survival. Little effort or time is available for the bulk of these people to consider longer-range economic and social problems.

Countries in the transitional growth stage make up about one-fifth of the world's population. Some countries in eastern and southern Europe and parts of Latin America are examples. In this stage, although the birthrate is falling, use of medical technology has caused a correspondingly faster drop in the death rate. This exerts an even greater population pressure on the resources of the country, particularly on the food supply.

It is in the transitional stage that a society is faced with other immense problems of social, institutional, and economic change. Political instability, revolution rather than reform, and rigidly planned economic and social guidance are prevalent at this time. Potential opportunity, uncertainty as to the economic and social outcome of change, limited education, and a wide divergence between those who own and control

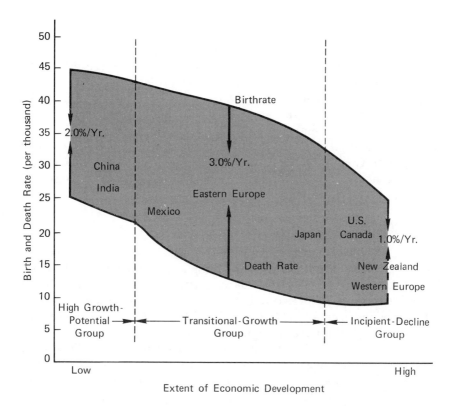

FIGURE 4-2

Relationship between Birthrates, Death Rates, and
Extent of Economic Development

property and those who do not—all these factors lead to resistance to change.

In the incipient-decline group of countries, there is a low birthrate and a lower death rate. Population may be expanding in these countries at a rate equal to those in the high growth-potential group. To test your understanding of this point, compare the vertical distance between the birth and the death rate in Figure 4-2 for these two groups. The incipient-decline countries, currently containing about one-fifth of the people in the world, include the advanced economies of the United States, Canada, northwestern and central Europe, Australia, and New Zealand. These economies have become relatively stable, and political and social change is more orderly.

THE LABOR FORCE

It should be clearly evident that farm people migrate readily to the city for any number of reasons—lack of opportunity at home and the promise of employment in town, more income in town compared to the farm, more cultural excitement, and so on. But migrate they do, and when they do, the consequence is an increasing number of people increasingly dependent on a decreasing number of people for their food production. Greater off-farm job opportunities lay the groundwork for increased on-farm specialization and nonfarm dependency on farm people. Let's take a closer look.

Labor Force Defined

The labor force is not the same thing as the population. The labor force of a country is described most generally by age: In the United States, it is composed of everyone between the ages of 14 and 65 who is physically and mentally able to work. Although 65 years has been accepted for a long time as an upper limit, it was only around 1920 that the lower limit was raised from 10 to 14 years. Children had long been exploited for their labor, and as a result of the institution of child-labor laws and legislation affecting mandatory school attendance, the lower age limit of the labor force was raised.

The labor force contributes the two catalytic agents of labor and management to the factors of land and capital. The whole population, as consumers, helps decide what the labor force will produce, how it will produce it, and who will share in the profits.

Employment

In 1820, three out of every four people employed in the United States worked on a farm. By 1972, only one out of every 25 employed people worked on farms. There are many reasons for changes in employment and the labor force. Probably the primary causes for shifts in demand for farm labor are secular changes in commodity prices, new technology, and the relative ease with which a farmer can substitute capital for labor.

Most farm employment is family labor. For the last 30 years, only

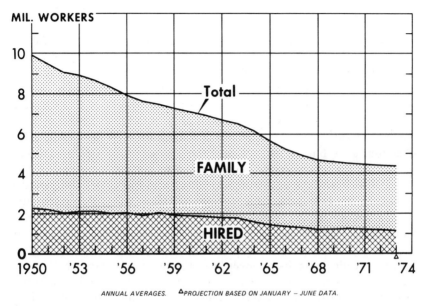

FIGURE 4-3
Sources of Farm Employment, 1950–1973

about one out of every four workers on farms has been hired (Figure 4-3).

Changes in employment. The economic development of a country or area can usually be traced from its trade patterns. Channels of commerce and trade change over the ages and, correspondingly, so does the country's or area's development. For example, in the United States, early settlers establishd a north-south coastal pattern based on cotton. Dependence upon cotton as a "one-crop economy" dictated shipment to the cotton mills in the North and export to England. Advancing technology in communications, the advent of the railroad, and an attitude of "manifest destiny" toward the undeveloped West began to exert an east-west trade pattern. The Civil War, with its ensuing depression in the South, boom in the industrial North, and expansion westward, combined to swing the bulk of trade into an east-west trade pattern that dominated the north-south pattern. People began to move from the comparatively disadvantaged South to the North and West.

Employment pattern changes with growth. Economic development of a country or area can usually be measured by adjustments in three sectors of employment: *primary employment*—people employed in extractive industries of farming, forestry, fishing, and mining; *secondary employment*—those people having jobs in the manufacturing industries, processing or fabricating materials into semifinished and finished goods; and *tertiary employment*—people whose job it is to service the needs of the other two employment sectors, as well as to provide much of the maintenance of the total economy (finance, education, transportation, construction, government, etc.). Using these three employment categories, let us trace the typical economic-growth pattern.

Historically, the economic growth of a country goes through three phases. In the first phase, the economy is almost solely dependent upon primary employment. Typical productivity per farm worker is quite low, and the vast majority of the population must engage in farming for survival. The second phase is introduced by an increase in farming productivity, which permits a movement of some workers from employment on farms to various types of nonfarm work. The first migrants out of farming generally manufacture materials and utensils for use on farms. Increases in secondary employment bring increases in both the size and quality of the labor force and in number and quality of manufactured goods. The technology contained in the use of the new agricultural implements is reflected in the continued movement of people from primary to secondary employment. This sets the stage for the more rapid growth of the third phase. As the number of people in secondary employment grows over time, there is a more than proportionate increase in the number of people employed to service the needs of the primary and secondary sectors. Fewer and fewer people are needed in farming. Technology permits more food to be raised by fewer people. Workers can thus move from producing food to the production of other goods and services desired by society.

Productivity of the Labor Force

Productivity of farm labor is largely influenced by (1) applying work methods that emphasize labor efficiency itself, (2) the quality and capabilities of the agricultural worker himself, (3) increased use of particular agricultural inputs, and (4) the adoption of new production, processing, and distribution technologies. Although the productivity of nonfarm labor is dependent upon the same factors, productivity per

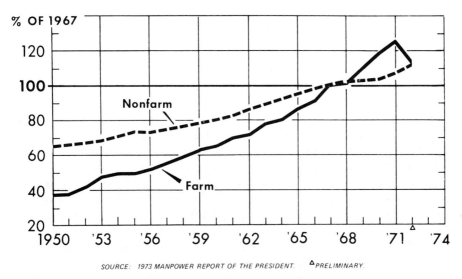

SOURCE: 1973 MANPOWER REPORT OF THE PRESIDENT.   △ PRELIMINARY.

U.S. DEPARTMENT OF AGRICULTURE   NEG. ERS 8858 73 (8)   ECONOMIC RESEARCH SERVICE

FIGURE 4-4
Labor-Force Productivity in the United States,
1950–1972

man-hour in farming has increased more rapidly than for the nonfarm
worker since the mid-1940s (Figure 4-4).

Increasing productivity in farming has had several consequences
upon the total economy. It has, first of all, freed labor to undertake new
jobs off the farm in manufacturing and services. Second, although the
productivity increases have not been distributed evenly throughout our
agricultural history (hindered partially by wars, depression, and such
natural disasters as flood, drought, plant disease, and insects), they did
allow farmers to provide for an ever-increasing number of people. In
1820, one farmer could supply enough food and fiber for only an additional four persons. It took 100 years for him to be able to double this
effort and provide for eight people. The number doubled again in only
30 years, reaching 16 by 1950. But by 1972, one farmer could take care
of the food and fiber needs of about 50 people, more than doubling
again. Not only has the time required to double productivity of farm
labor been reduced substantially, but the number of people provided for
has risen rapidly with significantly higher levels of population. If part-
time, hobby, and institutional farms are removed from productivity

calculations, and only workers on farms grossing over $10,000 annual sales are included, a full-time worker comes close to providing for an average of 200 people.

Labor-Force Characteristics

It is virtually impossible to talk about the labor force as if it were a single homogeneous mass. Members of the labor force are dissimilar in some respects and similar in others. In order to permit discussion of the working people of this nation with any degree of understanding, several characteristics have been developed by which they may be described. In general, these characteristics are qualitative in nature. The most common are occupation, sex, place of residence and urbanization, mobility, productivity, income, part-time and full-time work, unemployment, race, and education.

Work on the world's farms has usually been a total family commitment. It has had to be, both because of access limitations to capital and because of the reality of large families who offer an available labor force. Most of the time labor given by a farmer's children, wife, and relatives has been classified as unpaid family labor. Often there has been little or no ready cash to pay family members for their help, or it has been considered a simple condition of life—work or there is no food. This type of working condition has led to much abuse of children and others, but realistically there may not be many alternatives open in the markets of labor surplus economies.

In this country, as in others, women workers on farms have long played an unappreciated role. They have worked at field tasks as the equals of men, and have also been expected to cook, sew, and rear children. For their efforts they have received few wages. Farm wives often know as much, or more, about the farm business as their husbands, and often act the part by being the accountants and preparers of tax returns. They are an indispensable part of the farm labor force.

As noted elsewhere, population and the labor force move about primarily in response to the relative productivity and income differentials between farm and nonfarm employment opportunity. Throughout the world, migration is motivated by an effort either to escape the unevenness of fluctuations in food production or to gain access to greater income, social, and cultural opportunities outside of farming. It is of historic significance that population growth and economic development do not occur at an equal rate throughout a country or region. Pockets of economically and socially underdeveloped areas occur in the most developed nations of the world. There is a constantly changing comparative production advantage between nations and regions. Such a change is based on changing conditions of production technology, on the goals of local people and their government, and on a myriad of other political, social, institutional, and economic forces at work in a society.

The rise and fall of city centers follows much the same pattern described for regions. As cities grow, certain cost economies can be found for some industries. Creation of nonfarm jobs beckons to farm workers who are not fully satisfied with rural living, and they eventually move close to this new source of work. An increased population in turn brings about an increased demand for goods and services. More jobs are created by these demands; more rural people come to fill them, and they also exert further demands on the local economy.

Coincident with the development of urban life has been the development of suburban society. An ever-increasing number of people seeking the attributes of a rural life by living in the country and commuting to work in the city has caused a closer relationship between rural and urban people. Suburbs are a result of the decentralization of the central cities and often develop at their expense. Part of the urban growth comes about because of annexations by big cities of smaller surrounding suburbs. More people now live in suburbs than in other areas of the nation.

The consequences of people's leaving rural areas and of rapid urban growth cause differences in approach to employment and land use. In rural areas, the employment problems revolve around issues of finding economic uses for land that will help retard the migration, while in the city, the problems concern choosing between competing demands for intensive land use.

Mobility, immigration, and emigration are closely linked. Mobility simply refers to the rate at which people move about or change residence. The unemployed are usually more mobile than the employed.

Immigration and emigration put directions to mobility. Movements of people into and out of an area depend to a large extent on the relative economic and social attractiveness of the area. Lack of jobs and food, or escape from political repression, may actually push people out of a specific area. On the other hand, high paying jobs, plentiful food, and political security may attract people. There may be movements of people between (inter) nations or states, or there may be movements within (intra) a country or state.

Signs of population pressure on a country's resources are evident primarily from its efforts to obtain food. Elaborate terracing and highly intensive cropping systems designed to utilize the last possible bit of land tend to indicate the degree of the food–population crisis. Extremely low wages in agriculture and industry also show that labor is plentiful relative to the demand for it. A low value set on human life is another characteristic of population pressure.

The results of extreme population pressure on the food resources of a country from which emigration is slight can usually be identified in the death rate and the causes of death. Malnutrition and famine are usually felt sooner by the young and the old. However, lowered levels of nutrition also mean a lowered resistance to disease and hence a raised incidence of death from ordinarily preventable sicknesses.

European and Far Eastern history relates accounts of waves of emigration from areas when food production fails. The history of the United States and Europe shows that when agricultural productivity is high, labor tends to migrate from farm to nonfarm jobs. This is a basic factor underlying urbanization. However, in times of economic depression and severe dips in the business cycle, some people move from the city back to the farm, where food is cheaper to obtain.

The concept of a "net migration" allows people interested in economic growth and agriculture to analyze local trends closely. Fertility and death ratios coupled with census counts provide part of the data necessary to help determine relative rates of economic growth. Suppose the 1970 census of population indicated that there were 10,000 people in one county and that natural increase would be expected to add 2,000 additional people by 1980. If in 1980 only 11,000 people were actually living there, the areas would show a net loss to migration of 1,000 people.

Example:

1970 actual	10,000 people
1970–80 natural increase	2,000 people
1980 expected	12,000 people
1980 actual	11,000 people
1970–80 net loss to migration	1,000 people

If in 1980 the actual population was over 12,000, there would be a net gain to migration. Typically, a net loss to migration means there are not enough job opportunities in the area to provide employment for everyone who wants to work; likewise, a net gain to migration may indicate a surplus of nonfarm jobs, which induces labor from outside the area to move in.

Since 1948, the mobility rate of our entire population has remained at about 20 percent. This means that every year since 1948, one out of five persons has changed residence. More people move within the same county than move between counties, and more people move to another county in the same state than from one state to another.

Mobility should not be confused with the migrant or the migratory worker. The migrant worker and the migratory worker both have a degree of mobility. A migrant farm worker is broadly defined as a farm wage worker who has left his home country temporarily to do seasonal farm wage work in another country. A migratory worker is commonly understood to be one who follows a crop, planting it, cultivating it, or harvesting it. The Mexican *bracero* who works in this country is an example of a migrant worker. The wheat-harvest crews who begin in Oklahoma and follow the ripening crop through into Canada are examples of migratory workers.

Wages and salaries paid to workers vary with the kind of job and with the capabilities of the person working. Also, wages paid for the same type of job and for the same quality of employee will vary from region to region throughout the country. In general, farm workers are not paid as much as nonfarm workers, even though many farmers work seven days a week and up to 18 hours a day during peak labor seasons of planting and harvest. Cost-of-living differences account for part of the farm–nonfarm differential, as does the fact that many farm people prefer to live in the country and raise their families there rather than in the city, despite the difference in income.

In recent years, there has been a rapid increase in part-time employment. In fact, many jobs have been modified in an attempt to obtain competent adult women employees, for example, who prefer not to be away from their families all day on a full-time job. Students working their way through school have also helped develop the institution of part-time employment.

Since the numbers of farmers declined drastically during the 1950s, the statistics for those employed in part-time work or in off-farm work of 100 days or more either stayed constant or increased for most states. These part-time jobs became necessary if farmers wanted to stay in the business of food production. The most common kinds of part-time jobs obtained included custom work on somebody else's farm, driving a school bus, highway jobs, or some type of nonfarm work in town.

SUMMARY

Population growth inevitably puts pressures on our physical and human resources. At the same time, differing responses to those pressures by nations or groups of people can and do lead to economic growth, and consequently a shift of people off farms into nonfarm residences and jobs. The growing dependency of our growing nonfarm population on our dwindling farm population is one result of "successful" social and economic adaptation to these forces. How successful do you really think it has been?

5

Capital Resources
in Agriculture

WAYS TO DEFINE CAPITAL

There are many definitions of capital.[1] Until the early 1950s, most people thought of capital in terms of such tangible items as physical plant and equipment, construction of all kinds, machinery, and producers' inventories. Since 1950, certain intangible items such as education have been added to the physical kinds of capital recognized above.

Much of the recognition of intangible capital is due to the work of T. W. Schultz, who attempted to assess economic growth in America and abroad. He estimated that between two-thirds and three-fourths of the total output of developed countries was attributable not to the traditional forms of capital investment, but rather to investment in human beings, through education, technical training, and managerial knowledge. It was Schultz's idea that expenditures on education, training, health, and the like were not consumption expenditures but were really investments of a sort that produced a flow of income over time.[2]

---

[1] See W. G. Murray and A. G. Nelson, *Agricultural Finance* (Ames: Iowa State University Press, 1960), for a definitive discussion of capital in agriculture. Also, see E. L. Baum, et al., "Capital and Credit Needs in a Changing Agriculture" *Symposium* (Iowa State University Press, 1961), for a discussion of historical and projected capital and credit needs in agriculture.

[2] T. W. Schultz, "Investment in Human Capital," *American Economic Review*, Vol. 51, No. 1 (March 1961), 1–16.

Up to Schultz's time, capital had been defined traditionally as all forms of reproducible wealth or goods used directly or indirectly in the production process. A different perspective of capital was provided by the addition of intangible capital items. Capital could still be defined as an input in production that embodies technology; it was still consistent with the definition that capital is produced from goods and services saved from consumption and used by, or as a part of, the human agent in further production. But it went further; it recognized that investment could be made in the human being himself, and that he could produce an income flow directly as a result of this investment. Under this new perspective, capital might well be defined as a factor of production that generates a flow of income spread over a certain period of time.

Capital used in agriculture is composed of both equity and debt capital. Debt capital comes into being when borrowed money (credit) is used to purchase inputs for production processes and generates money income over time. Credit facilitates the process of economic development by supplementing equity funds when the latter are not sufficient to provide for such capital-consuming necessities as machinery. Equity capital is the capital that is fully owned and free of debt. It is important to distinguish between equity and debt capital (arising from credit) only insofar as they come from different sources, for they are essentially the same in their capacity to generate income flow.

Capital may also be classified as private or social capital. Any capital such as farm buildings, houses, stores, factories, and even education owned by a private individual, partnership, or corporation, can be classified as private capital. These items comprise a major share of the fixed assets of private business. Expenditures made by authorized local, state, or federal public agencies as well as the roads, highways, schools, courthouses, bridges, and parks they create belong in the social-capital category.

As a society grows, both kinds of capital grow and constitute the visible form of the country's wealth. A growing population calls for more businesses, for more construction, and for more factories. More people also increase the need for better communications. People also want better roads, better schools, and more parks and zoos.

WAYS TO MEASURE CAPITAL

The total amount of capital can be measured in three general ways. One way is to simply total the accumulation of funds spent on plant and equipment over a certain period of time. A second way is to total all expenditures. The third way is to enumerate and evaluate the production of all physical goods. Each method has certain advantages and disadvantages. Much depends on the purpose for which the particular measurement is being made.

CHARACTERISTICS OF CAPITAL

Physical-capital items have varying life cycles (usefulness). Some items of capital, such as a bag of fertilizer, are used up in one production cycle. Other capital items are very durable: Capital items like plant and equipment, housing, barns, and dams are things that will last a relatively long time; these items usually involve large expenditures of money and are often put in a fixed location; and finally there is usually quite a long time between the time such a project is initiated and the end of construction.

Note that these characteristics also apply to education and technical training. An education lasts for one's lifetime and can be constantly supplemented; it involves considerable costs in time, money, and effort; it is fixed in the individual, who in turn may teach someone else; and it generally takes a minimum of 16 years of formal education to get a bachelor's degree from college.

EVALUATION OF CAPITAL

There are three general methods of evaluating capital items. One is to capitalize the anticipated income stream over its expected lifetime.[3] This method can be misleading at times, because the capital item may not last as long as expected, or at the end of its expected lifetime it may still be in excellent condition, still generating a stream of revenue.

The second method is simply to record the item's market price. This is perhaps the easiest method. However, market prices are often deceiving because of inflation, variation from one year to the next, and different markets in different parts of the country.

The third way is to note the initial price and subtract a certain allowance for depreciation. This method can also be standardized by formula, but it is liable to the same difficulties mentioned above in the first method.

All three methods are used widely. However, the evaluation of capital assumes meaning only within a given framework of technology

---

[3] The formula is to divide the annual income stream in dollars by an imputed interest rate. For example, suppose you bought a piece of machinery that would increase your net income $300 a year. If your money is worth 5% a year to you, the piece of machinery would be worth $6,000 in capitalized value ($300 ÷ .05).

and institutions. For example, even though the looms and cloth markets of Great Britain during the Industrial Revolution had great significance at that time, both the looms (capital items) and marketing methods (institutions) are obsolete today. Advances in technology have shown new methods of weaving, and the innovation of new marketing institutions has opened new and different channels of product distribution.

There is probably more difficulty in measuring and evaluating social capital goods than private capital goods. Part of the reason for this is that the private business is interested in making profits, and this is not generally true for social-capital investment. How should one value public harbors, roads, bridges, parks, museums, and schools? Many of the items, like roads and bridges, are indispensable for the operation of a dynamic society; some, like museums, are priceless outgrowths of a society's cultural development. Does one measure and evaluate social-capital expenditures in the same manner that he does a private expenditure? Should the tolls we pay on certain roads and bridges be determined on a maintenance-and-repair basis or on a profit framework designed to return a "fair" amount to all input factors?

Another difficulty in capital evaluation arises when one attempts to standardize and evaluate either private or public capital expenditures on an international basis. Besides currency differences, different cultures place different emphasis upon different items, so that what might be highly valued in one country might have a relatively low value in another.

ROLE OF CAPITAL IN AGRICULTURAL DEVELOPMENT

Capital is a critical factor in determining the kind, amount, and quality of a society's total output or production. Use of capital follows the general law of variable proportions (discussed sometimes under its other name, the "law of diminishing returns"), which says (with reference to capital) that output can be increased by adding more capital if capital is the limiting factor in a production process. However, even though economists may be in general agreement with this law, they are not in general agreement on (1) what kinds of capital to add, (2) when they should be added, and (3) into what sector they should be added and through which enterprises they should be introduced into the economy. Most of this disagreement can be traced to different judgments of the relative roles to be taken by the private and public sectors of our economy, in differences in opinion of how capital should be raised, and in differences in viewpoint over rates of repayment.

It has been commonly said that relatively underdeveloped countries and certain areas in the United States lack capital to develop their industry and agriculture properly, and that there is a dearth of both private and public capital immediately available for investment in these areas. However, in many instances, it is people's attitudes toward credit and toward acquiring and using capital, and their managerial ability and desire that constitute the limiting factors, and not the availability of capital per se.

In our economy, capital has generally been used to increase the productivity of labor in farming. One can see this readily by noting the increasing value of assets per farm worker, a decreasing amount of farm labor (Chapter 4), an increasing total farm output, and an increasing output per farm worker (Table 5-1). For certain other kinds of capital (such as education), see Chapter 6 and 7.

Increased use of capital in farming has been facilitated by the adoption of yield-increasing technology. These new technologies usually concern an intensive use of capital which lowers per-unit costs of production, but tends to increase total capital costs per farm.

Total Capital Investment in Farm Production

Total investment in physical assets on farms has increased by over 10 times in the last century, and has increased sevenfold in just the last 33 years (Table 5-2). By separating capital investment into real

TABLE 5-1
Index of Farm Output and Average Value of
Production Assets per Farm Worker, Selected
Years, 1940–1973 (1967 = 100)

	1940	1950	1960	1972	1973
Index of total farm output[a]	60	73	90	112	116
Per unit of total input	61	73	93	110	112
Per man-hour	21	35	67	131	129
Average value of production assets per farm worker[b]	$3,300	$9,400	$21,100	$61,900	$70,700[c]

[a] Economic Report of the President (Washington, D.C.: U.S. Government Printing Office, 1974).
[b] U.S. Department of Agriculture, Balance Sheet of the Farming Sector, October 1973, Agr. Info. Bull. 365.
[c] Estimate for 1973.

TABLE 5-2

Comparative Balance Sheet of Agriculture, United
States, January 1, Selected Years, 1940–1973
(in billions of dollars)

Item	1940	1950	1960	1973 [a]
ASSETS				
Physical assets:				
Real estate	33.6	75.3	129.9	258.7
Non–real estate:				
Livestock and poultry	5.1	12.9	15.6	34.2
Machinery and motor vehicles	3.1	12.2	22.3	39.0
Crops stored on and off farms	2.7	7.6	7.8	14.1
Household furnishings and equipment	4.2	8.6	9.6	11.0
Financial assets:				
Deposits and currency	3.2	9.1	9.2	14.0
U.S. savings bonds	.2	4.7	4.7	3.9
Investments in cooperatives	.8	2.1	4.4	8.6
Total	52.9	132.5	203.5	383.5
CLAIMS				
Liabilities:				
Real estate debt	6.6	5.6	12.1	34.5
Non–real estate debt—Excluding				
Commodity Credit Corporation	3.0	5.1	11.6	37.3
Commodity Credit Corporation	.4	1.7	1.2	1.8
Total liabilities	10.0	12.4	24.9	73.6
Proprietors' equities	42.9	120.1	178.6	309.9
Total	52.9	132.5	203.5	383.5

[a] Preliminary.

estate (land and buildings) and non–real estate, several trends can be
identified.

The fixed investment in real estate has increased by about 15
times since 1870 and almost eight times since 1940, but almost half this
increase has been due to inflation and rising prices. Rising land prices
mean that the generation of farmers holding real estate will benefit by
getting appreciably higher prices for their land than they paid, although
they may have done nothing to it but hold onto it, while the generation

of farmers that buys land from them assumes a new, higher cost structure for the same land. When analyzing increases in land values, it is
well to remember that if one deflates land values to hold them in constant comparable dollars, the figures he compares are not the prices
that a farmer getting into business today will have to pay—and it is the
current land prices in which most farmers are interested.

The net adjustment in livestock capital has been upward, even
though the introduction of the gas engine and the electric motor eliminated the need for much of the animal power on farms. The rise in
value of implements and machinery capital is consistent with this shift
and also with the decrease in farm population and labor force.

Recent data on capital assets in agriculture shows that since 1940,
real estate values have risen by about eight times, livestock and poultry
values by over six times, and investment in machinery and motor vehicles
by over 12 times. At the same time, farmers' assets in the form of deposits
and currency have risen by a factor of 4, and investments in cooperatives
have increased by a factor of over 10.

Less than one-third the labor was used in 1972 as compared to
1929 (Table 5-3). The use of mechanical power of some type on farms
was about three times greater in 1972 than it was in 1929, while the use
of fertilizers, feed, seed, and livestock purchases had increased almost 11
times. Miscellaneous items such as taxes and interest just about doubled
during the same time.

Greater specialization in farming, combined with a trend toward
larger farms and fewer farmers, has helped cause an increased depen-

TABLE 5-3
Index of Major U.S. Farm Inputs, Selected Years,
1929–1973 (1967 = 100)

Year	Total	Farm Labor	Farm Real Estate	Mechanical Power and Machinery	Fertilizer and Lime	Feed, Seed, and Livestock	Taxes and Interest
1929	100	302	103	39	11	31	69
1940	98	269	103	42	14	43	68
1950	101	199	105	79	32	64	77
1960	97	134	99	91	54	84	87
1973	104	89	97	105	124	109	109

SOURCE: *Economic Report of the President* (Washington, D.C.: U.S. Government
Printing Office, 1974).

dence upon farm inputs produced in the nonfarm sector of the economy. Farmers purchased about three times as many agricultural inputs in 1972 than they did in 1929, and used about half as many farm-produced non-purchased inputs.

One should realize that increased productivity per worker and man-hour is associated with the quality of resources (inputs) used, as well as their quantity. Increased managerial know-how and improved farm organization also help account for farming's spectacular productivity increases.

It should be remembered that although these figures are for the entire country and all its agricultural production, there are differences between types of farming regions. The data presented here show only the aggregate trend and are not meant to apply to specific regions.

Capital investment per farm.   The average capital investment required in modern-day farming has increased rapidly during the last two decades (Table 5-4). In just a 33-year period, the average value of land and buildings per farm increased by 19 times, the value of machinery and motor vehicles rose by a factor of 19, and the total average farm value was almost 19 times greater in 1973 than it was in 1940.

Capital investment varies with the size of the farm and with the type of farming. Differences in capital investment related to size of farm come about principally because there is usually a higher dollar investment associated with more acres and more buildings. Differences in investment associated with types of farming can usually be traced to the number of acres needed for the various enterprises and to the differences in the type of equipment needed. For example, tillable acres tend to be

TABLE 5-4

Average Value of Production Assets per Farm,
48 States, Selected Years, 1940–1973
(in current dollars)

Year	Farm Real Estate	Livestock	Machinery and Motor Vehicles	Other	Total
1940	4,600	600	600	400	6,200
1950	11,800	2,200	2,000	1,200	17,200
1960	31,700	3,800	4,800	1,800	42,100
1973	89,400	12,100	11,600	3,400	116,500

SOURCE: U.S. Department of Agriculture, Economic Research Service, *Balance Sheet of the Farming Sector, October 1973,* Agr. Info. Bull. 365.

lower on Indiana dairy farms than on the hog and cattle-feeding operations.

Studies have shown that the lower-risk enterprises that produce frequent and regular incomes are associated with comparatively lower capital-investment requirements than high-risk once-a-year-income enterprises. For example, small poultry and dairy farms in general fit the low-risk category, as compared to specialized crop and livestock farms.

Capital Accumulation and Control in Farming

Capital accumulation is generally understood to be capital owned by individuals or legal business entities, such as partnerships or corporations. All capital accumulation occurs because someone or some group saves. Individual farmers accumulate capital from income that is not all spent on current consumption or maintenance items.

Control of capital, on the other hand, means that an individual or legal entity can use capital without necessarily having ownership of it. This is especially relevant in farming, where a large initial investment is necessary if a beginning farmer is to make a living on the farm equal to that which he could make off the farm. Acquiring control of capital usually means that a particular individual or group chooses the lending institutions from which to borrow, determines the debt load, and then makes investment decisions concerning a total set of capital assets, both borrowed and owned, as if all capital were owned by him.

Both capital accumulation and control of capital permit the adoption of new technologies and allow their adopters to reap initiator's profits, which in turn are an incentive to adopt other technologies. When capital accumulation is greater than population growth, the nation's stock of capital grows. The most economic growth that exists, the more new technologies are introduced into the production process and the institutional environment. These innovations also lead to further capital accumulation and economic growth.

SOURCES OF CAPITAL IN AGRICULTURE

Capital in agriculture comes from three main sources: from the equity of landlords, from the equity of farm operators, or from credit. The equity sources give rise to capital directly through savings; the credit source gives rise to capital directly through borrowing (although these funds have been saved previously for investment). "Mixed" types of equity and credit sources include gifts, inheritance, marriage, inflation, and certain legal entities such as rental or purchase contracts (including vertical integration), partnerships, and corporations.

The volume of savings is influenced by psychological and social values as well as economics. The desire of the individual to save, his evaluation of the worth of future risk versus the pleasure of current consumption, his expectations of profit, and his personal evaluation of the size of investment all enter into the savings decisions. The current tone of business activity and the outlook for both short- and long-term economic activity also influence the volume of saving and investment.

In many underdeveloped areas, the savings level tends to be low because the income level is low. In these situations, capital formation may be difficult, since the major portion of income is consumed by current necessities.

Capital for loans may come from home or abroad. The rate of interest is both the market price of credit and the investment incentive to which most potential lenders look. The rate of interest and the volume of credit outstanding at any one time both fluctuate. This is true for both short-term and long-term credit. Those seeking capital for investment on farms must compete for borrowed funds in the domestic and foreign capital markets along with all those who seek capital resources for investment in the other sectors of the economy.

The principal sources of farm credit in this country are private individuals, commercial banks, insurance companies, merchants and dealers, authorized government agencies, and the cooperative agricultural credit system. These sources make loans available in one or more of the following ways:

1. The direct method, in which the loan is made directly from the investor to the borrower without an intermediary of any kind. This is typical of the way most private individuals make loans.
2. The agency or middleman method, in which the agency or individual who makes the initial loan sells it to another investor, who, in turn, holds the mortgage or note.
3. The pooling or bond system, in which the agency or individual pools all its (his) loans and sells bonds through a broker to investors. However, these investors do not hold the mortgage(s) or note(s), but can only claim title to the bond itself as an income-yielding investment.
4. The indirect method, in which the credit agency borrows from many investors and then lends to farmers without knowledge on the part of the investors of the specific loan into which their funds went. Commercial banks and insurance companies are included in this category.

Repayment plans vary with the type of loan made, the security given for the loan, the length of time for which the loan is outstanding, the expected risk involved, and the tradition of the lending institution. There are three main types of repayment plans. The straight end payment plan is one in which the borrower pays interest annually or semiannually, making a principal lump-sum payment at the end of the loan period. The second method is the partial-payment plan, in which the borrower makes payments that include interest and part of the initial principal, closing the loan with a lump-sum payment of the remaining balance plus accrued interest at the end of a designated time period. The third method is the amortization plan, in which principal and interest are combined into one constant payment, and the payments are kept up at regular intervals until the initial sum is entirely repaid.

Another way to classify the sources of the money used in agricultural credit is according to whether they come from the private sector of the economy (individuals, banks, merchants, insurance companies, and the cooperative agricultural credit system), or from the public sector (government agencies, like the Commodity Credit Corporation and the Federal Housing Administration, that are legally authorized to make loans to farmers). These two broad classifications would apply equally well to short-term loans, intermediate or long-term credit, and real estate and non-real estate loans.

Private and public sources of loanable funds serve to dampen the effects on farming of the fluctuations caused by the business cycle. For example, in the depression of the 1930s, when the agricultural role of commercial banks declined because of unprofitable loans and shrinking deposits, government-sponsored credit agencies were created to help the farmers. When times are good, the role of the private sector of the economy in providing farm credit increases, but it tends to diminish in times of recession or depression. On the other hand, the role the public sector plays in providing agricultural credit increases when the country's economic activity slackens. The two sources tend to offset each other and thus reduce what might otherwise be disastrous effects of credit fluctuation on the people in agriculture.

Individuals

Individuals currently account for over one-third of the loans made to farmers. These loans are usually made directly. Loans are made for real estate, capital improvements, and operating funds. As a result of the person-to-person responsibilities, there is no established method of loan supervision (except by legal suit) or loan limit.

Commercial Banks

Commercial banks are corporations chartered under state or federal law. They are owned by stockholders and controlled by boards of directors. All the banks are supervised under laws that specify systems of audit and inspection.

Commercial banks are unique among credit institutions for their ability to create money in the form of bank deposits for purposes of making loans. This ability directly affects the supply of credit available to agriculture. The money used by commercial banks for making loans is, in a sense, not the bank's money. It belongs to the depositors and stockholders; the banks only hold a type of investing trusteeship over these funds.

Although the goal of a bank is to make profits for its stockholders, it must also be responsible for the safety of the depositors' money and the economic soundness of its overall loan policy. The most general criteria used by commercial banks when making farm loans are (1) service to the borrowers involved, and (2) satisfactory evaluation of the risk involved in making the loan.

Many commercial banks have agricultural representatives attached to their regular staffs. These men usually have an agricultural orientation either from their own farming experience or through their college training; they are well acquainted with old and current techniques of farm production and with new production technology that might be adopted by farmers. They are also usually familiar with the geographic area over which the bank makes its loans, and with the people who live in the area. These trained agricultural representatives help to evaluate farm loans from both the bank's and the borrower's viewpoints. They review the purpose of the loan, its expected return to the enterprise, the person or persons to whom the loan is to be made, the interest rates to be charged, the security required to back the loan, the length of time for which the loan is made, and the repayment schedule. Frequently, commercial banks maintain contact with the farmer after the loan is made, providing technical production and finance information when called upon. Banks make both operating and real estate loans. Although each bank has a state-regulated loan limit, the use of correspondent banks makes the financing of loans past these limits possible.

Insurance Companies

Insurance companies constitute the largest institutional lender in the farm-mortgage field. Their loans generally cover real estate, and repayment schedules extend over relatively long periods of time. The loans are generally larger than those made by commercial banks, because real estate loans are usually larger than non–real estate loans.

There are two general types of insurance companies that make loan funds available to farmers. One type is the stock company, which is owned by stockholders who provide the capital from which the loanable funds arise; the other type is the mutual company, in which loanable funds originate from cooperative associations organized under state law and controlled by boards of directors in much the same manner as banks.

They are supervised by state insurance departments, which perform audits and inspections.

Loan policies of insurance companies are only slightly different from those of banks. In general, loans must not be too risky, they must be profitable and backed by collateral, and they must also promote goodwill for the company involved. The total loan policy of the company indicates that the total investment portfolio also be of a diverse nature so that there is a certain amount of stability throughout.

The major insurance companies now employ trained agricultural personnel to handle their farm-loan business in much the same manner explained earlier for commercial banks.

Merchants and Dealers

The majority of merchants and dealers lend capital resources for current production purposes. This is especially true of businesses that manufacture and/or sell agricultural inputs. Feed and seed dealers, distributors of petroleum products, and fertilizer sales agencies are good examples. These businessmen extend credit via notes, open accounts, or chattel mortgages. However, mortgages are used most often when equipment items, such as new tractors or combines, are involved.

The time over which credit is extended by merchants and dealers depends upon many things. In some instances, personal friendship is the key to the length of the loan time. In other cases, harvest time determines loan repayment. In areas where livestock and poultry are fed in large numbers, it is not at all uncommon for dealers to extend open-account credit for feed bills of $150,000–$200,000 payable when the "feeders" are sold. Company salesmen keep the company management informed of the farmer's progress, his progress with his "feeders," and the approximate time when they can expect repayment. This type of credit is not usually budgeted in the same manner as loans from banks, insurance companies, or the cooperative agricultural credit system.

Commodity Credit Corporation

The CCC was created by executive order in October 1933. This credit agency was to make loans connected with farm commodity price-support programs. The CCC originated as a corporation wholly owned by the government, with $100 million capital and borrowing authority to obtain additional funds for loans on farm commodities. There is a current borrowing-authority limit of $14.5 billion. In July 1939, the CCC became part of the U.S. Department of Agriculture, and in 1948 it received a permanent federal charter from Congress.

One of the initial objectives of the CCC was to act as a stabilizing influence on selected farm commodity prices. If the loan rate went below the market price, few loans would be made; if the loan rate rose above the market price of a commodity, there would be relatively more loans made. The CCC makes a nonrecourse loan to farmers that is different from the loans made by most lending agencies. In a CCC loan, the commodity acts just like cash. Here is how the loan works: The CCC makes a loan based on the support price of the agricultural commodity in question. However, the borrower is not under obligation to repay the loan in cash. Instead, if the market price goes below the loan rate, the farmer can pay off the loan in kind, with the commodity he has already mortgaged in order to get the loan. On the other hand, if the market price goes above the loan rate, the farmer can sell the commodity and pay off the loan (principal plus interest) in cash. In addition, if the farmer stores the commodity on his farm (particularly in the case of grain), he is paid for storage if the commodity is stored past the first season. Commodity loans may also be made by private agencies, such as banks, under contract agreement with the CCC.

THE FARM CREDIT SYSTEM

There were 31 major pieces of legislation or executive orders affecting farmers' credit between 1916 and 1960. The Federal Land Banks and the Joint Stock Land Banks were established in 1916. Since that time, major revisions have included the Federal Intermediate Credit Banks, the Rural Electrification Administration, the Bankhead-Jones Act providing for tenant purchase loans, the farmer-owned credit cooperatives, the Farm Home Act, provisions for veterans, emergency credit programs, and permission for interagency mergers and incorporation of federal credit agencies into the Department of Agriculture.

The Farm Credit System was initially a government-sponsored attempt to set up a means by which farmers could provide their own cooperative credit. There are three principal parts to the Farm Credit System. They are the Federal Land Banks, the Production Credit System, and the Banks for Cooperatives. Each of these three agencies operates under the supervision of the District Farm Credit Boards, set up in twelve Farm Credit Districts spread over the entire United States.

Federal Land Bank System

This system is composed of twelve Federal Land Banks (FLB) and 831 FLB Associations (as of January 1, 1960), scattered throughout the twelve Farm Credit Districts. Each of the FLBs is a corporation chartered under the Federal Farm Loan Act of 1916. Each is supervised by a board of directors, and each district board determines its own loan policies. The Federal Land Bank Associations have been completely owned by farmers since 1947, at which time they completely repaid the initial capital given to them by the government.

Under present FLB loan policy, area credit needs are pooled, and the funds necessary to handle these loans are obtained by the sale of debenture bonds in the regular capital markets or investment centers of the economy. Loans are made directly to individual farmers at interest rates that vary depending upon the cost obligations undertaken at the time of the bond sales.

Production Credit System

The Production Credit System is made up of the Federal Intermediate Credit Banks (FICB) and the Production Credit Associations (PCA). Chartered in 1923, the twelve FICBs held provide the funds necessary to operate the 494 PCAs (as of January 1, 1960). This system operates under the policies of the District Farm Credit Board in the same manner as do the FLBs discussed above.

The PCAs are the farmers' contacts and make short-term and intermediate-term loans. These loans are "budgeted" loans, with repayment only on the outstanding balance, a specialized type of repayment plan initiated by the PCAs. Trained field personnel discuss the farm budgets, made out as a loan requirement, with the farmers, and offer technical help wherever they can.

The Production Credit System is owned partially by the government and partially by the farmers. The PCAs are almost entirely owned by farmers, and it is intended that government ownership be gradually retired as the PCAs absorb the FICB stock.

Sources of funds for the PCAs are funds borrowed from the FICB, from rediscounting farmer's notes with the FICB, and from rediscounting farmer loans made by other financing institutions. The FICB, in turn, obtains funds to lend to the PCAs by sales of debenture bonds to the investing public. The rate of interest charged by the PCAs depends on what rate of interest they must pay on their debenture bonds, plus the cost of operation.

Banks for Cooperatives

These banks were chartered under the Farm Credit Act of 1933 in an attempt to provide credit that farmers could obtain to operate their cooperatives. There are thirteen Banks for Cooperatives, one in each of the twelve districts and one central bank located in Washington, D.C.

Each bank has a board of directors that is served by the District Credit Board. These banks are owned jointly by farmers and the government, but final ownership will ultimately rest with the farmers through stock acquisition.

Types of loans made by the Banks for Cooperatives include loans for facilities, for operating capital, and for various commodities. Interest charged is variable, depending upon the type of loan, its term, and the cost of borrowed funds.

Sources of loan funds for the Banks for Cooperatives are capital and surplus, sales of debenture bonds on established capital markets, and funds borrowed directly from the FICB, the FLBs, and commercial banks.

Farmer's Home Administration

Despite the cooperative Farm Credit System, many farmers were once unable to get adequate financing for their operations. This situation is typical for many beginning farmers and for those with limited resources. For this reason, the Farmers Home Administration Act of 1946 created the Farmers Home Administration (FHA). This agency replaced two other government credit agencies that handled direct loans and emergency loans in the U.S. Department of Agriculture. Under this act, FHA loan services were considerably broadened past the responsibilities of the two agencies it replaced.

The objectives of the FHA were to provide supervised agricultural credit to farmers unable to get adequate credit from other sources on reasonable terms. In order to get a loan from the FHA, the farmer had to certify that other credit was not available. He also had to agree to refinance his farm operation until such time as regular commercial credit channels were willing to accept his risk. The second major objective of the FHA is to provide emergency credit in times of drought, hail, flood, and other conditions beyond the control of the individual.

The FHA has a National Office in Washington, D.C., that determines loan policies, interprets legislation, controls budgets, and gives technical training to FHA field personnel. There is also a National Finance Office in St. Louis, Missouri, which handles all the fiscal and business management matters as well as the accounting procedures. There are 43 state FHA offices and about 1,450 county offices.

The FHA has three main sources of loanable funds: It can borrow from the federal treasury, it can use a revolving fund set up by Congress principally to handle emergency loans, and it can borrow from banks.

All applications for loans are made at local county offices and are reviewed by a county committee of three people, at least two of whom are farmers. This committee determines the applicant's eligibility, certifies as to the validity of the loan request, and reviews the borrower's progress. Operating loans are secured by chattel mortgages, and farm ownership loans are secured by real estate mortgages.

There are six main types of loans made by the FHA: operating loans, farm ownership loans, soil and water conservation loans, farm housing loans, emergency loans, and watershed loans. Operating loans, available to tenants as well as owner-operators, are designed primarily to enable farmers to make more profitable use of their existing land and labor resources. Loan size is variable, with a ceiling of $20,000. Repayment schedules may not exceed seven years.

Farm ownership loans are given for buying farms, for enlarging existing farms, for developing land, and for refinancing debts. Repayment schedules extend up to 40 years, but they may be repaid sooner at the borrower's discretion. Soil and water conservation loans are made to individuals and groups of farmers to carry out conservation measures, irrigation developments, and farm water systems. An individual's total indebtedness may not exceed $250,000. Maximum repayment periods are 20 years for individuals and 40 years for groups or associations.

Farm housing loans are made to farmers for the construction and repair of farm outbuildings and farmhouses. Emergency loans are made in areas designated disaster areas. These funds may be made for operating loans or to replace fixed capital resources. The size of the loan is variable (averages about $2,500), and the repayment schedule is based on the ability of the borrower to repay. Watershed loans are made to local organizations to finance projects designed to develop and conserve land and water resources in small watersheds. However, loans are made only on the basis of project approval by the Soil Conservation Service, and only specific soil and water organizations are eligible to receive funds.

THE FUTURE OF CAPITAL IN FARMING

What are the trends in capital accumulation and use that might continue in American agriculture? The amount of capital per farm worker and the amount of capital per farm will continue to rise. As farmers try to lower per-unit production costs and obtain higher net farm incomes, they will increase the size, volume, and specialization of their farm businesses. These adjustments will call forth an increased need for the use and control of capital. Although capital requirements per farm will rise, it is not so clear that the total capital requirements for all agricultural production will also increase. The reason for this situation is that the rapid decline in the total number of farms may offset the total capital increases needed by the remaining farm units.

The composition of the capital used will probably continue to shift in the direction of its current trends. There will most likely be more machinery, livestock, feed, seed, and fertilizer used; and there will probably be relatively less capital investment in land and buildings.

Most of the capital requirements on farms will probably continue to be satisfied from current gross income from farming, but there will be more capital flowing into farming from external sources. Capital raised both from within the farm sector and outside it will undoubtedly provide relatively more non–real estate credit to farmers than real estate credit. Shares of stock may be sold in corporate farms or in specific types of farming operations, such as feedlots or feed mixing plants.

There will be more corporate farming in order to control capital, although corporate members will by no means monopolize the field. There will also be an increase in the number of part owners. These people will be full-time farmers but will own only a small portion of the agricultural assets they use. Farmers in this category will be permanent residents of the farm community, but they will use the land they own primarily as a base of operations for production work in related fields rather than as the principal source of their farm income.

Determining the proper cash-flow pattern will continue to be a problem for some farmers, but integration may help in solving it. Firms providing managerial, production, or marketing services will be in a position to help finance their farmer clients.

APPENDIX TO CHAPTER 5:
INDEX NUMBER CALCULATIONS

Simple Index

Index numbers are commonly used in economics to describe factual data, particularly in situations where it is useful to compare data and relate one number to another. It is often easier to interpret index numbers than raw data because they are usually smaller. Index numbers are used most frequently to describe trends.

To compute a simple index number, the first task is to decide what piece of information is to be used as a "base." The base is the point from which all comparisons will be made and is given an index number of 100. For example, suppose 42 students attended class last week and 47 attended this week. The teacher wants to compare this week's attendance with last week's. The base for comparison is the 42 who attended class last week. In this case, the number 42 is given an index number value of 100. To compare 47 (attendance this week) with last week, divide 47 by 42 and multiply the answer by 100. The answer is 111.9. This answer is the index number for this week's attendance based on last week's attendance. It means, specifically, that there were 11.9 percent (111.9 minus 100) more students in class this week than last.

On the other hand, one could use this week's class attendance as the base and compare last week's to it. In that case, this week's attendance, 47, is given an index value of 100. The index number for last week's attendance is computed by dividing 42 by 47 and multiplying by 100. The index number answer of 89.4 means, specifically, that attendance last week was 10.6 percent less than this week (100 minus 89.4).

The convenience of using index numbers becomes more apparent in the following example. The production of corn in the United States for the five-year period from 1967 to 1971 was:

Year	Thousand Bushels
1967	4,760,076
1968	4,393,273
1969	4,582,534
1970	4,099,493
1971	5,540,253

How much higher was corn production in 1971 than (based on) 1967? If you computed simple index numbers for each year based on 1967, you could give a quick precise answer. Let's do it. The production in 1967 of 4,760,076,000 bushels is given the index number of 100—really computed by dividing the number by itself and multiplying by 100. Each of the following years' bushel outputs is divided by the base-year output and multiplied by 100 to yield the following index numbers:

Year	Computation	Index Number
1967	$4{,}760{,}076 \div 4{,}760{,}076 \times 100 =$	100.0
1968	$4{,}393{,}273 \div 4{,}760{,}076 \times 100 =$	92.3
1969	$4{,}582{,}534 \div 4{,}760{,}076 \times 100 =$	96.3
1970	$4{,}099{,}493 \div 4{,}760{,}076 \times 100 =$	86.1
1971	$5{,}540{,}253 \div 4{,}760{,}076 \times 100 =$	116.4

Now you can say quickly and accurately that there was 16.4 percent more corn produced in 1971 than in 1967. Or that the production was 3.7 percent less in 1969 than in 1967. Practice computing and interpreting index numbers. For example, change the base for comparison to 1970 in this example. The production in 1967 was 16.1 percent greater than in 1970. Right? Note that you could have obtained the same answer of 16.1 percent increase by using the two index numbers (100 for 1967 and 86.1 for 1970). Since you wanted to compare 1967 to 1970, you can calculate what percent more 100.0 is than 86.1. Thus, 100.0 minus 86.1 divided by 86.1 gives the answer of a 16.1 percent increase.

In the corn-production example, there was no clear trend exhibited. The index number went down for 1968, up for 1969, down for 1970, and way up in 1971. You should be able to interpret the index numbers and make statements concerning trends.

Weighted Index

A weighted index number is used to combine several different items that are common to a group into one statistic. All the price indexes reported for the cost of living, the cost of food, industrial prices, farm prices, and so on are weighted indexes. The word "weighted" is used to indicate that not all the items to be considered in the group are of equal importance. Suppose that a comparison were needed of the prices received for major livestock and livestock products by farmers for the year 1971 compared to 1969—not a price comparison for each kind of livestock, but one index number that would represent the whole group. The following information is given as base data:

Item	Unit	Actual Price 1969 (dollars)	1971	Total Sales Value, 1969–71 Average (thousand dollars)	Percent of Total Sales
Beef and veal	cwt.	26.20	29.00	6,088,735	31.2
Hogs	cwt.	22.20	17.50	2,838,221	14.5
Lambs, mutton	cwt.	27.20	25.90	146,183	0.7
Broilers	lb.	.152	.137	1,224,268	6.3
Turkeys	lb.	.224	.226	386,136	2.0
Eggs	doz.	.400	.314	2,160,636	11.1
Milk	cwt.	5.49	5.87	6,674,370	34.2
				19,519,179	100.0

The objective is to compute one weighted index number that will represent all the price changes above for 1971 compared to 1969. There are two steps to the process:

Step 1. Compute simple index numbers for each item for 1971 based on 1969:

Item	Computation	Simple Index for 1971 (1969 = 100)
Beef and veal	$29.00 ÷ $26.20 × 100 =	110.7
Hogs	$17.50 ÷ $22.20 × 100 =	78.8
Lambs, mutton	$25.90 ÷ $27.20 × 100 =	95.2
Broilers	$.137 ÷ $ .152 × 100 =	90.1
Turkeys	$.226 ÷ $ .224 × 100 =	100.9
Eggs	$.314 ÷ $ .400 × 100 =	78.5
Milk	$ 5.87 ÷ $ 5.49 × 100 =	106.9

Step 2. Multiply the simple index number by the appropriate weight and add together for all items. The sum is the weighted index number. The weighting factor is the percentage of total sales generated by each item. In this example, the average value of sales for the three-year period 1969–71 was used in determining the weights for each item. The percentage weights are put into decimal form for multiplication.

Item	Percent of Total Sales	Decimal		Simple Index	Contribution to Weighted Index
Beef and veal	31.2	.312	×	110.7 =	34.54
Hogs	14.5	.145	×	78.8 =	11.43
Lambs, mutton	0.7	.007	×	95.2 =	0.67
Broilers	6.3	.063	×	90.1 =	5.68
Turkeys	2.0	.020	×	100.9 =	2.02
Eggs	11.1	.111	×	78.5 =	8.71
Milk	34.2	.342	×	106.9 =	36.56
	100.0	1.000			99.61

The weighted index number is 99.6 and means, specifically, that the prices of major livestock and livestock products in 1971 was 0.4 percent less than in 1969 weighted by contribution to total value of sales. It is the best single number that can be computed to show the price comparison for the two periods for the total group of products.

6

Technology

WHAT IS TECHNOLOGY?

Technology is the knowledge applied by man to improve production or marketing processes. It is reflected in tractors, combines, and corn pickers. It is embodied in hybrid seed corn, improved crop varieties, pesticides, commercial fertilizer, contour plowing, automatic hog feeders, and rural electrification. Technology is in the workshop, chemistry laboratory, barn, field, and office. Its objective is to provide greater output from a given amount of land, labor, and capital resources. Technology is vital to the economizing process.

Technology causes rapid changes in farm production. Within two short decades after hybrid seed corn was developed, it was used on 24 million acres. The estimated increase in yield during that time was 100 million bushels. This great increase in production, coupled with a more slowly developing demand, resulted in lower corn prices. Mechanization of American agriculture occurred so swiftly that from 1915 to 1940, the tractor, truck, and automobile cut down the human labor force by thousands and resulted in nearly 10 million less horses and mules being needed on farms. Hence, as scientific knowledge about improving crops and animals grows, and as engineers perfect labor-saving machinery,

113

other problems such as unemployment and falling commodity prices may be created.

TECHNOLOGY IS CUMULATIVE

"I entreat you send me thirty carpenters, husbandmen, gardeners, blacksmiths, masons, and diggers-up of trees' roots rather than a thousand such as we have," wrote Captain John Smith in 1609, in a desperate effort to save the settlement at Jamestown, Virginia. Of what significance is this? Simply that technology was a necessary ingredient to survival. The bare necessities of life (food, clothing, and shelter) required the application of man's knowledge of production processes in using the resources on hand. The initial settlement at Jamestown included a majority of traders, goldsmiths, and silversmiths—men who were sent to search for gold and other valuable items and who knew little about food production. What the New World needed was men who had brainpower oriented toward technical food-production processes. The mistake made at Jamestown was not repeated by the Pilgrims of Plymouth, who in 1620 brought skilled husbandmen, artisans, and tools to the first permanent settlement in New England.

Technology passes from father to son, from teacher to student, from generation to generation as knowledge once learned becomes a permanent resource. To say that the new settlers' technology was merely a replica of the Old World would be a grievous error. The native Indians offered much in helping the white man understand his environment. In 1609, Captain John Smith captured two Indians with the avowed purpose of making them "teach us how to order and plant our fields." Forty acres of corn were planted with the assistance of the Indians, and within five years, the Jamestown Colony was planting 200 acres of corn.

The important point is that as time passes, the fruits of technology —increased production at lower cost, or better-quality produce for the same cost—become cumulative. Not only does the amount of technical knowledge increase, but its growth in all directions tends to grow at a continually faster rate. It is probably safe to say that if an Egyptian farmer on the Nile River in 1000 B.C. could be transported through time to an 1850 colonial farm in America, he would not be too surprised by the agricultural technology in use. But should that 1850 colonial farmer be transported to a modern commercial farm, the technology employed would be almost entirely past his understanding. Thus, in a real sense, if technological knowledge is likened to a snowball rolling down a hill, the snowball rolled very slowly and increased in size very little for many years; but currently the snowball's momentum is great and its size is overpowering.

Another important element contributing to the rapid use and implementation of new technology is the advancement in the field of communications. The flow of new technology can be rapidly distributed through the mass media of television, radio, books, and newspapers. The rapid movement of people from one place to another owing to developments in transportation also contributes to the rapid dissemination of new technology.

At this time, however, the point should be made that simply disseminating the knowledge concerning new technology does not guarantee its adoption and implementation. Many Americans are so conditioned by living in a country of rapid technological change that they are used to seeing a new production idea tested quickly and implemented immediately if it proves successful. This is not so in other parts of the world. George M. Foster points out the complexity of the process of technological development.[1] He argues there can be no such thing as technological development in isolation and proposes the term "socio-technological development" instead. The acceptance of technology is a complex cultural, social, and psychological process much more than it is the overt acceptance of material and technical improvements. The failure of some American technical-aid programs overseas is in part due to our lack of understanding that for every technical and material change, there must be an accompanying change in attitudes, values, and beliefs of the people affected by the change. Foster argues:

> . . . These nonmaterial changes are more stable. Often they are overlooked or their significance is underestimated. Yet the eventual effect of a material or social improvement is determined by the extent to which the other aspects of culture affected by it can alter their forms with a minimum of interruption. In newly developing countries, for example, the introduction of factory labor brings changes in family structure. If the workers and their families can accept these new social patterns and reconcile their attitudes toward traditional family obligations with new conditions, industrialization need not be disruptive. But . . . reconciliation is often difficult, and the process of development is accordingly slowed.[2]

So we see that the use of new technology is not magical and is indeed a complex process. It is cumulative in its effect and the reservoir of technology is always growing.

---

[1] George M. Foster, *Traditional Cultures: and the Impact of Technological Change* (New York: Harper & Row, 1962), p. 2.
[2] *Ibid.*, p. 3.

EFFECTS OF TECHNOLOGY

By definition, if the input–output ratio is improved by the introduction of a new technology, it must eventually result in a greater output at a lower per-unit production cost. New mechanical technologies in the form of improved machines and equipment tend to decrease total inputs without any decrease in outputs. New biological technologies such as improved seeds, pesticides, or cross-breeding of animals, for example, tend to increase output with little or no change in total inputs. Both these types of technology permit economizing by improving input–output relationships.

Technological change, therefore, nearly always has an important effect on the level of agricultural prices. As new technology is introduced and per-unit costs of production decline, the quantity and quality of output increases. Under some demand conditions for certain commodities, there may be an eventual price decline. Therefore, part of the benefits of technology are passed on to food consumers through lower prices or a better-quality product for the same price. Whether the benefits of technology are equitably distributed among the farmers, the marketing middleman, and the food consumer is another question, one almost constantly under debate.[3] There are many factors that affect farm prices. The generalization that can be made with regard to farming technology is that the application of new technological advancements generally results in lower production costs, expanded output, and lower prices.

The effect of technology on the farmer's gross income is determined largely if and when a new technology is adopted. For example, the farmer who was an "early adopter" and used hybrid seed corn before the majority of his neighbors did was able to increase his gross and net income considerably. With the hybrid seed resulting in higher yields per acre harvested, his dollar return per acre was higher with relatively little additional cost. However, now that practically all commercial corn producers use hybrid seed, no individual farmer increases his net income very much as a result of using it; but if a farmer were *not* to use hybrid seed corn now, his low yields would lower his income. The old adage, "The early bird catches the worm," is directly applicable in the case of technology. The producer who adopts the new technology before others do gets higher net returns as a result. After every producer has adopted the technology, the income benefits to producers are generally lowered,

---

3 The theoretical and technical aspects of technology are examined later, in Chapter 11.

while all society benefits from increases in the quantity and quality of products available.

This generalization, however, does not preclude the fact that some technologies are adopted without any influence on dollar income. The intangible return of enjoying greater convenience and satisfaction is often reason enough to adopt some technologies. The use of a tractor instead of manual labor on a farm in certain tasks does not necessarily reduce the cost of producing or handling a crop. But the work can be done more quickly and easily, freeing more time and energy for leisure-time activities or additional productive effort elsewhere. Much of the technology that influences food-preparation time does not reduce the cost of feeding a family, but it does free much of the home-maker's time for other enjoyable activities. Numerous examples are in evidence, but these important ideas remain: A new technology will be adopted if the extra return generated as a result of adoption is greater than the added cost of adoption, remembering that returns may be of either an intangible or an actual dollar nature.

As technology changes costs and output, it also influences the level and distribution of income. Further, the use of existing technology and the infusion of new technology are strong stimulants to the rate of economic growth.

TWO KINDS OF TECHNICAL KNOWLEDGE

Dennison distinguishes between technological knowledge and managerial knowledge as follows:

> Technological knowledge consists of knowledge concerning the physical properties of things, and of how to make, or combine, or use them in a physical sense. . . . Managerial knowledge consists of advances in knowledge concerning the techniques of management construed in the broadest sense, and in business organization.[4]

Certainly, any discussion of advances in productivity and economic growth should recognize both kinds of knowledge and the contribution each makes. Advances in the technological sense are more obvious, with the familiar references to the steam engine, telephones, computers, rockets, synthetic fibers, and so on. Less obvious are the effects of better business organization and management procedures embodied in improved inventory-control procedure, office-building designs, self-service

---

[4] Edward F. Dennison, "The Sources of Economic Growth in the United States and the Alternatives Before Us," Supplementary Paper No. 13, published by the Committee for Economic Development, January 1962, pp. 231–32.

supermarkets, labor–management negotiations, and integration of production and marketing activities as exemplified in the broiler industry.

Some 20 percent of the increase in the measured growth rate of total real national product has been ascribed to the increase of knowledge and its application. To separate the contribution to this total into the components of technological knowledge and managerial knowledge is difficult. In many cases, the two are complementary. For example, improvement in inventory-control methods was speeded by both managerial knowledge and high-speed data-processing machines. Integration in the broiler industry was speeded both by new managerial organization methods and by machines, buildings, equipment, and genetic strains of broilers that functioned well in a controlled environment.

Another way of viewing technologies is to differentiate between changes in the use of a given bundle of resources and changes in the composition of resources used. Under the first grouping, the proportion of inputs remains the same while output increases. Timing of operations, organizational efficiency, and new production and marketing procedures are examples of this type of technology. The second grouping includes technology that changes the proportion of resources used. Under this category, inputs may be substituted in varying amounts and recombined in such a way that output increases relative to the amount of inputs used.

THE DIFFUSION OF TECHNOLOGY AND TECHNICAL CHANGE

The fruits of technology are not realized in a society until the new knowledge is utilized. The change that occurs in using technological knowledge is called technical change. Technical change cannot occur until new inventions and scientific discoveries take place.

Knowledge is a universal commodity whose increase depends greatly on a country's level of economic and social development; the greater the development, the more knowledge exists and is applid. The rate at which technological knowledge is adopted by countries and by individuals varies widely. Some of the obstacles to its adoption with regard to culture have already been discussed. Tradition, habit, and general attitude toward change are important factors affecting the use of technology.

What incentive does a person have to be inventive and create a new idea? There are many. Often, people are creative merely for the personal satisfaction it gives them. Others are spurred by the hopes of large profit. A productive scientist in an academic institution, business, or government job will sometimes find this paycheck increased if he is a productive generator of new ideas. The federal and state governments, as well as private businesses, allocate funds for research and development. The competitive nature of our economy requires commercial and industrial businesses to constantly search for better methods of production of goods and services. Estimates of total funds spent for research and development were $30 billion in 1973, over twice the amount in 1961.[5] About two-thirds of these funds are used by industry, but over half comes from federal sources. Thirty-seven percent of the funds were for defense and space-related research programs. Most of the R&D funds go to improve existing products, or to develop new prototypes capable of being market-tested. Funds used solely to improve efficiency in production methods, thereby lowering production costs, play a relatively minor role in industrial research.

Our system of patents also encourages the generation of new ideas, since the owner is protected from other inventors with similar ideas as soon as the patent is given. This means he has exclusive opportunities to make profits for a limited amount of time. The number of patents issued is sometimes used as another indicator of the rate at which new knowledge is being generated, although it is at best a very rough indicator. Patents issued averaged 40,000 per year for the 1900–1960 period. However, 78,183 were issued in 1972.

Diffusion of Technology

The rapidity with which technology is actually used in production processes depends on (1) the receptivity of the society to new ideas, (2) the efficiency of the communication or education system, (3) the size of the cash outlay required to use the technology, and (4) the degree of obsolescence of existing production equipment. How receptive the population is to new ideas is a function of many social, economic, and political factors that have already been discussed. There is little impediment to the use of technology from lack of communications in the United States. In addition to a free press and the mass media of radio and television, the Agricultural Extension Service created in 1914 by the Smith-Lever Act established a communications network reaching the "grass-roots" farmer in an educational system that is unsurpassed in any part of the world.

When the application of a new technology involves a considerable cash outlay, such as the initial purchase of a tractor or combine or the replacement of existing equipment with an improved model, other considerations become important. The decision depends on the answer to

---

[5] *Statistical Abstract of the United States,* 1973, p. 522.

such questions as, "Should I invest my money in a new tractor or should we put it aside for the children's education?" In contrast, whether or not a farmer should use hybrid seed rather than open-pollinated varieties is a much easier decision, because relatively little cash outlay is required. The important generalization is that technology requiring a large initial money outlay in order to implement its use is likely to be adopted more slowly than one that requires only a small cash outlay. The rate of depreciation and obsolescence of existing machinery and equipment, the extent of desire to maximize profits, the weights of risk and uncertainty, and the individual's personal preferences and values also influence the degree to which technology is created, adopted, and used.[6]

Measuring Technological Progress

To estimate the impact of the application of technological knowledge on output in agriculture is a complicated and difficult task. The rapid growth in food production in the United States is necessarily the result of an increase in the total level and quality of inputs as well as technology. One estimate claims that in the 1929–57 period, the annual growth rate of total real national income was 2.93 percent; and that of this amount, 2 percent was from an increase in total inputs, 0.59 percent from increased knowledge and its application (technological and managerial), and 0.34 percent from other sources.

Changes in the productivity of labor in terms of output per man-hour and output per farm worker have also been used to indicate technological progress, but Ruttan points out that the differences in substitutability of one input for another distorts its use.[7] An example is the extent to which capital can be substituted for physical labor. Not only may this substitution reduce operating costs, particularly when labor costs are high, but it may also provide intangible satisfaction because of the freeing of time for other uses. Thus, in an industry such as farming, where the increase in labor productivity has stemmed largely from substituting capital for labor, the index of output per man-hour overstates the contribution of technology. On the other hand, in an industry such as meat-packing, where technological progress has been primarily capital-saving rather than labor-saving, the indicator of change in labor productivity understates the contribution of technological change to

---

[6] In Part IV, costs will be separated into two categories—fixed and variable—and the significance of this aspect of implementing technology will become better understood at that point.

[7] Vernon W. Ruttan, "The Contribution of Technological Progress to Farm Output: 1950–75," *Review of Economics and Statistics*, Vol. 38, No. 1 (February 1956), 62.

output. If output per man-hour is used as an index for comparing technology in the farm and nonfarm economies, the farm index moved above the private nonfarm index in the late 1940s for the first time since pre–World War 1.[8] Several other studies indicate that the rate of technological change in farming is about twice that of all manufacturing.[9]

Technology and locational change. When a production process utilizes new technology, there are bound to be changes in the location of production, of the input markets, of the markets where the product is sold, or in all three locations at once. For example, when technology was adopted by those in the home arts and crafts industries at the beginning of the Industrial Revolution, it soon became clear that a factory system of production was better adapted to production methods than was the home. Technological improvements usually required machines powered by more than man himself. As a consequence, new inventions in the use of energy through the steam engine, water power, electricity, gas, and atomic power have all been increasingly away from the use of man or animal power to run machines.

Technology led to the use of improved, more costly, and physically larger units of machinery. Increasingly, inputs were used for a more mass-like type of production. For example, improvements in the mining of coal led to cheaper steel and an increased demand for it by other industries that was fulfilled only through the use of massive rolling mills and open-hearth furnaces. None of the new steel technology and machinery could be used in the homes of those previously employed in the homecraft industries.

When the production process shifted from the home to the factory, there was a simultaneous emphasis upon the division of labor and the degree to which it was specialized. Labor was now utilized by the production process in an entirely different way from before. New skills were required and new responsibilities were demanded of supervisors and management. A man was forced to specialize, since he could not be fully competent in all phases of the skills required for a top-quality production job.

With specialization also evolved the technologies associated with materials utilization and materials handling. One input was made substitutable for another in the production of a good, the amount of substitu-

---

8 "Technology and the American Economy," Report of the National Commission on Technology, Automation, and Economic Progress, Vol. 1 (Washington, D.C.: Government Printing Office, February 1966).

9 See R. M. Solow, "Technical Change and Aggregate Production Functions," *Review of Economics and Statistics,* Vol. 39 (August 1957), 312–20; and Lester B. Lave, *Technological Change: Its Conception and Measurement* (Englewood Cliffs, N.J.: Prentice-Hall, 1966).

tion depending upon the price of the necessary factors of production. As new inputs were used, the markets for inputs widened. The use of business specialists emerged—men who were trained in assembling the needed factors of production for various business and manufacturing concerns.

Improved methods of transfer were evolved. The railroads made new cars that refrigerated or froze the products en route. Trucking lines established new routes and express schedules, and also instituted new handling techniques, including refrigeration. New standards of quality were used and improved methods of communication relayed the current news about standards.

When the total impact of technology is assessed on location, it simply points up the fact that new processes generally reach increasingly further into input or final-product markets. They bring the country closer together through an improved network of transportation that includes cheaper rates, influences relative input and product prices, changes the locational pattern of distance and time, influences mass production of an item, and also tends to raise the quality of production.

As a consequence of an increased division of labor and specialization, there is an increased sensitivity concerning the moves of one firm, plant, or industry on other firms or industries. This sensitivity is caused by changing responses established in markets and supply areas. Sensitivity to these changes can lead to intense competition between producers and between the suppliers of inputs to these producers.

It should be noted that although new ideas and machines are invented, invention is only the *scientific* fact—innovation is the *economic* fact that determines which inventions are used and which are not. There are certain permissive conditions for innovation or for the acceptance of an invention into the production process. In many cases, these conditions resolve themselves into the ability of the labor force to absorb the technical changes brought about by use of the new technology. Although some labor displacement is tolerated socially and politically, extreme unemployment is not tolerable. Automation and the resulting unemployment are an example of a problem in the adoption of technology that is not yet solved.

In addition to the permissive conditions imposed by society, the individual entrepreneur has to be willing to risk the chance of using the new idea. He must be convinced that the potential profits are worth the costs necessarily incurred to put the technology into his production process. Credit institutions must be willing to finance the effort. Distributors must be paid for handling the new product. And finally, the individual household or businessman must be convinced that the new product would be a good thing to buy.

There is little doubt that we now live in an era of exploding technology, which can contribute rapidly to any country's growth rate if it is utilized in production. The use of atomic energy and major contributions by geneticists in improving plant and animal life are on the horizon.

A BRIEF CHRONOLOGY OF
TECHNOLOGICAL DEVELOPMENT IN
UNITED STATES AGRICULTURE

Many pages have been written about the dynamics of farming methods in the United States. For purposes of discussion here, technological development will be classified as to change in machines, animals, plants, land-use improvements, and food-processing methods.[10]

Technology in Machines

Beginning with Whitney's cotton gin in about 1820, the revolution in agricultural farm machinery began to take place rapidly. The reaper, the mower, the seed drill, the steel plow, and the threshing machine made farming possible on an extensive scale, particularly in the prairie regions of the Midwest. The pioneer colonial farmer was neither the traditional landlord nor the peasant type typical in Europe. He was enterprising, a pretty good mechanic, and when convinced a machine would aid him, he was fairly quick to adopt it.

The steel plow was perfected by John Deere in the 1840s. It evolved from the wood and cast-iron plows that failed to scour the moldboards in sticky prairie soils. Corn planters and wheat drills greatly simplified the planting process, and the reaper mechanically harvested grain that for centuries had been cut with a hand sickle. The McCormick reaper, patented in 1831, sold rapidly after a Chicago factory opened in 1844. The stationary threshing machine appeared at about the same time. This introduction helped to initiate the construction of grain elevators by Dart, who was given a patent on a granary (grain elevator) designed to be "heat and moisture proof."

But it was probably the tractor more than any other piece of equipment that revolutionized farming, particularly after 1910, when the

---

[10] This material draws heavily from U.S. Department of Agriculture, Bureau of Agricultural Economics, "Technology on the Farm," Special Report (Washington, D.C.: U.S. Government Printing Office, 1940); John W. Oliver, *History of American Technology* (New York: Ronald Press, 1956), Chapter 16; and U.S. Department of Agriculture, Agricultural Research Service, "Consumer Products by Design," Agr. Info. Bulletin 355, June 1972.

old cumbersome model was replaced with a lighter machine of a "jack-of-all-trades" sort. "Drawbar power" rapidly replaced "horsepower" and made it much more feasible for farmers to use large equipment, in addition to greatly speeding each process. Belt pulleys provided mobile power and the power takeoff increased both the efficiency and dependability of mechanical equipment. Tractor numbers doubled on farms in the decade of the 1930s, and the substitution of rubber tires for steel wheels decreased fuel consumption and extended the life of the general-purpose tractor.

To complement the all-purpose tractor, tillage implements have become lighter (in their relative size groups), more flexible, and more versatile. Erosion control and new fertilization and seeding practices have also influenced tillage-machinery developments. The combine and mechanical corn picker were in widespread use by the 1940s, but the perfection of a mechanical cotton picker was more difficult. Mechanical harvesting equipment has been introduced in orchards and for some perishable vegetables. The 1960s brought the fresh-tomato harvester, and in the 1970s, a mechanical harvesting system for red tart cherries was adopted.

Automated feeding systems for livestock will gain prominence in the 1970s. A new method first moves various ingredients from storage; measures, blends, and grinds them; and then conveys the mixed ground feed to feed bunks. Getting feed into an automated pipeline feeding system is accomplished by an auger-type feed injector, which also promises wide adaptations in other industries.

In supermarkets, a computerized system to speed up checkouts promises greater efficiency than present systems by eliminating ring-up error, providing customers with itemized printouts of purchases, cutting labor costs, automating the ordering of shelf replacements, and providing continuous inventory.

Technology in Animal Production

As time passes, Americans change their mode of living and eating habits. These changes have prompted biological scientists to search for ways to change animals and plants to meet the desires of food consumers. As a whole, physical labor has been reduced and a large number of people have more sedentary tasks. As an example, weight consciousness and disease prevention have reduced the desire for animal fats, with the result that hogs and cattle are bred to provide a higher proportion of lean meat. Nutritional studies are often applicable to farm animals as well as humans, and new knowledge of insects, pests, germs, and minerals controlling animal disease are in wide use.

Animal-feeding research has been directed toward learning the importance and use of such elements as vitamins, forage, and minerals in rations. The results appear in converting feeds to edible meats more efficiently. The broiler is a prime example. In the late 1940s, it required some fifteen pounds of feed to grow a three-pound broiler over a 15-week period. Currently, the figure is more likely to be slightly over seven pounds of feed input for an 8-week growing period. Recently, poultry geneticists have crossbred chickens and turkeys with wildfowl species. A new bird with a new taste for consumers could be the result.

New knowledge concerning diseases and parasites, the use of progeny testing, crossbreeding within all types of animals, and artificial insemination have all contributed significantly to an increase in livestock and livestock products. Some of the most dramatic successes are occurring with sheep. A new type of sheep called "Morlam" (more lambs) has been developed from over ten years of selective breeding. The ewes have lambing intervals of six to ten months, rather than twelve. Additionally, crossbreeding with a strain imported from Ireland is increasing the frequency of multiple births. The combined result is a greatly stepped-up rate of reproduction.

Technology in Plant Production

Plant technologists continually battle crop failure, and some of their greatest achievements are in breeding new varieties to withstand drought, disease, and plant parasites, as well as developing higher-yielding varieties. Plant innovations make available new species for regions that formerly could not grow them. Much has been already learned about hybrid plants, and new research on plant hormones and other growth and food substances continues to bring new revolutionary developments in our forests, fields, and gardens.

Hybrid seed corn, which has been already mentioned, increased corn output by 100 million bushels in the 1930s after the first commercial seed was produced in Connecticut around 1922. In addition to providing increased output, hybrid varieties may be more resistant to disease and possess better durability, allowing for more efficient use of mechanical corn pickers. Although developments in wheat do not show results comparable to those in corn, new wheat varieties have met the challenge of increased production in the face of depleted land fertility, increasing insect pests, and the extension of grain production into high-risk areas. In oats, the contribution of plant technologists has been in perfecting varieties resistant to stem rust, crown rust, and smut. For cotton, an important development is standardization of production in single-variety communities, a procedure whereby all farmers in a locality grow one improved strain of cotton.

In any one year, the U.S.D.A. Agricultural Research Service's plant explorers bring about 9,000 new plants into the United States. These are tested for their crop or breeding potential. From these plant-breeding efforts, food consumers in the 1970s can expect such new and improved foods as tastier sweet corn, thornless blackberries, tomatoes with more vitamin C, the Chinese gooseberry or Kiwi berry, sunflower-oil margarine, low-fat peanuts, greener lima beans, large-fruited persimmons, a new leafy green vegetable that has a productivity five times that of spinach, and leguminous beans and cereal grains with more protein of better quality.

Technology in Land Use

There is a fixed amount of land, but technology continually affects its productivity. The merit of good conservation practices of soil and forest resources was firmly established by the formation of the Soil Conservation Service in 1935. The primary objective of conservation is to control soil-erosion losses and the depletion of fertility. The use of cover crops and suitable crop rotations and proper tillage practices are necessary technologies in maintaining the basic soil resource. The stimulus to shifting of land use from grain crops to legumes and grasses was aided by increased yields that allowed the total grain production needed in the United States to be produced on fewer acres.

Terracing, contour farming, and sod waterways are important technologies that serve to make better use of the land resource and increase its productivity. Terracing and sod waterways provide a system of drainage that conserves water in areas of low precipitation and disposes of excess water in areas of high precipitation. Terraces are used primarily by farmers in the South. Contour farming controls erosion and conserves moisture on regular slopes.

The use of commercial fertilizer gained momentum after World War I, slowed down during the depression, and has risen continuously since 1937. In conjunction with cropping practices in improving soil productivity, commercial fertilizer has tremendously increased yields. Some plant diseases have been traced to the deficiency of certain trace elements in the soil. These losses have been stemmed or replaced by increased use of commercial fertilizer. Encouraged by agricultural legislation in 1938, the application of phosphate and lime contributed to large increases in hay and forage output as well as in grain yields.

Much of the efforts in improving land use have been from the standpoint of redirecting its use to serve human needs more effectively, for both present and future generations. Farm woodlands, for example, are now thought of as commercial farm enterprises, and wildlife management practices have enhanced the recreational value for many areas. In some desert areas, former lakebed land with virtually no agricultural potential for conventional crops or livestock is being used for commercial fish farming.

Technology in Food Processing

New methods in processing, packaging, preparing, and serving foods to the consumer have increased at a rapid rate. Most of these innovations are aimed at giving the housewife more convenience and less difficulty in providing the family with meals.

Frozen-food packing. Preserving fruits, vegetables, and meats by freezing is not only more convenient for the consumer, but also provides him with a higher degree of food nutrients, food flavor and aroma, and color than does canning. Proper freezing techniques also retard deterioration and keep the product fresher. Accompanying the rise in frozen-food processing were the developments of efficient retail dispensing cabinets to facilitate mass supermarket distribution. Other adjuncts to frozen-food packing are freezer lockers, home freezers, and freezing-compartment space in refrigerators.

Canning. The canning of fruit, vegetables, and fruit juices was an important technology in preserving foods, and it is still growing in importance. Commercial canning began in the United States in 1819, when a firm packed various meats and fish in glass containers. The tin can was patented in 1825; machine-made cans were manufactured after 1847. Early canners experienced difficulty with spoilage losses. When they found that this could be solved by higher sterilization temperatures, a new problem of exploding cans arose; but this was taken care of by the steam retort, invented in 1874. Large-scale canning operations are aided by machines such as the pea viner and the bean snipper, which cuts the ends off pods and reduces the cost of canned string beans. Other equipment of importance includes the machine that peels the hard shell of pineapple, removes the core, and cuts off the end in one operation; and the "Iron Chunk," a machine that eviscerates salmon and removes fins, tail, and scales.

Dehydration. The challenge in dehydration is to make the dried product taste as good as it did when fresh. Additional shelf life is also an advantage. In the 1970s, consumers can expect instant orange crystals, made by dehydrating concentrated orange juice through a special process. They can be reconstituted for drinking or used to flavor foods. Osmovac fruits are sugar-dried fruit slices that have a crisp, honeycomb-like texture. These dried fruits—which include bananas, apples, peaches, and strawberries—can be eaten with cereals or as snacks. They can also be used in baked goods, desserts, and salads. Explosion-puffed apple pieces and precooked dehydrated sweet-potato flakes are other foods on the horizon.

Technology in Fiber Processing

Cotton. Cotton has been a familiar fabric for centuries, but it has recently lost ground to synthetic fibers. Technological breakthroughs propose to revive the cotton industry. Some of the innovations are durable-press apparel that keeps its creases after many launderings; flame-resistant cotton goods that retain their flame resistance after repeated washing; stretch-cotton fabrics and yarns that have greater tear strength, warmth, and wrinkle resistance; cotton canvas (for tents, awnings, etc.) that is strong and does not fade or rot from mildew; and water- and wind-resistant cotton fabrics that can stand up to mildew, rot, and harsh weather.

Wool. The estimated damage in the United States from insects that feed on fabrics ranges from $100 million to $350 million annually. New compounds in the class of insecticides known as organophosphates show promise as effective mothproofing materials. Current research is also expected to bring the consumer, in the next decade, washable woolens that won't shrink, flame-resistant woolens, and permanent-press wool fabrics.

SUMMARY

Technology results from man's efforts to make a new piece of equipment, to breed new varieties of plants, or to adapt existing products to new human uses. In essence, technology improves the physical input–output ratio in our production processes and, in so doing, promotes efficiency in satisfying human wants from scarce resources. Technology is a cumulative process, because knowledge is passed from one generation to another and tends to grow at an ever-increasing rate. The rate at which new technology is adopted varies considerably among technologies, producers, and countries. The adoption process is sometimes slowed because of cultural and social factors. Technologies requiring little initial cash outlay will tend to be adopted faster than those requiring large cash outlays. Measuring this contribution of technology to society is a very complex task, but it has been estimated to have contributed about 20 percent of the total growth in per capita real national output.

PART THREE

PART
THREE

7

Characteristics of Farms and Farm Production in the United States

Many changes have taken place over the years in American farming and on the country's farms.[1] These changes have implications for the future that merit study and analysis. This chapter describes the principal characteristics of the farming industry; some have been omitted here because they are noted in other chapters, where discussion of them is more appropriate.

It is difficult to separate any one farm characteristic for analysis. Although data can be isolated and tabulated, nothing in farming moves by itself. There are many forces within farming and the rest of the economy that move at the same time. What stimulus causes exactly what response is sometimes extremely hard to discover. For this reason, we must remember that farmers do not operate in a vacuum, but do things for reasons that make good sense to them. To find out these reasons, analyze their consequences, and predict future farmer decisions is a serious and involved challenge.

---

[1] The words *ranch* and *farm* in this text are used interchangeably.

FARM DEFINITIONS

The first nationwide census of agriculture was taken in 1850. It itemized the number of farms, the land in farms, and the value of land and buildings. The census definition of a farm has changed several times, but it basically includes all the land on which some agricultural operations are performed by a person, either by his own labor alone or with the assistance of members of his household or hired employees. Agricultural operations consist of the production of crops or plants, vines, or trees (excluding forestry operations); or the keeping, grazing, or feeding of livestock for animal products, animal increase, or value enhancement. Included as farms are such enterprises as nurseries, greenhouses, hothouses, fur farms, mushroom houses, apiaries, and cranberry bogs. Excluded are fish farms, fish hatcheries, oyster farms, frog farms, kennels, game preserves, and the like. The Bureau of the Census in 1969 defined a farm on the basis of a combination of "acres in the place" and the quantity of agricultural resources on the place or the quantity of agricultural products produced. Detailed computer-editing specifications on land use, crop and livestock resources, and harvested acres were applied to determine if places of ten acres or more, or places less than ten acres, were farms.

There is some concern that the census of agriculture will be eliminated. The reasons given are that it is costly and that the information it provides is no longer as useful in an urban society as it once was in an evolving rural-oriented society.

Family Farms

Reference to family farms is often made in discussing American agriculture. Usually a family farm has simply meant a farm operated and managed by the labor of one family, and may include a small amount of part-time hired labor. Some people refer to a family farm on the basis of acreage. However, defining a family farm by size is misleading, because farming operations run by one family range from a few acres of intensive vegetable farming to several thousand of acres of cattle range.

Commercial Farms

A commercial farm is defined (as of 1969) as any farm with a value of sales from agricultural products of $2,500 or more. Farms with less than $2,500 sales were counted as commercial only if the farm operator was under 65 years of age, or if he reported less than 100 days of non-farm work.

RELATIVE IMPORTANCE OF FARMING

The total income from farming during the early 1800s comprised a large part of national income, because our society was primarily agrarian. However, with the advent of the Industrial Revolution, the relative importance of farm income began declining. A continuing stream of scientific knowledge and applied technology aided a high rate of growth in nonfarm industries. This trend has become more pronounced in recent times. Since 1955, farm income has been less than 5 percent of total national income (Table 7-1).

Despite this dramatic decline in relative income contribution, farming still comprises nearly half the total business units. This fact is remarkable, considering that farm numbers have been cut almost in half since 1914, that farm population and the number of farm workers in the labor force has fallen from about a third to slightly less than 4 percent of the total, and that only since the 1950s has farm income per capita risen to be more than half of per capita nonfarm income. It was still under 80 percent of nonfarm income by 1972 (Figure 7-1). No wonder it has often been said that farming is a way of life for many people, in addition to being a business. However, it cannot be denied that this is becoming less and less so. The management, capital, and technical requirements necessary to earn a good money income in farming call for an increased business perspective. Farming is big business

TABLE 7-1

National Income, Farm and Nonfarm, 1940–72

Year	Farm (millions of dollars)	Nonfarm (millions of dollars)	Total (millions of dollars)	Farm as a Percentage of Total
1940	5,967	75,157	81,124	7.4
1950	16,883	224,191	241,074	7.0
1960	15,857	398,665	414,522	3.8
1972	27,967	913,825	941,792	3.0

SOURCE: U.S. Department of Agriculture, Economic Research Service.

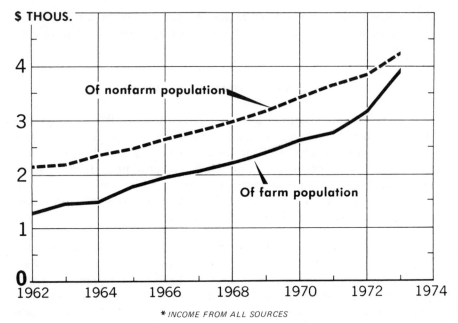

U.S. DEPARTMENT OF AGRICULTURE   NEG. ERS 8438-74 (4)   ECONOMIC RESEARCH SERVICE

FIGURE 7-1

Disposable Per Capita Income for Farm and
Nonfarm Population, 1960–1972

in America, and although it is difficult to separate farming as a business from living on a farm, the trend is clearly away from a general family farm to a more specialized, highly efficient commercial farming business.

FARM CHARACTERISTICS

Number of Farms

There was approximately the same number of farms in the United States in 1973 as between 1870 and 1880 (Table 7-2). When the first census of farms was taken in 1850, there was one farm for every 16 persons living in the United States. Despite rapid population growth and the movement westward to new lands, there was still approximately the same ratio of farms to population (one farm for every 16.4 persons) in 1920. But during the next few decades, the picture changed so rapidly that by 1969 the ratio was one farm for every 68 persons living in this country.

During the late 1800s and early 1900s, growth in numbers of farms was stimulated not only because of population growth, but also because food was produced in the new territories opening in the West, and transportation was not sufficiently developed to handle either the quantity or the quality of food needed to support the settlers there. Food had to be produced where the people lived. Limited agricultural technology and reliance on animal power rather than mechanical power also necessitated a growth in farm numbers into the early 1900s if food production was to keep pace with total population.

From 1910 to 1940, farm numbers stayed relatively stable. A downward trend in farm numbers has been evident since 1920, except for a brief increase during the depression years, when more than half a mil-

TABLE 7-2
Number of U.S. Farms, Selected Years, 1860–1973

Year	Total Number (thousands)	Average Farm Size (acres)	Average Farm Value (current dollars)
1860	2,044	199	3,251
1870	2,660	153	2,799
1880	4,009	134	2,544
1890	4,565	137	2,909
1900	5,740	147	2,905
1910	6,366	139	5,480
1920	6,454	149	10,295
1930	6,295	157	7,624
1935	6,812	155	4,823
1940	6,102	175	5,532
1950	5,388	216	14,005
1960	3,962	303	34,825[a]
1973	2,831	385	75,725[b]

[a] 1959 data.
[b] 1969 data.
SOURCE: U.S. Census of Agriculture; and Bureau of the Census, *Statistical Abstract of the United States*, 1973, p. 585.

lion families returned to the land. In 1935, the numbers of farms reached a new high of 6.8 million.

Farm Size and Value

The average size of a farm (Table 7-2) was almost the same in 1950 as it was in 1850, while the average value increased approximately sevenfold and total farm numbers increased about fourfold. Farm size reached the smallest average acreage around the turn of the century. It dropped from about 203 acres in 1850 to 134 acres in 1880, rose to 139 acres in 1910, and reached 216 acres in 1950.

In spite of this hundred-year "stability" in farm acreage, there have been relatively large increases since 1935. During the period between 1935 and 1969, average farm size increased 223 acres, or 145 percent. The most rapid increase in farm size was between 1954 and 1964, when average farm size increased 109 acres, partly owing to definition change. Average value of farms also increased the most during this period.

Consolidation of small farms into larger operating units has been an important cause of the reduction in farm numbers. Consolidation has been aided by the increased use of mechanized technology in farming that has made it possible for one man to handle increasingly larger acreages.

Number of farms by size.   While there have been large changes in total farm numbers, there have also been large changes in sizes of farms. Since 1880, farms with 500 or more acres have increased steadily, with the number of farms of 1,000 acres or more growing more rapidly than that of farms between 500 and 1,000 acres (Table 7-3).

In 1969, farms of 1,000 or more acres comprised only 5 percent of all farms, yet accounted for over half the total farmland. Farms with less than ten acres increased fairly rapidly until 1940, then declined sharply. Farms in the 10-to-99 and 100-to-499 acre categories comprise about 75 percent of the total, showing increases in numbers up to 1920 and declines ever since.

Regional differences in farm numbers and size.   Increases and decreases in farm numbers have not been spread evenly across the land. In the East, the abandonment of some of the poorer farming land in the mountain and hill regions has led to significant declines in farm numbers. There have been consistent decreases in the number of farms in the Northeast since 1880.

New technology and new legislation affecting land for farms have allowed other areas to increase their farm numbers. The institution of conservation, drainage, and irrigation districts and new laws affecting payments for land development projects have contributed to this increase.

The largest decreases in the number of farms between 1959 and 1969 were in the South, where there was a loss of 485,000 farms. Most of these were share-tenant and sharecropper farms that were absorbed into larger operating units. The largest percentage losses in number of farms were in the South Atlantic states and New England. These areas lost almost one-half their farms from 1959 to 1969. However, this decrease came primarily from marginal and part-time farms with sales of farm products of less than $2,500.

Even though every state except Alaska reported a decrease in farm numbers, all but one (Rhode Island) reported increases in farm size. However, the average size of a farm covers a wide range. In 1969 the average size of farms varied from 98 acres in Rhode Island to 6,486 acres in Arizona. The reason for this wide range lies primarily in the differences between types of farming: the fairly intensive type of farming in Rhode Island and the extensive dryland range operations in Arizona.

Land in Farms and Tenure of Operator

Total land in farms has little more than doubled from 1880 to 1969. From 1880 to 1950, there was a steady increase in the number of

TABLE 7-3
Number of Farms by Acres for the United States,
Selected Years, 1880–1969

Year	Less than 10 Acres	10–99 Acres	100–499 Acres	500–999 Acres	1,000 or More Acres
1880[a]	139,241	2,069,133	1,695,983	75,972	28,578
1900	268,446	3,030,964	2,290,561	102,526	47,160
1920	288,772	3,488,521	2,456,729	149,826	67,409
1940	509,347	3,080,389	2,255,396	163,711	100,574
1950	488,530	2,527,671	2,068,466	182,297	121,473
1959[b]	244,328	1,471,206	1,658,530	200,012	136,427
1969	162,000	933,000	1,268,000	216,000	151,000

[a] Data for Hawaii and Alaska not included.
[b] Change of census definition of a farm contributed partially to the decline.
SOURCE: Bureau of the Census, U.S. Census of Agriculture, 1972.

acres in food production. However, from 1950 to 1969, there was actually
a reduction of over 93 million acres in land in farms. This reduction can
be attributed to many things: increased application of farm-production
technology, participation in land-retiring government programs, Social
Security, high production costs, low farm income, and the movement of
farmers to nonfarm jobs.

Perhaps the most significant trend in tenure and land in farms is
the increasing importance of the part-owner (Table 7-4). The importance of part-owners is much greater than that indicated by the number
of farmers who reported farms operated, particularly since part-owner
farms are larger than those operated by full owners or tenants. Although
full owners operated about 62 percent of all the farms in 1969 as compared to about 25 percent by part-owners, the latter controlled over 51
percent of the land in farms compared to only 35 percent for full owners.

The fact that part-owners control more farmland than any other
single tenure group, and over half of all farmland, heralds a new approach to the business of farming. Increased capital requirements and
high land values tend to restrict a man entering farming from owning
his land outright. If he buys much land, he will have a large percentage

TABLE 7-4

Percentage Land in Farms and Tenure of Operator
for the United States, Selected Years, 1900–1969

Year	Full Owners	Part-Owners	All Tenants
	Percentage of Farms		
1900	55.8	7.9	36.3
1940	50.5	10.0	39.5
1950	57.1	15.3	27.6
1959	57.1	22.0	20.9
1969	62.5	24.6	12.9
	Percentage of Land		
1900	51.2	14.8	23.2
1940	35.9	28.3	29.4
1950	36.1	36.4	18.3
1959	31.0	44.3	14.8
1969	35.2	51.8	13.0

SOURCE: Bureau of the Census, U.S. Census of Agriculture, 1972.

of his capital resources tied up in it and there will be little left for production operations. Instead, a farm operator may choose to own a portion of the land he farms and rent the rest. Part-owners must be skillful managers if their operations are to be profitable. It takes additional management ability to profitably farm land owned by people other than the operator, because fixed rent charges must be paid and the tracts may be far apart.

In 1969, individuals or families farmed two out of every three acres and accounted for just over half of all farms. Corporations controlled less than 10 percent of the acreage, and partnerships accounted for around 17 percent. Trusts, estates, and other minor categories accounted for the rest of the acreage. These data must be considered, however, in terms of the productive quality of the acres controlled.

There are five main classes of tenants: crop-share, share-cash, croppers (in the South only), cash tenants, and livestock-share tenants. There are more crop-share tenants than any other group and fewer livestock-share tenants than any other group. Crop-share tenants are most frequent in the cash grain areas and where cotton and tobacco are grown. Livestock-share tenants tend to concentrate where feed grains and livestock production are found. Adjustments in agricultural operations have brought about the biggest share of reductions in farm tenancy. These adjustments include consolidation of farms, the growth of part-owner-operated farms, and farm mechanization.

Specialization on Farms

The decrease in number of farms and the increase in the average size of the farm have been accompanied by a trend toward greater farm-enterprise specialization. Specialization in farming means that one farmer will tend to concentrate production in one enterprise rather than have many different agricultural enterprises on the same farm. For example, rather than two or three milk cows, a hundred chickens, four or five feeders, and twenty sows, the farmer may have only the sows and the land necessary to provide feed for them. Without the other enterprises, he is free to attempt more intensive production from his hog enterprise. To gain the production he wants and to fill his time efficiently, he will get more sows and pigs than he used to have under a multienterprise farm organization. The best example is milk cows. In 1900, over three-fourths of all farms had milk cows; by 1970, less than one-third had milk cows. The same situation existed for hogs and pigs and for chickens (four months and older) during this same period.

There is a growth in size of enterprise associated with enterprise specialization. However, in spite of the tendency to specialize and intro-

duce large-scale enterprises, the continuing smallness of the average enterprise is noticeable. Large numbers of small enterprises tend to offset
the large, specialized farm operations that have been so widely publicized.
Whether this situation will continue in the future depends on many
things. Capital limitations, adjustments in farm organization, management capabilities, technology, and the risk and uncertainty preferences
of the individual managers all influence the decision about whether a
farm enterprise should be expanded or eliminated from the farm.

There also tends to be a specialization in the production patterns
across the country (Figure 7-2). This type of regional production specialization is defined very broadly, and the farms in each region are by no
means limited to only the major type of farming for that area. However,
the climate, markets, topography, soils, and institutional patterns have
combined to provide certain areas with certain production advantages.

Value of Production Assets Per Farm and Farm Worker

There have been large increases in the amount of capital assets
needed to carry out enterprise specialization and farm consolidation.

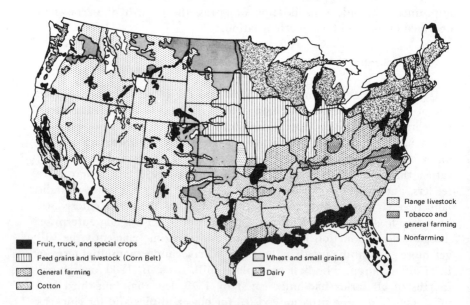

FIGURE 7-2
Major Types of Farming in the United States

Although the average value per farm has been going up since 1850, the increase has been especially rapid since 1940. From 1940 to 1973, the average value of production assets per farm in current prices increased by 18 times. During this same period, the average value of production assets (in current prices) per farm worker increased by 21 times.

For review, read again the material in Chapters 5 and 6 that refers to capital resources and technology used in farming.

FARM PRODUCTION, YIELDS, AND EXPENSES

Farm Production

Farm production increased 137 percent from 1910 to 1970, and has risen almost 50 percent since 1950 (Figure 7-3). Livestock and livestock products have increased more rapidly than crops during this

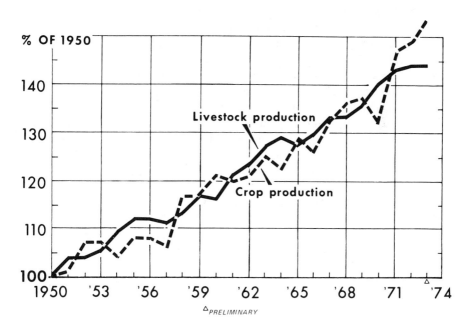

U.S. DEPARTMENT OF AGRICULTURE   NEG. ERS 1357 73 (8)   ECONOMIC RESEARCH SERVICE

FIGURE 7-3
Index of Crop and Livestock Production, 1950–1973

period; both categories more than doubled, while poultry and egg production rose fourfold. In crops, the most spectacular increase was in oil
crops, owing primarily to the introduction of soybeans and to increased
plantings of peanuts. Tung nuts were introduced in the late 1930s and
the tung oil substituted for whale oil as a lubricant for many intricate
mechanical parts. Neither feed-grain output nor hay and forage output
kept pace with the output of meat animals. The reasons include the
facts that many meat animals consumed the feed initially needed for
horses, which were replaced by mechanical power; that the number of
dairy animals (some of which were used for meat) was reduced; and that
gains in efficiency due to breeding and nutritional technology were
made.

When the gains in production efficiency are compared for livestock
and poultry, it is easy to see that they are not spread evenly through
the various enterprises and that additional feed-conversion efficiencies are
likely. For example, from 1935 to 1971 the amount of feed necessary to
produce 100 pounds of broilers was about cut in half, while the amount
of feed necessary to produce 100 eggs dropped slightly. However, in
order to get 100 pounds of milk, of cattle and calves, or of hogs, a
farmer actually had to feed more in 1966 than he did in 1935, although
the time necessary for production was lowered. When one compares
these rates of gain in farm production and feed efficiencies to population
growth, it is easy to understand why research efforts continue in the
animal sciences, horticulture, agronomy, soils, and plant breeding.

Crop yields per acre have tended to increase rapidly since the figures
of 1935 to 1939 (Table 7-5). Before that time, the opening of new lands
acted as an inducement to move to better soils rather than increase
yields on existing land. The years of depression during the 1930s also
restricted the amount of technology that farmers were able and willing
to buy and apply to their croplands. Crop yields projected to the year
2000 show an approximate doubling of yield from the 1960 level for
corn and cotton—from 53 bushels to 100 bushels per acre, and from 446
pounds to 800 pounds per acre, respectively. Wheat and hay yields will
probably increase about one-third.

Productivity

Farm productivity has been dramatic and closely linked to the
increases in quality of capital items used in the production processes
(Figure 7-4 and Chapter 5). In addition, there has been an effective substitution among production inputs—fertilizer, water, and better seeds
for land. Output per unit of input has risen fairly steadily since 1950,

TABLE 7-5

Yields per Harvested Acre of Four Major Crops,
Selected Periods with Projections, United States[a]

Years	Wheat Corn (bushel/acre)		Cotton (lb./acre)	Hay (tons/acre)
1878–82	13.2	25.6	179	1.14[b]
1920–24	13.9	27.2	154	1.21
1930–34	13.3	23.8	185	1.08
1940–44	17.1	31.9	262	1.35
1950–54	17.3	38.5	297	1.43
1960	26.2	53.0	446	1.76
1970	28.0	70.0	560	2.00
1980	31.0	80.0	640	2.30
1990	33.0	90.0	720	2.60
2000	35.0	100.0	800	3.00

[a] U.S. Department of Agriculture, *Agricultural Statistics and Crop Production, Annual Summary*. Projection estimates are a medium projection. The way these estimates were made is explained in detail in the source listed below.

[b] Estimated from data on tame hay alone.

SOURCE: Hans H. Landsberg, et al., *Resources in America's Future* (Baltimore: The Johns Hopkins Press, 1963). Adapted from Table A 18-1, p. 972. Published for Resources for the Future, Inc.

while the total of all farm-production inputs has remained almost constant.

Animal Power and Mechanical Power

Much of the productivity of farming in America can be attributed to the change from animal power to mechanical power. In 1910, there were virtually no mechanical aids to help the farmer. The farmer did have a few automobiles, and some dairymen had milking machines. But nearly everything, from breaking ground for planting to harvest, was done by hand or with animal power, principally horses and mules. By 1960, this situation had just about reversed itself. Horses and mules were down to a fraction of their 1910 numbers; almost every farm had at least one tractor. Many of the larger farms had three tractors: a large, 4 to 6 bottom-plow tractor for heavy work, a medium-sized tractor for lighter field jobs, and a small "runabout" tractor to work in the barns

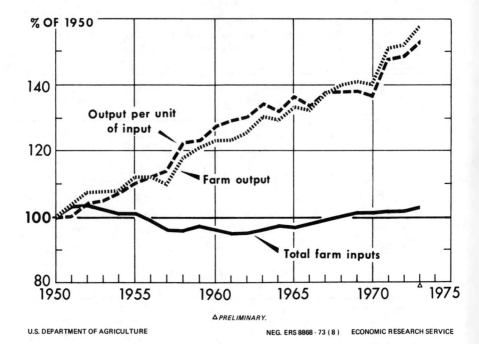

U.S. DEPARTMENT OF AGRICULTURE   NEG. ERS 8868 - 73 (8)   ECONOMIC RESEARCH SERVICE

FIGURE 7-4
Productivity of Farm Inputs, 1950–1973

and supply power for specialized equipment like augers, hay loaders, and stationary forage choppers and blowers.

The use of trucks on farms grew more rapidly than did the use of combines. Pickup balers and field harvesters also increased rapidly, but neither of these implements was used much prior to the early 1940s. Milking machines on farms increased until the early 1950s, when their number declined, primarily because of the reduction in the numbers of dairy farms and farmers.

Acres Harvested

The cropland harvested dropped by 7 million acres from 1910 to 1971 (Table 7-6), but an approximate doubling of crop production per acre filled the needs of our population, which also doubled. Acreage needed to produce the farm products for one person in this country fell from 2.17 acres in 1910 to 1.2 acres in 1971. The number of acres used to produce products for export has undergone large fluctuations, from a low in 1940 of 8 million acres to a high in 1965 of 76 million acres.

TABLE 7-6

Acres of Cropland Harvested for Export and Domestic Use, Selected Years, 1910–72

Year	Total Cropland[a] (millions of acres)	Cropland Harvested[b] (millions of acres)	Index Crop Production per Acre (1957–59 = 100)	Acreage Used for Producing Export Crops[c] (millions of acres)	Acreage Used for Producing Products for Domestic Use[d] Total (millions of acres)	Per Capita (acres)
1910	330	317	68	37	200	2.17
1920	368	351	74	60	210	1.98
1930	382	360	64	39	265	2.15
1940	368	331	76	8	290	2.20
1950	377	345	84	50	295	1.94
1960	355	324	109	64	260	1.44
1972[e]	336	296	136	85	211	1.01

a The difference between total acres and cropland harvested is in the number of acres of crop failure or summer fallow.

b Land from which one or more crops were harvested.

c Acreages for exports relate to exports for year beginning July 1, or month representing beginning of crop season. Acreage includes seeds for crops and feed for livestock that are exported.

d Includes products used by our military forces in this country and abroad, and by our domestic civilian population.

e Preliminary.

SOURCE: U.S. Department of Agriculture, Changes in Farm Production and Efficiency, 1962 and 1973, Statistical Bulletin No. 233.

Farm-Production Expenses

The costs necessary to produce agricultural output have fluctuated over the years, corresponding closely with the ups and downs of total agricultural income. For example, during the early 1950s, agricultural income declined and so did the total production expense of farmers (see Table 5-3). However, some expenses did not fluctuate as much as others. While expenses for feed, livestock, seed, and hired labor took a relatively large decline, expenses for fertilizer and lime showed only a slight dip.

Costs not associated directly with a level of production, such as taxes and interest charges, have increased steadily since 1940. Rising tax costs reflect the pressure of population on rural areas. More intensive land uses and suburban development projects of all kinds require financing that is often drawn from the land. For this reason, many farmers are paying higher taxes for schools and highways even though they may not use these facilities very much, if at all.

GROSS AND NET FARM INCOME

Gross cash receipts from farm marketings in current dollars have risen almost every year since the mid-1930s, except for a six-year period in the 1950s. However, when the net income of farm operators is adjusted to a constant 1967 dollar basis, it shows a decline from 1949 to 1960 (Table 7-7). Inflation and the competitive structure of agriculture contributed to this situation. It takes continually increased amounts of farm sales just to maintain a given level of net farm income.

Realized gross income per farm in the United States almost quintupled from 1949 to 1973, in current dollars. This is what one would expect from continually increasing receipts from all farm marketings. However, realized net income per farm increased by only about 56 percent in constant dollars. Increasing production costs, falling farm prices, rising fixed costs of owning land and of debt, and inflation all reduced the margin of profit.

The farm-income components are shown in Figure 7-5. One can easily see how rising production expenses have caused a rising realized gross farm income to yield a fairly constant net income.

Number of Farms and Value of Farm Products Sold

When U.S. farms are grouped by the value of farm products sold, several trends become apparent. Since 1939, there have been reductions

TABLE 7-7
Realized Gross and Net Incomes, All Farms and
per Farm, United States, Selected Years, 1949–1973

Year	United States		Per Farm[d]	
	Realized Gross Farm Income[a] (millions of current $)	Operators' Realized Net Farm Income[a] [b] (millions)	Realized Gross Income[a] [c] (current $)	Operators' Realized Net Income[a] [c]
1949	31,628	12,780	5,527	2,385
1955	33,138	11,464	7,121	2,417
1960	38,088	12,079	9,614	2,962
1965	44,926	14,987	13,452	4,190
1967	48,998	14,882	15,572	4,520
1973	91,200	24,400	31,831	9,469
	Index: 1967 = 100			
1949	65	86	35	53
1955	68	77	46	53
1960	78	81	62	66
1965	92	101	86	93
1967	100	100	100	100
1973	186	163	204	209

a Includes Alaska and Hawaii after 1960.

b Of farm operators.

c Realized gross income includes cash receipts from farm marketings, government payments, value of home consumption, and gross rental value of farm dwellings. Realized net income deducts farm-production expenses and accounts for net changes in farm inventories.

d Per-farm estimates prior to 1960 have not been corrected for change in definition of farm.

SOURCE: U.S. Department of Agriculture, Economic Research Service, *Farm Income Situation*, February 1974; and supplements to F.I.S. 187, 211, 218, and 229, 1962 and 1971.

in the number of farms selling less than $5,000 worth of farm products, and gains in the number selling more than $5,000 worth. In addition, the loss in farm numbers is intensified in the lower-income groups while relatively large increases in numbers of farms are recorded in high-income groups. For example, there was a loss of almost 67 percent in the number of farms selling less than $5,000 worth of farm products from 1949 to 1972. Farms that sold between $5,000 and $10,000 worth

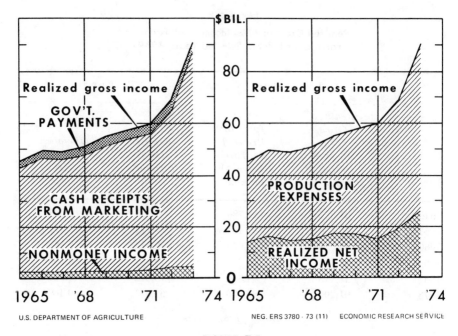

FIGURE 7-5
Production Expenses, Realized Growth and Net
Farm Income, 1965–1972

of farm products decreased in numbers by only about 50 percent, whereas the number of farms that sold over $10,000 worth of output increased by about 117 percent.

The number of farms selling more than $10,000 worth of farm products in 1939 was slightly under 5 percent of the total. By 1949, it had increased to almost 9 percent, by 1959 to over 21 percent, and by 1972 to almost 37 percent (Table 7-8). In 1972 this group, comprising slightly over one-third of all farmers, sold approximately 90 percent of our country's agricultural output.

Ranking of Farm Products Sold

When the farm production is analyzed in terms of income contribution, livestock and livestock products head the list. Field crops and fruit are quite far down the list. This is to be expected because livestock must convert the field crops into meat, eggs, and milk, and the value of these

TABLE 7-8

Number and Percentage of U.S. Farms by Value of Farm Products Sold—1949, 1959, and 1972

Value of Farm Products Sold ($)	1949				1959				1972			
	Number and % of Farms by Sales Class		Amount and % of Farm Sales		Number and % of Farms by Sales Class		Amount and % of Farm Sales		Number and % of Farms by Sales Class		Amount and % of Farm Sales	
	Number (thou.)	%	Dollars (bill.)	%	Number (thou.)	%	Dollars (bill.)	%	Number (thou.)	%	Dollars (bill.)	%
10,000 +	484	9.0	11.3	50.9	794	21.5	21.9	71.6	1,054	36.7	58.3	90.2
5,000–9,999	721	13.4	5.1	23.0	653	17.6	4.7	15.4	359	12.5	3.1	4.8
2,500–4,999	882	16.4	3.2	14.4	617	16.7	2.3	7.5	420	14.6	1.8	2.8
Less than $2,500a	3,292	61.2	2.6	11.7	1,637	44.2	1.7	5.5	1,037	36.2	1.4	2.2
Total	5,379	100.0	22.2	100.0	3,701	100.0	30.6	100.0	2,870	100.0	64.6	100.0

a Not fully comparable. The more restrictive definition of a farm used in the census of 1959 resulted in exclusion of approximately 232,000 places that would have qualified as farms under the definition used in the census of 1949. By definition, the farms excluded were small places selling less than $250 worth of farm products. Their exclusion affects total number of farms much more than the total value of farm products sold. For a discussion of the change in the census definition of a farm, see Introduction, Volume 2, 1959 Census of Agriculture.

SOURCE: U.S. Department of Commerce, *Statistical Abstract of the United States*, 1968, p. 596; and U.S. Department of Agriculture, Economic Research Service, *Farm Income Situation*, July 1973, p. 68.

products must be correspondingly higher than the feed that the animals producing them must eat.

One can also pick up the reasons for differences in regional farm incomes from a priority ranking of farm products. The most prosperous states in terms of farm income are those that produce both the feed and the finished livestock or livestock products. Those states with lower farm incomes are more crop-producing states, or states that produce the cattle and other livestock for finishing elsewhere.

Government Payments

Government payments for farmers were first introduced in legislation of the early 1930s. The initial objective was to stabilize incomes and protect against widely fluctuating farm prices. Gradually, an income-level objective was added to the justification of price supports. This income objective of supports has not been realized for the low-income farmers to whom it was politically aimed, but this issue will be discussed more fully in Chapter 23.

Payments are made to farmers under a variety of programs (Table 7-9). They are made only to farmers who are legally eligible for compensation and who have filed application or notified the proper officials of their actions.

Government payments, or price supports, are achieved through loans, purchases, and direct payments to producers—all at levels announced by the secretary of agriculture. For most commodities, loans are made directly to producers. Some commodities may also be purchased directly from producers at the time of loan maturity for the crop. Price-support loans are "nonrecourse," which simply means that farmers are not obligated to make good any decline in the market price of the commodity they put up as collateral. Direct payments are made to producers who participate in certain of the land-retirement provisions of the Feed Grain Programs or in cotton-acreage diversion programs, or sell wool under the Wool Act.

Government payments have comprised an increasing share of gross farm income since the late 1940s. In 1949, government payments amounted to only $185 million, but rose to $554 million by 1956. The next year they almost doubled, reaching $1,016 million. In 1961, payments hit $1,493 million, and rose to a high of $3,961 million in 1972, falling in 1973 to $2,600 million.

Farm Home Consumption and Rent

The amount of food consumed in farm homes and the rent for the farm dwellings are two items that are not generally accounted for when

TABLE 7-9

Government Payments by Programs, Selected Years, 1950–1972
(in millions of dollars)[a]

Year	Conservation[d] ACP	Conservation[d] Great Plains	Soil Bank	Sugar Act	Wool	Feed Grain	Wheat	Cotton[b]	Cropland Adjustment	Total
1950	246	—	—	37	—	—	—	—	—	283
1955	188	—	—	41	—	—	—	—	—	229
1960	217	6	370	59	51	—	—	—	—	702
1965	215	9	160	75	18	1,391	525	70	—	2,463c
1966	220	11	145	71	34	1,293	679	773	51	3,277c
1967	225	12	129	70	29	865	731	932	85	3,079e
1968	229	—	112	75	66	1,366	747	787	81	3,462
1969	204	—	43	78	61	1,643	858	828	78	3,794
1970	208	—	2	88	49	1,504	871	919	76	3,717
1971	173	—	—	80	69	1,054	878	822	67	3,145
1972	198	—	—	82	110	1,845	856	813	52	3,961e

a Details may not add to totals because of rounding.
b Includes cotton price adjustment and cotton option and producers' pool payments.
c Includes milk indemnity payments ($194,000 in 1965, $150,000 in 1966, and $275,000 in 1967).
d Includes Great Plains and other conservation programs.
e Includes $2 million miscellaneous such as milk indemnity, 1971; $6 million in 1972.
SOURCE: U.S. Department of Agriculture, Economic Research Service, *Farm Income Situation*, 222, July 1973, Table 21H.

farm incomes are calculated. It has been estimated that in 1949, the value of food both produced and consumed by farmers was $2,399 million. With the reduction in the farm population, this amount had fallen to $886 million by 1973, about half what it had been in 1959.

Although the value of food consumed declined, the rental value of farm dwellings increased. In 1949, the gross rental value of farm dwellings was $1,408 million; but by 1973, it had climbed to $3,590 million. This increase has been caused primarily by the increased capital investments by farmers in dwellings and in their equipment. Many have made improvements in their houses and have added offices for more efficient farm organization.

Farmer's Nonfarm Income

With the increase in farmers doing more nonfarm work, there has also been an increase in the number of farmers who report income from nonfarm sources to be greater than farm income. In 1954, 29.8 percent of the farm operators reported nonfarm income to be greater than farm income. By 1959, this proportion had increased to 35.8 percent, and by 1969 to almost 40 percent.

Farmers and farming continue to be a big business in America. However, there are significant changes going on in production, in farm income, and in the numbers of people who farm. There are problems of agricultural adjustment that will not be solved easily, including not only the quality and quantity of farm production but the number and quality of people who farm. The changes in farms and farmers have come about primarily through the interplay of free-market forces and voluntary individual management decisions. What will take place in the future?

8

Farm-Supply Businesses

HISTORICAL PERSPECTIVE

As you read in Chapter 2, less than 200 years ago the typical farm family produced its own food, fuel, shelter, draft animals, feed, seeds, tools, and implements, and even most of its clothing. For most practical purposes, including education and health care, such a family operated either as a self-contained unit or as part of a closely knit community of farm people. Some 80 percent of the labor force were actually engaged in farm production, and only a few items were bartered or purchased from off-the-farm sources.

The technological revolution of the mid- and late nineteenth century changed the situation. Machinery and the goods and services associated with its use by farmers and their families spawned a rapid growth of farm-supply businesses. From the early peddlers, tinkers, and drummers, there evolved a host of specialized sales and service jobs. The invention, manufacture, and sale of farm machinery gave economic impetus to a number of related businesses, such as binder-twine factories, belt factories, implement stores, wire and nail factories, and repair shops.

Sources for information in this chapter include the U.S.D.A.'s *Farm Income Situation Reports* and *Farm Cost Reports*.

With the farm tractor came the need for the petroleum industry and for skilled mechanics to serve farmers. The change from steel to rubber tractor tires called on the rubber manufacturer for a new product, and new tires are still evolving for specific needs. The electrification of farm homes and buildings created a market for motors, milking machines, pumps, waterers, heaters, welders, and power tools of all kinds. The electronic age has brought solid set sprinklers, timing devices based on heat or light, and even more complicated computerization of farm operations. These are just a few examples.

Biologically-oriented technology helped foster the commercialization of chemical fertilizers. Seed companies applied the genetic principles discovered in land-grant schools, the Department of Agriculture, and privately financed laboratories all over the country. The agricultural-chemicals and pharmaceutical industries have also grown at a fast pace. All in all, farm-supply industries now sell farmers in excess of $30 billion worth of products annually. Over the years, the proportion of a farmer's expenses to produce food that requires cash outlays has constantly increased.

In another vein, commercial dependence has invaded even the farmer's kitchen. Rural milk-delivery routes provide most dairy-farm families with bottled pasteurized milk and cheese, and the family freezers are filled with custom-butchered and wrapped meats and sausages.

SCOPE OF BUSINESS ACTIVITIES

The scope of the farm-supply businesses used by farmers and ranchers annually is partially portrayed in the summaries of farm-production expense in Chapter 7. Goods purchased include manufactured feed, seeds, fertilizers and lime, pesticides, and petroleum fuel and oil, all of which amounted to $12.7 billion, or 31 percent of all production expenses, in 1971. Services purchased include repairs and maintenance for vehicles, buildings, machinery, and other farm equipment; banking services (reflected by interest costs); insurance; and veterinary, transportation, accounting, legal, and telephone services. Together, these services accounted for over $7 billion of expenses in 1971, or about one-fifth of the total. Of the remaining $20 billion of expenses in 1971, purchased livestock and hired labor comprised about $8 billion, taxes on farm property about $3 billion, rents $1.3 billion, and depreciation on buildings, machinery, equipment, and land improvements of $6.7 billion. Miscellaneous supplies accounted for the remaining billion.

Manufacturers sold $2.6 billion worth of machinery and equipment to farmers in 1970. Farmers also spent $2.4 billion for vehicles and $826 million for buildings. Thus, total capital outlays representing purchases from these farm-supply industries totaled $5.8 billion.

Feed Industry

There are more than 10,000 feed mill and mixer establishments in the United States. This does not include the many small units and mixers privately owned and operated on farms. Some of the commercial operations are small custom mills where local grain is brought in by farmers and mixed with concentrates supplied by and purchased at the mill. Other operators are large-volume mills that prepare many different feed formulas. Special feed preparations can be sold for a particular type and age of animal, or for a particular feedlot or dairy herd.

Mills tend to be located closer to the point of feed consumption (final feed sales) rather than in grain-producing areas (area of raw-feed production). The reason for this has to do with assembling the fairly cheap and bulky large amounts of feed inputs, and selling relatively smaller lots of more costly mixed feeds.

Corporations and cooperatives predominate as major types of business organizations in the commercial feed industry. A majority of these firms develop brand names for their feeds and attach a great deal of competitive pride to their products. Competition is on both a price and a service basis. As in almost all cases within the farm-supply business, the ability of a firm to provide on-site service for maintenance situations as well as emergencies is increasingly making the difference as to which firm gets the farmer's account. Price is important, but service may be relatively even more important where large capital investments necessitate a continuous flow of materials. There's little sense in installing an expensive self-feed dairy system if the feed does not arrive just before it's needed.

Sales of feed may be directly to farmers or through farm-supply stores, which number more than 20,000. The larger-volume feed manufacturers may distribute through a farm-supply-store dealership. In terms of total dollar farm-production expenditures, purchased feed represents the largest single cost component—17.5 percent in 1971. Beef cattle consume nearly one-half of purchased feeds, dairy cattle about one-fifth, hogs about one-seventh, poultry about one-eighth, and other animals the remainder. The consumption of feed by animal groups will change depending on the physical supply of breeding animals and the effective demand for meat and meat products.

Farm-supply stores tend to carry a rather complete line of farm and home needs, with their primary sales volume coming from feed, seed, fertilizer, chemicals, veterinary supplies, and hardware. Most are sole proprietorships and partnerships. In addition, there are about 3,500 home and garden supply stores.

Fertilizer Industry

In 1970, farmers used about 40 million tons of commercial fertilizers, double the amount they used in 1950. Approximately 2,500 fertilizer-mixing plants now prepare over 3,000 grades of mixed fertilizers. Any farmer or horticulturist can obtain a specially mixed blend of nitrogen, phosphate, potash, and trace minerals according to his needs. An equal number of bulk blending plants blend two or more fertilizer grades in combinations to meet farmer's needs. Distribution channels are direct to farmers through company-owned outlets, or to farm-supply stores. Many large farm operations buy train carloads of fertilizer. Handled in bulk, it can be applied by spreader in the field, or by airplane.

Farm Machinery and Equipment

Manufacturers of commercial farm machinery and equipment are of two basic types: tractor manufacturers, and large-machinery and equipment makers. In total, there are more than 1,500 machinery and equipment plants in the United States, not including the many machine shops on farms, in which farmers make much of their own new machinery or create adaptations to machines they buy. About two-thirds of these firms' sales are accounted for by only seven full-line farm-machinery manufacturers.

The larger full-line companies typically operate regional branch houses that, in turn, serve more than 15,000 local dealerships throughout the country. Besides these outlets, there were 1,568 farm cooperative associations in 1970, which handled $108 million of sales, or about 4 percent of the total. Many local dealers are franchised; others are classified as independent merchants. Capital requirements can be substantial, and as a result, most dealers are legally organized as business corporations. Brand-name advertising is common, particularly among the small group of leaders, with severe competition oriented toward the provision of excellent service rather than only sales. Provision of good repair and service facilities is an important economic contribution to a dealer's financial success. In most dealers' operations, services account for about one-third of total annual dollar sales volume.

Power

As farmers increase their use of power-driven tractors, combines, forage harvesters, pumps, and conveyors, their use of gasoline, natural gas, diesel fuel, oils, other petroleum products, and electricity has risen dramatically. Gasoline is distributed by the manufacturers through local dealerships to all types of customers, including farmers. Deliveries are made on both a scheduled and an "on-call" basis, and since most commercial farmers have bulk-storage facilities on their own farms, purchases are sometimes made directly from wholesale distributors. In any case, there are often discounts, depending on the volume purchased. In 1970, there were 2,774 cooperative associations handling petroleum products for farmers; they accounted for about 45 percent of the $1.8 billion total sales volume. There were also about 900 rural electric cooperative associations in 1970, with nearly 6 million member participants. Many of these associations were connected with the government-sponsored REAs (Rural Electrification Associations).

Agricultural Chemicals

Farmers purchased about $800 million worth of pesticides and herbicides in 1969, and almost $1 billion in 1972. About $400 million was spent to control weeds or grass in crops, $400 million for control of crop insects, $65 million to fight crop diseases, $30 million to control insects in livestock and poultry, $23 million for defoliation or growth control in crops, and the remainder for nematode control and insect control on hay crops.

There are many outlets through which farmers may purchase agricultural chemicals. Corporate conglomerates often have acquired firms that have direct sales outlets, or field salesmen who will visit a farmer, appraise his needs, and take his order based on their recommendations. In many states, the Cooperative Extension Services have fully qualified entomologists and chemists who offer advice and free consultation to individual farmers. Also, 3,640 farm cooperative organizations distributed farm chemicals in 1970, handling about 18 percent of the total sales volume.

Under various national and state legislation passed since 1970, most of the more potent farm chemicals must be applied by a licensed technician. For example, in 1972 there were almost 2,500 licensed agricultural-chemical applicators in California. However, even with the many precautions against indiscriminate use of toxic materials, accidents and deaths owing to exposure to chemicals occur every year.

Seeds

Farmers purchased almost $850 million worth of improved seeds in 1971. The seed industry differs somewhat from other farm-supply industries. For example, it needs much acreage for experimental plots, germination tests, and harvest maturity coordination. The seed industry also requires large amounts of initial and continuing research efforts.

Basic plant breeders and producers typically sell to wholesalers and distributors. These outlets in turn sell directly to farmers, to farm-supply stores, to home and garden stores, or to nursery and greenhouse outlets. In 1971, there were almost 4,000 farm-cooperative organizations also involved, accounting for about one-fifth of the total business. Many of the seed breeders rely on research done by private firms, the Department of Agriculture, and the Agricultural Experiment Stations scattered across the country. These research sources can incorporate regional climatic and geographic differences into their products.

Vehicles

Farmers purchase over $2 billion worth of autos, trucks, and trailers for farm use annually. The manufacturers that farmers buy from are the same major companies that produce vehicles for private families and other uses. Vehicles are distributed primarily through franchised dealerships.

Some farmers are leasing an increasing amount of vehicles and equipment. Lease expenses are all tax-deductible, and this tax benefit helps some large operations.

Buildings

New construction of buildings for farm use totaled $826 million in 1971. In addition, farmers probably spent close to half that amount for building repairs and maintenance. There is always a building, fence, or gate that needs fixing on a farm or ranch.

To cope with this huge market, there are some 30,000 lumber and building-materials dealers in the United States, which also serve the general public. These dealers are typically organized as corporations and are locally owned and operated, although there are also regional chains of building-supply outlets. The approximately 2,200 cooperatives that sell building materials to farmers account for about one-fifth of total sales.

Services

Financial services to farmers were discussed in Chapter 5. There are no specific data to detail the use farmers make of accounting, legal, and professional management services. However, all these services have become increasingly important as the average size of businesses grows and the interrelatedness of sectors in the overall economy becomes more complex.

Many services are being contracted for on the basis of an annual retainer fee, with extra charges for emergency or special performance. For example, services of veterinarians are moving toward an annual contractual arrangement, with emphasis on disease-prevention programs. Accountants and lawyers increasingly fit the retainer situation. Management fees for absentee owners have long set an example in this category, whereby there is a fixed fee of so many dollars per acre (or head), depending on the value of the crop. Other production costs are paid in addition to the management fee.

In addition, there is a growing contracting business for specific farm-production and harvest operations: for example, for the licensed technicians who apply agricultural chemicals. Some farmers contract their spring fertilizer spreading by air, since the ground may be too wet. Some may contract harvesting of their crops, particularly when the harvesting-machinery expense is high. Grain combining and fruit and nut harvesting are other situations where contracts are often seen.

SUMMARY

The farm-supply and farm-service industries will continue to grow in relative importance. New technology is embedded in farm inputs that must be purchased by the farmer for economic survival. New organizational forms may evolve. There are now more persons employed in the farm-supply industries than in direct farm production.

9

Marketing Food Products

The advent of commercial agriculture separated the farm producer from the urban consumer and created the need for a different kind of marketing system. Marketing activities arise primarily because of form, distance, and time variables. These variables require that food be processed, transported, and stored. Thus, the job of our commercial farm marketing system is to get food to the consumer at the proper place, at the proper time, in the proper form, and at acceptable prices.

MARKETING ACTIVITIES ARE
CONSUMER-ORIENTED

The focus of all marketing activities is to satisfy the consumer. Food-processing and distributing firm managers must keep this in mind. Consumer purchases are signals to the marketing men about what is wanted. Every time a housewife buys a pound box of frozen peas, she is in a sense saying to the marketing men, "Continue to freeze peas and package them in one-pound boxes." In turn, the marketing men pass the signal back to the farmer by placing an order that prompts the farmer to continue pea production. If the consumer stops buying—or voting for a product with dollar bills—at the retail store, the production of the item will soon slow down. For example, weight-conscious Americans no longer prefer cuts of meat with much fat attached. As a result, the signals pass back to the farmer, and more lean-type hogs are being produced.

Businessmen attempt to influence consumer votes through advertising. The American Dairy Association reminds us to continue to drink milk, and consumers are bombarded with commercials describing the merits of various brands of cereals, meat products, and ice cream. These efforts have varying degrees of success. Efforts to advertise butter, for example, have failed to stem the tide of consumer taste changing to margarine.

WHAT SOCIETY WANTS FROM ITS MARKETING SYSTEM

The public wants a marketing system that provides food at the lowest possible cost. Although efficiency in marketing activities is also highly desired, output is still measured in terms of consumer satisfaction and the number of "repeat customers" a firm can attract. From another viewpoint, society allows those people working in the marketing system a reasonable return for their inputs of property and personal service. The marketing system should also function to find and develop new markets, in the sense of making new products or bettering old products for sale at home and abroad.

From the farmer's viewpoint, a marketing system that can entice consumers to buy more food is a good one. To make goods continuously available to consumers at prices that allow the consumer to raise his standard of living and increase his satisfaction is a goal that requires much of both the farmer and the marketing man. They are partners, dependent on each other.

THE DEVELOPMENT OF OUR MARKETING SYSTEM

As we have already discussed, self-sufficient colonial farmers marketed few of their products commercially. Food was grown, processed, and stored primarily for family sustenance. But with the rapid development of commercial agriculture in the nineteenth century, the business of processing and distributing food grew quickly. The Chicago Board of Trade was founded in 1848 and quickly became the nation's leading grain market. The Union Stockyards of Chicago, established in 1865, followed by the development of the refrigerated railroad car in 1880, allowed the meat industry to commercialize quickly. About the same time, the grain-milling industry centered in Minneapolis. New technologies in food containers allowed the canning industry for both fruits and vegetables to develop.

With farms increasing production at a record pace, new marketing businesses were under great pressure to move food to markets at home and abroad. Rapid growth led to the use of various unethical business practices, particularly as some of the huge firms wielded monopoly power. By 1900, with federal antitrust legislation passed and regulatory agencies such as the Interstate Commerce Commission established, the situation eased. The steady and regular growth of the marketing system aided the quarter-century of agricultural prosperity enjoyed by the farmer before World War 1.

THE FUNCTIONAL APPROACH
TO MARKETING

A framework is needed in order to study marketing problems. One of the most useful is the functional approach. Marketing functions are synonymous with business activities, and the functional approach classifies each of them into three groups: exchange, physical, and facilitating.

Exchange Functions

Buying and selling. The exchange or transfer of title of food as it moves from the farm to the consumer is vital to the marketing system. Buying and selling functions are part of the cost of marketing. Every time a buyer and seller agree to exchange money for goods or goods for money, price negotiation takes place. A detailed study of prices will come later.

Buying costs often include the time and effort involved in seeking out sources of supply, in addition to the negotiating phase. Selling, on the other hand, may include the cost involved in preparing, advertising, and promoting a product for sale. Merchandising is a term sometimes used to describe these kinds of costs.

Physical Functions

Transportation. Physical functions are those of transportation and storage, which are directly associated with the physical handling of the products. To move the raw-food production from several million scattered farms to a population of over 210 million consumers domestically and many more abroad is a big job. Transportation activity creates place utility, becoming a major factor with the assembly of raw food at the farm. The network of railways, airways, waterways, and highways is an integral and essential part of our marketing system. In addition to assembly and actual costs in transit, the cost of loading and unloading goods is included in transportation.

Storage. Most farm products are harvested in one season, but because consumers desire to obtain all sorts of foods at any time, storage activities that create time utility are another vital element in our marketing system. Storage of perishable commodities is more expensive than storage of nonperishables, since costly refrigeration or other equipment may be necessary to maintain proper product quality. The farmer often performs the storage function himself. A farmer who stores grain after harvest through the winter for sale in the spring is creating time utility in the same manner that a large grain elevator would. The farmer's return for storing the grain is in the form of a higher selling price. However, owners of commercial storage usually charge a fee based on amount stored and time held.

Facilitating Functions

The costs of marketing arising from the facilitating functions of standardization, financing, risk bearing, and market information are commonly overlooked. These functions do what their name suggests: they facilitate the smooth performance of the market and hold down the costs of the exchange and physical functions. They are the grease that makes the wheels in our marketing system perform easily.

Standardization. Did you ever stop to think how difficult it would be if a bushel of wheat weighed 60 pounds in Kansas but only 50 pounds in Indiana? This certainly would complicate the exchange of wheat between the two areas. Or what about the complexities that would arise if the criteria for a choice steer in three different livestock markets were all different? Immediately the necessity for a uniform measuring system for quantity and quality becomes apparent. In a complex mass economy such as ours, standardization greatly simplifies the exchange process of buying and selling, and at the same time reduces the cost. You can call your broker, order 5,000 bushel of Number 1 hard red winter wheat, and know exactly how much you will get and what qualities it will possess. In other words, accepted and uniform standards allow sale by description, and buyers feel no compulsion to see the physical product before purchase.

The nature of standardization requires a regulating agency. This is most often a public body of the local, state, or federal government.

Financing.   The financing function creates a cost to the person or agency owning the product because of time lags between purchase and sale. It is impossible to escape this type of cost, because someone must always own the product at all times. When a grain elevator buys wheat from the farmer, the elevator exchanges money for wheat and must finance the wheat until it exchanges the commodity for money with the miller. The retailer who buys a can of beans and places it on the shelf in his store has money tied up until some consumer purchases the beans, which may be six months later.

Risk bearing.   Another cost associated with ownership is risk bearing. This function is distinct from financing and includes the assumption of both physical risk and market risk.

Physical risk arises with ownership because of the possible deterioration of a product owing to excessive moisture, heat, contaminating metals, bacteria, insects, and rodents, and because of possible physical loss from accidents, fire, or theft. There is no escaping this cost, although it may be converted to a different form. Sometimes the owner elects to take out insurance against possible physical loss and pays a premium to a company willing to assume the risk for the premium fee.

Market risk arises with ownership because of a possible decline in the product's price. Whether a commodity is held by a farmer, warehouseman, processor, wholesaler, or retailer, the risk of a lower market price is always present. Various devices are available to the owner to shift or spread the risk involved. For certain commodities, the farmer may be able to get nonrecourse loans from the government. Another method is to sell products now for later delivery. Still another widely used method is to buy or sell futures contracts on a commodities exchange. A grain elevator that purchases corn on October 1 for $1.10 a bushel can "hedge" by selling a futures contract to deliver corn at some future date at some specified price—say, $1.20.[1] If the price of corn declines such that the elevator can get only $1.05 a bushel for its corn when sold to a miller two months later, the elevator manager will try to buy a futures contract for $1.15 a bushel at that time. The 5-cent loss on the actual corn bought and sold ($1.10–$1.05) is offset by a 5-cent gain on the corn futures contract ($1.15–$1.20). The gain and loss in this situation would be referred to as a perfect "hedge." Actual grain prices and futures prices

---

[1] A corn futures contract is a commitment to take (if contract is bought) or deliver (if contract is sold) a specified amount of corn at a specified date in the future. Typically, no actual corn shipments ever take place, as a person buying a contract will sell it again before the specified date in the future is reached, and vice versa.

generally move in the same direction, with a difference that approximates storage costs over the specified period of time.

Market information. It is vital that both buyer and seller possess adequate and up-to-date information about the market conditions when negotiating price. Also, good market information can greatly expedite the physical functions. Jobs in market information include the collecting, analyzing, and disseminating of a large variety of data. As with the standardization function, much of the marketing information is provided by government agencies.

The Functional Approach—A Summary

The functional approach looks at the various activities that are performed to increase the utility of the product as it moves from the farmer to the consumer. It is of considerable help in making cost studies. Some marketing businesses specialize in one function, such as the owner of refrigerated storage, while others, such as a retail food merchant, may perform nearly all eight functions.

Although it is impossible to eliminate any marketing function, it may be possible to improve its efficiency and thus lower its cost. The farmer who sells his produce via roadside stand (frequently referred to as "direct" marketing) carries the burden and cost of all eight functions.

The functional approach also helps us to understand why one product has a higher marketing cost than another. For example, the cost of the storage function would be higher for eggs than for corn because of the more perishable nature of eggs; they require controlled storage temperatures and involve more risk because of possible breakage. Sometimes the consumer performs marketing functions. When a housewife pushes a grocery cart around the supermarket, she simplifies the selling task and reduces the retailer's cost.

THE INSTITUTIONAL APPROACH
TO MARKETING

The institutional approach to marketing describes the people who perform the various functions in the marketing system. The business firms that engage in marketing activities vary widely in size and ownership. There are the small concerns owned and operated by individual proprietorships; there are partnership concerns and huge corporations. Cooperatives, owned and operated by farm producers, are also prominent in the marketing of agricultural products. The institutional approach to marketing gives primary emphasis to people and business organizations. The people engaged in performing marketing activities are called middlemen. There are more than 600,000 establishments engaged in marketing food products.

Merchant Middlemen

Retailers and wholesalers. Some middlemen, such as retailers and wholesalers, are classed as merchant middlemen, because they actually take title to and thus own the products they handle. The merchant middleman buys a product, performs functions that add utility to it, and sells it for gain. He hopes to cover the costs of the functions he performs, and in addition to realize a profit for his efforts. A retailer is the market agency closest to the consumer, and in most cases his marketing job is the most complex. Retailers are also the most numerous of marketing agencies.

Wholesalers are more heterogeneous than retailers and generally include those agencies referred to as jobbers, carlot receivers, and country assemblers, such as the local livestock buyers and grain elevator. The wholesaler performs fewer functions than does the retailer and usually deals in larger volumes of goods.

Agent Middlemen

Agent middlemen act as representatives for their clients and are differentiated from the merchant middlemen by the fact that they do not take title to any products. The principal function performed by most agent middlemen is providing market information, in which they become specialists. Their income is generated by fees and charges in exchange for services rendered.

Brokers and commission men. Brokers act to bring buyers and sellers together in negotiating favorable terms of exchange. If either a buyer or a seller feels he does not have enough market information to bargain effectively, does not have the time, or wishes to remain anonymous, he can secure a broker to represent him for a fee.

Usually, when products are consigned to a commission firm on a market, the commission agent has a relatively broad degree of control. His job is to sell the product at the best possible price, with no obligation to check with the owner as to whether the selling price is acceptable. The difference between brokers and commission men is largely one of degree of control. The commission firm normally supervises the physical handling of the product. Conversely, the broker works much more closely with the client and will not buy or sell except at a specific price after consultation with him.

Speculative Middlemen

Although the word "speculation" connotes something evil to many people, the speculative middleman is important to an efficient marketing system. Remember the device used by the grain elevator operator in "hedging" against market risk. This hedge merely shifts the responsibility of performing the market function of market risk to someone else—a speculative middleman. A speculator is one who seeks out market-price risks and is willing to accept them in the hope that the price will move in a direction that will afford him a profit. Speculators deal mostly in futures contracts rather than physical goods and most often attempt to earn their profits from short-run price fluctuations.

Facilitative Organizations

These organizations do not take part directly in marketing activities, but are important to any market. Examples include the stockyard companies, which own the real estate or physical parts of the market and which receive rent and fees for their use. They usually stipulate the trading hours and terms of sale on the market.

Trade associations are also considered a type of facilitative organization. An example is the American Meat Institute. Trade-association activities are varied and typically include the gathering and dissemination of market or other information of particular value to their group. Lobbying in state and federal legislative bodies in an effort to influence legislation important to their industry is also an important task.

Meal Services

The meal-service industry may be classified into businesses that exist primarily to sell a product or service for profit, and institutional outlets where food may be sold for a profit and is served to large groups of customers. Food service to small groups or individuals may be provided as an auxiliary facility in other stores, such as a drugstore soda fountain or bowling-alley snack bar, or as a major kind of restaurant business. There are more than 200,000 separate eating places and 50,000 separate drinking places in the United States. The institutional sector contains about 80,000 schools and colleges, and more than 11,000 hospitals, sanatoriums, and rest homes.

Food Processors

Since about two-thirds of the food consumed needs to be processed to some degree, processors must also be considered in the institutional approach. In many cases, processing is only one kind of activity of large business concerns that often act as their own buyers, wholesalers, and retailers. There are about 20,000 food-processing establishments in the United States. They include processors of dairy products; meat; grain-mill products; bakery products; canned, cured, and frozen fruits and vegetables; sugar; confections; and fats and oils products.

THE COMMODITY APPROACH
TO MARKETING

A third way to study marketing is to concentrate on a particular commodity, such as wheat, and follow it through its various processing stages as each market function is performed by each institutional organization. Actually, this combines the two previous approaches in studying the marketing of a single commodity. For those interested in a specific commodity, this is probably the best approach. It helps to focus attention on the physical differences of products that result in different marketing costs.

All three approaches to marketing may be utilized to gain a thorough understanding of marketing principles. Moreover, owing to the wide variety of technical and physical data necessary to solve many marketing problems, the economist must obtain the cooperation of horticulturists, food technologists, entomologists, engineers, transportation specialists, and many others.

ORGANIZATIONAL ASPECTS OF MARKETING

In addition to the functions and kinds of middlemen, there are organizational aspects among the various market agencies that merit study. A market channel is simply the path of a product from its raw to its finished form. For example, after production on the farm, a product may pass through the hands of a local assembler, a food processor, a wholesaler, and finally a retailer before its ultimate destination—the consumer. The nature of the market channel for any product may vary depending upon the region of the country, the season of the year, and the methods employed in handling. Also, one or more channels may be employed to market any single product.

Integration is a marketing organizational feature that has gained recent attention. Where various marketing agencies are grouped together under the control of the same management, integration exists. Vertical integration occurs when two agencies at different levels performing unlike market functions are bonded together. If a food processor controls his wholesaler either by contractual agreement or ownership, vertical integration exists. Horizontal integration, however, exists when management control is extended over another firm performing like activities or functions. Examples of horizontal integration are the retail chain food stores. A single firm may expand its activities both horizontally and vertically. In the poultry industry, feed mills initiated vertical integration by extending control over the farm-production phase and, in some cases, over marketing agencies as well. More attention to integration will be given later in the chapter.

THE COSTS OF MARKETING FOOD

The Marketing Bill and Its Composition

In 1972, consumers spent $116 billion for food products at the retail level, up about two-thirds in ten years (Table 9-1).[2] The costs of marketing accounted for two-thirds of the total. The remaining one-third, commonly referred to as the farmer's share (Farm Value, Table 9-1) declined until 1960 and has been relatively stable since. Factors accounting for the rising marketing bill include an increase in the amount of processing and other services sold with food, an increase in prices of marketing services, and an increase in volume of food sold.

Price changes reflect increases in the prices of marketing inputs such as labor and packaging materials. Volume of sales is influenced mainly by growth in population and disposable income and consequent changes in per capita consumption. Increased marketing services also include an increasing share of prepared foods, such as convenience foods, and eating away from home. The trend toward providing services with food items shows that they are quite responsive to periods of rapid economic growth. Services increased very little during the late 1950s and early 1960s, but the mid-1960s was a period of rapid growth for them.

---

[2] Part of the data in the following sections is taken from various issues of *Marketing and Transportation Situation,* a publication of the U.S.D.A.'s Economic Research Service, between 1968 and 1972.

TABLE 9-1

Total Marketing Bill, Farm Value, Consumer
Expenditures, and Farmers' Share of Consumers'
Dollar, 1947–49, 1957–59, 1960–64, 1965–69,
1970, and 1972[a]

	Total Marketing Bill[b] (billion dollars)	Farm Value[c] (billion dollars)	Civilian Expenditure for Farm Foods (billion dollars)	Farmers' Share of Consumers' dollar (percent)
1947–49	24.5	18.9	43.4	43.5
1957–59	39.9	20.9	60.8	34.4
1960–64	48.1	23.6	71.7	32.9
1965–69	60.0	30.0	90.0	33.3
1970	71.2	34.8	106.0	32.8
1972[d]	77.2	39.0	116.2	33.6

[a] Data for 1960–72 include Alaska and Hawaii.

[b] Difference between farm value and domestic expenditure.

[c] Payment to farmers for equivalent farm products, adjusted to eliminate imputed value of nonfood by-products.

[d] Preliminary.

SOURCE: U.S. Department of Agriculture, Economic Research Service, *Marketing and Transportation Situation,* February 1968 and 1973.

Cost components.   Labor costs for marketing domestic farm food products account for nearly half the marketing bill (Figure 9-1). Labor costs include wages and salaries of employees, wage supplements such as Social Security taxes, and tips. Increases in labor costs come from both higher hourly pay and total man-hours worked. The farm food marketing system employs more than 10 million workers.

Packaging costs account for about 12 percent of the total marketing bill. Prices of most food-packaging materials rose substantially in recent years—up 17 percent from 1967 to 1972. Food packaging costs can amount to one-fourth of a manufacturer's selling prices.

Rail and truck transportation costs were 8 percent of the marketing bill in 1972. About three-fourths of recent cost increases have resulted from rail rate increases granted by the Interstate Commerce Commission (ICC), and the remainder come from increased volume handled. Regulated truckers were also allowed rate increases in 1970 and 1971, but

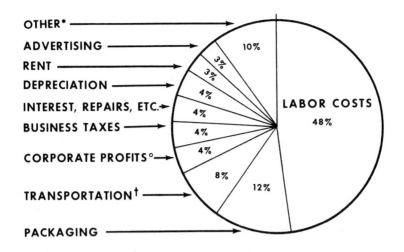

OTHER* ──────────────────►

ADVERTISING ─────────────►

RENT ────────────────────►

DEPRECIATION ───────────►

INTEREST, REPAIRS, ETC.─►

BUSINESS TAXES ─────────►

CORPORATE PROFITS°──►

TRANSPORTATION† ─────────►

PACKAGING ──────────────────►

10%

3%
3%
4%
4%
4%
4%
8%

12%

LABOR COSTS
48%

*RESIDUAL INCLUDES SUCH COSTS AS UTILITIES, FUEL, PROMOTION, LOCAL FOR-HIRE TRANSPORTATION, INSURANCE.
°BEFORE TAXES.   †INTERCITY RAIL AND TRUCK.   PRELIMINARY DATA.

U.S. DEPARTMENT OF AGRICULTURE   NEG. ERS 8452 · 73 (8)   ECONOMIC RESEARCH SERVICE

FIGURE 9-1
Components of Bill for Marketing Farm Foods, 1972

generalizations about rates are difficult to make because good information is not generally available.

Capital costs (depreciation, rent, and interest) totaled $6.7 billion in 1972, over 7 percent of the marketing bill. Recently, annual increases in these costs have been about 4 percent. A major factor causing increases is rising construction costs, which increase depreciation costs and commercial rental rates for food-marketing firms.

Advertising accounts for 2 to 3 percent of the marketing bill. Food processors expend about half that total. In 1971, expenditures for advertising on television were three times greater than for print media.

Corporate profits before taxes take 4 to 6 percent of the marketing bill each year. After-tax profits run about half of before-tax profits. Business taxes make up another 3 to 4 percent of the marketing bill. "Other costs"—for utilities, fuel, insurance, professional services, and so on—constitute the remaining one-eighth.

Food eaten away from home. The U.S. Department of Agriculture began publishing estimates in 1972 of the marketing bill for food consumed at home contrasted to away from home. We have already discussed the retail meal-service industries—public eating places and institutions.

In 1972, consumers spent $34.9 billion (30 percent of the total food expenditure bill) on food eaten away from home. Of this amount, $27.7 billion paid the marketing charges and $7.2 billion represented farm value. Thus, marketing costs represented 79 percent of total consumer expenditures for food eaten away from home, contrasted to 67 percent for food eaten at home. This reflects the added cost of preparing food consumed away from home. Public eating places such as restaurants, cafeterias, and snack bars account for three-fourths of consumer expenditures for food consumed away from home, and institutions (hospitals, schools, rest and nursing homes, colleges, etc.) account for the rest. Money spent on eating away from home rose 94 percent from 1963 to 1972, while expenditures for meals cooked at home rose only 45 percent. This contrast in trends is likely to continue for some time.

Middlemen's marketing charges.   Another way to view the total marketing charge would be to divide it up among the various important groups of middlemen. Studies in 1939 concluded that retailing took 39 percent of the total farm-to-consumer cost; wholesaling, 11 percent; local assembly agencies in production areas, 6 percent; transportation agencies, 10 percent; and processing firms, 34 percent.[3] For the 1970–72 period, processors accounted for 35 percent, wholesalers and assemblers 13 percent, and retailers 29 percent of the total marketing bill. Eating places accounted for the remaining 23 percent.

A rising marketing bill, however, is not sufficient reason to reach the conclusion that the marketing system is inefficient. Remember that there were some 25 million more consumers in 1970 than in 1960 and that they continually demanded more services with their food, such as packaging, credit, and changes in physical facilities. Efficiency can be determined only if consumer satisfaction is adequately measured and considered. ,

The Farmer's Share of the Consumer's Food Dollar

The farmer's share has been given considerable attention by various groups investigating the high cost of marketing. Farm groups point to any decline in their share and conclude that the middlemen are getting rich at the farmer's expense. Consumer groups use any rise in their marketing share to justify their conclusion that the marketing middlemen are the cause of high food prices. Each group's conclusion, if based solely on this one measure, is faulty.

Relationship of retail value to farmer's share and marketing costs.   The

---

[3] *Series of Margin and Cost Studies by Commodities,* U.S.D.A. Technical Bulletins 932, 934, 936, and 939, 1946–48.

amount that consumers spend for food products is primarily affected by the level of disposable income. If the general economy is prosperous and there is little unemployment, the public will spend more freely for all goods and services, including food. On the other hand, if the economy is experiencing a depression, consumers have less disposable income and hence spend less.

The farm value is the amount left after subtracting total marketing costs from the total amount spent for food (retail value). Here, two ideas are important: First, changes in the farm value vary directly with changes in retail value; and second, marketing costs fluctuate less than farm value. Marketing costs are slower to change with changing economic conditions and hence might be called inflexible relative to retail value. This characteristic of marketing charges causes the farmer's share to fluctuate widely. For example, when the economy was depressed in the early 1930s, retail value fell 17.9 percent. Marketing charges fell only 13.1 percent. As a result, farm value suffered a 25.4 percent decline. The opposite situation occurred in 1964 to 1965. A 4.6 percent increase in the retail value was accompanied by an 8.8 percent increase in farm value but only a 2.7 percent rise in the marketing bill (Figure 9-2). The statement that farm value fluctuates to a greater degree than retail value can also be made about individual commodity prices. Farm value reflects farm prices times quantities sold, whereas retail value reflects retail prices times quantities sold. It follows that that farm prices will fluctuate more widely than retail prices.

Marketing costs are inflexible because many of them are based on volume rather than value, particularly those associated with physical functions. For example, the cost of transporting 100 pounds of beef is the same for the trucking company regardless of whether the meat eventually sells for 80 cents or $1.20 per pound at retail. And the situation is the same for storage costs. In the meat-packing plant, the labor required to kill the animal and cut it up is the same in hours of time regardless of the meat's final selling price. Rigidities have also been built into the labor cost by labor–management contracts that stipulate pay based on hours worked rather than meat prices per pound.

Are Marketing Costs too High?

As we have already noticed, marketing is more important today than it was a century ago. The role of the home and the housewife has changed. Instead of stocking flour and sugar to be sold for processing into bread and cakes in the home, the grocer today must stock more finished products, many of which require a large amount of prior processing. In addition, the housewife wants to buy in relatively small food

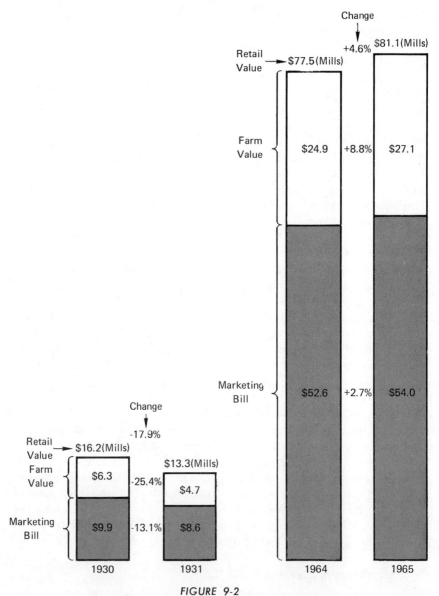

FIGURE 9-2

Comparison of Changes in Retail Value, Farm Value,
and Marketing Bill for 1930–1931 and 1964–1965

SOURCE: U.S. Department of Agriculture, Economic Research Service, *Marketing and Transportation Situation*, MTS 147 (November 1962), and MTS 186 (August 1972).

units, which increases handling and packaging costs. To provide and offer an increased variety of products in convenient and attractive packages, merchants and distributors have had to assume new risks and take on additional tasks, all of which contribute to costs.

To ascertain whether marketing costs are too high, it is necessary to assess consumer satisfactions. Studies dwelling on the duplication of services in the marketing system and the almost frenetic drive of merchandisers to add services and promote their products' consumption through advertising may well suggest that costs are too high. However, the fact that consumers buy additional services with food is an indication that a forced sale does not take place and that costs are considered reasonable.

This is not to say there are not inefficiencies in the marketing system that require correction and close scrutiny. However, as long as consumers continue to receive higher incomes, marketing costs will tend to rise as more services are demanded and added.

Marketing Costs Differ among Products

The alert student will already be able to see why marketing costs and farmer's share vary among products. It has been noted that marketing costs took two-thirds of the consumer's dollar during the 1960s. However, they took only 35 percent on the average for choice beef but a whopping 86 percent for canned tomatoes. (Table 9-2). The following four reasons can account for such differences:

1. *Amount of processing.* The more processing a product requires, the higher the marketing cost will be. Bread and canned foods are good examples.
2. *Degree of perishability.* A perishable product will require more careful physical handling, both in storage and during transportation. To prevent deterioration, special kinds of storage facilities and transporting vehicles may be required. Refrigerated railroad cars and fluid-milk tanker trucks are examples.
3. *Bulkiness relative to value.* Fresh cabbage is not only a perishable product; it is bulky and takes up a relatively large amount of storage and transportation space. This bulkiness makes cabbage marketing cost high relative to its low retail value.
4. *Seasonality of production.* Consumers want to be able to buy nearly all food products the year round. Some foods can be produced only in certain areas of the United States. While producers attempt to even out the seasonality of production, they are able to do so only within limits. When oranges are out of season, their price is seasonally high to defray the costs of storing them until that time.

TABLE 9-2

Farm Food Products: Retail Price and Farm Value; Farmer's Share of Retail Price, 1971–73 Average[a]

Product	Retail Unit	Farm Equivalent	Retail Price	Net Farm Value[b]	Farmer's Share
Beef, choice grade	Pound	2.28 lb. choice cattle	117.9 ¢	76.8 ¢	65 %
Lamb, choice grade	Pound	2.43 lb. lamb	123.0	64.6	53
Eggs, grade A large	Dozen	1.03 dozen	61.1	38.2	63
Chicken, frying	Pound	1.41 broiler	47.3	24.9	53
Milk, fresh, at store	½ gal.	4.39 lb. Class I milk	61.4	31.3	51
Milk, fresh, delivered	½ gal.	4.39 lb. Class I milk	70.6	31.3	44
Cheese, American processed	½ lb.	Milk	55.8	25.6	46
Apples	Pound	1.04 lb. apples	26.2	8.7	33
Oranges	Dozen	1.03 doz. oranges	97.8	22.3	23
Cabbage	Pound	1.08 lb. cabbage	15.1	4.9	32
Carrots	Pound	1.03 lb. carrots	21.4	7.4	35
Lettuce	Head	1.88 lb. lettuce	36.6	12.4	34
Potatoes	10 lbs.	10.42 lb. potatoes	105.0	30.3	29
Canned peaches	No. 2½ can	1.52 lb. Calif. cling	38.4	7.2	19
Canned tomatoes	No. 303 can	1.52 lb. tomatoes	23.3	2.7	12
Orange juice, frozen	6-oz. can	3.35 lb. oranges	24.5	8.7	36
Peas, frozen	10 ozs.	0.68 lb. canning peas	22.8	3.8	17
Margarine	Pound	Vegetable oils	34.4	10.8	31
White bread	Pound	0.87 lb. wheat	25.7	3.2	12
Corn flakes	12 ozs.	2.87 lb. yellow corn	32.3	2.5	8

a Retail price and farm value for second quarter 1972. Farmer's share, average 1969–72.
b Payment to farmers for equivalent quantities of farm products (gross farm value) minus imputed value of by-products obtained in processing.

SOURCE: U.S. Department of Agriculture, Economic Research Service, *Marketing and Transportation Situation*, MTS 184 (February 1972), and MTS 192 (February 1974).

176

SOME IMPORTANT TRENDS IN MARKETING

The marketing system is continuously changing to meet new market conditions, as businessmen experiment to find new market channels and new organizations that reduce costs and enhance their competitive advantage. To outline and discuss in detail the developments in marketing over the past century would fill many pages. Some of the more important ones will be discussed here.

Market Decentralization

The initial developments of the large terminal markets at strategic transportation points in large cities accompanied the development of railroads that could move large loads over long distances. Local markets in the country complemented the terminal market, because of their collection and assembly functions. The goods were sold on the central market by commission firms representing the farmer. Processors were usually located near the terminal market.

One of the drawbacks of this early market organization was the relatively costly process of concentrating the huge quantities of goods at the central market. To the farmer, the typical deduction of 1 to 2 percent from his sales value for sending his goods to the central market seemed large, particularly if these costs could be avoided by selling on a local market.

After World War I, developments in transportation, communications, storage, and retailing favored market decentralization. Decentralization essentially means that the large terminal market is bypassed, and goods move from the farmer or local market directly to processors and wholesalers. The relocation of meat-packing plants and other food processors nearer the producing areas was favored by the freight rate structure. More trucking and improved highways also facilitated the assembly of goods in local areas.

Any market must place accurate values on its products, including considerations of quality differentials. Farmers will want to sell on a market only if the price is as high as they could get elsewhere. Buyers want to purchase at a market where products are available at prices no higher than elsewhere. Market information is one of the keys to efficient market pricing. With improvements in the gathering and dissemination of market news information, it became possible for buyers and sellers on local markets in producing areas to have as much price information as those buying and selling on the central market. As a result, prices could be established at local markets that would adequately reflect quality differentials. In addition, the development of standards and grades facilitated sale by description. Consequently, since World War I, the volume of products moving through the terminal markets has been constantly decreasing.

There is considerable controversy over the effects of market decentralization, the majority of problems concerning how "good" competition is and how "efficient" prices are at local markets. Physical presence of buyers, sellers, or products is hardly necessary for competition to exist if telephones are available and product standards are known. However, if decentralization is to be successful, market grade and price information must be provided comparable to that found at terminal markets.

Food Systems Management

In recent years, businessmen have been experimenting with various ways to coordinate food production with marketing activities, all the way from the farms through to the consumer. Most of the initiative has come from food processors and marketing firms, rather than the farmer. The concept of a "food system" that has evolved considers the total process of food production and marketing—farm supply inputs, raw-food production, food assembly, food processing, food wholesaling, and food retailing. Let's look at some of the more important ideas contained in this "systems" approach.

Vertical coordination and integration.[4] To achieve vertical coordination, agricultural production is integrated with factor-supply or marketing firms. This can be done through a production contract, which is an agreement between a factor supplier or commodity buyer and an agricultural producer. It can also be done through vertical integration, in which one firm assumes two or more stages of production that are traditionally handled by separate firms. Rapid vertical coordination of certain agricultural enterprises in the 1950s seemed to signal a radical change in market organization for farm and ranch products. This trend aroused concern that farmers were losing their freedom of operation, that competitive markets were being bypassed, and that giant corporations were taking over agricultural production. However, experience during the 1960s indicates that this concern was generally unfounded.

Basically, firms integrate to improve profit potential. Integration

---

[4] See Agricultural Extension Service, University of California, "The Structure of Agricultural Markets," *Major Economic Issues,* MA-36-1, November 1971; and Federal Reserve Bank of Dallas, "Vertical Coordination of Agriculture Flows," *Farm and Ranch Bulletin,* August 1972.

may improve bargaining power in buying and selling. It may enable market firms to get a more steady flow of product of a more consistent quality than before. The marketing rationale for vertical coordination is that it does a better job of balancing supply and demand in terms of quantity, quality, and variety; it reduces risk and increases efficiency, thereby leading to lower production costs. Other potential pluses include assured markets and better credit relationships with commercial lenders and between the contracting firms.

In 1960, about 19 percent of all agricultural production was vertically coordinated. In 1970, this figure had reached only 22 percent. In both these years, contract production was the dominant form of vertical coordination and accounted for 15 and 17 percent of total production, respectively. As was mentioned, most of the initiative for vertical coordination came from food processing firms that wished to stabilize and standardize the supply of raw farm product coming into their businesses. Farmer initiative to vertically coordinate came primarily through their cooperative organizations. Vertical coordination tends to be highly commodity specific, depending upon such factors as size of market, degree of processing needed, perishability of the product, size and number of producers, nature of demand, and seasonal factors of supply and demand. In the final analysis, its success depends upon the profitability it yields to parties involved in the agreement.

Livestock enterprises are generally more coordinated than crop enterprises. On the average, one out of every three livestock producers was involved in some vertical coordination in 1970. Production of fluid-grade milk is about 98 percent vertically coordinated. Broiler production has also become highly coordinated, resulting in relatively few large producers throughout the country. The production of broilers, as well as turkeys and eggs, provides a noteworthy example of supply coordination between feed companies and producers, and of degree of vertical integration.

In cattle feeding, there has also been a significant transition to vertical coordination. This trend is attributed to the proliferation of large commercial feedlots that engage in custom feeding and often have predetermined contracts with packers. In marked contrast to beef, there has been little coordination with hogs. Most hog feeders combine hog and corn production. They raise the feeder pigs and the feed for fattening, a situation quite unlike that in cattle feeding.

Crops tend to be either highly coordinated or virtually uncoordinated. Specialty crops, highly perishable crops, and crops that require extensive processing are the major candidates for vertical coordination. Just over 14 percent of all crops were vertically coordinated in 1970, compared with 13 percent in 1960. In vegetable production, however, about half the fresh market and 95 percent of the processing market were vertically coordinated in 1970. At the same time, 80 percent of the seed crops and all the sugar beets and sugar cane were vertically coordinated. Grains and oil-bearing crops were usually not vertically coordinated, since they are relatively nonperishable, have a fairly uniform quality, and are produced by a large number of farmers. Moreover, there are well-established marketing channels and futures markets for these crops, which apparently provide a satisfactory substitute for direct coordination.

Joint ventures.   Joint ventures are sometimes used in managing food systems. In a joint venture, two or more companies combine all or part of their business for a single undertaking, exercising control and sharing in earnings on some agreed basis. The joint venture appeals to small or medium-sized firms because they can compete more effectively with large firms in geographic areas and stages of business often closed to them because of their size. Farmer cooperatives are beginning to use joint ventures to tap new areas of development, including expanding sales to international markets, entering the food service area, and manufacturing production input such as fertilizers and containers. Farmer cooperatives have interjoint ventures with regular corporations as well as with other cooperatives. Joint ventures between cooperatives and general corporations may become an increasingly important means of insuring market participation and finance.

Meal fabrication.   The commodity approach to marketing is beginning to give way to coordination of the stages of activities required to convert commodity items into meal components. The rapid rise in food consumed away from home was noted earlier. A newly emerging food business entity is the "meal fabricator," who prepares meals for restaurants, institutional food-service units, and cafeterias. Meals can be prepared thousands of miles away from where they are consumed. Airline meals are perhaps an outstanding example of this industry. Quality of meals offered is high, and often of gourmet standards.

If the meal-fabricator businesses do expand, much primary food-ingredient and processed-food buying will be done in a different manner, replacing many traditional wholesale suppliers. At present, between 15 and 20 percent of their food-ingredient purchases are from parent firms. In some cases, food manufacturers have integrated forward into the fabricator and food-service stages.

Retailers, meanwhile, view the prepared-foods development with concern. Responding to the 20 percent annual increase in retail store sales for fast-food items in recent years, some chain grocery firms have integrated into the meal-service area, with facilities for sandwiches, entrees, and complete meals. Some chain managers consider fast foods as a great opportunity for sales and profit improvement.

Red meats, poultry, fish, processed fruits and vegetables, and fresh vegetables now seem to comprise the broad category of food lines that will be involved in closer coordination and integration. These are the major components of meals. Their supply fluctuates considerably because of differences in demand expectations of firms and farmers, so that supplies are sometimes far off from actual market needs. Uncoordinated production by individual producers has resulted in chronic oversupplies in the fruit and vegetable processing industry and sharp cyclical variations in the supplies of some meats.

The large meal-fabricator firms that do not coordinate sources of supply with long-term contracts will most likely shift their purchases to substitute products as relative product prices change. This means that producer bargaining groups and processing firms must have a thorough understanding of the competitive alternatives perceived by such meal fabricators. The role of bargaining groups will be more difficult as a coordinated system expands and the farmer membership depends more on them.

Individual producers will find their alternatives sharply reduced with a system coordinated around the meal fabricator. Most purchasers will have contracted or produced their basic requirements, so that the traditionally uncoordinated market will essentially be a residual source of supply, much as the terminal livestock markets have become. Producers will have to become a part of the emerging system either through membership in the cooperative linked to the system or by contractual arrangements with the processors integrated with the system. As a coordinated system evolves within the food industry, new procedures for allocating returns to each level of the system must be devised. Prices offered by different handlers and processors are gradually becoming more difficult to compare because of the variation in services they offer. The problem will become even more difficult as new methods of income allocation, like profit-sharing schemes, evolve.

Summary. The food industry can be viewed as consisting of four sequentially linked subsectors: the farm-input sector, the farm-production sector, the food-processing sector, and the food-merchandising sector. All the subsectors have been experiencing a decrease in number of business firms involved and a corresponding rise in the size of businesses. Experiments in managing the "food system" that includes all the subsectors are of several types, and the final outcome as to what type of business firms will control the system—if any—is not clear. Following is a discussion of some of the more important specific changes occurring in the food-marketing industry.

Changes in Food Wholesaling and Retailing

One of the most striking institutional innovations in recent years is the rise of supermarkets and large food retailing organizations.[5] Declining in importance are the small grocery stores that usually waited on each customer, extended credit, and often doubled as a social center for the neighborhood "philosophers." In 1967 supermarkets (if defined as stores with annual sales of $500,000 or more annually) represented 15 percent of all grocery stores but accounted for 75 percent of total sales. Moreover, 19,000 supermarkets (9 percent of total food retail stores) had sales of over $1 million, and accounted for almost two-thirds of total sales. Stores with annual sales under $100,000 were 61 percent of the total in 1967 but accounted for under 10 percent of total sales.

This concentration of business is dramatic because as late as 1940, supermarkets had only 25 percent of the business. The division is one of the large and small groceries, not one of chain stores as opposed to independents. Even with the concentration of sales into a smaller number of stores, there is intense competition in the food retailing business. High volume and high turnover are the primary features of a supermarket, with typical profits of one cent out of each dollar of sales.

Another development in food retailing is the shift in sales from single-unit firms to multiunit firms. In 1948, single-unit establishments averaging only $42,000 in annual sales did 59 percent of the grocery business. In 1967, however, multiunits accounted for 61 percent of the total. As the multiunit firms increased their share of total grocery-store sales, each multiunit size category—in terms of number of stores operated —increased its share. For example, firms operating 51 or more stores increased their market share from 29 to 42 percent from 1948 to 1967. As grocery-store sales have become more concentrated among multiunit firms, the market share of the 20 largest chains also has increased, to 40 percent in 1970 compared to 30 percent in 1954.

The rise of the self-service, multiunit food market is both the cause and the effect of other trends. Size of stores increased, wages of employees rose, the amount of advertising increased, more items were stocked, and margins fell. The impersonal nature of selling in the supermarket has

---

[5] Information in this and the next section from U.S. Department of Agriculture, Economic Research Service, "Market Structure of the Food Industries," Marketing Research Report No. 971, September 1972.

resulted in changes in the marketing channel. Because the single retailer moves a larger volume of goods than ever before, he has increased his power in negotiating price with food processors and wholesalers. This is particularly true of the chain stores, which may have one purchasing agent for a region or area.

Changes in grocery wholesaling are also significant. In order for the retailer to assure himself of adequate amounts of uniform and quality products when needed, many have acquired their own wholesaling facilities or have vertically integrated the wholesaling functions into the retailing functions. Others have joined cooperative wholesaling groups or entered into contracts with private wholesaling firms, which stipulate a rigid procurement policy. Sales of independent stores declined from about one-fourth in 1963 to less than one-tenth in 1969.

Thus, affiliated grocery establishments—those sponsoring voluntary groups of retailers and those cooperatively owned by retailers—were a major new force in the general-line wholesale grocery trade in the mid-1960s. Sales of affiliated grocery wholesalers now account for sales about equal to those of food stores performing their own wholesaling function. Moreover, the recent growth of affiliated wholesalers and their retailers is increasing at a faster pace than growth in integrated food stores. This trend will probably slow in the 1970s. The number of affiliated wholesale establishments increased by more than a third from 1958 to 1967, and sales per establishment were five times greater than those of non-affiliated wholesalers. Sales of retailer-owned cooperative establishments grew at a faster rate but started from a much smaller base. The growth of affiliated wholesalers has been due to the realization of both wholesalers and retailers that in order to compete effectively, they had to achieve the economies of scale accruing to their chain competitors.

Sponsoring a voluntary group of retailers affords the wholesaler a relatively stable base of loyal customers. In return for this loyalty, the wholesaler provides the retailer with a merchandising and promotional program and the services of specialists in store operation. Moreover, many voluntary-group sponsors provide financial assistance, store-employee training, and other services to improve retailer effectiveness.

Retailers have also placed new demands on processors. As a result, some have resorted to vertical integration backward toward the farmer. For example, an egg processor, by contracting with an egg producer, could extend his supervision over the production of eggs on the farm. By integrating, the processor would be assuring a source of eggs as well as more carefully controlling product quality. This would enable the processor to meet the demands of the modern supermarket operator for large quantities of uniform-quality eggs. There is a power struggle between large-scale retailers and national processors as to who will control whom.

In any event, there is less open-market negotiation in the marketing channel as concentration at the retail level has favored vertical integration.

Fewer and Larger Food-Processing Firms

A general trend in evidence throughout the food-marketing industry is toward fewer but larger firms. A notable exception is meat slaughter and packing firms; where the four largest firms accounted for 51 percent of the slaughter in 1950 but only 26 percent in 1967, owing to the growth of medium-size operations. The pattern of changes varies with commodity orientation.

The number of fluid-milk bottling plants decreased from 8,484 to 1,864 between 1948 and 1971. Fluid-milk plants packaged an average of slightly more than 20 million pounds per plant in 1970, compared with less than 13 million pounds in 1963 and about 5.6 million in 1948. The number of plants manufacturing dairy products fell 42 percent in the period 1961–71, while the average value of milk (milk equivalent basis) that they made into manufactured dairy products rose—from 10 million in 1963 to 17 million in 1970.

For poultry and eggs, the trend is also toward fewer plants and increased average size. In 1970, there were 87 plants processing frozen and 24 plants processing dried eggs under federal inspection. Hatchery numbers decreased by nearly half from 1965 to 1971. Poultry-meat-processing plants in 1970 numbered 412, compared to 482 in 1964, while volume slaughtered was up 45 percent. Nearly half the plants processed 30 million or more pounds, accounting for three-quarters of the total.

The number of country grain elevators was about the same in 1967 as 1954 (6,500). Terminal elevators increased 67 percent in the 1954–67 period. The number of plants producing flour and meal decreased 33 percent during 1954–67. Establishments in the blended and prepared flour industry showed a substantial increase in the same period, while rice-milling and cereal-preparations plants declined. Numbers declined sharply in the bread and related products industry, while biscuit and cracker companies increased.

From 1954 to 1967, the number of establishments canning fruits and vegetables in the United States declined 30 percent. In contrast, firm numbers in the frozen fruit and vegetable industry more than doubled, and dehydration plants were up one-fifth.

Soybean oil and cottonseed oil are the two major vegetable oils produced in the United States, accounting for 90 percent of total production. Both are used primarily in the production of edible commodities. The number of cottonseed processors decreased 48 percent from 1954 to 1963, while the average size of plant increased 30 percent. Soybean processing establishments increased 16 percent in number while production was up $2\frac{1}{2}$ times in the same period.

In summary, the trend toward fewer but larger firms can be found throughout the food-marketing industry. Technological developments, such as changes in equipment and improved transportation and communications, have intensified the trend. Changes in ownership by purchase or merger have also furthered the movement. A surviving company often concentrates its operations in the most efficient plants, which often were its largest plants.

Market Orders and Bargaining Programs

Agricultural producers are becoming more and more interested in developing producer-administered group action programs to increase their market power, manage the supply of farm commodities, and thereby improve farm prices and income. The possible abandonment of federal price and income support, possible surpluses of some commodities, and the continued concentration of buyers in farmers' markets are some of the factors contributing to current interest in group action.

Several national farm organizations and commodity groups advocate collective bargaining by farmers to establish commodity prices and other terms of sale. National legislation has been proposed to require buyers to negotiate with certified farmer bargaining groups. There is renewed interest in the use of state and federal marketing orders for supply management and other purposes. Marketing boards like those that operate in some other countries have been proposed in Congress in recent years as a way to give producers the authority to regulate production, entry of new producers, and farm-commodity prices.

Some basic issues concerning bargaining and group action are:

Can producers organize and successfully manage supply?
Should they be permitted or encouraged to do so?
What are the magnitude and sources of potential gain?
Are changes needed in public policy to assist the development of market power through group action?
Do public policies and legislation need to be changed to protect consumers from excess use of farmers' market power?

Marketing orders emerged from the efforts of cooperative associations to regulate farm-product marketing in the 1920s and 1930s. Those purely voluntary efforts met with only limited success, largely because recalcitrant producers were unwilling to adhere to the proposed marketing plans. The marketing order, authorized and enforced by the federal or state government, was developed to ensure industry-wide adherence to programs favored by a majority of producers.

Bargaining programs evolved to complement marketing orders and cooperative marketing. It was recognized that, even under industry-wide regulations established by marketing orders, terms of sale of farm products were still negotiated individually between many producers and a relatively few large buyers. Several of these buyers were in a position to exercise market power to influence price and other terms of sale. It was believed that collective bargaining would complement the efforts of cooperative marketing associations by regularizing marketing arrangements and influencing terms of sale between producers and independent buyers.

Some of the more recent developments in bargaining seem to be based more directly on labor's use of collective bargaining and market power. There have been attempts to implement collective action and bargaining on a regional and national basis for feed grains, which are not under marketing orders or other closely related supply-management programs.

Despite the many years of experience with marketing-order and bargaining programs, their potential and limitations are not well understood. Some view the programs as a temporary phase in the development of a highly commercial, integrated agriculture. Some regard them as the embryo of a self-managed food and fiber system similar in structure and conduct to other sectors of the American economy in which organized labor confronts a highly concentrated set of buyers. Others believe they have little potential effectiveness at best, and are an impediment to the efficient functioning of "free" markets at worst. As with most such programs, their potentials and limitations fall between the extremes. They should be examined pragmatically in terms of the realities of agricultural markets—current and emerging.

Economic aspects. Both marketing-order and bargaining programs try to modify economic conditions in agricultural markets to the producers' advantage. In some cases, the alterations may also be advantageous to other firms in the marketing system and to consumers. For example, a marketing order might establish quality standards favorable to all. Or a bargaining program might benefit processors if services like delivery scheduling or contracting for supply were provided at lower cost than they would be if the processors themselves made such arrangements with individual producers. However, in many cases, there are conflicting interests, so that economic gains to one party mean losses to other parties. Although consumer interests should be considered when marketing orders are formulated and operated, it is clear that both orders and bargaining programs are primarily intended to benefit producers.

The extent of the economic gain to producers, the source of gain, and the distribution of costs and benefits that the programs give depend on many economic variables. These include market structure, supply–demand relationships, the provisions employed, and the extent to which producers are willing and able to discipline their market behavior. Discussion of the principal features of the programs will illustrate these points.

Marketing orders, whether federal or state, are based on statutes that enable producers to combine in specified marketing activities. A majority of producers and (in joint orders) handlers must approve the order. Once approved, the order is binding upon all in the industry, unlike bargaining programs or marketing cooperatives, in which participation is voluntary. Orders are usually written for a single commodity produced in a specific area for either a definite or indefinite period of time, subject to amendment, suspension, or termination. Final approval for actions taken on the order resides with the U.S. secretary of agriculture or the state director of agriculture, depending on whether the order is enabled under federal or state statutes. Producers and handlers initially bear the operating costs of orders, including, in state orders, their governmental administrative costs.

There may be differences among states as to commodities covered by orders. For example, under California statutes, any agricultural commodity is eligible for an order, but federal statutes exclude some commodities. In California, marketing of milk is regulated under a special law. Federal laws permit establishment of minimum prices to producers.

An order may contain one or more of the following eight provisions:

1. *Grade, size, maturity, and/or quality control*—prohibits shipment of products not conforming to standards.
2. *Surplus or total quantity control*—limits the quantity of the product shipped in total or in specific market outlets.
3. *Rate of flow control*—limits, within season, shipment by day, week, or other appropriate time period.
4. *Pack and/or container regulations*—prohibits shipments not meeting specifications.
5. *Unfair trade practices*—defines and prohibits such practices.
6. *Inspection and certification*—ensures conformity to prevailing standards.
7. *Promotion and/or advertising*—generally limited to nonbrand promotion and, in the case of federal orders, advertising for specified commodities.
8. *Research*—production, processing, and/or marketing research and surveys; federal orders limited to market research and development.

The most common provisions included are those related to quality control, promotion and/or advertising, and research. Relatively few orders have quantity control provisions, although those containing such provisions attract the most attention and controversy. The California-Arizona orders for lemons and navel and Valencia oranges are examples of programs with rate-of-flow provisions.

As currently authorized, orders may provide a means of dealing with occasional or seasonal commodity surpluses. They have not adequately resolved problems of chronic oversupply caused by excess resources in an industry. Because enabling legislation is generally interpreted as precluding production control, most orders do not regulate the entry of new producers or the use of farm-production resources. Orders may allocate production among markets, and they may cause a portion of the production to be destroyed "on the tree" or in the processing plant, but, with few exceptions, they do not regulate production capacity itself.

An order that substantially increases farm-product prices may bring greater resources into the industry and cause increased production with mounting set-asides, "green-drops," or other forms of surplus disposal. But if the surplus is occasional or temporary, judicious use of the order may mitigate the pronounced price decline that frequently accompanies such a surplus.

From time to time, amendments have been proposed to give marketing orders the authority to control production. To date, all such proposals have failed. In recent years, however, government administrative interpretations and rulings have sometimes granted orders an authority that approaches production control.

Whether marketing orders should be authorized to control production through acreage allotments, as in federal price-support programs, is a controversial question. Opponents argue that such approaches have not worked well in federal price-support programs. When they do work initially, the value of the quota becomes capitalized into the value of the land, thereby affecting production costs. Acreage allotments impede resource-use efficiency by "locking in" inefficient producers if quotas are nontransferable. If transferable, they tend to speed up consolidation of the industry in the hands of larger firms.

Proponents, on the other hand, suggest that farm prices and incomes can be significantly improved only by rigorous supply management, which requires the ability to control production and entry into the industry. They see agriculture becoming more and more concentrated even without such controls. Some seek authority to regulate entry to protect those who depend on farming as their sole or major income source against the competition of large, well-financed firms that may consider farming secondary to their other economic interests.

In most cases, the positions of both proponents and opponents are heavily laced with value judgments involving ethics, politics, and sociology, as well as economics. The economic effects of quotas can be evaluated only by considering the economic circumstances of the regulated industry and of related industries affected by the accompanying "spillover" effects.

Orders have functioned most successfully in relatively small geographic areas and under technical and economic conditions that are comparable among farm firms. It is easier to administer the programs when the product moves through relatively few handlers. Ideally, the order should encompass all or at least a high percentage of the product harvested or marketed during the relevant control period. The long-run effectiveness of an order may be jeopardized if it stimulates production outside the regulated area. Of course, if all major producing areas agreed to cooperate under an order, prices might rise. But such agreements are difficult to establish and enforce. Efforts to set up such arrangements have usually failed because of disagreements over how much each area should withhold from the market.

Even if supply can be controlled, the extent to which prices and incomes can be increased may be limited. If consumers respond to reduced supply by bidding up prices proportionally more than the supply reduction, income will increase. But where consumers respond by shifting their purchases to competing products or simply by doing without the product, prices of the regulated commodity may rise very little and the producers' gross income may decrease. Thus, the nature of the demand for the regulated commodity is an important consideration in operating quantity control and rate-of-flow provisions.

With the exception of federal marketing orders for milk, price cannot be directly fixed under marketing orders. The price effect is achieved by manipulating supply and/or demand (promotion and advertising). Bargaining programs, however, seek to directly negotiate price on behalf of cooperating member firms. Many of the same principles and considerations for successfully using orders also apply to successful bargaining—for example, the effective control of a significant part of the relevant market supply, and the nature of the demand for the commodity. The bargaining group may also face added problems associated with its voluntary nature. It must be able to persuade or force handlers to bargain with the group, either by offering the handler a service or advantage, or by withholding or threatening to withhold supplies the handler needs.

Bargaining-group members must be prepared to bear the possible costs involved in gaining the handlers' recognition and in withholding products from markets to obtain desired terms of sale. If the product is perishable, considerable losses may occur unless terms are negotiated well before harvest, and preferably before planting or beginning the production process. Terms of sale for some crops are, in fact, negotiated well before harvest, sometimes on a sliding scale whereby the negotiated price declines as total production increases. In any case, bargaining costs fall directly on participating members, not on all members of the industry as they do under marketing orders. But all producers in the industry may share, to some extent, the benefits of bargaining under voluntary arrangements.

Because bargaining is voluntary, one crucial question concerning its potential effectiveness is the producers' ability to organize and discipline themselves to rigorous supply management. Exhortations and rhetoric are insufficient to bring about significant, lasting improvement in terms of sale. The group must be able to exercise market power to punish or reward its bargaining opponent. In the past, purely voluntary marketing arrangements to manage supply have usually been unsuccessful. It remains to be seen whether producers are now willing and able to exercise market discipline to avoid failure.

Most discussions of bargaining focus on price enhancement by limiting supply. But terms of sale other than price may be negotiated through bargaining. The negotiation may ensure uniform contract terms among group members. Standardized credit terms, premiums, and discounts for raw products may be negotiable. Other possibilities include long-term contracts between the association and handlers, varieties to be planted, and delivery scheduling. If the group provides services that otherwise the handler would perform, their value might be negotiated, perhaps to the mutual benefit of producers and handlers. Many bargaining groups have been slow to develop these services—services that may be increasingly important in improving vertical coordination in the food industry.

If marketing orders and bargaining programs improve farm prices and incomes, how do they affect consumer prices and handlers' profits? Again, there is no unequivocal answer. The structure of the food industry suggests that much of the farmers' gain might be reflected in higher consumer food prices. However, depending on the market power of handlers in relation to buyers of their products, the handlers' profits might be lowered. Of course, some actions taken under marketing orders and by bargaining groups may benefit consumers. Improvement in grades and standards, more uniform quality, and a more stable supply, when in accord with consumer demands, may be of value to consumers, producers, and marketers. Given present food price levels and the current consumer movements in the United States, it is doubtful that either orders or bargaining programs could operate for long in a highly restrictive manner that increased consumer prices.

Air Transportation

Although air transportation is only a small part of the total movement of agricultural products now, it is in a period of rapid growth.[6] Juicy pineapples and papayas fly from Hawaii to the United States mainland. Ripe strawberries and freshly cut flowers are flown from Florida to Chicago and from California to Europe and the Far East. Air shipments of strawberries from California to markets in seven European countries in the first six months of 1968 totaled almost 2 million pounds. Vine-ripe melons and crisp lettuce fly from California to Boston. In one four-month period, 100,000 head of veal calves were shipped from one U.S. air terminal to Italy. Hatching eggs, baby chicks, and nursery and floral stocks fly to Europe, South America, and the Far East from the United States.

With the coming of wide-bodied jumbo freight jets, air transport for farm products will help spark a distribution revolution that will give consumers more fresh food at—it is hoped—lower costs than ever before. These changes can be expected to enhance the diets of rural and urban consumers alike, while at the same time creating new worldwide marketing opportunities for farmers able to use the service. New cargo-handling systems are being developed to speed loading and unloading of the huge airfreighters and to hurry the shipments through the air-cargo terminals. Plans for computerization of the shipping paperwork, and the design of insulated and refrigerated containers to protect the products, are well on their way.

In 1968, domestic airfreight of all types totaled about 1,900 million ton-miles. Agricultural products accounted for about one-third of this amount. Projections show total ton-miles increasing to about 14 billion by 1980. If the proportion of agricultural products shipped by air remains about the same during the 1970s, farm commodities will make up almost 5 billion ton-miles of the total annual domestic airfreight by 1980.

These estimates may be too conservative. Although domestic airfreight of all types is increasing by about 20 percent a year, air shipments of agricultural products have been growing at least twice as fast. Domestic shipments of fruits and vegetables by air in 1968 totaled 1.16 billion pounds, or about 2,904 rail carload equivalents. In traffic-volume terms, this total amounted to about 128 million ton-miles. California

---

[6] Information in this section from Philip Breakiron, "Putting Wings on Your Food," *Yearbook of Agriculture* (Contours of Change), U.S. Department of Agriculture, 1972, pp. 333–37.

alone shipped more than 25,000 tons of fruits and vegetables by air in 1969—an increase of almost 150 percent over the 1965 volume.

In the 1960s, the level of airfreight rates was reduced about 20 percent. Further reductions can be expected as the larger jets with greatly increased cargo capacities come into use. Already in the planning stage for the 1980s is a six-engine giant subsonic airfreighter capable of carrying 500,000 pounds. To accompany this giant airfreighter, on the planning boards are helicopters with lifting capacities of 25,000 pounds, which can be used to pick up and deliver containers to and from the freighters in a matter of minutes. This development will, in turn, generate further increases in air shipments as field-fresh products are placed within reach of more freight budgets and more consumers. Total operating cost per ton-mile for the big jets is expected to range from 5.2 to 5.4 cents, compared with 8.6 to 9.8 cents for today's jet freighters, and 20 to about 31 cents for the piston-driven aircraft in use in 1960.

Some 30 percent of total jet-freight costs today are incurred in ground handling of the cargo. New cargo terminals, planned or already under construction, will have their loading platforms at plane-door height for direct movement of cargo into and out of the planes. Intermodal containerization is another technique that will cut air-terminal delays and handling costs. The loading of refrigerated and insulated food containers at the shipper's plant allows products to be carried directly to the receiver's loading dock without rehandling or transfer of individual packages. Controlled temperatures, humidity, and atmospheric makeup will be maintained inside the containers. Handling damage, spoilage, and quality losses will be minimized. Special types of containers for livestock will allow live animals to be carried with the same comfort and care as human passengers.

Ground transport of shipments to and from the airports is also receiving attention. Mathematical simulation and systems-analysis techniques will be used to find the fastest, lowest-cost routing of trucks picking up and delivering air shipments. These analytical techniques will also be used to coordinate cargo flight schedules and pick-up–delivery schedules with the shippers' and the markets' requirements. These are but a few of the many steps that will be taken to speed shipments of agricultural products to market by air in the 1970s.

Selling Livestock on a Grade-and-Yield Basis

The livestock industry is constantly searching for ways to improve the pricing of animals in order to reflect desired meat-quality attributes. Grading on a quality-grade and yield-grade basis is one method sometimes used by farmers selling at auction markets or directly to packers, but widely used when wholesalers and retailers buy from packers. In 1971, about 13 percent of all cattle, 12 percent of all sheep and lambs, 6 percent of calves, and 4 percent of hogs sold direct to packers were sold on a quality- and yield-grade basis.

This method of selling has an inherent marketing advantage, as it is a more accurate way to determine carcass quality and value. For animals sold on a live basis, only an estimate can be made of the carcass quality and weight of salable cuts. However, a disadvantage of grade-and-yield selling is that the "shrink" occurring from hot-carcass weight to cold-carcass weight of 1.5 to 3 percent is price-discounted among packing plants.

Since grade-and-yield prices are not directly comparable to live prices, the producer has difficulty in comparing and evaluating markets. Until producers gain confidence in procedures used at the packing plants to grade, weigh, and identify carcasses, the use of this method will grow rather slowly despite the economic advantage it offers.

Other major changes in livestock marketing include a significant drop in cattle shipments by rail as the growth and development of highways has spurred truck transportation. Also, futures trading in live animals is a recent innovation. Since there is virtually no delivery of livestock on futures contracts, futures trading has not altered directly the way in which livestock are sold, but it is an important vehicle for establishing prices for livestock and for transferring price risks.

AGRICULTURAL COOPERATIVES

About 27 percent of the farm products sold by farmers in the United States are marketed through cooperatives. There is nothing magic about the way that a cooperative performs marketing functions. Nor is a cooperative always successful. It is only one of the legal types of business organizations, as is the partnership or corporation. The differences between a corporation and a cooperative lie in the way the business is owned and controlled and in the basic objectives and policies for organizing and carrying on business activities. The key to a business's success is management, corporate or cooperative.

The old-fashioned husking bee or barn raising was an example of cooperative action to solve tasks by groups for their mutual good. The stimulus for group cooperative action by farmers was often initiated by low market prices or by the inability to buy quality inputs at reasonable prices. Farmers, feeling that perhaps the middleman was taking advantage of his situation, thought that by banding together they could set up a cooperative business to do a better job. Most cooperatives in the United States are among farmers, and with the passage of the Capper-Volstead Act in 1922, the concept of a cooperative as a type of business organization was legally established.

Mutual insurance was the earliest form of organized cooperation in the United States. Benjamin Franklin headed the board of directors of the first one, the Philadelphia Contributorship for the Insurance of Houses from Loss by Fire, established in 1752. Cooperatives of many kinds have been formed and can be easily classified by tasks performed; there are purchasing, marketing, service, and manufacture or processing associations.

Three distinctive characteristics of a cooperative differentiate it from other forms of business organization.

1. Ownership and control are exercised by those who patronize the business. Although you may own stock in Ford Motor Company and still buy and operate a Chevrolet, this is not the case with a cooperative. If you own stock in a cooperative business, you use its services; in fact, wanting to do business with the cooperative is the reason you become a part-owner in it. To assure that this concept will be maintained, cooperatives usually restrict the amount of business they do with non-members to a certain small percentage of the total. In addition, each member in a cooperative has an equal voice—one member, one vote. In a corporation, however, each *share* gets the privilege of a vote, and one person gaining control of 51 percent of the stock can effectively control the business. In a cooperative, then, there is a patron-owner relationship rather than an investor-owner relationship. Most cooperatives also give control over the transfer of capital-stock shares to their board of directors, which limits transfers to those utilizing the services of the cooperative.

2. Another basic principle is that the cooperative business will be operated to just cover costs, and any excess will be returned to the patron-owners, based on patronage. This is not to say that the desire for profits does not motivate the management to perform in the most efficient manner for its patron-owners. But the incentive for ownership is to gain from group action, not to earn a large return on money invested, as it would be in owning stock in a corporation.

3. The third differentiating characteristic in a cooperative is that there shall be limited returns on owner's invested capital. The fact that investors join a cooperative to gain from utilizing its services gives a very distinctive feature to the capital invested in a cooperative. To reduce speculation on capital shares, their transfer is carefully controlled and they are commonly given a top value. To raise new funds for financing an expansion of a cooperative, patronage refunds are often given in stock rather than cash. However, since there is no market where shares can be bought and sold, this method merely forces patrons to increase their capital holdings in the cooperative.

Marketing Cooperatives

Marketing cooperatives may be organized to perform one or more of the marketing functions already described. Their objective is to maximize returns to the producers. A cooperative livestock commission may only perform the function of market information. Other cooperatives, such as a grain elevator, may mix and sell feed as well as buy and store grain and thus act as a purchasing cooperative. In the late 1960s, the proportion of various farm products marketed through cooperatives was as follows: cotton, 24 percent; dairy products, 69 percent; fruits and vegetables, 31 percent; grain, 34 percent; livestock, 14 percent; and poultry, 9 percent.

How Cooperatives Function

Cooperatives have all the problems associated with performing business activities that private concerns have. They must compete with corporations and all other forms of business organization. They must be able to do a job as well or better than their competitors in order to survive. Many times, farmers are unwilling to meet their competition, and try to cut costs by hiring poor management or constructing inefficient physical facilities. This practice eventually leads to failure.

Since business is conducted on a cost basis, the cooperative theoretically has no profits, the excess returns above costs being regarded as return payments to patrons and not as profit. In this way, it does not pay a tax equivalent to the corporate income tax. This information is used by noncooperative firms as a way to generate public opinion against cooperatives. The public has generally favored cooperatives, particularly in the 1920s, when it was felt that cooperatives could achieve orderly marketing and solve "the farm problems."

Although cooperatives are not technically outside antitrust laws, the Capper-Volstead Act of 1922 makes prosecution of them unlikely. The act gives the secretary of agriculture restricted jurisdiction over cooperatives; a complaint must come from him if a cooperative is to be charged with an antitrust suit for monopolizing or restraining trade. No complaints have ever been issued.

The role of the cooperative must change with the times. Present operational methods designed to serve small farmers will probably not be adequate to meet the challenges associated with larger and more specialized production units. Bargaining cooperatives, common in the marketing of milk, are diversifying in other products. The concept of countervailing power is important when concentration and integration of firms take place in the marketing channel. The bargaining cooperative is one avenue to offsetting the increased market power of large retailers and vertically integrated market agencies. In any case, the future of cooperatives as a surviving type of business organization rests with the ability of their management to adapt to competitive conditions and to continue to serve their patron-owners in the best fashion possible.

As previously noted, some cooperatives are taking the lead in experimenting with various kinds of joint ventures and coordinated systems in the production and marketing of food. They will most likely continue as a major form of business organization in agriculture. In addition, the concept of cooperatives has been extended to consumer buying organizations, specific health-insurance programs, travel programs, and living establishments.

10

Consumption of Food

Although man's most persistent efforts have been spent in acquiring food, it is only during the last century that investigations have been made into food consumption and man's needs for various nutrients. A study of the economics of food consumption centers around what foods man consumes, what good they do, and the factors that influence choice of foods.

Today, an estimated 20 percent of the world's population suffers from not having enough food to eat. Almost two out of every three people suffer from malnutrition, not having the proper quality of diet in terms of essential amino acids or protein for adequate nutrition.[1]

The most striking contrast in the current world food situation is the relative surplus of food in the West and the shortages that prevail in the less-developed countries. This situation results in a great difference between countries in the composition of diets. In the poorer and more heavily populated sections of the world, the diet is composed largely of cereal grains (Table 10-1). Estimates are that while virtually all types of cereal grains are eaten by man in the poorer areas, nearly 70 percent of the grain production in the United States, excluding

---

[1] *The World Food Problem,* a report of the President's Science Advisory Committee, Panel on the World Food Supply (Washington, D.C.: U.S. Government Printing Office, May 1967), Vol. II, 5.

TABLE 10-1

Composition of Diet for Selected Regions and
Countries in Terms of Caloric Intake,
1959–61 Average

Region	Wheat	Rice	Other Grains[a]	Fats and Oils[b]	Meat, Fish, Eggs	Milk Products[c]
			(percent of total caloric intake)[d]			
United States	17.4	0.9	2.5	20.5	16.9	13.5
Northern Europe	23.4	0.6	4.0	17.8	16.4	11.3
Mexico	11.1	1.6	42.2	8.1	6.1	5.3
Brazil	8.6	14.5	11.2	5.9	8.4	3.9
West Asia	48.0	4.2	8.8	8.1	4.0	4.2
India	11.3	33.1	19.0	4.2	0.9	5.5
East Asia	1.8	50.1	7.7	5.7	4.1	0.7
West Central Africa[e]	1.2	5.7	27.2	9.0	2.0	0.6
East Africa	2.3	8.4	55.9	3.4	3.6	2.4
Communist Asia	12.2	44.3	18.1	3.1	2.3	0.1

[a] Corn, barley, oats, rye, millet, sorghum, buckwheat, quinoa, spelt, and teff.
[b] Butter (fat content), edible animal fats, marine oils, and vegetable oils used for food.
[c] Except butter.
[d] Percents do not add to 100. Data not shown for following groups: other starchy crops, pulses and nuts, sugar, and vegetables.
[e] Other starchy crops, mostly manioc, account for 47.1 percent.
SOURCE: U.S. Department of Agriculture, Economic Research Service, *The World Food Budget, 1970*, Foreign Agricultural Economic Report No. 19, October 1964.

sorghums, is consumed by animals. It is easy to see that it takes a rich country to be able to convert its grain into meat. An average of eight pounds of grain is required to produce a pound of meat. In addition, a pound of milled rice contains 50 percent more calories than a pound of beef.

Cereal grains are deficient in at least one of the essential amino acids for proper nutrition. Only meat, milk, eggs, and other livestock products are complete proteins, in that they have all the essential amino acids for complete and proper nutrition. As the real per capita income of a country grows, people shift the composition of their diet from grain-oriented protein intake to more livestock products. Fortunately, this shift is in concert with good nutrition, with one exception: People tend to eat more sugar as their incomes rise, which is not in their best nutritional interests.

FACTORS INFLUENCING FOOD
CONSUMPTION

Consumer Wants and Desires

The strategic position of consumers at the end of the marketing process has been discussed. The basis of the consumer's desire for food is rooted in the physiological requirements of the human body. The standards necessary to maintain adequate health have been constantly reviewed by the Food and Nutrition Board of the National Research Council.

In some parts of the world, particularly the industrialized West, the standards necessary to satisfy physiological requirements are met so easily that they are seldom thought about. People who are "food rich" eat food for enjoyment as well as for nutrition. A person may want a particular food merely because it tastes good or looks good to him.

We are also influenced by our cultures and want to eat the kind of food that is customary. If our neighbors eat a wide variety of foods, we want to consume a similar variety. Certain tribes in Africa keep cattle for the purpose of drawing and drinking the blood from them. This is socially unacceptable as a food in most places, but each new generation in those tribes not only is willing but desires to consume blood as a food. This example illustrates forcefully the influence of social environment on food consumption.

Physical environment is also important. For example, rice grows well in Southeast Asia; people there are accustomed to eating rice early in life and this habit continues. People in Northeast Asia, where the climate is suitable to wheat production, prefer wheat products.

Food preferences arising from social, cultural, and physical environment do not change quickly or often. When they do occur, changes are important; some of the more recent examples in the United States are (1) the decline in consumer preference for fat meats as compared to lean meats, (2) the decline in consumer preference for animal fats as compared to vegetable fats, (3) the decline in fresh fruits and vegetables as compared to canned and frozen fruit and vegetable products, and (4) the decline in grain consumption as compared to meat consumption.

Consumer Income

Consumers in the United States spend about 15 percent of their disposable income for food. This proportion averaged about one-fourth from 1920 to 1950 but has since declined except for sharp increases in

1973–74. It was a bit higher during the depression, when total family incomes were lower. However, the average covers up the fact that poor families may spend half or more of their income for food while the rich spend a small percentage. In 1857, Ernest Engel propounded his famous law of consumption: The poorer a family is, the greater the proportion of total expenditures it must use to procure food.

Economists are vitally concerned with what happens to a family's food-consumption pattern when its income changes. The change that occurs in consumption of an item when income increases is measured by what is called *income elasticity*. For example, if consumption of food increases 1 percent as a result of a 1 percent increase in income, the income elasticity of food would be +1.00. The formula is:

$$Income \ elasticity = \frac{Percent \ change \ in \ consumption \ (quantity)}{Percent \ change \ in \ income \ (dollars)}$$

Income elasticity for food varies with (1) level of family income;[2] (2) type of product; (3) whether measured at farm or at retail level, or the effect of services added to product in marketing channel; and (4) family residence.

Level of family income. The absolute level of family income is the most important factor affecting income elasticity of demand. The coefficient tends to be higher for low-income families and lower for higher-income families.

Type of product. It has already been mentioned that diets of families in general change from a grain-oriented protein diet to an animal protein diet with more processed foods as income increases. If consumption of a food increases with an income increase, it is called a *superior* food (income elasticity coefficient is positive); if its consumption decreases with an income increase, it is called an *inferior* food (income elasticity coefficient is negative). Some foods exhibit no particular trend one way or the

---

[2] Rockwell reports the following income elasticities of expenditures for all food and beverages at mean value for nonfarm household groups by income (based on arithmetic regressions of individual observations, per person average): low income, 0.25; medium income, 0.21; and high income, 0.15. See George R. Rockwell, "Income and Household Size; Their Effects on Food Consumption," Marketing Research Report 340 (Washington, D.C.: U.S. Department of Agriculture, Agricultural Marketing Service, June 1959), p. 58.

Income elasticity estimates for the United States for specified food groups are: cereals, −0.5; vegetables, 0.25; milk, 0.05; meat, 0.35; eggs, 0.0; and fish, 0.3. In contrast, estimates for India, where the per capita income level is only 1/35 of the United States average, are: cereals, 0.5; vegetables, 1.0; milk, 1.7; meat, 1.4; eggs, 2.2; and fish, 1.5. See U.S. Department of Agriculture, Economic Research Service, "The World Food Budget 1970," Foreign Agricultural Economic Report No. 19, October 1964, Table 8, p. 21.

other and might be called *neutral*. Beef, fresh tomatoes, frozen fruits, and cookies are examples of superior foods; potatoes, evaporated milk, and flour are good examples of inferior foods (Table 10-2). For food purchased away from home, the income elasticity of demand is estimated at 0.8.

Measured at farm or retail level.   The income elasticity for farm food products is in the neighborhood of 0.1, while the income elasticity at retail is 0.4–0.5. The difference is associated with the high income elasticity (1.0 to 1.3) of the services added by agencies in the marketing channel. Consumers are more willing to purchase added convenience with their food than more basic food. As this trend continues, the income elasticity of food approaches zero as income increases.

Family residence.   The rural population consumes more home-produced food than urban consumers do, and this influences income elasticity. Excluding services, the quantity of all food consumed per person varies with the level of income from farm to nonfarm to urban, but has quite a low income elasticity. In addition, "the quantity of purchased foods consumed per person varies much more with level of income among rural families than does the quantity of all foods, which includes home-produced supplies." Also, "the value of food-marketing services per person bought with food, both in retail stores and in eating places, varies with level of income two to three times as much as the quantity of food per se consumed among families within each urbanization category."[3]

Prices of Competing Products

If the consumer finds the price of beef high, he may substitute pork for it as meat for the family table. It should be apparent that there are various degrees of substitutability among foods. Fruits may not be appropriate substitutes for meat, but chicken may be substituted directly when chicken prices are lower than pork. Cheese and egg dishes with brown rice and yogurt salad may be an even more nutritious substitute, as well as a cheaper one.

Supply of Products

Basically, whatever food is produced is consumed. If nature cooperates to produce an abundant crop of carrots, per capita consumption of carrots will tend to increase. The increased quantity on the market will drive prices down and induce consumers to purchase the extra

---

[3] Marguerite C. Burk, "Relationship Between Income and Food," *Journal of Farm Economics,* Volume 44 (February 1962), 122.

TABLE 10-2

Household Food Use in Families of Various Income
Levels, Selected Families, Spring 1965

	Average Household Use per Week (pounds)	Income After Taxes (percent of average)			
		$2,000– $4,000	$6,000– $8,000	$10,000– $15,000	Over $15,000
Meat:					
Beef	5.43	75	123	128	153
Pork	3.60	99	115	108	115
Chicken	2.62	106	111	107	122
Eggs (dozen)	1.84	107	109	102	112
Vegetables:					
Potatoes	4.82	113	113	98	89
Fresh tomatoes	1.09	83	119	123	172
Fresh cabbage	0.65	108	103	83	83
Fresh lettuce	1.30	81	118	146	183
Canned	2.93	105	119	104	98
Frozen	0.62	73	119	177	221
Fruit:					
Fresh citrus	2.51	85	115	140	148
Fresh bananas	1.45	86	121	123	135
Fresh cantaloupe	0.37	65	138	162	308
Canned	1.59	81	118	123	129
Frozen	0.05	40	120	440	480
Fluid milk (quarts)	8.90	82	121	124	131
Evaporated milk	0.62	160	95	100	63
Cheese	1.16	74	121	130	141
Flour	1.56	147	87	53	45
Prepared flour mixes	0.48	81	121	123	146
Cornmeal, grits	0.61	179	56	36	23
Cookies	0.89	78	125	133	142

SOURCE: Calculated from data in U.S. Department of Agriculture, Agricultural Research Service, "Food Consumption of Households in the United States, Spring 1965," Report No. 1, 1968.

amount. This will be particularly true of perishable foods, where storage cannot help to even out the variations in annual supplies.

TRENDS AND PATTERNS IN FOOD
CONSUMPTION IN THE UNITED STATES

Consumers in the United States are fortunate to have adequate supplies of practically all kinds of food. Because of the changing nature of the average diet, total pounds of food consumed per capita annually has decreased by about 100 pounds since World War II. Curiously enough, with one out of three adults overweight, many Americans spend more money losing weight than buying food. Food abundance is also reflected by the fact that on the average, 600 calories per person per day are thrown away with garbage—almost 20 percent of the total purchased for use.

Extensive surveys of food consumption in households of the United States were conducted by the U.S. Department of Agriculture in 1955 and 1965.[4] In 1965, the average size of household was 3.29 persons, with a per capita expenditure for food of $10.64 per week. Of total expenditures, 83 percent was expended for food used at home and the remaining 17 percent for meals and snacks eaten away from home. One-third of the families used some food produced at home, another third received food without direct expense in the form of a gift or pay, and 3 percent received federally donated foods. Seventy percent of the households bought meals and between-meal snacks in restaurants and other eating establishments.

About a third of the dollar spent on food consumed at home went for meat, poultry, fish, and eggs. The next largest proportion, about a fifth, went for vegetables and fruit, including juices. A little over 10 percent was used for milk and milk products other than butter; flour, cereals, and bakery products; and coffee, tea, soft drinks, and alcoholic beverages. Fats, sweets, and all other foods took the remaining money.

The money value of all food averaged about the same for urban and farm households, $36 per week at that time; but the average was slightly lower for rural nonfarm households, $33. Although the money value of their total food was the same, urban and farm families divided this total differently between food used at home and food bought and eaten away from home. Urban families used only $29 worth of food at home per week while farm families used $32 worth. Urban families spent

4 U.S. Department of Agriculture, Agricultural Research Service, "Food Consumption of Households in the United States, Spring 1965," Household Food Consumption Survey 1965–66, Report No. 1, 1968.

more on eating out—$7 per week, compared with $4 for farm families. The effect of income on the level of individual foods has already been discussed.

Home production added greatly to the average value of food used at home by farm families. Nearly all farm families used some home-produced food. They raised nearly one-third of their home food in terms of its money value. Relatively little was raised by nonfarm families.

Changes from 1955 to 1965 showed a decrease in the proportion of the food dollar that went for milk and milk products, an increase in the proportion for grain products because of more purchases of bakery products, and an increase in the proportion for beverages. (See Table 10-3.)

Food Eaten Away from Home

About one meal out of seven eaten by food consumers is eaten away from home. Meals eaten out were either purchased, received free as hospitality, or obtained at school or work.

TABLE 10-3

Consumption of Selected Food Groups by
Households, United States, 1955 and 1965

Food Group	Unit of Measure	Quantity per Household per Week		1965 as Percent of 1955
		1955	1965	
Milk, cream, cheese (calcium equivalent)	Quarts	14.82	13.39	90
Fats, oils	Pounds	2.97	2.70	91
Flour, cereal	Pounds	5.87	4.69	80
Bakery products	Pounds	6.70	7.63	114
Meat, poultry, fish	Pounds	13.78	15.08	110
Eggs	Dozens	2.04	1.84	90
Sugar, sweets	Pounds	4.15	3.70	89
Potatoes, sweet potatoes	Pounds	6.23	5.37	86
Other vegetables, fruit	Pounds	27.14	25.16	93
Soup, other mixtures	Pounds	1.53	1.95	127
Household size	Persons	3.33	3.29	99

SOURCE: U.S. Department of Agriculture, Agricultural Research Service, "Food Consumption of Households in the United States, Spring 1965," Household Food Consumption Survey 1956–66, Report No. 1, p. 3.

The proportion of some foods eaten away from home is related to their association with a certain meal. Seven percent of the morning meals were eaten out, compared to 23 percent of noon and 10 percent of evening meals. As a result, the foods with the lowest percentages consumed away from home were eggs, cereals, and fruits. The highest percentages were for candy, soft drinks, and alcoholic drinks.

Changes within Major Food Groups

Meat. From the economic viewpoint, meat is the most important food in the average diet of civilians in the United States. Since World War II, meat has represented about 25 percent of the total food consumed. Although consumption of pork was usually greater than that of beef in the first half of the century, beef consumption has recently gained over pork (Table 10-4). Beef now represents 61 percent of the total red-meat consumption. Per capita consumption of veal, lamb, and mutton declined in the immediate postwar years, rose between 1952 and 1954, and then drifted downward again. The decrease was sharper for veal than for lamb and mutton.

Although separate data are not available, there have no doubt been

TABLE 10-4

Per Capita Consumption of Red Meats in the
United States for Selected Periods, Primary
Distribution Weight with Percentage Comparison[a]

Period	Beef	Pork[b]	Veal	Lamb and Mutton	Total
		(pounds)[c]			
1909–14	66.2	65.2	6.7	7.0	145.1
1925–29	53.8	56.9	7.3	5.3	133.3
1935–39	55.6	56.5	8.1	6.8	127.0
1947–49	65.6	68.4	9.7	4.8	148.5
1956–59	83.0	64.3	7.7	4.4	159.4
1965–69	106.0	62.3	4.1	3.7	176.1
1970–73	113.1	67.1	2.4	3.1	185.7

[a] Civilian consumption only since 1941; calendar-year basis; 50 states beginning 1964.

[b] Excluding lard.

[c] Carcass weight.

SOURCE: U.S. Department of Agriculture, Economic Research Service, *Livestock and Meat Situation,* May 1967 and December 1973.

important changes in consumption patterns of canned and processed meats. Many new meat specialty items have been introduced in the post-war period. Altogether, canned meats represent about 6 percent of total meat consumption.

The principal factors influencing meat consumption are consumer incomes, consumer customs and habits, and meat production. Essentially, the amount that is produced is consumed. Thus, if cattle numbers are at a peak, there will be more beef produced and this will be reflected in per capita consumption. However, improvements in animal-production prac-tices and in their application, particularly in environmental control, have tended to reduce the cyclical pattern in beef production.

Income of consumers is among the most important factors affecting the demand for meat. Surveys indicate that beef, veal, and lamb con-sumption increase with income levels, while pork fluctuates over the in-come scale (Table 10-2). Families with high levels of income also tend to buy more expensive types and cuts of meat.

Custom and habit are also important influences on the type and cut of meat that people consume. These factors change slowly and have a moderating effect on consumption patterns. In the South, pork consump-tion is higher than in any other region and has not been altered much by rising incomes. Veal and lamb consumption is also highly concen-trated geographically. Education about nutrition, and food promotion and advertising also have their effects.

The United States is fifth in per capita meat consumption. Fifteen countries enjoy more than 100 pounds of meat per person per year, nine of which are in Western Europe. About half the 99 billion pounds con-sumed in the world in 1960, excluding Communist China, was beef and veal, 41 percent was pork, 8 percent lamb, mutton, and goat, and the remainder was horsemeat.

Fish. Total fish consumption has been relatively stable, at 10 to 11 pounds per capita (Table 10-5). In relation to consumption of all foods between 1947 and 1949, fish consumption reached a high of about 3 percent in 1929 and again in 1935 to 38. It declined to 2 per cent of all food consumed in World War II years and has stabilized at that point. These data reflect only commercial fish. It is difficult to estimate the extent of game fish caught and consumed, but the amount is thought to average about 1.2 pounds per capita.

Poultry. Fried chicken for Sunday dinner is no longer a treat for most Americans. Continuing improvements in breeding and rearing methods, along with relatively low feed prices, have resulted in making chicken one of the least expensive types of meat. Consumption of "ready-to-cook"

TABLE 10-5

Per Capita Consumption of Fish and Poultry Products
in the United States for Selected Periods, Primary ·
Distribution Weight with Percentage Comparisons[a]

| Period | Fish | Poultry | | |
	Total (pounds)	Eggs (number)	Chicken (pounds)	Turkey
1909–14	NA	302	14.8	NA
1925–29	NA	330	14.3	NA
1935–39	11.0	300	13.4	2.2
1947–49	10.5	385	18.7	3.3
1956–59	10.4	357	26.8	5.8
1966–69	11.0	319	37.5	8.2
1970–73	11.8	311	41.9	8.0

[a] Civilian consumption only since 1941. Data on a calendar-year basis. Includes available data for Alaska and Hawaii beginning in 1960.

NA = Not available.

SOURCE: U.S. Department of Agriculture, Economic Research Service, *National Food Situation*, No. 146, November 1973.

chicken has tripled since 1939, while consumption of turkey is up by four times.

Poultry-meat output expanded at a more rapid pace than demand, with the result that prices fell drastically. Low prices, in turn, stimulated consumption. Exports of broilers, turkeys, and other fowl have increased dramatically. Per capita egg consumption reached a peak in 1949, falling steadily since that time. Increased egg output per hen has been spurred by new technologies in breeding and rearing. The result is a sagging egg price. Technologists are searching for new uses for eggs to impede falling consumption, but as yet have not been successful. Breakfast cereals plus declining emphasis on the breakfast meal have had a negative effect on egg consumption.

Fats and oils.[5]   Total consumption in the past 40 years has increased about 20 percent, and major shifts have occurred in the use of food fats and oils. Substitution among the three major food-fat groups (table spreads, cooking fats, and cooking and salad oils) has continued. The

---

[5] Data in this section taken from U.S. Department of Agriculture, Economic Research Service, *The Fats and Oils Situation*, various issues.

reduced consumption of table spreads, particularly butter, has been off-set by increases in other edible oils. Butter consumption in 1972 was only 29 percent of that of 1935–39, while margarine consumption was nearly four times higher (Table 10-6). The combined consumption of table spreads (butter and margarine) averaged about 20 pounds per capita prior to World War II. In 1946 it was reduced to a record low of 14.4 pounds. Since then, recovery has been slow, and it appears stabilized at about 16 pounds. The increased use of mayonnaise and cheese spreads, along with declining use of bread and potatoes, are factors contributing to the fall in per capita fat and oil consumption.

The rapidly rising role of margarine is largely attributed to a favorable price ratio and the removal of restrictive legislation. In 1959, the price of butter averaged 2.7 times that of margarine. Also, government purchase programs and price supports have tended to keep butter prices relatively high. Beginning in July 1950, the federal excise tax of 10 cents per pound on colored margarine and one-fourth of a cent per pound on uncolored margarine was repealed. The same legislation lifted the annual retailer's, wholesaler's, and manufacturer's tax imposed on the

TABLE 10-6
Per Capita Consumption of Fats and Oils in the United States for Selected Periods, Primary Distribution Weight with Percentage Comparisons[a]

Period	Butter	Margarine, Actual Weight (pounds)	Lard	Shortening	Other Edible Fats and Oils[b]
1904–47	17.2	1.4	11.5	NA	NA
1925–29	17.7	2.4	12.5	9.5	NA
1935–39	17.0	2.9	11.0	11.8	6.5
1947–49	10.6	5.6	12.4	9.6	7.3
1955–59	8.5	8.6	9.6	11.3	10.8
1966–69	5.6	10.7	5.4	16.3	15.8
1970–73	5.0	11.2	4.0	16.9	19.1

a Civilian consumption since 1941.

b Includes fats and oils used in cooking; in salad oils, salad dressing, and mayonnaise; in bakery products; and in minor uses, such as fish canning.

NA = Not available.

SOURCE: U.S. Department of Agriculture, Economic Research Service, *National Food Situation*, No. 146, November 1973.

margarine industry. Acceptance of margarine has steadily improved with standardization and general quality improvement. Margarine manufacturers have also conducted a vigorous merchandising and promotional campaign, particularly since World War II. The increased consumption of margarine was made possible by the sharp growth in domestic output of edible vegetable oils in the last 25 years. The largest source of fats and oils for margarine—85 percent in 1959—was soybeans. Prior to the war, cottonseed oil was the major constituent.

Except during World War II, when use of all food fats declined, the "other edible" category (mostly cooking and salad oils) has shown a steady growth. Consumption per person rose from 3.5 pounds in 1921 to about 20 pounds in 1972. Of this total, about 30 percent is oil used in mayonnaise and salad dressing. Commercial use of oils in production of potato chips, frozen french fries, and other prepared foods and food mixes has been rising. For example, per capita consumption of frozen french fried potatoes increased from an estimated 6.6 pounds in 1960 to over 34 pounds in 1974. An increase also occurred in potato chips, from 11.6 pounds consumed per person in 1960 to over 17 pounds in 1974.

Dairy products.[6]   The study of consumption trends for dairy products is one of sharp contrasts. There has been a decline in the use of milk-fat solids and a rise in the use of milk nonfat solids. Fluid milk and cream consumption declined in the postwar period, after reaching a high of 359 pounds per capita in 1947–49. New low-fat and skim products have been introduced, with increasing consumer acceptance. Sour cream is an example of a new lower-fat cream product.

Use of cheese has more than doubled since 1930 and continues to increase steadily. Postwar increases have averaged 40 percent for a number of varieties of whole- and part-whole-milk cheeses, such as Swiss, cream, brick, Münster, and Italian varieties. Use of cottage cheese has been constant at 4–5 pounds since 1950.

Increased consumer incomes, the widening of the distribution system at retail, and increased use of refrigerators and freezer appliances are primary factors influencing ice-cream consumption. Ice milk, with a low fat content, has gained wide consumer acceptance (Table 10-7).

The major influences affecting consumption of dairy products are growth of the total population, changes in consumer's tastes and preferences, and changes in supply and price of competing products. This list is little different than for any other food product.

---

[6] Data in this section taken from U.S. Department of Agriculture, Economic Research Service, *The Dairy Situation,* various issues.

TABLE 10-7

Per Capita Consumption of Dairy Products in the
United States for Selected Periods, Primary
Distribution Weight with Percentage Comparisons[a]

Period	Fluid Milk and Cream[b]	Cheese[c]	Condensed and Evaporated Milk[d] (pounds)	Ice Cream[e]
1909–14	330	4.0	6.9	2.5
1925–29	338	4.5	12.0	9.9
1935–39	330	5.6	16.8	9.9
1947–49	359	7.0	20.1	18.7
1955–59	346	8.0	15.3	18.1
1965–69	286	10.2	9.2	18.1
1970–73	259	12.7	6.6	17.6

[a] Civilian consumption only since 1941. Data on calendar-year basis.
[b] Includes cream in terms of whole-milk equivalent.
[c] Whole- and part-whole-milk cheese; excludes full-skim, cottage, pot, baker's.
[d] Case and bulk goods, unskimmed only.
[e] Product weight.
SOURCE: U.S. Department of Agriculture, Economic Research Service, *Dairy Situation,* June and November 1962, and July 1967; and *National Food Situation,* No. 146, November 1973.

Because young people use more fluid milk than older people, any shift toward a younger population would tend to increase milk consumption. It would seem that this might be an important factor in the United States, but there is the tempering effect of an increased proportion of people in the older age group.

In recent years, new beliefs, often in conflict with each other concerning the effect of different foods on the human body, have come into vogue. Some have undoubtedly had an effect on the consumption of dairy products. The fact that one out of three adults is overweight has made many people conscious of low-fat diets for weight control. In addition, the controversy over the effect of cholesterol found in animal fats as related to the incidence of heart disease has tended to slow down the sale of milk products with high degrees of butterfat.

Rising per capita incomes have impeded the decline in dairy-product consumption, as evaporated milk is the only product that does not increase in consumption with income. However, despite rising incomes and more families shifting to higher income brackets, the actual consumption of dairy products on a milk-fat basis has declined. Adding further significance to the decline is the fact that retail prices for dairy products as a group have risen less than food products in general since 1949.

Institutional and technological changes in the dairy industry have also affected consumption. With increased specialization on dairy farms, the number of farms keeping cows has dropped. Many of the people who formerly consumed milk and cream in large quantities from home production now purchase milk and other dairy products. Technological developments have enabled dairy farmers to produce increased quantities of milk at the same relative prices. Developments in refrigeration, processing, and bulk handling methods have also made it advantageous for the farmer to sell a larger proportion of milk as whole milk. This has influenced available market supplies of milk solids.

For decades, the importance of milk in the diets of young people has been stressed. Two programs developed by the federal government have directly affected consumption of milk. Under the School Lunch Act of 1946, which endorsed the School Lunch Program, substantial quantities of milk, butter, cheese, and nonfat dry milk were distributed to schools. In addition, the Special Milk Program of 1954 was designed to stimulate consumption of fluid whole milk by schoolchildren. The government paid a major share of the cost. Milk distributed under these programs accounted for about 6 percent of total national consumption of fluid milk and cream in 1969. The government program of supplementing costs of milk and butterfat also influences consumption. Although the first effect is to raise prices to producers and consumers, it encourages farmers to produce larger quantities of milk.

Fruit.[7]   Per capita consumption of fruit in the United States since 1910 is characterized by a rising trend in volume consumed, which has leveled off since 1950, and by a continuing shift in emphasis from fresh to processed fruit. Fresh and processed fruit, combined on a fresh-equivalent basis, increased to a record level of 227.9 pounds per capita in 1946, 43 pounds higher than the 1910–14 average. Recently, the total has been fluctuating around 200 pounds, some 40 to 45 percent of which is citrus fruits. About half this total is fresh and half is processed.

Fresh-fruit consumption per capita has trended downward for 50 years and in 1970–73 was only slightly over half the average for 1909–14 (Table 10-8). However, citrus fruits, principally oranges and grapefruit,

---

[7] Data in this section taken from U.S. Department of Agriculture, Economic Research Service, *The Fruit Situation,* various issues.

TABLE 10-8

Per Capita Consumption of Fresh and Processed
Fruits in the United States for Selected Periods, Primary
Distribution Weight with Percentage Comparisons[a]

Item	1909–14[f]	1925–29	1935–39	1947–49 (pounds)	1955–59	1965–69	1970–73
Total fresh:[b]	146.1	142.6	137.0	130.3	99.6	80.2	79.0
Citrus	18.6	31.9	48.5	53.9	36.4	28.9	28.2
Apples[c]	65.9	46.3	30.3	25.2	20.8	15.9	17.1
Others[d]	61.7	64.4	58.4	51.2	42.6	35.4	33.7
Canned fruit	4.0	11.9	14.8	18.1	22.3	23.0	22.1
Canned juices	0.3	0.2	3.9	15.9	14.9	13.2	15.4
Frozen[e]	–	0.3	0.8	3.2	8.7	9.1	10.5
Dried	4.0	6.0	5.8	3.9	3.4	2.9	2.5

a Civilian consumption only since 1971. Data on a calendar-year basis except for dried fruits, which are on a pack-year basis, and canned fruits, on pack-year basis 1935–39.
b Farm weight.
c Commercial.
d Excluding melons.
e Including juices.
f Tangerines not included.
SOURCE: U.S. Department of Agriculture, Economic Research Service, *The Fruit Situation,* August 1962, August 1967, September 1971; and *National Food Situation,* No. 146, November 1973.

showed consistent increases into the 1940s but have since declined in favor of canned and frozen citrus fruits.

One of the most striking features of fruit consumption in the United States in the twentieth century is the fivefold increase in per capita consumption of processed fruits. These increases more than offset the decreases for fresh fruits. Processed fruits can be categorized broadly as canned, dried, or frozen. Canned fruits and fruit juices trended slowly upward into the mid-1930s and then jumped sharply until the late 1940s, leveling off since then. Canned citrus juices accounted for most of the increase and also the postwar decrease. The postwar decrease in canned juices, however, was more than compensated for by the sharp increase in frozen fruits and juices, especially orange concentrate.

The trends just discussed were the result of many factors. The increase in total fruit consumption was principally due to increased production of both citrus and noncitrus fruits. The shift in emphasis from fresh to processed fruits was largely due to new product and processing technologies that made canned and frozen products available throughout the year. The decline in dried-fruit consumption in the last 25 years is due to consumers' preference for fruit in canned and frozen forms. Consumers now have a wide selection of fruits in all forms throughout the year.

Vegetables.[8]   Fresh-vegetable consumption per capita reached a high of 120.4 pounds during 1947–49, declining 20 percent to just under 100 pounds in 1970–73 (Table 10-9). The current level is about 10 pounds less than fifty years ago. The total per capita annual consumption on a fresh-equivalent basis has remained quite stable at about 200 pounds, but there have been important changes in the form in which these vegetables are sold. Frozen-vegetable consumption has increased by over seven times since 1949, while fresh vegetables declined 20 percent (Table 10-9). Frozen vegetables retain many of the desirable characteristics of fresh vegetables, are easy to prepare, and are widely available throughout the year at relatively stable prices. Canned-vegetable consumption increased 30 percent in the same period. Fresh salad items, such as lettuce and celery, have maintained their position, but for most other vegetables, consumers now prefer frozen to fresh. Of the ten principal vegetables[9] used both in fresh and processed forms, only sweet corn and cucumbers escaped a decline.

Factors influencing the shift from fresh to processed forms are similar to those mentioned for fruit. The shift of the population from rural to urban areas, which decreases production for home use, rising consumer incomes, the increasing production and availability of processed vegetables throughout the year at relatively stable prices, and the convenience to the housewife in using canned and frozen vegetables have all contributed to the changing pattern.

Sugar.   Refined-sugar consumption has been steady at about 100 pounds for 50 years (Table 10-10). Over the years there has been a slow but steady decline in the proportion of sugar delivered in consumer-size packages. This merely means that people are consuming an increasing proportion of sugar in processed food products.

---

[8] Data in this section taken from U.S. Department of Agriculture, Economic Research Service, *The Vegetable Situation*, various issues.

[9] Asparagus, lima beans, snap beans, broccoli, cabbage, corn, cucumbers, green peas, spinach, and tomatoes.

TABLE 10-9

Per Capita Consumption of Vegetables in the United States
for Selected Periods, Primary Distribution Weight
with Percentage Comparisons[a]

Item	1909– 14	1925– 29	1935– 39	1947– 49 (pounds)	1955– 59	1965– 69	1970– 73
Fresh vegetables	NA	104.9	113.2	120.4	103.3	98.1	98.3
Melons	NA	32.4	27.0	27.4	26.4	22.7	22.7
Canned	17.0	24.2	30.1	39.2	44.4	51.0	51.8
Frozen	NA	NA	0.4[d]	2.9	7.9	16.7	20.4
Potatoes[b]	175.0	144.5	130.0	114.0	101.8	112.8	118.8
Sweet potatoes[b]	24.0	24.1	21.6	12.6	7.3	5.9	5.1
Dry edible beans	6.4	7.9	8.8	6.7	7.6	6.6	6.0
Dry field peas[c]	NA	NA	0.6	0.6	0.6	0.2	0.2

[a] Civilian consumption only since 1941. Excludes home-garden production. Calendar-year basis.

[b] Farm weight. Excludes quantities canned and frozen, which are included with processed vegetables except for 1965–69 and 1972.

[c] Crop-year basis.

[d] 1937–39 average.

NA = Not available.

SOURCE: U.S. Department of Agriculture, Economic Research Service, *The Vegetable Situation,* October 1962, November 1967, October 1972; and *National Food Situation,* No. 146, November 1973.

Cereal grains and products.   Per capita consumption of flour and cereal products has declined 20 percent since the end of World War II, a continuation of the decline registered for the past fifty years. Wheat is by far the most important grain, accounting for 80 percent of the flour and cereal products consumed as food. Corn contributes 10 percent, and oats, barley, rye, rice, and buckwheat make up the remaining 10 percent. On the other hand, per capita consumption of corn syrup has nearly tripled, and corn sugar is up nearly fivefold. Rice has maintained a per capita consumption of five to seven pounds since the 1920s.

One major cause of the decline in grain consumption is the increasing availability of meat, poultry, and vegetables at reasonable prices. Another factor is the decline in physical labor, bringing about a reduced

TABLE 10-10

Per Capita Consumption of Sugar, Grains, and Beverages
for Selected Periods in the United States,
Primary Distribution Weight with Percentage Comparisons[a]

Item	1909–14	1925–29	1935–39	1947–49	1966–69	1970–73
			(pounds)			
Sugar, refined	76.4	101.0	97.4	95.1	98.6	102.8
Corn products:						
Corn meal and flour	48.1	29.1	23.1	12.9	7.2	7.4
Corn syrup	5.1	7.7	7.7	9.9	14.4	17.1
Corn sugar	1.1	5.6	2.7	4.2	4.7	4.9
Wheat:						
Flour[b]	209.0	177.0	160.0	137.0	111.8	110.0
Breakfast cereals	2.7[c]	3.3[c]	3.3	3.2	2.9	2.9
Rice, milled[c]	6.8	5.6	5.8	4.9	7.7	7.1
Coffee[d]	9.2	11.7	14.0	18.2	14.6	13.7
Tea	1.0	0.8	0.7	0.6	0.7	0.8
Cocoa beans[e]	1.5	3.3	4.4	4.1	4.2	4.1
Peanuts, shelled[f]	2.4	3.7	4.3	4.4	5.7	6.1

[a] Civilian consumption only since 1941.

[b] Includes white, whole wheat, and semolina flour.

[c] Rice year beginning August 1. Includes some table rice used by brewers prior to 1934.

[d] Green bean equivalent.

[e] Includes cocoa-bean equivalent of cocoa products imported 1942 to date.

[f] Crop-year basis.

SOURCE: U.S. Department of Agriculture, Economic Research Service, *National Food Situation*, May 1962, February 1968, and November 1973.

need for such high-energy foods as grains. Emphasis on weight control and dieting is frequently mentioned as a contributing factor.

In cereal products, the decline in bread consumption has been in the home-baked form. Commercially baked bread has accounted for an ever-increasing share of the total bread supply. In contrast to bread, other wheat products, including spaghetti, macaroni, vermicelli, and noodles, have maintained a stable consumption level for many years.

NUTRITION AND FOOD CONSUMPTION
IN THE UNITED STATES

Compared to residents of many other countries of the world, the people in the United States spend only a small percentage of their disposable income for food. This fact implies a high standard of living. However, there is growing concern that the quality of nutrition is not keeping pace with food consumption. The proportion of family diets meeting the 1963 recommended dietary allowances of the Food and Nutrition Board of the National Research Council dropped 10 percent between 1955 and 1965. A primary factor appears to be the substitution of soft drinks for milk and of snacks for fruit and vegetables. The result is that more diets have dropped to below standard for calcium, vitamin A, and ascorbic acid. For seven important nutrients, only half the U.S. families met the recommended daily allowance in 1965, with 18.6 percent getting less than two-thirds the allowance in one or more nutrients. The solution to this nutrition problem would seem to be greater consumer education efforts, as much as it is further increases in family income.[10]

---

[10] U.S. Department of Agriculture, Agricultural Research Service, "Dietary Levels of Households in the United States, Spring 1965," Household Food Consumption Survey, 1965–66, Report No. 6, July 1969.

PART
FOUR

PART
FOUR

11

Production Principles

The role of agriculture and economic growth has been discussed in the preceding chapters, as well as the relationships between farming and farm people, and the nonfarm economy. Parts II and III included much data concerning production, marketing, and consumption of food products. Our concern now is with the tools necessary to analyze economic problems and manage businesses.

ELEMENTS OF THE PRODUCTION PROCESS

Production is the transformation of two or more inputs (resources) into one or more products. Transformation takes place by combining the inputs in various amounts for different needs and uses. The word *combining* necessarily implies that there must be more than one input to make a product. If nothing was added, the original resource would simply remain whatever it was. Thus, nothing can be made with less than two inputs, and some products take hundreds of different inputs for their creation.

Think of the various products we use. Each requires some sort of physical resource (metal, wood, cloth, chemicals, etc.), some labor, and some financial arrangement for the production process. Management is also necessary to conceive of the production idea, assume risks, make decisions about production, and solve problems related to the firm's production. Therefore, resources can be classified under four general headings: land, labor, capital, and management.

Land may be thought of as providing the space for production. Factory sites and farmsteads are both set upon land. However, land is not a resource whose quality is evenly distributed over the surface of the world. This uneven distribution gives rise to more production advantages in some areas than in others. Water is usually put in the land-resource classification.

Labor is the physical and mental effort spent in producing goods and services. Tractor drivers and harvest hands are examples of physical labor; draftsmen and engineers use much mental labor in their work. It is important to distinguish between the effort and the agent of labor. The effort of labor is the particular physical or mental skill one can employ. An agent of labor is the human being possessing the skills. The effort can be likened to a *flow* of services; the agent of labor can be compared to a *stock* resource—that is, a stock of human capital.

Capital also includes buildings, machinery, and livestock. The home you live in is a form of capital. Education is another form; it enables a person to contribute to the production process (review Chapter 5).

Management is the final broadly defined resource. Here the individual or group makes choices and decisions concerning the use of land, labor, and capital. Management is the human element in the production process, the element that initiates, modifies, and maintains the production process through its never-ending decisions regarding all the factors of production, including itself. *Management* is used synonymously with *entrepreneurship* in many economic writings.

Farmers producing crops and livestock use several different kinds of inputs. To begin with, they use land as the factory to help in producing the crop. Through this manufacturing plant, they pass machinery and labor to plant, cultivate, and harvest. Fertilizer is added at times decided upon by management. Water may be provided by rain, or supplemental irrigation may be used. The crops in turn are fed to animals, which produce meat, milk, eggs, and many other livestock and poultry products through complex biological processes.

GENERAL DIFFERENCES BETWEEN FARMING AND INDUSTRIAL PRODUCTION

Generalizations concerning both similarities and differences between farming and industrial production do not always hold true. Perhaps the similarities should be stressed more than the differences.

Goals of production and the need for management decisions concerning the allocation of inputs are strikingly similar between the two. However, there are some differences that can be noted in general.

For example, *weather* affects farming much more than it affects manufacturing production. Production indoors goes on despite showers outside, but the farmer cannot get into his fields because of the rain and mud. (Construction is another industry also greatly affected by weather and the seasons.) *Production scheduling* is another factor that differs between most farms and factories. Many production schedules (except feeding, milking, etc.) on a farm can wait a day or two, whereas in a factory operating on strict production schedules, timing of production processes and operations is often more crucial. The farmer is ruled by physical *seasons* of the year, in contrast to industrial production, which is primarily governed by the seasonality of demand for its products.

Hired labor tends to be less specialized on farms than in industrial work. Farm help is generally capable of working at many different jobs, whereas production-line processes, craft and trade unionization, and the emphasis on special skills (electronics, etc.) limit labor flexibility in industry. *Product perishability* is generally evident in farm products to a greater degree than industry. Spoilage of truck crops, bruising of livestock, and shrinkage are examples. Industry, in contrast, is faced with production-line rejects.

There is more invested *capital,* on the average, per worker on the farm than per worker in industry. However, the range in capital investment per worker is probably wider in industry than in farming. Agricultural products are produced by many relatively small production units; the majority of industrial output is produced by large corporations composed of many divisions and plants. The large number of farm firms, combined with their relatively small individual output, places individual farmers in the position of having no effective influence on market quantities and prices. The opposite is frequently true in industry, where a few large firms can exert an influence on the prices of the products they sell and the resources they buy.

Finally, farming, for the majority of people in agriculture, is a combination of home and business. On most farms, production is conducted at the same place the family lives. Work and leisure time are both spent on the farm. This condition does not exist to the same extent in manufacturing.

CONCEPT OF A PRODUCTION FUNCTION

The concept of a production function is really quite simple: Total yield, or output, varies with the quantities of inputs used in the production process. Management must decide the amount of production and the amount and kinds of inputs to be used, because production does not vary evenly as inputs are fed uniformly into the production process. Thus, differences in production response to evenly applied inputs open the doors to economics as an aid to managerial decision making.

Let us discuss a production function using only one varying input of production that, in combination with the fixed inputs, produces only one product. Remember that we are investigating only the *physical* input–output relationships at this time, beginning with the notion that an input has productivity when combined with other resources.

There are three types of production response to an input or factor of production: increasing, constant, or decreasing returns to the variable factor. For example, *increasing marginal returns* (productivity) occur when each unit of added input produces more product than the previous unit of input:[1]

Units of Input	Total Physical Product, or Units of Output	Added Output, or Marginal Physical Product (MPP)
1	1	1
2	3	2
3	6	3
4	10	4
5	15	5

In this case, the second unit of input adds one more unit of product than the first input, the third input adds three units of output compared to only two units of output produced from the second unit of input, and so on.

Constant marginal returns occur when each additional unit of input always yields the same amount of additional product:

Units of Input	Total Physical Product, or Units of Output	Added Output, or Marginal Physical Product (MPP)
1	2	2
2	4	2
3	6	2
4	8	2
5	10	2

---

[1] *Marginal product* is defined as the change in units of total product (total output) divided by the associated change in units of input.

Each additional unit of input produces two additional units of output.

Decreasing marginal returns occur when each additional unit of input yields a relatively smaller amount of additional product:

Units of Input	Total Physical Product, or Units of Output	Added Output, or Marginal Physical Product (MPP)
1	5	5
2	9	4
3	12	3
4	14	2
5	15	1

Less product is added to total product for each additional unit of input than was added by the previous unit of input.

A graphic presentation of these three relationships, taken from the foregoing tables, is shown in Figure 11-1.

The concept of constant returns to an input is the least important of the three. Such a condition is unusual in farming. However, the notions of increasing and decreasing returns are of utmost importance to the theory of production. These two ideas give rise to the laws of variable proportions discussed later.

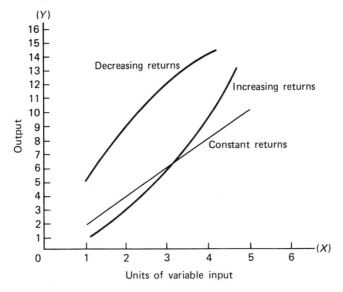

FIGURE 11-1

Increasing, Constant, and Decreasing Returns

Three methods to describe resource productivity have just been presented: verbally, arithmetically in tabular form, and geometrically in the graph. A fourth way to describe resource productivity is by means of an algebraic equation. This fourth method enables us to set up a functional relationship between input and output, which allows us to predict and analyze the consequences of varying the amounts of input used in the production process. The general equation for a production function that results in only one product using only one variable input is:

$$Y = f(X_1 \mid X_2, X_3 \ldots \ldots \ldots, X_n)$$

This equation states that output Y depends on (is a function of) the amount of the variable input (X_1) used in combination with a fixed quantity of other factors of production, X_2, X_3 . . . . . , X_n. In the equation, the bar between the inputs or factors of production separates those factors that vary from those that are fixed in the production process.

Limiting factors are those that are fixed in some way and finally slow down the production process, preventing the increase of total production. For example, the amount of land on any one farm used in crop production for any one crop year is generally fixed at a set amount of acres. Likewise, the amount of labor may be fixed—for example, at two people, the owner-operator and his tenant; capital may be fixed by the amount of the operating bank loan.

Law of diminishing returns. In farm production processes, limiting factors tend to set in at some level of production before total output becomes very great, and thus decreasing returns are the most common type of production response. The point at which increases in (additions to) total output stop occurring at an increasing rate (the same point where marginal physical product, MPP, begins to decline) is also the point where diminishing marginal physical returns begin. The economic law that says this point will always occur is called the *law of diminishing returns*. It states that when successive equal units of a variable resource are added to a given quantity of a fixed resource, there will come a point where the addition to total output will decline.

To test your understanding of the idea of diminishing physical returns, think of what would happen if increasing or constant returns were the case throughout all levels of possible output! It would be possible to feed the whole world's consumption need for milk from the production of one cow, by merely increasing her food intake. Or the world's needs for corn could be satisfied from the production of one acre of land, by simply adding more and more inputs to produce more from this single acre of land.

Production functions.   Combining the ideas of resource productivity and limiting factors, we can now show the concept of a typical production function (Figure 11-2a).

The total amount of output produced as a result of the variable

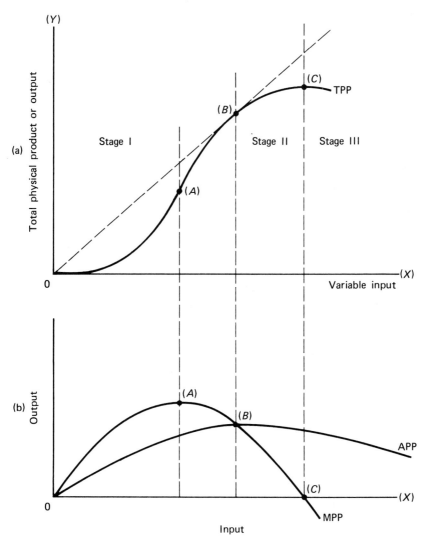

FIGURE 11-2
The Production Function: Total, Marginal, and
Average Products

input and the fixed inputs is known as *total physical product* (TPP). Its general shape is like that of a small hill. Increasing returns at an increasing rate are evident up to point *A* on Figure 11-2a; from *A* to *C*, returns are still increasing but the increase is slowing down (increasing at a decreasing rate); after *C*, TPP decreases because of the harmful effects that occur when the variable input increases.

Marginal and average physical product curves are shown in Figure 11-2b. Let us consider the marginal physical product curve (MPP) first. Marginal production (extra production occurring by adding one more unit of input) is zero when total physical production is zero. As total production increases as indicated by the TPP curve, the marginal physical product curve rises. At *A*, the point on the TPP curve where returns to the variable input shift from increasing at an increasing rate to increasing at a decreasing rate (also called the *inflection point*), marginal physical product is at a maximum. When TPP begins to decrease at *C*, marginal physical product is zero again, and any additional units of input produce a negative marginal physical product. Review the short tables just used to illustrate increasing, constant, and decreasing returns.

Average physical product (APP) is also zero when there is no production. Its maximum height occurs at *B*, the point at which the ratio of output to input is greatest. (This point can be found easily by drawing a line from the origin tangent to the TPP curve. This line has the greatest slope—the ratio of output to input—at the point of tangency to the TPP curve. Thus, the maximum height of the APP curve lies directly below the point of tangency.) Average physical product becomes zero again if and when TPP also becomes zero.

The production function (TPP) is divided into three stages. In stage I (up to point *B*), marginal physical product (MPP) is always greater than average physical product (APP). As long as it pays to produce at all, it will pay to add inputs and produce through stage I. In stage III (beyond point *C*), total production is decreasing and marginal physical product is less than zero, thus making it irrational for production because you simply get less and less product for increasing amounts of input. Stage II (from point *B* to point *C*) becomes the relevant part of the production function for profitable production to take place. However, physical conditions alone will not determine the profitability of production. One needs to know something about product prices and input (factor) costs. The points to remember from this discussion are that stage II is the only "rational" production stage, while stage I and III are "irrational" production stages; and that physical data alone do not decide the profitability of a production process. The data in Table 11-1 illustrate the three stages of the production function.

TABLE 11-1

Hypothetical Total, Average, and Marginal Products
Related to Production Stages I, II, and III

	Number of Units of Input	Total Product (TPP)	Average Product (APP)	Marginal Product (MPP)
	1	1	1	1
Stage I	2	6	3	5
	3	9	3	3
Stage II	4	11	2.75	2
	5	12	2.4	1
Stage III	6	11	1.8	− 1

Effect of New Technology

Technology has the effect of raising the production function; that is, of producing more product per unit of input (Figure 11-3). Generally speaking, more output is produced for each unit of input. This means that more total output can be produced by or from the inputs that were used prior to the technological innovation, or the same amount of total output can be produced with fewer resources. These effects are quantitative. Sometimes qualitative changes are included in the new products;[2] however, qualitative changes are extremely difficult to measure and are usually resolved through the pricing system rather than through analysis of the production function.

In either the quantitative or qualitative case, technology changes the production function. Changes in total output per unit of input cause changes in the most profitable level of use of the factors used in production. The technological change may call for increased use of certain factors because of a more complex production technique (special fertilizer and feed mixtures, for example); or they may call for decreased use of a factor (less labor is needed to produce a bushel of corn). Review Chapter 6, which dealt with technology in more detail.

Continuous and Discontinuous Factor and Product Relationships

A continuous input–output relationship may be thought of as a smooth curve with no breaks or bumps in it. Continuity implies that

---

[2] Some economists, notably T. W. Schultz, argue that the production function shifts simply because some input has not been identified. If all inputs could be identified, the production function would not shift. The point is that conventional accounting of inputs does not include technological change.

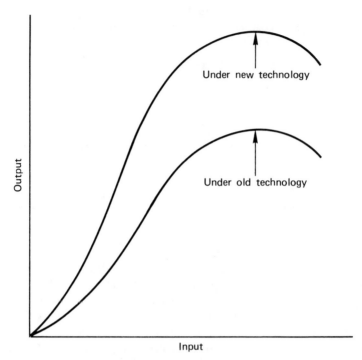

FIGURE 11-3
The Impact of Technology on the Production Function

minute fractions of inputs may be used to produce minute fractions of output. Feed and fertilizer may sometimes be bought and used in fractions of pounds, and the resulting output measured.

However, in agricultural production, there are few opportunities for such factor and product continuity to exist. Many factors of production are not minutely divisible. A farmer cannot buy half a tractor, a third of a combine, or a fourth of a cow. He has to buy "lumps" of inputs. Even most fertilizer and feed inputs are bought in bulk units to save money. Discontinuous relationships look like steps when graphed.

Input combinations. There are several types of input (factor) combinations: complements, substitutes, single, multiple, and fixed. Inputs are *complements* when they are combined in fairly definite proportions in the production process. An example is a one-man-one-tractor type of operation. Factors are *substitutes* when the production function allows one input to be substituted for another input. Livestock rations in the Midwest, which use corn as a carbohydrate, may have barley substituted if the ration is used in the West or if corn prices become too high relative to barley. Silage and hay are sometimes used as substitutes by cattle feeders and dairymen. Production processes can be studied by changing one variable while holding others constant (single-variable analysis), or by changing two or more inputs (multiple analysis). A *fixed* factor of production is one that remains constant in amount regardless of the production process with which it is concerned. For example, an acre of ground planted to corn remains an acre of ground regardless of how much corn is planted, how much fertilizer is applied, or how much labor is used to cultivate and harvest the corn crop.

There are three types of production management decisions directly related to the concept of a production function and input combination. These decisions may be classified as (1) factor-factor decisions, (2) factor-product decisions, and (3) product-product decisions. These help decide what products to produce, how to produce them, and how much to produce of any product.

Types of Production Decisions

Factor-factor decisions.   In this type of decision, the farmer must decide which inputs he will use in the production of a particular product and how the amounts of each used might vary in response to changes in their prices. For example, the dairy-farm manager may vary the combination of grain and hay in his herd's ration, letting the cows have free-choice silage. Criteria for changing the proportion of hay and grain will depend both on the amount of milk production desired and the relative prices of the two inputs. A factor-factor decision means a substitution of one factor of production for another. It does not necessarily mean, although it may by chance happen, that one factor will be substituted entirely for the other factor. It is more a process of varying input proportions within certain limits than of using mutually exclusive (one or the other) inputs. The degree of substitution will depend upon the price of the two factors and how well they will substitute for one another.

Factor-product decisions.   This is the general type of decision with which we began the discussion of a production function. Output is dependent upon the amount of a single variable input that was combined with certain fixed resources. Also included in the decision classification are multifactor single-product or multiproduct decisions. For example, corn and protein supplement are multifactors used in the production of pork. But corn and silage (multifactor) may also produce mutton and wool (multiproducts). A further example of multifactor, multiproduct relationships would be a farm on which fertilizer and water were used to produce a cover crop in addition to a seed crop later that same season.

Product-product decisions. In this decision category, farm managers decide how many enterprises they will have on the farm and how much production each enterprise will attain. If a farmer has a feedlot operation and a group of sows, he must figure how many cattle and sows he can manage profitably with the resources at his disposal.

Some enterprises are *complementary;* by increasing the production of one enterprise, you automatically produce more of another. An example of crop complementarity is grass and alfalfa; as alfalfa production is increased, up to a point, more grass is also produced. Crop rotations are also examples of complementary enterprises. The nitrogen-increased organic matter and improved soil structure left by producing legumes leads to increases in the next crop planted on the field.

Competition between enterprises occurs when the output of one can be increased only by reducing production of the other enterprise. Crop or livestock operations that require the same resources at the same time are competitive. For example, if two crops must be harvested immediately, they are competitive for the resources of labor and capital (the combine) used in harvest. Competition between enterprises occurs only when all production resources are being used.

Enterprise *supplementarity* is evident in those operations that use the same resources at different times during the production season. For example, the first crop of hay is usually made before the winter grains are harvested, and both of these are out of the way before the fall corn harvest. In this case, hay, winter grains, and corn harvest supplement each other with respect to using available labor and machinery. Livestock and crops may also be supplementary enterprises with respect to labor resources over the years. Feeder stock may be bought to feed throughout the winter when the farmer is not working in the fields.

Specialization, diversification, and intensive and extensive farm management. As farmers make decisions concerning enterprise selection and resource combination, they necessarily make decisions about whether they will operate a diversified farm or a specialized one. A specialized farmer is usually one who receives a major portion of his farm income from one source (crops, livestock, dairy, poultry, etc.). Specialization offers a farmer the opportunity to engage in intensive management and production, since he has the time and the motivation to dig deeply into the technology of a particular type of production and put it into effect. The result is to produce a relatively large amount of output from a proportionately small amount of input (often from a relatively small physical or geographic area).

Specialization offers farmers the chance to produce in volume and thus capitalize on the benefits of doing business on a big scale. Feed, fertilizer, and other resources may be bought in volume at lower costs for a large enterprise that would not be economic under small-scale management. Specialization also offers unique distribution and marketing contacts that might result in higher prices truly reflecting the quality of product produced.

Disadvantages of specialization are evident when the manager realizes that "all his eggs are in one basket." In many ways, a specialized farmer is more vulnerable to market-price fluctuation than is a diversified farmer. He tends to cash in when the market price is up, but he is also apt to lose relatively more when the market price declines. His enterprise inputs and management may not be flexible enough to shift over to another enterprise. For example, a milking parlor can effectively be used only to milk cows. It is not adapted to produce pigs or chickens. One way to eliminate much of the risk of being a specialized farmer and still remain specialized is to gain some control of the market channels. He may contract with a market agency to sell his output at some stipulated price (this practice is sometimes called *prearranged selling*), or he may organize and manage his own distribution outlets (a type of vertical integration). Examples of farmer groups organized to accomplish this goal include the citrus fruit growers, the walnut and filbert growers, and the cotton producers who organized a marketing cooperative to sell their product.

A diversified farm operation is one that has several production enterprises. The principal reasons that diversification appeals to many farmers, particularly smaller farm operators, are that (1) diversification tends to more fully utilize all the resources of the farm unit, and (2) diversification tends to reduce the risk of financial failure due to the failure of one or more crops or loss of animals through livestock diseases. Diversification is generally thought to spread the financial risks involved in farming. While prices of one enterprise may fall drastically, it is unlikely that all farm prices will fall to the bottom together.

A diversified farming operation may be intensive or extensive in the same manner as a specialized farm. Intensive production means that full use is made of all fixed resources through application of all relevant technology.

Intensity of production leads to relatively large amounts of output from a relatively small resource base. Extensive production can also be specialized production, but in this case a large quantity of fixed input is usually needed for production. An example of a specialized-intensive operation would be the "milk factories" in Los Angeles, in which cows are milked continuously 24 hours a day and all inputs are purchased and used on a small amount of land. An example of a specialized-extensive operation would be a cattle or sheep ranch, where a great many acres of range land are needed to feed the livestock.

Whether a farm is diversified or specialized depends primarily upon

the farm manager. His decision, based on his interests, experience, quali-
fications, desires, and goals, will determine the extent to which his farm
is specialized or diversified.

The Law of Comparative Advantage

At first glance it would seem that the advantage of any system of
farming in a given area would be determined by the physical yields possible, which are heavily influenced by climate and topography. However,
economic aspects must be included to get a truer picture. For example,
the Corn Belt region of the United States (from a physical-yield standpoint) produces more than other regions in many crop enterprises, including corn, wheat, potatoes, and fruit. The Great Plains region
specializes in wheat, and other areas specialize in fruit and other commodities. The answer to this phenomenon lies in the law of comparative
advantage, which says, "To maximize profits, one should produce those
things, considering yields, costs, and returns, from which the percentage
return above cost is greatest."

Let us look at an example. To keep matters simple, assume that
there are only two producers and consumers in the world, who will be
designated as farmers A and B. Their consumption needs are 60 bushels
of corn and 60 bushels of wheat each. Farmer A is the more efficient producer in both corn and wheat, since with his inputs he can produce six
bushels of corn in a day's work or four bushels of wheat, while farmer
B's efforts will get him only one bushel of corn or two bushels of wheat.
Farmer A has an *absolute advantage* in the production of both corn and
wheat, or is in a position similar to that of the Corn Belt region in the
production of corn and wheat.

Now, if both farmers provide for their own consumption needs,
farmer A will need to work 10 days to get his corn and 15 days to provide his wheat. Farmer B will work 60 days to get his corn and 30 days
for his wheat. In other words, farmer A will work a total of 25 days and
farmer B will have to work 90 days.

A logical question arises as to what benefits would be derived for
each if they would specialize in the production of one crop and trade
with each other. It seems clear that farmer B would gain from any such
proposition, but it is not immediately apparent that A would gain. Let
us check.

Using the principle of comparative advantage, farmer A should specialize in corn, where he has the *most* advantage (6 to 1), and farmer B
should specialize in wheat, where he has the least disadvantage (2 to 4).
Quick arithmetic tells us that total expenditure by farmer A to produce
corn for their combined consumption needs is 20 days. Farmer B needs

to work 60 days to provide wheat for himself and farmer A. Farmer A has thus saved five days work, and farmer B has saved 30 days. In total, 35 days have been saved.

In this instance, farmer A has a comparative advantage in the production of corn, and farmer B has a comparative advantage in the production of wheat. It is this economic law that makes it profitable for both rich and poor nations of the world to trade with each other. Each country specializes where it has a *comparative* advantage, even though it may have an *absolute* advantage or disadvantage in all products. An important idea in comparative advantage is that just because an enterprise is profitable (a positive difference after subtracting costs from returns), it does not necessarily mean that the product should be produced. A manager looks for those enterprises that are most profitable relative to all his production choices and his trade possibilities.

The following appendix can be studied by those who wish to delve deeper into production relationships and principles. However, it is not essential, since the stage is now set to move from the physical aspects of the production process to considerations of dollars and cents as they relate to production.

APPENDIX TO CHAPTER 11

This section is designed for those who wish to study the principles of production more deeply than the previous material permitted. This appendix is technical and should be treated as supplementary to the prior presentation.

Optimum Use of a Single Variable Input Used in a Factor-Product Relationship

The rule in this situation is to use an input until the value of the last unit of output it creates just pays for the last unit of input used. Another way of saying this is that optimum use of an input occurs when the marginal value product (MVP) of the resource is equal to the price (P) of the resource. Algebraically, the equation is:

$$(1) \quad MVP_{X_1} = P_{X_1}, \text{ when } MVP_{X_1} = MPP_{X_1} \cdot P_Y$$

or

$$(2) \quad \frac{MVP_{X_1}}{P_{X_1}} = 1$$

When:

> MPP = marginal physical product produced by last unit of input X_1
> P_{X_1} = price of a unit of input
> P_Y = price of product Y
> MVP_{X_1} = marginal value product of input X_1

This equation indicates that the use of input X_1 should be increased if MVP_{X1} is greater than P_{X1}; that less of X_1 should be used if MVP_{X1} is less than P_{X1}; and that the optimum use of X_1 is attained when MVP_{X1} just equals P_{X1}. What this algebraic rule says is this: Use a unit of X_1 to produce product Y if the value of product Y produced from a unit of X_1 is equal to, or greater than, the cost of X_1. Remember that although this is the general rule, changing factor and product prices and changing technology will change the answer to a specific problem.

Optimum Combination of Two or More Variable Inputs and One Product (Factor-Factor Relationships)

Equation (2) can easily be expanded to include the combining of two or of an infinite number of variable inputs. The form is:

$$(3) \quad \frac{MVP_{X_1}}{P_{X_1}} = \frac{MVP_{X_2}}{P_{X_2}} = \cdots = \frac{MVP_{X_n}}{P_{X_n}} = 1$$

where $X_1, X_2, \ldots, X_n$ are all variable inputs.
If equation (3) is divided through by the price of the product, P_Y, we have:

$$(4) \quad \frac{MPP_{X_1}}{P_{X_1}} = \frac{MPP_{X_2}}{P_{X_2}}$$

or

$$(5) \quad \frac{MPP_{X_1}}{MPP_{X_2}} = \frac{P_{X_1}}{P_{X_2}}$$

Equation (5) provides the formula for the optimum proportions of the use of inputs X_1 and X_2 at any set of prices in the production of a relevant product.

A graphic approach may serve to illustrate the algebra. We mentioned previously that the production function looked like a hill. Pretend that you have a huge knife and that as you walk up the hill you take horizontal slices out of the mountain. Then take these circular slices, lay them down in a stack, and look down on them, so that they look much like any topographic map you have seen. The resulting concentric rings (similar to topographic contour lines) are called isoproduct (equal product) lines, each line being a certain fixed amount of production created by varying the amounts of each input. Figure 11-4 shows this concept.

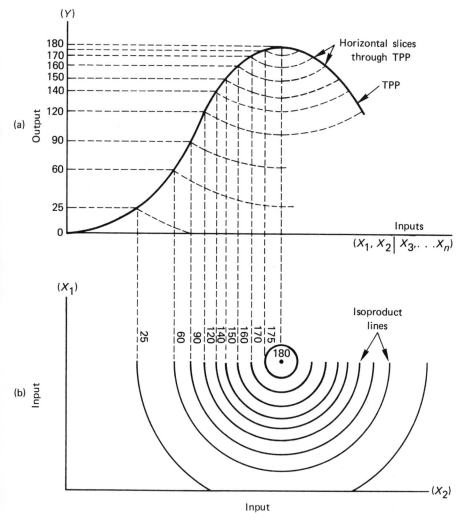

FIGURE 11-4

Production Function and Isoproduct Derivatives

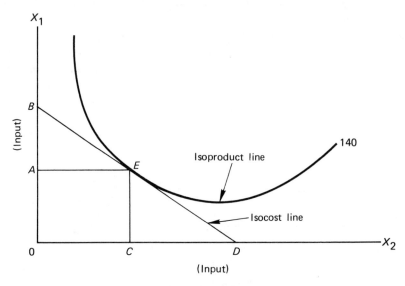

FIGURE 11-5

Diagram Showing the Different Amounts of Resources
X_1 and X_2 Necessary to Produce 140 Units of Product

Note the change in the axes. In Figure 11-4a, the axes are Output and Inputs; in Figure 11-4b, the axes are both Inputs, X_1 and X_2, with output shown on the isoproduct curves. The bunching together of the middle isoproduct curves (90–150) shows that the production-function hill begins to steepen beyond output of 90; the farther apart the rings are, the more gentle the slope of the production function.

Let us take out just one of the isoproduct contours and use it to illustrate the optimum point expressed by equation (5). Figure 11-5 shows this situation.

A given amount of money to be spent on inputs will buy either OB of X_2 or OD of X_1. It will also buy any combination of inputs possible along BD. BD is called the isocost (equal cost) line; that is, any combination of inputs X_1 and X_2 formed from this line cost the same amount. The slope of BD is $\dfrac{-P_{X_1}}{P_{X_2}}$. The slope of the isoproduct curve is $\dfrac{-\text{MPP}_{X_1}}{\text{MPP}_{X_2}}$. Where BD is tangent to the isoproduct contour, the two slopes are equal:

$$\frac{-P_{X_1}}{P_{X_2}} = \frac{-\text{MPP}_{X_1}}{\text{MPP}_{X_2}}$$

Hence, multiplying through by minus one to get rid of the minus signs:

$$(5) \quad \frac{\mathrm{MPP}_{X_1}}{\mathrm{MPP}_{X_2}} = \frac{P_{X_1}}{P_{X_2}}$$

Under the example we have chosen, OA units of X_2 and OC units of X_1 would produce 140 units of product at the given amount of resource expenditures.

This procedure also provides the *least-cost point of input combination* to produce a given amount of product. For example, no combination of resources other than OA units of X_2 and OC units of X_1 can produce 140 units of product at a lesser cost. This can easily be seen by examining the isocost line. The line runs straight from its extremes on the X_2 and X_1 axes to a point of tangency with the isoproduct curve. At no point, under the assumed input expenditures, does the isoproduct line intersect the isocost line. Thus, it can be concluded that E is the least-cost point, using inputs X_1 and X_2, to produce 140 units of product.

Substitution of One Input for Another Under Changing Factor Prices

Let us take the situation described by Figure 11-5, in which the least-cost combination of inputs was determined to produce a set amount of product (140 units), but let us change the prices of inputs to see what the new least-cost combination and production points would look like. Let us assume, as we did before, that there is a certain set sum of money to spend on factors of production. However, let us say that the price of input X_2 increases; we can now buy less of it with a fixed amount of money than we could before. The new isocost line is shown in Figure 11-6 (BF), and the new and old input amounts are compared with the new isoproduct lines.

Under the assumptions of a constant outlay of input expenditures and a price increase in X_2, 140 units of output cannot be achieved. Some lesser amount must be produced, because the amount of X_2 needed in the production of 140 units of output is not feasible under the new price structure. To determine the new lesser amount of production, we proceed as before. The amount of X_1 we can buy at a constant cost outlay is the same as before. The amount of X_2 is lessened because its price has risen, and accordingly the point (F) is nearer the origin. BF is the new isocost line. It happens to be tangent to the 120-unit isoproduct contour at I. This point then becomes the new least-cost combination of X_1 and X_2 to produce 120 units with the original input expenditures. It is also the highest amount of production possible under the new prices, and

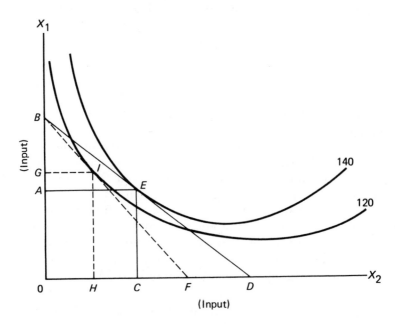

FIGURE 11-6
Factor Substitution under Changing Factor Prices

accordingly, OC and OH become the new amounts of X_1 and X_2, respectively, needed for production.

Optimum Output Combination With Two or More
Enterprises (Product-Product Relationship)

Combining enterprises is a difficult business, since preferences for various kinds of enterprises discount the economics of a situation. Despite these difficulties, the theory of enterprise combination is straightforward. It answers the question, "How can a maximum revenue be obtained from a given cost outlay?"

Figure 11-7a shows several types of production-possibilities curves. Production-possibilities curve (1) shows a decline in one product as the other is increased, but the decline is greater than the increase. This situation would be encountered when a farmer took on a new hired hand and was faced with the prospect of training him. Total production generally decreases in a training situation and can be tolerated only if the trainee improves his knowledge and skill level to the point where total production increases. If it does not increase, the farmer is most likely better off under the old system of management, without the

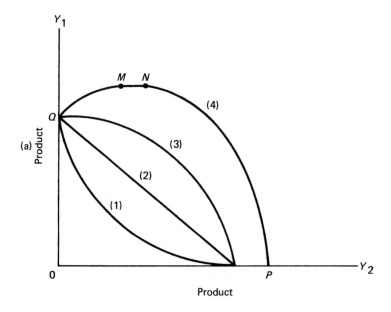

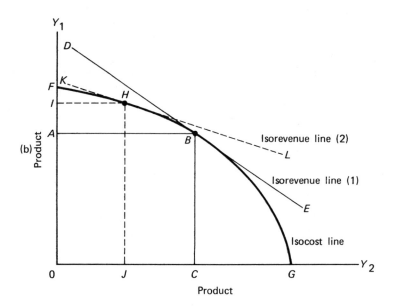

FIGURE 11-7
Isocost and Isorevenue Lines Plotted to Determine
the Optimum Combination of Two Enterprises under
a Given Total-Cost Outlay and a Change in
Product Price

cost of the extra man. Production-possibilities curve (2) shows a substitution of one product for another in some constant ratio. A situation like this often leads to specialization in one or the other product, rather than continued production in both enterprises. Curve (3) shows the most common type of production-possibilities situation. This curve is competitive throughout, but the curve permits substitution of one product for another for increased total production (not a straight-line substitution). Production-possibilities curve (4) combines complementary, supplementary, and competitive areas of production. Arc QM denotes an area of complementarity, where the increase in production of one product leads to an increase in the production of the other product. The marginal rate of substitution ratio for this arc is greater than 1. Arc MN is a supplementary situation, where the marginal rate of substitution is equal to 1. Arc NP illustrates the competitive relationship, where the marginal rate of substitution is less than 1.

Let us approach the product-product question in the same general manner as we did the factor-product and the factor-factor situations. Let us assume that we produce two products, Y_1 and Y_2, with certain variable and fixed inputs. We can trace an isoproduction-cost curve between the two outputs that shows the relative amounts of Y_1 and Y_2 that can be produced for a given cost outlay. Figure 11-7b provides this diagram. The isocost line may also be thought of as a "production-possibilities curve," indicating how much of each product it is possible to produce under a given cost condition.

The production-possibilities curve shown (FG) in Figure 11-7b is an example of a competitive relationship. The line DE is known as an isorevenue (equal revenue) line and shows the amount of Y_1 and Y_2 necessary to obtain the same total revenue. Its slope is determined by the ratio of the prices of Y_1 and Y_2. Revenue received is constant throughout the length of DE for any combination of Y_1 and Y_2 that falls on DE. B is the point at which the greatest possible revenue (shown by DE) is equal to the given cost outlay. Our question is answered: We produce OA units of Y_1 and OC units of Y_2 to maximize profits from the given cost outlay. At point B, the ratio of the marginal physical product of input X_1 in the production of Y_1 to the marginal physical product of input X_2 in the production of Y_2 is equal to the inverse price ratios of Y_2 and Y_1, equation (6):

$$(6) \quad \frac{\text{MPP}_{(X_1)\,Y_1}}{\text{MPP}_{(X_2)\,Y_2}} = \frac{P_{Y_2}}{P_{Y_1}}$$

If we multiply through by the product and the factor prices, we get:

$$\frac{P_{Y_1}}{P_{X_1}} \text{MPP}_{(X_1) Y_1} = \frac{P_{Y_2}}{P_{X_2}} \text{MPP}_{(X_1) Y_2}$$

Suppose now that a change in product prices was instituted and that the resulting isorevenue line was KL, Figure 11-7b. The new point of optimum product combination would be H. At this point, maximum returns for a given cost outlay would be obtained by producing OI of Y_1 and OJ of Y_2.

12

Production Costs and Supply

TYPES OF INPUT COSTS

The preceding chapter developed the concept of the production function and the law of diminishing physical returns. The three major types of production decisions regarding the choice of level of output, combination of inputs, and combination of products were discussed. In this chapter, analysis of the effect of varying the level of an input upon total costs and costs per unit of output is developed. These per-unit costs will be used to derive the levels of production for an individual producer that would result in the most profit for him for different prices of the product. The individual-producer supply schedule is related to the total-market supply schedule for the product. Finally, the concept of price elasticity of supply and the difference between supply in the short and long run are discussed.

Fixed Costs

Fixed costs are those costs that do not change as output (TPP) changes. The notion of being fixed is a static concept, meant for a relatively short period of time. In the long run, all costs become variable, because more opportunity exists to change all the factors of production,

242

including plant and equipment. Taxes on property, for example, are a fixed cost of production. Farmers must have land on which to produce agricultural commodities, and consequently they are obligated to pay property taxes on the land they own. The amount of this tax does not vary with production; a farmer pays the same property tax if he raises 150 bushels of corn per acre or if he lets his land lie idle. However, over the years, the amount of property taxes paid by the farmer may rise as more schools, roads, and other public facilities need to be built. The costs that are fixed include unpaid family labor, taxes, depreciation, insurance, interest, and some maintenance repairs.

Variable Costs

Variable costs are those costs directly related to production output. The level of these costs is dependent upon the level of output and is directly connected with the production function. Many examples of variable costs are evident on the farm. Total fertilizer costs rise as more plant-food inputs are used to increase crop production; feed costs rise as higher rates of gain are attempted, or if increased numbers of livestock are fed. Hired labor is also a variable type of cost.

Total Costs

Total costs of production are found by adding total fixed costs and total variable costs of production together.

Marginal Cost

Marginal cost is the additional cost necessary to produce one more unit of output. Marginal costs depend entirely upon the nature of the production function and the unit costs of the variable inputs. Marginal cost is comprised entirely of variable-type costs.

Summary of Costs

There are seven cost concepts derived from the production function that are used in economic analysis. They are:[1]

1. Total cost (TC)
2. Average total unit cost (ATUC)

---

[1] The student who attempts to gain an understanding of cost relationships merely by memorizing formulas or definitions will encounter difficulty in solving problems. For example, one must understand thoroughly why fixed cost is fixed, not merely some mechanical formula in its computation.

3. Total fixed cost (TFC)
4. Average fixed cost (AFC)
5. Total variable cost (TVC)
6. Average variable cost (AVC)
7. Marginal cost (MC)

The computation of each and their relationship to each other are as follows:

1. TC = TFC + TVC
2. ATUC = TC ÷ Number of output units
3. TFC = Simple sum of depreciation, taxes, maintenance repairs, interest, insurance, and unpaid family labor
4. AFC = TFC ÷ Number of output units
5. TVC = Simple sum of all variable-type costs
6. AVC = TVC ÷ Number of output units
7. MC = Change in TC or change in TVC, divided by marginal physical product (MPP)

TABLE 12-1

Hypothetical Cost Data Illustrating the
Relationships among the Various Cost Concepts

Units of Output	Total Cost (TC) $	Total Fixed Cost (TFC) $	Total Variable Cost (TVC) $	Average Total Unit Cost (ATUC) $	Average Fixed Cost (AFC) $	Average Variable Cost (AVC) $	Marginal Cost (MC) $
0	50	50	0	Undefined	Number	0	—
1	58	50	8	58.00	50.00	8.00	8.00
2	65	50	15	32.50	25.00	7.50	7.00
3	71	50	21	23.67	16.67	7.00	6.00
4	76	50	26	19.00	12.50	6.33	5.00
5	81	50	31	16.20	10.00	6.20	5.00
6	87	50	37	14.50	8.33	6.16	6.00
7	94	50	44	13.42	7.14	6.28	7.00
8	102	50	52	12.75	6.25	6.50	8.00
9	111	50	61	12.33	5.55	6.77	9.00
10	124	50	74	12.40	5.00	7.40	13.00

The relationships above are summarized in Table 12-1. Note that the total-cost and the total-variable-cost functions increase continually as output increases. This would be expected from the definitions. Variable costs are one of the two components of total cost and by definition are associated directly with output level. Total fixed cost is constant over all levels of output. Again, fixed costs by definition have nothing to do with level of output and therefore are a constant dollar amount even at zero units of output. Average fixed cost is a continuously decreasing function, since a constant dollar amount (TFC) is being divided by an ever-increasing number of output units. The rest of the cost functions—average total unit cost, average variable cost, and marginal cost—are U-shaped; they first decrease at lower levels of output but then begin to increase once a certain output level is reached, although the output level at which each begins to rise is different.

Next, let us draw a picture of the seven cost concepts and see how each is related to the other (Figure 12-1). The difference between TC and TVC is always the constant TFC. Measure the vertical distance between the TC and TVC curves with your pencil or a ruler. It is the same anywhere on the graph. AFC is continually declining as output increases; a constant TFC is divided by a constantly enlarging number (increasing output). The MC curve crosses both the AVC and ATUC curves at their minimum points. This is part of the *symmetry of economics*. The importance of cost structures and their relationship to output cannot be overemphasized. It is in these relationships that the symmetry of economics is found. An economist who fails to see these symmetries and relationships between output and cost is severely handicapped when he comes to solving applied economic problems.

The transition from the physical ideas discussed about the production function and the cost ideas is indicated in Figure 12-2, which illustrates the relationships graphically. The marginal and average cost curves are the mirror image of the marginal and average physical product curves. (Experiment with an actual diagram on a piece of paper and a mirror, to see if you can get the mirror image.) Note the change in the labeling of the axes. In Figure 12-2a and 12-2b, the vertical axes are labeled "Output" and the horizontal axes are labeled "Input." Measurements are in physical terms of output per unit of input. In Figure 12-2c, the vertical axis is "Dollars" and the horizontal axis is "Output." Measurements from this diagram are in economic terms of cost per unit of output. This is an important difference of notation and will be critical when we begin the discussion of profits.

Relationships between increasing and decreasing returns to mar-

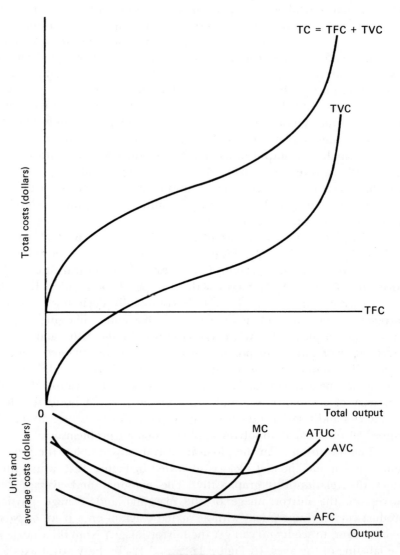

FIGURE 12-1
Seven Cost Concepts: TFC, AFC, TVC, MC, TC, ATUC

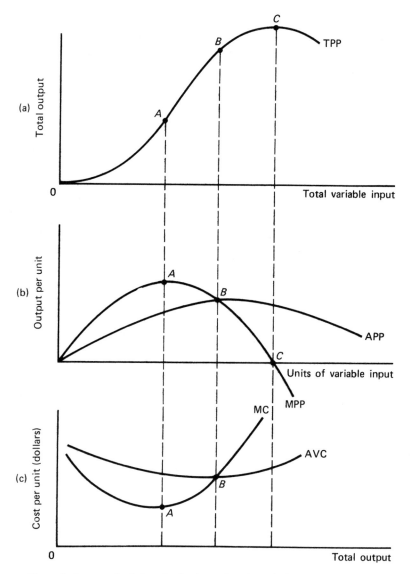

NOTE: It is recognized that the horizontal and vertical axes in each of the three figures above are not comparable on a quantitative basis. The importance is to show the relationship between various points on the physical product curves and the cost curves. Point *A* is the point of diminishing returns, where MPP begins to decline and the TPP curve begins to increase at a decreasing rate (inflection point). Since MPP is at its highest point, the MC of producing that extra unit of output is at its lowest point. Where the APP and MPP curves intersect is also where the MC and AVC curves intersect (point *B*). This point on the TPP curve is the beginning of stage II, or the beginning of the area of rational economic production. MPP reaches zero where TPP begins to decline. This is the beginning of stage III, an irrational area of production level.

FIGURE 12-2

The Production Function and Some of Its Derivatives

ginal and average physical production and marginal and average costs
may be summarized as follows:[2]

Physical	*Economic*
(*Input–output relationships*)	(*Output–price relationships*)
1. Where MPP is greater than APP, APP is *increasing*.	1. When MC is below AVC, AVC is *falling*.
2. When MPP is equal to APP (where the two curves cross), APP is at a *maximum*.	2. When MC is equal to AVC (where the two curves cross), AVC is at a *minimum*.
3. When MPP is less than APP, APP is *falling*.	3. Where MC is greater than AVC, AVC is *rising*.

EFFECT OF TECHNOLOGY ON COSTS

Technology and production costs are closely related. Remember
that the effect of the adoption of new technologies was to raise the production function—to increase TPP with a given quantity of inputs and
thus shift both marginal and average physical product curves upward
(Figure 12-3). Under the old technology, only production levels APP_1
and MPP_1 were attainable. Under the new technology, average and marginal output levels of APP_2 and MPP_2, respectively, can be attained.

Remember, too, what we said about the symmetry between production and costs, and you will see that increased marginal and average
production will cause decreased marginal and average costs of production. This is shown in Figure 12-4. Under the old technology, the lowest
costs possible were found at the intersection of the MC_1 and AVC_1
curves. Under the new technology, which permits increased output per
unit of input, MC_2 and AVC_2 are attainable. The minimum cost per
unit of output has declined from P_1 to P_2, and this lower cost is to be
found at an increased volume of production, Q_2 instead of Q_1 (Figure
12-4).

The effects above were discussed under the assumption of constant
factor, or input, prices. This assumption may not always be valid in applied problems, and care must be taken to include factor cost when considering the impact of technology. Often the individual farmer has too
small an operating unit for his actions to influence factor prices. But
volume purchases or inputs, or the ability to handle inputs in a cheaper

---

[2] These relationships assume the existence of perfect competition, which is discussed in Chapter 15.

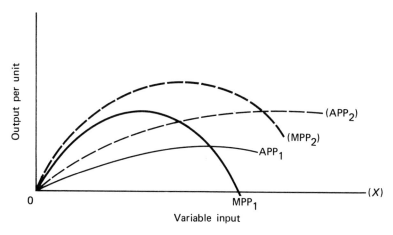

FIGURE 12-3
The Effect of Technology on Marginal and Average
Production

way through technological innovations (bulk fertilizer versus sacked fertilizer), do exert downward pressures on factor prices, a fact of which individuals may take advantage.

The principal purpose of adopting a new technology is to increase output or decrease costs per unit of output. Changes in output quality may also be affected, but differences of this nature are generally handled by changes in product prices rather than factor prices. New technology may increase total cost by increasing total fixed cost (buying a new self-

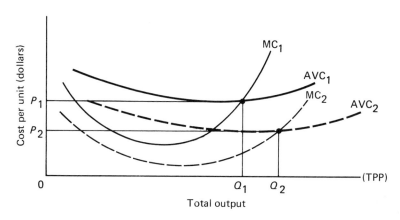

FIGURE 12-4
The Effect of Technology on Marginal and Average
Costs

propelled combine versus owning a small power-takeoff six-foot combine), or total costs may be increased through increased variable costs
(buying and using a new fertilizer). The important thing to consider
when making decisions about adopting a new technology is whether the
innovation will lower per-unit output costs and whether this total decrease will offset (or more than offset, in order to make a profit under
constant product prices) the increase in total costs accruing to the entire
farm operation.

CONCEPT OF SUPPLY

The concept of *supply* involves price–quantity relationships. A
farmer's supply of corn, for example, is defined as the different amounts
of corn he is willing and able to put on a market at a given time within
a relevant range of prices. The word *supply* as used in everyday language refers only to the variable of quantity offered to the market.
Statements such as, "The supply of corn last year was 100 thousand bushels in Jackson County," are misleading. Supply involves two variables,
price and quantity. To make the statement correct, we should say,
"Farmers supplied 100 thousand bushels of corn in Jackson County at
an average price of $1.15 a bushel." Since supply has two dimensions,
price and quantity, the relationship can be easily illustrated (Figure
12-5). The graph tells us that if the price of the product were $1, pro-

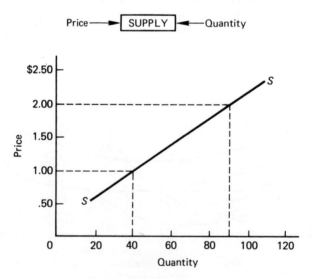

FIGURE 12-5

Hypothetical Illustration of a Supply Schedule

ducers would provide 40 units of product on the market, but if the price were $2, they would offer 90 units. Common sense would allow you to deduce the correct relationship between price and quantity with regard to supply. A higher price induces more production. A statement of the relationship between price and quantity constitutes the formal *law of supply*. The law says that the quantity of goods and/or services offered on a market varies *directly* with the price. The notion may be in an individual sense (individual producers) or in an aggregate sense (all producers in an industry).

The Supply Schedule

A *supply schedule* is a line (or a curve) showing the relationship between quantity of goods and/or services offered for a series of prices in a given market at a certain time. The supply schedule may actually be thought of as a boundary line beyond which no goods or services will be offered.

Determination of a supply curve. The supply curve is based on marginal cost in relationship to the price received when the product is sold. Its origin is illustrated in Figure 12-6. Look at P_1 through P_7. Think of them not only as costs but also as possible price levels for the product. Producers will be willing to place additional units of product on the market as long as the price they receive is equal to or exceeds cost of production (MC). Thus, the supply curve for the individual producer is the same as his marginal cost curve. The farmer will produce to the point where P_1 to P_7 just equal the marginal cost (MC). At $P_1 = $ MC in

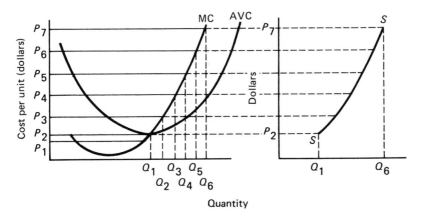

FIGURE 12-6

The Derivation of Supply

Figure 12-6 (left), even the variable costs of production are not covered, so that it is not profitable to produce at all. However, at $P_2 = MC$, AVC are covered, normal marginal profits are made, and the producer is willing to offer output quantity Q_1. This situation continues through $P_7 = MC$. The price–quantity-offered boundary relationship is the MC curve above AVC, from P_2 to P_7 and Q_1 to Q_6. These quantities (or up to these quantities) will be offered at the series of prices P_2–P_7. This portion of the MC curve thus becomes the relevant supply curve for the producer.

The aggregate supply curve, or industry supply curve, can be determined by horizontally summing all the price–quantity-offered relationships of all producers. The curve SS in Figure 12-6 (right) shows how this would be done, using Figure 12-6 (left) as an example. At every relevant price (P_2 to P_7, in this case) the quantities offered for sale are added up. The resulting total (Q_1 to Q_6, in this example) is then plotted against price, and the resulting curve is the supply function for this particular commodity in the particular market at a certain time.

A change in supply occurs whenever more or less of the good and/ or service is offered on the market for the same price or series of prices (Figure 12-7). A shift to the right is an increase in supply, and a shift to the left is a decrease. A movement from A to B on SS in Figure 12-7, however, does not constitute a change in supply but merely a change in the quantity offered as a result of a price change.

Assume that SS is the original supply response curve: An increase

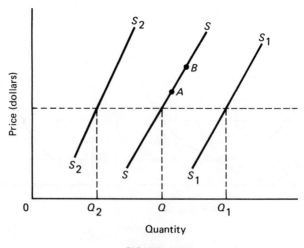

FIGURE 12-7
Shifts in Supply

in supply is denoted by a shift of the entire schedule to the right (S_1S_1), and a decrease in supply is shown by a shift to the left (S_2S_2). An increase means more (Q_1) will be offered for sale on the market at the same price; a decrease means less (Q_2) will be offered than before at the same price.

A contraction of supply may be the result of increased costs of production (losses, rising factor costs, etc.). An increase in supply is usually the result of a new technology or of production areas.

Supply Elasticity

Supply elasticity is a measure of the responsiveness of quantity offered to changes in price. More specifically, supply elasticity measures the percentage change in quantity offered in response to a designated change in price. The formula for calculating arc elasticity (an average elasticity between two known points of price and quantity) is:

$$E_s = \frac{\dfrac{(Q_2 - Q_1)}{(Q_2 + Q_1)}}{\dfrac{(P_2 - P_1)}{(P_2 + P_1)}}$$

There are three general types of supply elasticities—elastic, inelastic, or unitary. An elàstic response occurs when the percentage change in quantity offered relative to price changes is greater than 1 $(E_s > 1)$; an inelastic response occurs when the percentage change in amount offered relative to a price change is less than 1 $(E_s < 1)$; and a response of unitary elasticity occurs when the percentage change in amount offered is equal to the relative price change $(E_s = 1)$.

Instances of these three types of elasticity would take place when a 10 percent change in price was associated with a 15 percent change in quantity offered (elastic); when a 10 percent change in price was associated with a 5 percent change in quantity offered (inelastic); and when a 10 percent change in price called forth a 10 percent change in quantity offered (unitary elasticity).[3]

----

[3] For the student with a mathematical background, the equation for point elasticity, or that response taken at a specific point on the supply curve, is:

$$E_s = \frac{\dfrac{dQ}{Q}}{\dfrac{dP}{P}} = \frac{dQ}{dP} \cdot \frac{P}{Q}$$

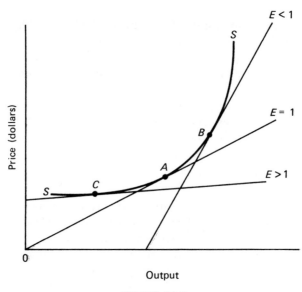

FIGURE 12-8
Price Elasticity of Supply

Supply elasticity graphed. A curved supply function has all three phases of elasticity (Figure 12-8). Any straight line supply curve through the origin has a constant unitary elasticity throughout. Let us utilize this information to devise a general rule of thumb about supply elasticity. Given a curved supply function SS, how can we determine general areas associated with the three types of elasticity? If we draw a line tangent to SS at A through the origin, we know that at A the slope of SS equals the slope of the tangent and therefore SS at that point has an elasticity equal to one (point of unitary elasticity). We can then easily see that the arc of SS to the left of *A* has an elasticity greater than 1 (see tangent at *C*), and the arc of SS to the right of *A* has an elasticity less than 1 (see tangent at *B*).

The elasticity concept in agriculture is of great importance when applied to questions of national agricultural policy. People estimating supply response in agriculture have recently been helped by rapid and far-reaching mathematical and statistical advances. However, much work remains to be done in this field, as it is one of the least-understood areas of agricultural economic research.

Supply in the Short and Long Run

The price elasticity of supply for farm products in the short run is relatively inelastic, because production is not easily changed in the short run. The reasons for this are that most commodity-production periods are long, and that few resources, if any, can be changed once the seed-bed has been prepared and the crop planted, or once the feed has been harvested and stored and the feeder livestock purchased. The longer the time period involved, the more opportunity exists for the farmer to respond to price (to change the quantity he produces with regard to farm-commodity price changes). A longer time period permits a farmer to be more flexible in his choice of production enterprises, and to allocate his resources in adjustment with his more flexible enterprise selections. In effect, then, elasticity of supply in agriculture depends more on the degree to which resources are fixed in their use than on time itself. Time allows for resources to lose their fixity and become variable. In the short run, supply response is relatively inelastic—in the long run, it becomes fairly elastic.

Much depends then on the length of the production period. If a farmer raises several crops a year, as in the case of truck crops in some of the southern, eastern, and western states, resource fixity is much less than in the situation faced by a Wisconsin dairy farmer who raises his own herd replacements.

The comments above pertain to the aggregate of farm production. However, there are differences between the response for individual commodities and the aggregate response. Response for meat products in general, for example, tends to be more inelastic than for any one meat source (beef, pork, etc.).

Factors influencing supply response.   The two main factors responsible for shifts in supply are technology and changes in input prices. The discovery and adaptation of new technologies to farm production create lower costs per unit of output and act as an incentive for the individual farmer to increase production. Changes in the prices of factors concerned with agricultural production are often influenced by nonfarm factor markets. For example, jobs in manufacturing may bid labor away from the farm. Changing demands for fertilizer, insecticides, and capital are constantly causing dynamic changes in the prices of farm inputs.

Added to this dynamic economic situation are the individual managerial responses to supply pressures. Differences in the attitude, understanding, and response of managers can be attributed to one or more of the following three factors: differences in information available to individual managers, differences in individual interpretations of available information, and differences in the necessity to sell.

13

Principles of
Profit Maximization

The purpose of this chapter is to show how the previous material covering input–output relationships, costs, and revenue may be combined into simple economic rules for profit maximization. The types of production decisions that managers must make were introduced briefly in Chapter 11. They included:

What to produce—a product-product problem
How to produce—a factor-factor problem
How much to produce—a factor-product problem

A graphical and mathematical discussion was given to these decision types in the appendix to Chapter 11. In Chapter 12, the cost relationships were discussed in greater detail. This chapter is designed to provide further understanding of the application of economic principles to these types of production decisions. First, the factor-product problem will be discussed.

TOTAL REVENUE

Revenue may be viewed from the standpoint of either input or output. That is, income to the producer may be measured in terms of either revenue per unit of input or revenue per unit of output. Either way, it can be measured in a total, average, or marginal sense. However, it is usually determined in terms of output. Let's consider total revenue (TR).

Revenue Per Unit of Output

Total revenue is determined by the amount of product sold, multiplied by the product price. There are so many farmers that no one producer can influence the product prices appreciably. This means that the only way a farmer can increase his total revenue (TR) without changing quality of product is to increase his total production, because total production multiplied by product price equals revenue. This revenue relationship is referred to as a linear one, a straight-line relationship. Constant marginal dollar returns accrue from each additional unit of output. Average revenue (AR) under these conditions is the price received for the product. It follows that marginal revenue (MR) is also equal to price, since marginal revenue is the change in total revenue produced by selling one more unit of output (or the price of the product times one additional unit of product). Figure 13-1 illustrates these relationships. It should be noted that although these relationships hold generally for the majority of agricultural production, they do not hold for some commodities under production and market quotas, or for the majority of products sold in the rest of the general economy. This situation holds

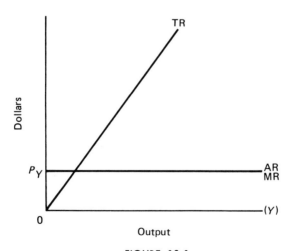

FIGURE 13-1

Total, Average, and Marginal Revenue in
Perfect Competition

true only under the limiting assumptions of perfect competition, which are discussed later.

MAXIMUM PROFIT IN TERMS OF OUTPUT

The concept of profit maximization is that profits are maximized when the revenue from the sale of the last unit of output just equals the costs necessary to produce it. At this point, marginal costs equal marginal revenue (MC = MR). An example of this situation would occur when the revenue from the last hundredweight of milk just paid for such factors as the feed, labor, and electricity necessary to produce it.

Figure 13-2 shows two marginal and average revenue curves. This is done simply to show that the least-cost point of production is not necessarily the point of maximum profits.

At a price of P_1, maximum profits occur at $MC = MR_1$. The amount of output produced is Q_1. Total profit is shown by the amount of profit per unit of output (line ab) times all units of output (OQ_1), and is represented by the rectangle $abcd$. This profit is sometimes referred to as *excess profit* (in the short run) and means that the manager is making more than is needed to keep him in production.

At price P_2, maximum profits are made at $MC = MR_2$. Output production stops at Q_2. Note that at $MC = MR_2$, the low point on the ATUC curve is reached. This is the least-cost point of production. Yet much less profit is made here as compared to operating at a higher cost

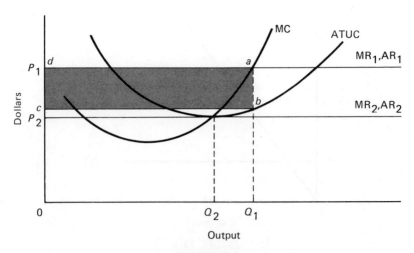

FIGURE 13-2

Maximum Profits in Terms of Output

of production and at a different output price. At $MC = MR_2$, the profit per unit of output just pays for the costs of production. Managerial salary, labor wages, and other inputs have been paid their relative prices, but no excess profit exists.

In each of the two cases, maximum profits are made when $MC = MR$. But in one instance, excess profits are made, whereas in the other instance, only a "breakeven" profit is earned. Note the relationship between these cost curves, price received (average revenue, AR), and profits.

Maximum Net Return (Profit) in Terms of Total Cost and Total Revenue

Net return (profit) is determined by total revenue (TR) minus total costs (TC). Net profit is greatest when the difference between TR and TC is greatest.

In Figure 13-3, total costs are less than total revenue only for the shaded area *ABCD,* which represents the area of profit. The breakeven

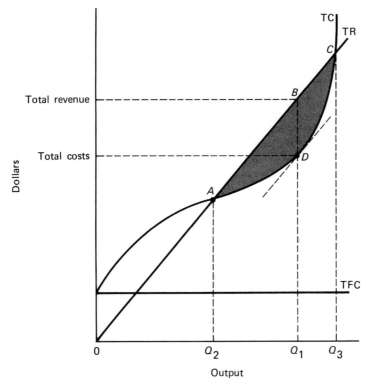

FIGURE 13-3
Maximum Profit from Total Revenue and Total Cost

point occurs at *A*, with Q_2 amount of output production. At this point, all fixed and variable costs of production are paid for, and for the first time revenue becomes greater than costs. To the right of point *C*, with production of Q_3, costs again become greater than revenue; hence, the area of profitable production lies between Q_2 and Q_3. The task is to find the production point at which maximum profits are earned. This can be done in either of two ways. One method is simply to take a ruler and measure where the greatest vertical distance between TR and TC is located. This distance is represented by the line *BD*. The other way is to draw a line tangent to the TC curve and parallel to the TR curve. At this point of tangency, the rate of change along the TR curve is just equal to the rate of change of the TC curve. Because rates of change are the same as the marginal concept, we again have MR = MC and have discovered the point of maximum profits at an output of Q_1.

ILLUSTRATIONS OF PROFIT-MAXIMIZING PRINCIPLES

Maximizing Profits with Unlimited Inputs (Factor-Product)

Let us work through an example using simple arithmetic. Suppose Table 13-1 represents a production situation where feed is the only variable cost incurred in producing the output of milk. Our fixed resource is one dairy cow, and feed is available in unlimited quantities at $60 per ton. Assume that total fixed cost is $50. The managerial decision facing the farmer is, "How much feed should I give the cow in order to maximize the profit from her milk production?" Milk is assumed to have a market value of $4 per hundredweight.

Maximum profit occurs where 1,300 pounds are fed to the cow or where 8,600 pounds of milk are produced. Note that up to this point, marginal cost (MC) is less than marginal revenue (MR), but beyond this point, MC is greater than MR. The correct answer can also be checked by looking at the total-cost and total-revenue figures. The greatest difference between total cost and total revenue is $255, and this occurs where 1,300 pounds of feed are being fed and 8,600 pounds of milk are being produced.

At this point, it would be well to check your understanding of many of the ideas that have been discussed since the beginning of Chapter 11. Let us review by asking some questions:

1. What kind of a production function is involved in the example above? Since the marginal physical product declines throughout, it can be concluded that only decreasing returns exist over the range of output

TABLE 13-1

Hypothetical Data Illustrating Profit-Maximizing
Principle when Inputs Are Unlimited

Feed Consumed (lbs.)	Total Milk Produced per Year (lbs.)	Marginal Physical Product (lbs.)	Marginal Cost ($)	Marginal Revenue ($)	Total Cost ($)	Total Revenue ($)	Profit ($)
			per Pound of Output				
500	5,000	—	—	—	65	200	135
600	5,800	800	.0038	.0400	68	232	164
700	6,500	700	.0042	.0400	71	260	189
800	7,100	600	.0050	.0400	74	284	210
900	7,600	500	.0060	.0400	77	304	227
1,000	8,000	400	.0075	.0400	80	320	240
1,100	8,300	300	.0100	.0400	83	332	249
1,200	8,500	200	.0150	.0400	86	340	254
1,300	8,600	100	.0300	.0400	89	344	255
1,400	8,650	50	.0600	.0400	92	346	254
1,500	8,675	25	.1200	.0400	95	347	252

levels represented. Therefore, it is not possible to delineate the inflection point on the total physical product curve, which is the same as the point of diminishing returns. This reminds us that the point of diminishing returns has nothing to do with what level of output is most profitable.

2. Total physical product never declines. Does this mean that stage III of the production function does not occur in milk production? No, it does not, but it does indicate that stage III does not begin until the production level is beyond 8,675 pounds, the highest level of output given in the data. This is also a reminder that it is not economical to push for the highest possible milk production per cow. The same would be true for crop yields, weight per steer, or any other physical yields level.

3. Does the example prove that the level of total fixed costs has no influence on the most profitable level of production? Yes. Suppose fixed costs were increased to $100. Note that only two columns of data would be altered. Each total-cost figure would be increased by $50 and each profit figure would decrease by $50. The maximum possible profit would then be $205, and it would still occur at 1,300 pounds of feed input and 8,600 pounds of milk output. The marginal-cost figures are not changed, because they are computed from variable costs only.

4. What is the effect of a change in the cost of feed or in the market price of milk? If the price of feed increased, each of the marginal-cost figures

would increase. An increase to $85 a ton would decrease the most profitable level of feed input to 1,200 pounds. Why? Because the marginal cost of producing each pound of milk between 8,500 and 8,600 would now be $.0425, which is greater than the marginal revenue of $.04. Therefore, this increase is not profitable. Now give yourself a test: How much would the price of milk have to change in order to change the most profitable level? The answer is below $3 or above $6 per hundredweight.

5. Would plotting the total physical product against the marginal costs trace out a supply schedule for the farmer with regard to this production process? Yes, it would. As long as marginal cost is equal to or less than marginal revenue, it pays to produce. Thus, the marginal costs trace out the output that would be produced at a set of milk prices per pound of the same amount. The supply curve has the expected positive slope. As milk price increases, so does the amount the supplier is willing to offer, since the most profitable level of output increases in a similar fashion.

Maximizing Profits with Limited Inputs and Where Several Enterprises Are Profitable (Factor-Product)

The example just discussed assumed that feed was the only variable input used in the milk-production process, that the feed was available in unlimited quantities, and that milk was the only profitable use of the dollars spent for feed. How realistic is this in a commercial farm operation? Not very. One of the input factors is usually available only in a limited amount. Since money will allow the manager to purchase added quantities of capital, it is usually the most limiting factor.

The other assumption, that of having only one profitable enterprise, is equally invalid for most farmers. Perhaps the wheat grower in western Kansas or the cranberry-bog owner in Massachusetts has only one profitable enterprise alternative, but most others have several. A new problem emerges with regard to the production levels that are most profitable in this situation. It would go something like this: How can the limited resource be allocated among the profitable enterprises so that the total amount of profit is maximized from the total farm unit?

The opportunity-cost idea. Before illustrating how this problem is solved, let us gain an understanding of a new idea. Every time one uses an input in a production process, potential income that could have been realized by using the resource in other uses is foregone or sacrificed. When one attends college, for example, he sacrifices or gives up income he could earn by being employed somewhere. Opportunity cost, as it is called, is the amount of income you sacrifice to do what you are doing, or the highest dollar return sacrificed by employing resources in some particular production process. You have probably already guessed that it is impossible to avoid opportunity costs.

Opportunity costs are not actual out-of-pocket costs, but they are real nevertheless. Perhaps some examples would help our understanding of this concept. What does a college education really cost? In addition to the $2,000 or so in out-of-pocket costs per year, several thousand dollars in opportunity costs are involved. Certainly, opportunity cost, although not an out-of-pocket cost in this example, is worth incurring in this case, since a college graduate's earning power in later years will more than make up for the income foregone. Nonetheless, there can be no dispute that there is money income foregone while one is in college.

How does all this relate to the economic principle of maximizing profit with limited resources when several enterprises are involved? It simply indicates that a smart manager will use his scarce inputs where the marginal return is greatest. Perhaps some profitable enterprises will not even be included in the "most profitable combination." The marginal idea is again put to use. The manager will maximize profits if he considers each unit of resource as a marginal unit and employs it where it will return the greatest amount.

The equal-marginal-return principle. The guiding economic principle for the manager, given this situation, can now be stated: Employ the scarce units of input until the marginal returns are equated in each enterprise.

Let's work through an example, given the data in Table 13-2. The production function tells us that variable input X_1 can be used to produce Y_1, Y_2, and Y_3 types of outputs, representing corn, soybeans, and cotton, respectively. All other inputs, $X_2 \ldots X_n$, are fixed in quantity and will cost $20.00. The price (cost) of X_1 (the variable input) is $20.00 per unit. The selling price, or output value, is $1.20 per bushel for corn, $4.00 per bushel for soybeans, and $.30 per pound for cotton.

Marginal physical products (MPPs) are given for up to five units of input X_1 in each enterprise. A new concept, marginal value product (MVP), is introduced for the first time. It is equal to MPP times the price of Y. For corn, the first unit of input X_1 gives a marginal value product of $48 calculated by multiplying the MPP (40) by the price of corn ($1.20).

If the quantity availability of X_1 was *unlimited* to the manager, he will push production in *each* enterprise until MC = MR. This is the same point at which the price of X_1 equals the marginal value product of X_1, $(P_{X_1} = \text{MVP}_{X_1})$. Thus, for corn, the manager will put in three units of input; for soybeans, four units of input; and for cotton, three

TABLE 13-2
Hypothetical Data Illustrating the
Equal-Marginal-Return Principle

Assumptions:

Production function: $Y_1, Y_2, Y_3 = f(X_1 \mid X_2 \ldots X_n)$
Price (cost) of $X_1 = \$20.00$ per unit
Price (value) of Y_1 (corn) $= \$1.20$ per bushel
Price (value) of Y_2 (soybeans) $= \$4.00$ per bushel
Price (value) of Y_3 (cotton) $= \$.30$ per pound
Total fixed costs: $(X_2 \ldots X_n) = \$20.00$

Input X_1	Marginal Physical Product			Marginal Value Product		
	Corn	Soybeans	Cotton	Corn	Soybeans	Cotton
1st	40	20	300	$48	$80	$90
2nd	30	14	200	36	56	60
3rd	20	10	100	24	40	30
4th	10	7	50	12	28	15
5th	5	2	20	6	8	6

Inputs Used (total)	Input-Use Combination			Marginal Value Product (dollars)	Total Return	All Enterprises	
	Corn	Soybeans	Cotton			Total Cost (dollars)	Net Return
	(units of input)						
1	0	0	1	90	90	40	50
2	0	1	1	80	170	60	110
3	0	1	2	60	230	80	150
4	0	2	2	56	296	100	196
5	1	2	2	48	344	120	224
6	1	3	2	40	384	140	244
7	2	3	2	36	420	160	260
8	2	3	3	30	450	180	270
9	2	4	3	28	478	200	278
10	3	4	3	24	502	220	282

units. Another unit of input in the enterprise will return an MVP less than the price (cost) of the input. Ten units of input used in the 3-4-3 combination will result in a total physical output of 90 bushels of corn, 51 bushels of soybeans, and 575 pounds of cotton. Total revenue would be $502, total cost ($220 — $20 TFC + $200 TVC), leaving a net return of $282. Using another unit of input in any of the enterprises would reduce net return. Prove it to yourself.

The assumption of unlimited inputs is not a very realistic one for any manager. Input availability will probably be limited; at some point the banker won't loan any more money to buy the input. Data in the bottom half of Table 13-2 show the effect of various input limitations. If only one unit of input were available, the profit-maximizing manager would employ it in cotton production, where the highest return (MVP = $90) is possible. If the second input were available, it would be used in soybeans (the next highest MVP, $80), and so on. In the process of continually choosing the next highest MVP as more units of input are available, the manager is applying the "equal-marginal-return" principle. He is trying to equalize marginal returns in all enterprises. This goal is not ideally achieved in this problem, nor is it likely in real-life production processes. But this does not diminish the importance of the guiding principle.

In summary, finding profitable enterprises where returns are above cost is not quite good enough. Managers must search for the *most profitable combination* of enterprises.

Let's look at this problem of finding profitable enterprise combinations in another way.

Selecting and Combining Enterprises (Product-Product)

The types of plant and animal enterprises that are profitable for any manager are determined to a large degree by the law of comparative advantage (review Chapter 11).

The rule of comparative advantage in farm production holds equally true whether the comparison is made within a single farming region or between farming regions. The Corn Belt, the tobacco states, the citrus states, and the dairy states (review Figure 7-2) offer explicit evidence that certain areas of the country have, and try to maintain, an advantage in either the production or the marketing, or both, of a particular product. Location of urban centers, technology adoption, and transportation costs have much to do with influencing the location of farm production.

The first enterprise consideration with which most farm managers must deal is determining the cropping system; the second is the livestock program. In each case, selection of enterprise combinations within crops and livestock and between crops and livestock are important decisions. The choice of enterprise(s) depends in part on the farmer's personal preferences and family goals, in part upon the farm manager's ability to

TABLE 13-3

Illustration of Enterprise Relationships on Two Different Soil Types for Crop Rotations, Including Corn, Oats, and Hay

	Rotation[a]	Acres Planted Grain	Acres Planted Hay	Per-Acre Yields Corn (bushels)	Per-Acre Yields Small grain Hay (tons)	Production Grain (pounds)	Production Hay (pounds)
	Soil Type: Drummer Silt Loam, Illinois						
(A)	C	100	0	24.3	—	136,248	0
	C – O/SCl	100	0	33.6	34.5	— 149,212	0
	C – O – Cl	67	33	51.1	49.8	0.82	149,891	54,200
	Soil Type: Clarion-Webster Silt Loam, Iowa						
(B)	C	100	0	40.0	—	—	224,000	—
	C – C – O – Cl	75	25	59.9	56.5	1.79	212,920	89,600
	C – O – Cl	67	33	59.5	50.1	1.46	166,194	96,400

[a] Rotation abbreviations: C = Corn; O = Oats; SCl = Sweet Clover; Cl = Clover.
SOURCE: Earl O. Heady et al., "How to Choose the Most Profitable Crop Rotation for Your Farm," *Iowa Farm Science,* June 1952.

apply his technical ability and economic reasoning, and in part upon the resources with which the manager must work. The profitability of alternative enterprises is influenced by the law of comparative advantage. In a majority of cases, the product-product relationships and the equal-marginal-return principle are most important.

Developing the cropping system. After an inventory of the physical characteristics of the farm, such as the kind of soils, topography, and so on, the manager first considers the cropping system. The physical factors of soil type, rainfall, length of growing season, topography, and temperature will in most cases eliminate a large number of crop enterprise possibilities. A general guide is to attempt to grow the highest profit crops that are adapted to the natural conditions of the area.

But there are other pertinent questions. Is a crop rotation necessary to maintain fertility and/or prevent soil erosion? How much will a crop rotation reduce risk by diversifying production? What are the relationships among enterprises when put together in various crop rotations? Each of these merits consideration.

Let us review our understanding of enterprise relationships (discussed in Chapter 11) by using the data from Table 13-3. In part (A) of the table, when grain acreage was reduced by one-third and clover hay was introduced, production of grain was slightly increased. Over 27 tons of hay were also harvested. This illustrates a *complementary* relationship between grain and forage. It always pays a farm manager to take advantage of any complementarity that he can find among his enterprises. In part (B) of the table, however, introducing hay into the rotation reduced the amount of grain that could be produced, illustrating a *competitive* relationship. All enterprises (both crop and livestock) become competitive with each other at some point. The manager must search for the combination that will return the highest total return to his limited resources; in the case just illustrated, only 100 acres of land were available.

To determine the most profitable rotation, the price of each product and the production costs per acre for each crop are needed. Assuming that production costs are equal (to make calculations easier) and the prices of corn, oats, and hay are at $1.10 a bushel, $.80 a bushel, and $20 a ton respectively, the most profitable rotation—part (B) of Table 13-3— would be C-C-O-Cl, the four-year one. Check it:[1]

Rotation	Corn		Oats		Hay		Total Value
	(bushels)	(value)	(bushels)	(value)	(tons)	(value)	
C	4000	$4400	—	—	—	—	$4400
C-C-O-Cl	2995	3295	1413	$1130	44.75	$895	5320
C-O-Cl	1983	2181	1670	1336	48.66	973	4490

Developing the livestock system. The kind of livestock kept will be determined partially by the kind of feed produced from the cropping system. In general, the *minimum* amount of livestock kept on most farms should not be less than enough to utilize profitably the roughage and pasture produced. The *optimum* amount of livestock for a farm depends upon many factors.

Management is highly important to the successful operation of livestock enterprises. Livestock efficiency (the principal source of variation in income on livestock farms) is directly influenced by many livestock-husbandry factors. The manager must have knowledge of good, eco-

---

[1] The optimum (most profitable) combination for two competitive enterprises is where the marginal rate of substitution is equal to the inverse price ratio. See appendix to Chapter 11.

nomical feeding practices, be able to control disease, be familiar with and have a knowledge of breeding, have ability to judge feeding efficiency, know what the basic requirements are in shelter and equipment, know when to buy and sell, and have the ability to organize work and get it done well and on time.

The amount, cost, quality, and distribution of available labor will influence livestock enterprise selection. Expansion of livestock enterprises is often justified on certain farms because of the relatively large amounts of family labor (a fixed cost). On small farms, where the problem is to profitably utilize labor, livestock with high labor requirements and with a yield of high returns for feed (dairy cattle and poultry) are usually better adapted. But on farms where labor is scarce, livestock that yield lower returns for feed but higher returns for labor (hogs and feeder cattle) are often better choices. Most farms with above-average management should keep enough livestock to utilize labor not required for the cropping system.

Returns per hour of labor and returns for dollars worth of feed vary widely. But in general, *dairy and poultry* enterprises pay high returns for feed but comparatively low returns for labor. Capital requirements per man are relatively low. These enterprises fit best on farms where labor utilization is a problem and where capital and feed are limited. *Hogs* pay high returns for labor and medium returns for feed. They require moderate capital investment per man. *Beef and lamb feeding* enterprises pay high returns for labor over the long run, but are highly speculative in any one year. They pay relatively low returns on feed. Their financial requirements are moderate. They fit best where it is necessary to utilize roughage with little or no grain, or where available grain is fed to higher-yielding classes of livestock. *Poultry* (*eggs*) returns are average as to feed and require little labor. Often a poultry enterprise is supplementary to other crop and livestock enterprises.

Input Combinations to Achieve Least Cost (Factor-Factor)

After a given level of output for enterprises has been selected, factor-factor analysis aids in finding the least-cost combination of inputs that will produce the desired product. Look at the data in Table 13-4. The least-cost combination of hay and grain for cows producing 8,000 pounds of milk is $111.30, where 8,000 pounds of hay are fed in combination with 1,565 pounds of grain. For 9,000 pounds of milk production, the least cost is $127.50 at two different combinations—either 8,000 pounds of hay and 2,375 pounds of grain, or 8,500 pounds of hay and 2,125 pounds of grain.[2]

TABLE 13-4

Grain-Forage Combinations for Various Outputs of
Milk by Good Cows[a]

8,000 Lbs. Milk			9,000 Lbs. Milk		
Pounds of Hay[b]	Pounds of Grain	Total Cost[c]	Pounds of Hay[b]	Pounds of Grain	Total Cost[c]
4,500	3,875	$122.50	4,500	5,000	$145.00
5,000	3,450	119.00	5,000	4,500	140.00
5,500	3,050	116.00	5,500	4,050	136.00
6,000	2,700	114.00	6,000	3,625	132.50
6,500	2,365	112.30	6,500	3,275	130.50
7,000	2,075	111.50	7,000	2,950	129.00
7,500	1,820	111.40	7,500	2,650	128.00
8,000	1,565	111.30	8,000	2,375	127.50
8,500	1,330	111.60	8,500	2,125	127.50
9,000	1,115	112.30	9,000	1,890	127.80
9,500	900	113.00	9,500	1,690	128.80

[a] A 1,200-pound cow capable of giving 10,000 pounds of 3.5 percent fat content milk when fed a grain milk ration of 1:4.

[b] Includes silage and pasture converted to hay equivalent consumed. This does not include the portion of hay fed but not consumed, which is normally about 8 percent.

[c] Assumes a hay cost of 1 cent per pound and a grain cost of 2 cents per pound.

SOURCE: Kentucky Agricultural Experiment Station, *Station Bulletin 648* (Lexington, July 1956).

Summary of Production Principles

If resources were unlimited, the manager would push the production of each enterprise where there was a return above cost until marginal cost was equated with marginal revenue (Chapter 13). Limited resources, however, do not permit the manager to push production this

---

[2] The least-cost combination is where the marginal rate of substitution between grain and hay is equal to the inverse price ratio. At the least-cost combination, the marginal rate of substitution and the inverse price ratio are both 2.0 in this case. See appendix to Chapter 11.

far for all enterprises. He must therefore employ the equal-return principle. A summary of principles guiding decision making where the objective is profit maximization would be as follows: (1) Produce products in such a combination that the last unit of resource used in the production of any product will result in an equal value of production. (2) Use such a combination of resources for the production of any product that the last dollar invested in each resource (input) will result in the additional production of the same amount of product. (3) Add inputs to the business until the last unit of input produces just enough to cover marginal cost or until capital is exhausted.

Everyday uses for maximizing principles. The profit-maximizing principles just discussed are very important. They can be applied to practically any situation involving a decision. The equal-marginal-return principle, for example, can be a guide for college students in allocating time. The restricted resource is 24 hours of time in a day. The problem for students is to allocate their limited time among their academic and nonacademic pursuits so as to maximize their scholastic achievement and personal satisfactions.

The housewife tries to allocate a limited amount of money in the food budget among the various foods to maximize the satisfaction of the family (to be discussed in detail in the next chapter). A person usually attends a movie only once, because after he has seen it, the marginal return from a second viewing is below the price of admission; it is thus a poor decision to see the movie twice. In addition, considerably more satisfaction is realized by seeing a different movie, where the satisfaction return (utility) is higher; hence, opportunity costs are held to a minimum. Numerous examples could be given. See how many you can think of and put into use.

14

Economic Principles of Consumption and Demand

Economists are interested in people as receivers and spenders of money. In this chapter, we are particularly concerned with the how and why of consumer decisions with regard to purchases of goods and services.

How can we explain the decision of the Smith family to buy a new green car with automatic shift? Was the purchase made because the Jones family had one? Or was it made because, after checking all the cars on the market, the Smiths found that this model gave them the most for their money? Keeping up with the Joneses could be called a noneconomic reason; comparing the cost of different autos is an economic one. Most consumer decisions are based on a combination of economic and noneconomic factors. Both are determined by personal and social values.

CONCEPT OF UTILITY

Economists invented the concept of *utility* as a way to measure the personal satisfaction that people derive from owning and using goods and services. If eating ice cream satisfies a human want, then we can say that the ice cream (a good) possesses utility. It is a little harder to think of services possessing utility, but the idea is the same. A haircut and the daily mail are examples of services received that also satisfy needs and desires.

Let us use numerical units to signify different amounts of utility. A banana may yield 5 units of satisfaction or utility to Johnny. But if Billy does not like bananas, he may get no units of utility at all. In fact, if Billy is allergic to bananas and gets sick, a banana will yield him a number of units of negative utility (*disutility*). The amount of utility obtained from any good or service may be different for each individual. The difference depends on individual taste and preferences.

A THEORY AND ILLUSTRATION OF CONSUMER BEHAVIOR

To formulate a theory or framework for studying and predicting consumer behavior, it is necessary to make several assumptions. To begin with, we assume man to be rational if he tries to maximize his satisfaction. When economists use the term *rational,* they mean that people try to get the most income they can to use in reaching individual and family goals.

A second assumption is that man is aware of the relative amounts of utility or satisfaction he gains from each of the many goods and services available to him. All of us can rank goods and services by comparing them in terms of more or less satisfaction. Given a dollar to spend at an amusement park, some people prefer to ride the merry-go-round, and others choose the more daring roller coaster.

A third assumption is that man has limited income. The notion of limited resources forces man to make decisions based upon his satisfaction priorities.

Diminishing Marginal Utility

The utility of any one good or service varies according to how much of that good or service we have in our possession. For example, the satisfaction of an apple just received depends upon how many apples we already have. A formal statement of diminishing marginal utility is this: As additional units of a good or service are consumed, the utility derived from each successive unit declines. Marginal utility is the extra or additional utility derived from consuming one more unit of product or service. When you decide to visit an ice-cream stand, the first cone tastes exceptionally good and gives you, let us say, 15 units of satisfaction. However, if you order a second one, the extra satisfaction you gain may be only 10 units (Table 14-1 and Figure 14-1).

Note that in the title of Table 14-1, time and place is specified.

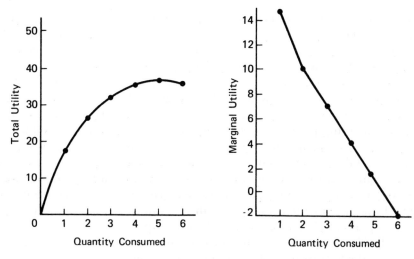

FIGURE 14-1

Graph Showing Total and Marginal Utility (data
taken from Table 14-1)

This is important. A number of other variables could also be specified, such as health, sex, age, climate, and necessity of purchase.

Utility-Maximization Principle

The economic principle states that one can maximize his total satisfaction by *allocating limited money income so that the last dollar*

TABLE 14-1

Utility Received by Mr. John Doe from Ice Cream
at a Stand at a Specific Time and Place

Ice-Cream Cones Consumed (number)	Total Utility Received (units)	Marginal Utility Or Disutility Received (units)
0	0	0
1	15	15
2	25	10
3	32	7
4	36	4
5	37	1
6	35	− 2

spent on each good and service yields an equal amount of marginal utility.[1] When the consumer equalizes his marginal utilities in accordance with this principle, we say his consumption pattern is in equilibrium and any change he makes will decrease his total satisfaction.

To illustrate the utility-maximization principle, let us assume there are only three goods available on the market, A, B, and C. Also, assume that we have a weekly income of $15 to spend and that we can exactly order our utility preferences from each of the three products. Product A costs $1 per unit, product B costs $3 per unit, and product C costs $5 per unit (Table 14-2). Note that diminishing marginal utility sets in immediately for each of the three products. Marginal-utility information is described on a per-dollar basis, because a consumer's choices are influenced not only by the amount of additional utility successive units give him, but also by how many dollars he gives up to get them.

Let us consider one dollar of expenditures at a time. Looking at the marginal-utility-per-dollar columns in Table 14-2, we see that a dollar spent on product A provides the most satisfaction. On neither B nor C is the marginal-utility return as high as A's 14 units. A dollar would buy only $\frac{1}{3}$ unit of B, which yields 9 units of increase satisfaction per dollar spent on B. A dollar spent on C would buy $\frac{1}{5}$ unit of C,

TABLE 14-2
Price and Utility Information for Products A, B,
and C[a] in Units

Unit of Product	Product A (price $1)		Product B (price $3)		Product C (price $5)	
	Marginal Utility	Marginal Utility per $1	Marginal Utility	Marginal Utility per $1	Marginal Utility	Marginal Utility per $1
First	14	14	27	9	30	6
Second	10	10	18	6	25	5
Third	8	8	9	3	20	4
Fourth	6	6	6	2	15	3
Fifth	4	4	3	1	10	2

[a] It is necessary to assume that the amount of marginal utility received from extra units of each of the three products is independent of the quantity of the other product.

[1] This idea has also been called the *equal-marginal principle* (see Chapter 13).

which gives only 6 units of added utility for that dollar. Continuing our expenditures, if the second dollar is spent on A, it again buys the most marginal utility. However, when we are spending a third dollar, a switch to product B returns 9 units of added satisfaction, as opposed to 8 if the dollar is spent on A. Continuing in this fashion and considering each dollar of expenditure in marginal terms, the best combination we can purchase with $15 would be 4 units of A, 2 units of B, and 1 unit of C. Total utility generated would be 113 units. Four dollars spent on A gives 38 units of satisfaction; $6 spent on B gives 45 units; and $5 spent on C yields 30, for a total of 113. No other combination will result in a total this high with an expenditure of $15.

If you have remembered the formal statement of the principle, you will note that the example worked out perfectly. The last dollar that was spent for each of the products yielded an equal amount of marginal utility—6 units. "Balancing," or equalizing, our marginal utility per dollar spent is the best we can do. In real life, we seldom get such a neat solution. Nevertheless, if we operate our lives using this principle, we will gain greater satisfactions.

DEMAND

The theory of consumer behavior will help us understand the concept of demand. The word *demand* as commonly used in everyday language refers only to the variable of quantity consumed. Statements such as, "Consumers demanded 12 billion pounds of pork last year," are common, but this reference to demand is misleading. Demand really involves two variables—price and quantity at the same time.

Price ───▶ DEMANDS ◀─── Quantity

To make the statement above correct, we should say, "Consumers demanded 12 billion pounds of pork last year at an average price of $.75 per pound." Now the idea is complete.

The concept of demand involves price–quantity relationships. Your demand for apples is defined as the different amount of apples that you would be willing and able to buy within a reasonable range of prices. Since demand has two dimensions, we can easily illustrate the relationship between the two variables (Figure 14-2).

The graph tells us you would buy one apple if the price were 10 cents, but should the price drop to 2 cents, you would be willing to purchase 6 apples. This is just good common sense; anyone would have been able to tell us that people tend to buy larger quantities if the price is low. Be sure to remember that the concept of demand en-

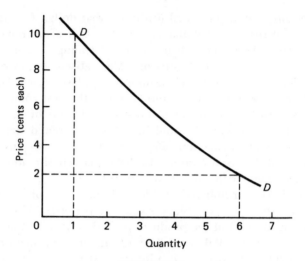

FIGURE 14-2
A Hypothetical Demand Curve for Apples at Some
Specified Place and Time

compasses the entire curve labeled *DD*. It is a line (schedule) that shows the quantities you would buy at various prices. Remember that although demand is an abstract notion, it is also operational in the real world. There need be no apples present in order for us to conceptualize the demand for apples and predict what might happen under various price and quantity changes.

The Negative Relationship between Price and Quantity

The commonsense statement that "consumers will buy a larger quantity as price is reduced" states the relationship between the two variables of price and quantity and is usually referred to as the *law of demand*. Other terms to describe the relationship are *negative* and *inverse*. We will increase our understanding of demand by investigating the various reasons why this relationship exists.[2]

First, as noted before, not all people have equal desires for the same commodity. Let us take fresh strawberries. Some people desire strawberries enough to pay $2.00 a quart for them. However, the number of people with this intense desire for strawberries is small relative to the number of people with more usual desires, who will buy at 80 cents a

---

.[2] This relationship has often been explained in terms of an "income-substitution effect."

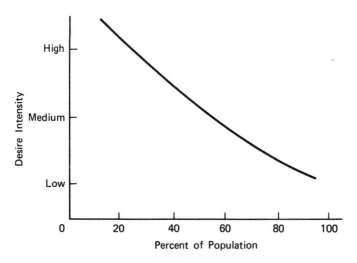

FIGURE 14-3

Hypothetical Illustration of Consumer Desires for
Strawberries

quart. Figure 14-3 helps us understand the idea. Although only 20 percent of the population desires to purchase berries at 70 cents (a high
level of desire intensity), virtually 100 percent would purchase them at
10 cents (a low level of desire intensity). This, then, is one reason that
there is an inverse relationship between price and quantity.

Second, there is wide variation in the income of individuals and in
their ability to buy goods and services. Although a millionaire oilman
and a poor ditchdigger may have the same size stomachs and an equal
desire for strawberries, it is not hard to understand that the millionaire
can afford to pay $2.00 a quart while the ditchdigger may not. As the
price of berries is lowered, a greater quantity can be sold because more
and more people can afford them. This is the second reason why a
demand curve slopes downward to the right.

Third, price varies inversely with quantity because of diminishing
marginal utility, discussed earlier in this chapter. As a person consumes
additional units of a commodity, the added or marginal utility he gains
diminishes. With regard to food, this is basically because our stomachs
cannot expand indefinitely.

Building Market Demand From Individual Demands

Until now, we have discussed only an individual's demand for a
commodity. In order to study the total market for a commodity, it is

necessary to think of the total or aggregate demand for commodities. As might be expected, the market demand for apples is derived by summing up the amounts of apples that are demanded at each price by each consumer. Taking an unrealistic situation of 10 million consumers with identical individual demands and assuming that these people make up the entire market, we could then think of the market demand as a 10-million-fold enlargement of the individual demand curve (Figure 14-4).

A Change in Demand

A change in demand is not the same thing as a change in the quantity demanded. For example, using the data in Figure 14-2, when the price is lowered from 8 to 6 cents for apples, the quantity demanded increases from 2 to 3. This is not a change in demand, but merely a movement from one point to another on the demand schedule. What has happened is merely a reflection of the law of demand working; the two variables of price and quantity have moved in opposite directions.

To have a change in demand, it is necessary for one of the variables (price or quantity) to remain constant while the other variable changes. A change in demand also occurs if both variables move up or down together. For example, if consumers purchase 5 million tons of oranges this year at an average price of 50 cents a dozen, and next year they buy 5½ million at 50 cents a dozen, then demand has changed. At the same set of prices, consumers are purchasing greater quantities all along the line. Thus, a change in demand constitutes a shift in an entire demand schedule (Figure 14-5). A movement from *A* to *B* would be a change in quantity demanded. A move from *B* to *C* is a change in de-

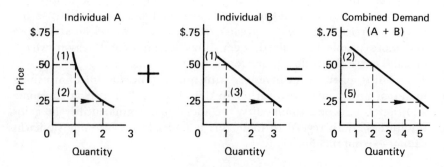

FIGURE 14-4
Deriving Market Demand by Adding Individual
Consumer Demands

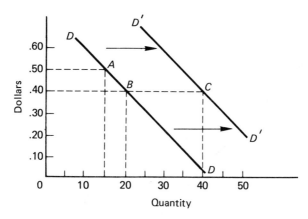

FIGURE 14-5

Hypothetical Illustration of a Change in Demand

mand. The concept of a change in demand for an entire demand schedule is shown by going from *DD* to *D'D'*.

Price Elasticity of Demand

The law of demand is applicable to virtually all products. However, although demand curves slope downward to the right, there is considerable difference in the steepness of the slope for individual commodity curves. Price elasticity of demand indicates whether the demand curve slopes steeply or whether it lies flat. The word *elasticity* brings to mind something that can be stretched. Price elasticity of demand refers to the "stretchiness," or the extent to which quantity changes in response to some given price change.

We know that when price is increased, less will be bought. The concept of elasticity is concerned with the question of how much less. When the percent change in quantity taken is greater than the percent change in price, we say that the demand is elastic. If the price of T-bone steak is reduced from $1.20 a pound to $.60 (a 50 percent decline), it is quite likely that consumers would buy more than a 50 percent greater quantity.

In a situation where demand is elastic, the total expenditures by consumers will increase as you go down the demand curve (Figure 14-6). As the price falls from $.70 to $.40, the quantity taken increases from 2 to 14 units. As a result of the relatively larger change in the quantity taken than in price total, expenditure (revenue to sellers) increases from $1.40 ($.70 × 2 units) to $5.60 ($.40 × 14 units). If total expenditures

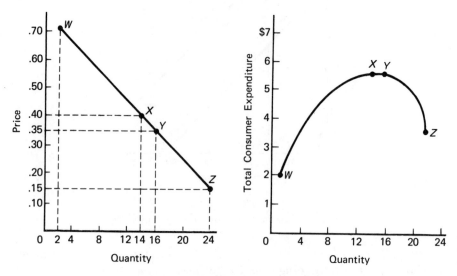

FIGURE 14-6

Illustration of the Various Types of Price Elasticities
of Demand and Corresponding Total-Revenue Functions

Computation of price elasticity $= (E_d) = \dfrac{\dfrac{(Q_2 - Q_1)}{(Q_2 + Q_1)}}{\dfrac{(P_2 - P_1)}{(P_2 + P_1)}}$

Portion of demand curve WX: $\dfrac{\dfrac{(14-2)}{(14+2)}}{\dfrac{(.40-.70)}{(.40+.70)}} = \dfrac{\dfrac{12}{16}}{\dfrac{-.30}{1.10}} = \dfrac{12}{16} \times \dfrac{1.10}{-.30} = \dfrac{13.20}{-4.80} = -2.75\ E_d$ (Elastic)

Portion of demand curve XY: $\dfrac{\dfrac{(16-14)}{(16+14)}}{\dfrac{(.35-.40)}{(.35+.40)}} = \dfrac{\dfrac{2}{30}}{\dfrac{-.05}{.75}} = \dfrac{2}{30} \times \dfrac{.75}{-.05} = \dfrac{1.50}{-1.50} = -1.00\ E_d$ (Unitary)

Portion of demand curve YZ: $\dfrac{\dfrac{(24-16)}{(24+16)}}{\dfrac{(.15-.35)}{(.15+.35)}} = \dfrac{\dfrac{8}{40}}{\dfrac{-.20}{.50}} = \dfrac{8}{40} \times \dfrac{.50}{-.20} = \dfrac{4.00}{-8.00} = -0.50\ E_d$ (Inelastic)

Elasticity coefficients:

$-\infty$ -1.5   -1.0   -0.5   0

Elastic   Unitary   Inelastic

increase as one moves down the demand curve, that portion of the demand curve examined is elastic. The demand for most luxury-type items or those not considered necessities is elastic.

Total revenue can decrease as you sell a larger quantity. This may be surprising, but the classic example of salt will quickly prove this point. Most people consume about the same quantity of salt regardless of its price. With salt at 10 cents a box and with a 50 percent reduction in price, one certainly would not expect consumers to buy much more salt. Figure 14-6 (*YZ* portion) illustrates this inelastic type of demand. In this situation, where price is falling but quantity taken is not increasing at as fast a rate, total consumer expenditure will fall. This is exactly what happens as we move from point *Y* to point *Z* in Figure 14-6. Total expenditures decrease from $5.60 ($35 × 16 units) to $3.60 ($15 × 24 units). It is not difficult to think of a number of items that have an inelastic demand. For the most part, items in this group are necessities. If you smoke, it should not be hard to understand this idea.

There is a third type of price elasticity, called unitary elasticity. A commodity has unitary price elasticity of demand if relatively equal changes occur in both price and quantity. Since the change in both the variables is identical, total expenditure remains constant. Looking at Figure 14-6, note that as price falls from $.40 to $.35, the quantity taken increases from 14 to 16. As a result, the total revenue is $5.60 at both points.

A quantitative measurement.   In addition to applying the test of total revenue to indicate whether a demand curve is elastic, inelastic, or shows unitary elasticity, we can also derive a precise coefficient of elasticity of demand. The formula for measuring price elasticity of demand is:

$$E_d = \frac{\dfrac{(Q_2 - Q_1)}{(Q_2 + Q_1)}}{\dfrac{(P_2 - P_1)}{(P_2 + P_1)}} \text{(see computations in Figure 14-6)}$$

P_1 and Q_1, and P_2 and Q_2, refer to two points on a demand curve. The formula describes the way to measure the elasticity between these two points. This may appear to be a rather complicated formula, but it is quite easy to manipulate. The price-elasticity coefficient will always have a minus sign in front of it, because there is a negative (inverse) relationship between the variables of price and quantity in demand. A price elasticity of demand coefficient between zero and −1.0 is inelastic. A coefficient of -1.0 is unitary elasticity, and a coefficient of less than -1.0 is elastic (Figure 14-6).[3]

Factors Affecting the Level of Demand

The term *level of demand* refers to the horizontal distance of the demand curve from the price axis. As the demand level increases, the curve will shift farther and farther to the right. Conversely, if the demand curve shifts to the left, there is a decrease in the level of demand.

The general factors affecting the level of demand are categorized as follows:

Consumer disposable income. Disposable income means income left for spending on goods and services or for saving, after taxes have been paid. This is probably the most important factor affecting the level of demand. For "superior" food products such as T-bone steak and ice cream, there is a direct or positive relationship between income level and demand level. For "inferior" food products such as evaporated milk and cornmeal, there is a negative or inverse relationship between income level and demand level. The positive effect that an increase in income level has on the total demand for goods and services is not difficult to understand. Let us assume that a man's limited income of $100 a week is so arranged that it will purchase an amount of goods and services that will maximize his satisfactions. Now let us assume that he gets a raise of $20 per week. The increased income allows him to rearrange his purchases of goods and services so that he will be able to derive a greater amount of satisfaction. He may want to save some of his increased income, but he will probably spend a high percentage of the increase. As incomes increase, the proportion spent on food diminishes even though the total dollars spent are greater. This is the idea of income elasticity of demand, which was discussed in Chapter 9.

Population. Many people believe that a rapidly expanding population will directly increase demand, contributing to general economic prosperity. However, we need only compare the per capita consumption levels of various products in the United States and India to see that this is not altogether true. An increase in population will definitely have a positive effect on demand level, provided that per capita income levels are maintained or increased. Whether or not this is possible depends upon the total productivity of the country. In the United States, the

---

[3] The price elasticity of demand can also be calculated by dividing the percentage change in price by the percentage change in quantity. However, with this method, the midpoints must be used as the basis for calculating the percentage change.

rate of real per capita income has more than kept pace with the rate of population increases. To date this has not been true in India, for example. The population elasticity of demand for food in the United States is thought to be about 1.0. This means that a 1 percent increase in population is accompanied by a 1 percent increase in food consumption.

Changing consumer tastes and preferences.   A change in consumer tastes and preferences affects the demand for individual commodities more than it affects the total or aggregate demand. For example, as a result of the emphasis on weight-consciousness, supplemented by the warnings from health authorities about the intake of large amounts of animal fats, the demand for lard has decreased while the demand for vegetable oils has increased. At the same time, the demand for all fats and oils has remained fairly constant.

The introduction of completely new products also tends to shift demand levels among commodities. When the motorcar was introduced, the demand for buggy whips and carriages declined.

Substitute products.   Oleomargarine is a substitute for butter, and its low price makes it attractive. The demand for oranges is directly conditioned by the possible substitution of grapefruit. If there were no synthetic fiber available, consumers would have to use more cotton and wool even if prices were higher.

Other factors.   Environmental and cultural factors also affect demand levels. More ice cream is consumed in the summer than in the winter (at equal prices). Holidays alter the demand for turkeys and flowers. National customs and religious beliefs are other factors that influence demand.

THE DEMAND FOR FOOD PRODUCTS

The generalization already made that necessities have inelastic demands would lead to the correct conclusion that the demand for food is highly inelastic. However, as one would suspect, the demand for individual food items varies widely.

Demand for food items can be measured at two levels in the marketing channel: the retail level and the farm level. The demand for commodities at any point prior to the retail level is called a derived demand—derived from retail prices. For example, the demand for live beef animals as they are ready to leave the farm is derived from the demand for beef in retail stores. In order to derive the demand curve for live animals at the farm level, it is necessary to subtract the costs of

slaughtering, processing, transporting, and packaging from the retail demand curve. The costs are all necessary to transform a live steer to edible
beef. The demand curve $D'D'$ was derived from the demand curve DD
in Figure 14-7 by subtracting (vertically) a constant 50 cents for marketing charges. Of red meats, veal, lamb, and mutton show quite elastic demands at retail, beef shows about unitary elasticity, and pork is the least
elastic (Table 14-3). Turkey is more elastic than chicken. If retail prices
of each red or poultry meat would increase or decrease 1 percent, which
might occur if overall livestock supplies generally decreased or increased,
changes in consumption would be smaller, because there would be no
incentive to substitute one meat for another. Brandow estimates the
expected changes in consumption to be .67 percent for beef, .47 percent
for pork, .54 percent for chicken, .70 percent for turkey, and .60 percent
for all red and poultry meats collectively.[4] This illustrates the principle
that since there are fewer substitutes for meat than there are for beef,
the price elasticity for meat as a category of competing products is less
elastic than the weighted average for beef. There exists greater substitutability within a class of meats (beef, pork, and mutton) than between
groups of meat (red meats, poultry, fish). The greater degree to which
the consumer can substitute, the more elastic is the demand.

This principle helps explain the low price elasticity of demand for
all foods and why a relatively small increase in the total quantity of food
will drive farm prices down substantially if "dumped" on the market.

In our discussion of marketing, we learned that farm prices are
lower than retail prices in accordance with the amount of the costs of
marketing (marketing margin). In Figure 14-7, the derived demand at
the farm was illustrated by subtracting the marketing margin. Demand
at the farm level for food is less elastic than retail demand for foods—
much less elastic when marketing margins are large. For example, the
price elasticity of eggs, for which the marketing margin is relatively low,
changes only from .30 to .23 from retail to farm, whereas that of evaporated milk, a more highly processed product with a relatively high marketing margin, changes from .30 to .15. The difference in elasticity at
retail and farm levels is another reason why small changes in total farm
output cause considerably larger changes in farm prices. The application
is equally valid for individual products. At the farm level, only calves
and sheep appear with elastic demands.

The grain and livestock economies are highly interrelated, because

---

[4] George E. Brandow, "Interrelations Among Demand for Farm Products and
Implications for Control of Market Supply," Bulletin 680, Pennsylvania Agricultural
Experiment Stations, August 1961, p. 4. These elasticities assume that prices of all red
meats and poultry change simultaneously.

TABLE 14-3

Price Elasticities of Demand for Various Food
Products[a]

Item	Elasticity Retail Level	Elasticity Farm Level[c]	Item	Elasticity Retail Level	Elasticity Farm Level
Beef	− .95	− .64	Fluid milk and cream	− .29	− .15
Veal	−1.60	−1.08	Evaporated milk[d]	− .30	− .15
Pork	− .75	− .45	Cheese	− .70	− .38
Lamb and mutton	−2.35	−1.78	Ice cream	− .55	− .11
Chicken	−1.16	− .74	Fruit	− .60	− .20
Turkey	−1.40	− .92	Vegetables	− .30	− .10
Fish	− .65		Cereals, baking		
Butter	− .85	− .66	products	− .15	− .03
Shortening	− .80		Sugar and syrups	− .30	− .18
Margarine	− .80		Beverages	− .36	
Other edible oils	− .46		Potatoes, sweet		
Lard, direct[b]	− .40	− .40	potatoes	− .20	− .08
Eggs	− .30	− .23	Dry beans, peas, nuts	− .25	− .08
			All foods	− .34	− .23
			Nonfoods	−1.02	
			All goods and services	−1.00	

[a] Assumes that prices of all substitutes remain constant.
[b] Does not include lard contained in shortening and margarine.
[c] Raw product at farm (cattle for beef, hogs for pork, etc.).
[d] Includes condensed milk.
SOURCE: George E. Brandow, "Interrelations Among Demands for Farm Products
and Implications for Control of Market Supply," Bulletin 680, Pennsylvania Agricultural Experiment Station, August 1961, data in Tables 1 and 10, pp. 17 and 50.

grains and other concentrates are the major input in meat production.
Demand for corn, wheat, and other feed grains can also be thought of as
derived demands. Brandow's results indicate that:

> . . . with no changes in rates of feeding and apart from the upward
> trend in total feed requirements, an increase of one percent in the ton-
> nage of concentrates fed increases hog production 1.3 percent, broiler
> production 1.8 percent, egg production .66 percent, and milk produc-
> tion .33 percent. . . . Weight added in cattle-feeding operations rises 1.9
> percent and, with the same number of head slaughtered, the total live-
> weight cattle slaughter increases .23 percent. Farm prices of hogs decline

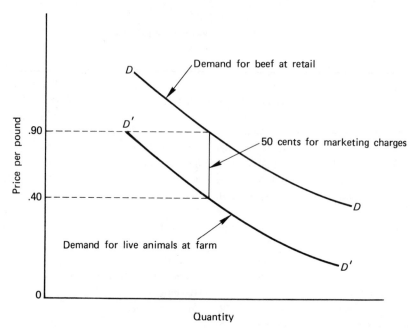

FIGURE 14-7

Hypothetical Illustration of the Derived Demand for Beef

3.5 percent, chickens 3.4 percent, turkeys and eggs 3.2 percent, and beef cattle 1.0 percent. Increased production of lard and butter fat reduces prices of soybean and cottonseed oils about 1.5 percent if their production remains the same. Concentrate prices decline 4.4 percent. . . . Thus the elasticity of demand for feeding purposes is low, only about −.23. Livestock is the principal means by which a large share of total crop production is or might be utilized, but this low elasticity shows how difficult it is to expand utilization through livestock by reducing feed prices. . . .[5]

Cross-Elasticities of Demand

It is possible to compute a coefficient to show the effect that a price decrease or increase for one food has on the consumption of another food. This notion is called the cross-elasticity of demand between the two commodities. The formula for calculating cross-elasticity coefficients is:

$$\frac{\dfrac{(Q_2 - Q_1)}{(Q_2 + Q_1)}}{\dfrac{(P_2 - P_1)}{(P_2 + P_1)}} = \text{Cross-elasticity coefficient}$$

---

[5] Brandow, "Interrelations," p. 7.

where **Q** is the quantity of one food and **P** is the price of another.

If two products are easily substitutable for each other (beef and pork), the cross-elasticity coefficient will be much greater (more elastic) than for two products that are not good substitutes (beef and coffee). Cross-elasticities are also lower at the farm than at retail. For example, Brandow estimates the total cross-elasticity of the quantity of cattle demanded on prices of other livestock and poultry to be .18, and the corresponding figure for beef .28.[6] The effect of the price of one farm product on purchases of another is reduced if the first product has a high marketing margin.

Another general relationship is that when all prices of a group of competing products advance, the consumption of the highest-ranked luxury item within the group will be affected most. Again, using Brandow's estimates, a 1 percent advance in *all* fat and oil prices at retail decreases butter consumption by .52 percent but margarine consumption by only .08 percent. Coupled with this is the fact, already mentioned, that the marketing margin is lower for butter than for vegetable-oil products.

The tools needed to study how prices are determined in markets will now be considered. The next chapter uses the concept of supply from Chapter 12 and the concept of demand just discussed to study market-price determination.

----

6 *Ibid.*, p. 51.

15

Principles of
Market-Price Determination

One of the major characteristics of capitalistic economies is their heavy reliance upon a price system as a means for allocating society's scarce resources. The importance of resource allocation has been emphasized as being at the very heart of the study of economics. It should be no surprise then that considerable time in the study of economics must be devoted to an understanding of the price system, which embodies an understanding of individual market prices.

Even the most casual observer of the American business scene will observe that there are many different kinds of market arrangements in the purchase and sale of goods and services. There is no such thing as a "typical" industry, yet all industries use some form of a price system that, except in a few instances, is not directly regulated by a central government authority. For example, at one extreme we may find only a few firms producing aluminum, whereas at the other extreme there are several million farmers who produce corn. In between is a myriad of situation far too numerous to study individually.

A more reasonable approach is to look for certain similar characteristics in industries and classify them. Traditionally, economists have envisioned four relatively distinct market situations: pure competition, monopolistic competition, oligopoly, and monopoly. Although some

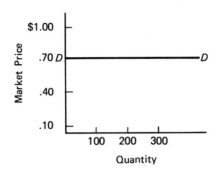

FIGURE 15-1

An Illustration of the Demand Situation Faced by
an Individual Firm in Pure Competition

business firms do not fall neatly into one of the classifications, the framework is very useful in understanding markets and prices.

This classification by economists is not that typically employed by businessmen or laymen. Furthermore, these classifications are necessarily abstractions and do not purport to present a clear picture of the operation of any single business or industry.

MARKET MODELS

Pure Competition

The most distinguishing feature of pure competition, which sets it apart from all the others, is that the individual firm in the industry faces a perfectly elastic demand function (Figure 15-1). As a result, individual firms exert no influence over market price by themselves. They are price takers and therefore at the mercy of the market.[1]

The reason the individual firm is in this situation stems from two other characteristics of pure competition. The first is the presence of a large number of independent sellers acting individually. The second is the fact that firms in pure competition produce a virtually standardized or homogeneous product. This means that the buyer or consumer of the product is indifferent as to the seller from whom he purchases, since

---

[1] A distinction is often made between pure and perfect competition. Perfect competition does not exist in any market; it is an abstract model helpful to the theoretician. In addition to the requirements for pure competition, perfect competition is typically thought to mean that buyers and sellers have perfect market knowledge and that no other frictions exist; therefore all sales would take place at equilibrium, and the price-discovery process would be nonexistent.

FIGURE 15-2
Hypothetical Demand Situation Facing the Industry
Group in Pure Competition

the products are, for all practical purposes, perfectly substitutable for each other. It is fruitless for any particular firm to attempt to extract a price higher than the going market price from the consumer, since the purchaser can buy the same product from many other firms at the going market price. Because of the large number of firms, the output of each producer makes up a negligible part of the total industry's output. If there were two million corn producers each producing 1,000 bushels, market supply would be two billion bushels. If one producer increased or decreased his output 50 percent, total supply would change by only 500 bushels, or .00025 percent. It is apparent that this small change in total supply would not affect market price noticeably. The individual producer, then, sells all he can at the going price. He must adjust to market price, since he has no influence on it.[2]

All firms in an industry can, *as a group,* cause market price to vary, and the demand situation facing the industry may be highly elastic or inelastic (Figure 15-2). For example, using the same illustration, if *all* firms producing corn changed production by 50 percent the total industry supply would change by a similar amount. This would have a very large effect on the going price for corn. Thus, even though price to an

---

[2] However, even though the farmer may sell all his wheat at the going price, variation probably exists in the prices at various elevators that is not the result of transportation-cost differentials. Farris has shown that a band of prices exists on both sides of the average market price and that the width of the band (magnitude of price differences) varies by commodity and the amount of market information possessed by the buyer and seller. Farris further points out that if either the buyer or the seller were more skillful than the other, it would be expected that he would influence the location of price transactions within the band of his advantage. See Paul L. Farris, "The Pricing Structure for Wheat," *Journal of Farm Economics,* Vol. 40, No. 3 (August 1958), 622.

individual producer is fixed, the market price is free to move up and down in accordance with changing conditions in total demand or total supply.

For pure competition to exist, it is necessary that new producers be free to enter production and that existing firms be free to discontinue production.

When purely competitive firms produce nearly identical products, they have no reason to try to compete with one another on a nonprice basis. If there are virtually no differences in product quality, buyers will recognize the products as the same, and advertising efforts by individual farm producers will be of little avail.

These characteristics of pure competition are quite restrictive. However, farming is the one industry that in many instances could be classified as purely competitive. Using wheat as an example, there are a large number of producers. Farmer Brown's wheat may not be identical to Farmer Smith's wheat, but through our systems of grading and standardization, each market grade of wheat is made to be identical. Similarly, for corn, eggs, and many other commodities, the same situation exists. Even though the eggs produced on several farms are in many ways different, by the time they are graded into quality classes and size classes, each market grade class becomes identical and thus meets the criterion of homogeneity necessary in pure competition. Each producer grows a negligible part of the total industry's supply and has no effect on price. The homogeneity of farm products is also reflected by the fact that little advertising is carried on by individual farmers. There is free entry into and exit from the industry, with minor exceptions. It is difficult to find examples in American industry other than farming that meet the requirements of pure competition so well.

Monopoly

At the opposite pole from pure competition is monopoly. Instead of an extremely large number of firms, there is only one firm. This single firm's output is thus also the industry's output. The demand situation facing the monopolist firm is likely to be inelastic.

Although in a broad sense all goods and services compete for the consumer's dollar and are substitutable for each other, a television set is not a good substitute for an automobile. Buying taxi service is a better substitute for a family-owned automobile but is still an inferior service to most people. Following from the definition of a monopolist as a one-firm industry and applying the idea of substitution in a narrower sense, the monopolist produces a product for which there are no close substitutes. This means that a buyer has no alternative but to purchase from the firm or do without the product.

In direct contrast to the firm in pure competition, which has no control over price, the monopolist could exert direct influence (if allowed) on price by manipulating the quantity of product put on the market. It is immediately apparent that the producer or seller could take unfair advantage of the consumer or buyer by charging very high prices. Thus, monopolies are illegal unless franchised and regulated. Examples are the U.S. Postal Service and the utility companies. It is also apparent that such industries, because of the nature of the production process, lend themselves to a monopolistic structure. Imagine the cost if ten or twenty electric-power or telephone companies each strung wires down our highways. To utilize just one set of wires for all is certainly most economical. But to make sure that the electric company does not exploit the public, the rates charged are reviewed and approved by a public utilities commission. The rates set are determined to yield a fair return to the input factors of the electric-power company. Typically, after expenses for labor's wages, management's salaries, and other operating costs are subtracted from gross profits, the utility company is allowed to earn some "fair" percent on capital invested.

Why is there lack of competition for monopolists? The case of industries in which the production process lends itself to monopoly has already been mentioned. To perpetuate a monopoly, barriers of an economic, legal, or some other nature must exist to prevent other concerns from entering the field. For example, it would be extremely difficult for a private firm to compete in the mail-delivery business.

The extent of advertising by monopolists varies with the product or service offered. It would hardly seem necessary for a water company to advertise, since everyone uses water, wants to continue to use water, and will probably not use more water as the result of advertising. It is common, however, to find advertisements by utility companies in local papers, television, and other media. The advertising is mostly of a public-relations or "goodwill" type, rather than the advertising of the attributes of water or electricity. The monopolist wants the public to feel good about his company so that consumers do not feel they are being hurt by too-high rates or charges. The monopolist is usually quick to point out his firm's technological progress or contribution to civic projects in the community.

To summarize, in monopoly there is a single firm in the industry, producing a product for which there are no good or close substitutes. There are barriers of some nature preventing entry of other firms. Advertising is designed to promote goodwill toward the public and to explain the company's service to the community. Private-industry monopolies are illegal except those that exist under regulation. Examples are the public utility companies: water, gas, and electricity.

Monopolistic Competition

As the name implies, monopolistic competition has some aspects of both pure monopoly and pure competition. It is somewhat closer to pure competition, in that a large number of sellers are involved, each of whom produces a fairly small share of the total industry output and thus has a very limited amount of control over market price. However, products of these industries are not homogeneous or standardized as in pure competition. Differences among products are usually slight and may be real or imagined. Many times, the only difference is in brand name. Differences in workmanship and the imaginary differences implanted in the consumer's mind by effective advertising and attractive packaging are difficult to separate.

Product differentiation is important in two respects. First, to the extent that consumers have preferences for the products of a particular firm, they will be willing to pay a higher price than for competing products. This allows the seller some small degree of price control and acts as an incentive for him to win the consumer to his slightly differentiated product. Second, in order to win the consumer, the seller will probably also engage in nonprice competition, adding a complicating factor to the analysis. The primary emphasis in competing is to win a larger share of the market by offering such things as better services, by extending credit, and by having a more attractive looking store, prettier salesclerks, or giving away trading stamps.

Another important characteristic of monopolistic competition is that no one firm recognizes its rival or feels any mutual interdependence with any other firm. This would seem reasonable in a market of many sellers. Any form of collusion would be ineffective unless a fairly large number of firms were involved. And any gain an individual firm might make by lowering its price would be spread so thin over its many rivals that their sales loss would be negligible and hence bring no retaliation.

Strict adherence to this characteristic—that of no mutual interdependence among firms—would seem to rule out practically all real-life situations. However, firms typically listed as in monopolistic competition include some in the apparel and furniture industries.

Entry into monopolistically competitive industries tends to be easy from the standpoint of capital requirements, since individual firms are small. However, if existing firms hold patents and have been successful in building consumer allegiance via advertising, costs of entry and operating may be higher for rivals, making survival difficult.

To summarize, monopolistic competition is a situation in which a fairly large number of firms produce slightly differentiated products. No firm recognizes its rival in deciding on price policy. Nonprice competition is emphasized, as each producer strives to win consumers to his particular product, thus affording him a small degree of price control. Price competition is still important, however, since entry of new producers is relatively easy.

Oligopoly

Where a few firms dominate an industry and where sellers think of their rival's reaction before setting a price policy, the industry is labeled an oligopoly. A moment's reflection brings convincing evidence that oligopoly is the dominant form in American capitalism, not in terms of numbers, but in the total volume of commerce and business.

To the extent that oligopolists produce identical products, they are called pure oligopolists. Basic steel and aluminum are examples. However, most oligopolists are differentiated in that they produce differentiated products. Examples are numerous and would include firms manufacturing automobiles and electrical appliances.

The prime feature of oligopolies—namely, a few firms with each controlling a significant share of the market—necessarily brings about mutual interdependence. One cannot lower its price without considering what its rival will do. If firm A cuts its price and increases its share of the market, firms B and C may note a sizable loss in sales and in retaliation may also lower price to recapture their previous market shares. The net result is that everyone is worse off, with the consumers the only beneficiaries. It is not long before price competition of this nature is recognized by the sellers as futile. Price wars, or competing on a price basis, most often hurts every seller.

The reason that oligopolists most often choose to compete on a nonprice basis is clear. The oligopolist, being rather powerful, is usually in a better financial position to compete on a nonprice basis. More funds are available for advertising and product development, and he must advertise not only in order to expand his market share, but merely to hold it steady.

The paucity of firms in oligopoly suggests some barriers to entry; otherwise firm numbers would increase considerably. In some of the manufacturing industries, such as automobiles, there are considerable economies in large-scale production. As a result, huge amounts of capital would be required to enter the industry and produce at an efficient size. Also, any new competitor would need to have large amounts of operating capital to carve out a niche in the market, as each existing firm already has a great number of consumers convinced that its product is best. In the past half-century, where economies of size do exist, the trend has been for firm numbers to decrease, because some firms have not been able to produce efficiently or to gain a large enough share of the market, owing to ineffective advertising or lack of funds for advertising and product development. Other barriers to entry may include such factors as ownership of strategic patents or control of raw-material sources. In terms of advertising outlays creating an effective barrier by themselves, the cigarette industry is the classic example.

Some industries must be classified as oligopolies even though firm numbers are large and entry is easy. These include gas stations, barber shops, and restaurants, where, within a given locality, the reaction of rivals must be considered in setting price policies. Some of the most vicious price wars have occurred in retailing gasoline. Here again, the most common form is for all to charge the same price and compete for share of the market solely on a nonprice and service basis. Entry and exit occur continuously in these industries; they are often referred to as the "sick" or "overcrowded" industries. The rigid price charged by all is usually excessively high, since fixed resources are highly underutilized. Total returns and profits to owners are usually low, because the large number of firms forces market shares to be quite small for each seller. For firms in these industries to succeed, they need a particular desirable location or a unique ability to compete successfully on a nonprice basis.

In summary, the two primary factors of oligopolies are fewness of firms and recognition of rivals' existence in establishing pricing policies. Nonprice competition is prevalent, and advertising expenditures may be heavy to assure consumer loyalty in holding a share of the market. There is often a going industry price maintained by tacit collusion. Entry is difficult in those oligopolies where capital investment is high and large economies of size exist. Some oligopolies, such as gas stations, afford easy entry, but excessive numbers of firms make financial success difficult because market shares are low in most instances. Oligopoly is the predominant market form in American industry.

MARKETS IN AGRICULTURAL AND NONAGRICULTURAL INDUSTRIES

The only industry that approaches the conditions of pure competition is farming. The farmers producing corn, wheat, cotton, feed grains, soybeans, hogs, cattle, sheep, broilers, eggs, and so on have no control over market price. However, for some raw food products, such as cranberries or walnuts, the number of producers is relatively small, and they may be able to exercise some control over prices through joint

action. Often the group of producers exercises control through a market-
ing-cooperative association. Also, in the case of milk, for example, producers may exercise control via bargaining associations. These latter
situations are encouraged where the production of the commodity is
geographically concentrated or where the perishability of the product
keeps it from moving long distances before consumption. The tendency
for a greater amount of collective action on the part of farmers is stimulated by the lack of price control by the individual.

In the agribusiness complex, including both the farm-supply industries and the processing and food-distribution industries, one finds many
degrees of imperfect competition. The poultry-breeding, farm-machinery,
and meat-packing industries are examples of a few large firms dominat-
ing the industry and therefore meeting an important criterion of oligopoly. A common situation can be noted in the food-retailing and feed-
processing industries, where there are several large firms and many small
ones. In these cases, small independents seem to be surviving and competing successfully. The relative use and importance of price versus nonprice competition varies widely. Food retailers compete heavily in both
kinds, whereas bankers loaning money to farmers compete virtually entirely on a service or nonprice basis. Thus, there is no general rule.

Again, the delineation of the four market models is just an analytical aid in helping to understand the real world. Except in a few
instances, businesses cannot be classified neatly into any of these categories. The four-model framework does allow us to understand and perhaps predict the policies that will be followed in particular cases.

AN ALTERNATIVE APPROACH

Another framework for explaining how markets behave and the differences among them has been outlined by Bain.[3] Bain is concerned with
the environmental setting within which similar enterprises operate and
perform as an industry. Elements of market structure and conduct are
outlined and discussed with reference to their effect on market performance, crucial in an enterprise economy.

Market structure refers to how a market is organized, with particular emphasis on the characteristics that determine the relationship
among the various sellers in the market, among the various buyers, and
among the buyers and sellers in a market. In other words, market structure deals with the organization of a market as it influences the nature

---

[3] Joe S. Bain, *Industrial Organization* (New York: John Wiley & Sons, Inc., 1968).

of competition and pricing within the market. Bain discusses four strategic elements:

1. *The degree of seller concentration.* How many sellers are there in the industry? How large and how important are they? Are there a few large ones, several large ones and many small ones, or only many small ones?
2. *The degree of buyer concentration.* How many buyers are there for the product? How much do they buy?
3. *The degree of product differentiation.* Product differentiation has the same meaning here as in the previous discussion of market models.
4. *The condition of entry to the market.* Is the market open to new producers, or are there barriers to entry? How much influence can existing firms exercise in keeping new competitors out? Do existing firms own strategic patents or raw-material sources that make entry difficult?

Market conduct refers to the ways firms adjust to the markets in which they are engaged as sellers or buyers. Generally, market conduct is concerned with the pricing policies of a firm as a seller and with its recognition of other firms in decisions regarding product development, advertising, and so on. Specifically, Bain outlines five dimensions of market conduct:

1. *The principle and the method employed by the firm or group of firms in calculating or determining price and output.* Is the objective to maximize profits to an individual firm or to a group of firms, or is the concept of a "fair" profit used in setting prices? Are all buyers charged the same price?
2. *The product policy of the firm or group of firms.* Are efforts made to improve the product's quality through individual efforts or group efforts? What orientation does product change take?
3. *The sales-promotion policy of the firm or group.* How much advertising is done by individual firms and by group action? What determines the volume of advertising expenditures?
4. *Means of coordination and cross-adaptation of price, product, and sales-promotion policies of competing sellers.* Are there any collusive agreements with regard to prices, products, or sales-promotion expenditure? Is there tacit collusion in the form of price leadership by one major firm in the industry? Are collusive agreements abrogated by secret price cutting, leading to imperfect collusion? How closely are rivals' prices analyzed when changing prices?
5. *Presence or absence of, and extent of, predatory or exclusionary tactics.* Is there price cutting with the objective of wiping out competitors? Are there attempts by individual firms to monopolize strategic raw materials? Are there binding contracts with buyers, so that other competitors cannot sell to them? Are there restrictive uses of patent licensing?

Market performance refers to the end results that are essentially brought about by the nature of the market structure and the way firms conduct themselves.

Market performance includes:

1. *The price relative to the average cost of production, and thus the size of profits.* From society's viewpoint, a price that just covers the cost of production is ideal. This price assumes a fair return to the inputs used in production but allows no excess profits. This ideal would be reached under conditions of pure competition.
2. *The relative efficiency of production, so far as this is influenced by the scale or size of plants and firms relative to the most efficient, and by the extent, if any, of excess capacity.* Are firms operating with a plant of sufficient size to avoid excess capacity resulting in higher costs? If excess capacity exists, is it because there are too many firms trying to operate in the industry, or because of a temporary lack of demand?
3. *The size of sales-promotion costs relative to the costs of production.* Are promotion costs excessively high? What percent are advertising costs of the total costs of production?
4. *The character of the product, including choice of design, level of quality, and variety of product within any market.* Is the quality of the products of the industry high? Is there any variety available to the consumer? Are products excessively improved, to the point where buyers would prefer lower quality at a lower cost?
5. *The rate of progress of the firm and industry in developing both products and techniques of production.* Are firms attempting to find cost-reducing techniques? One indication might be the scope of their research activity. Do firms try to discover what the consumer wants? Does the firm have a good public image?

Bain's approach to looking at the various kinds of markets is not in any way contradictory to the previous discussion or to the four market models of pure competition, monopoly, monopolistic competition, and oligopoly. The approach is different. Understanding it should be helpful in understanding the markets for goods and services where buyers and sellers meet.

PRICE DISCOVERY AND DETERMINATION

The concepts of supply and demand have been explained in detail in Chapters 12 and 14 respectively. Now let us examine the interactions of supply and demand in price determinations. Since we have discussed both purely competitive and imperfectly competitive markets, it will be necessary to talk about price determination for each.

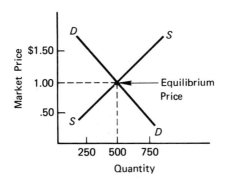

FIGURE 15-3
A Graphic Portrayal of Equilibrium Price
Determined by Intersection of Supply and Demand

Purely Competitive Market Pricing

Although it is correct to say that market price is determined by
the forces of supply and demand, let us delve a bit deeper. Why is this
so? Consider the situation depicted in Figure 15-3, where the market
price settles at $1.00 per unit and 500 units are sold. How and why did
this come about?

As you remember, demand represents what buyers are willing to
take from a market at a given price, and supply represents what producers or sellers are willing to offer. Because the relationship between
price and quantity is negative for demand but positive for the supply
relationship, the two functions must intersect each other at some point.
This point of intersection traces out the equilibrium price and quantity
in a purely competitive market. This is not to say that the sale of each
unit of the commodity will move at exactly the equilibrium price; although, theoretically, if all buyers and sellers had perfect and complete
market information, all sales would take place at this one price.

In a sense, then, buyers and sellers are trying to discover the equilibrium price. And as sales are made in a market, the market price of any
one transaction adds to and makes more complete and valid the actual
supply and demand situation in the market. In the hypothetical case
posed in Figure 15-3, as soon as a buyer who paid $1.25 noted others
paying less, he would probably tell himself that he had paid too high a
price and would not do so again. On the other hand, the seller who received the $1.25 probably feels quite fortunate and would not expect to
do that well again. The opposite situation with regard to the feelings of
a buyer and a seller would exist after a sale transaction at a price of $.75.

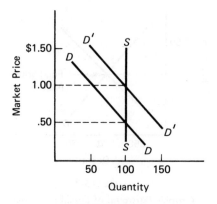

FIGURE 15-4
Equilibrium Price Determination in a Very Short
Time Period at Two Demand Levels

Thus, in a competitive market with a large number of transactions taking place, the price will tend to settle closer and closer to $1.00, the true equilibrium price. Markets approximating this situation would be grain, fruit, and livestock auction markets. The prices quoted in the newspapers for these and other commodities can be thought of as approximating or equaling the true equilibrium prices. Of course, each new day brings a changed set of supply and demand conditions, which result in price fluctuations.

It should also be remembered that the elasticity of the supply function depends upon the time period involved. It is often said that market price is demand determined in a very short time period—perhaps one market day (Figure 15-4). In a time period short enough so that sellers cannot offer more to the market than the amount on hand, as indicated by the perfectly inelastic supply function in Figure 15-4, a very high level of demand would push the price to $1.00. In this sense, price is determined virtually by demand alone. We shall see later, however, that whether one of these prices persists or not is considerably dependent on supply, which is in turn determined by the producer's cost of production and profit potential at the particular price. The situation depicted in Figure 15-3 would tend to represent more of a long-run situation, as indicated by a greater elasticity in the supply curve.

Effect on equilibrium price of changes in supply and demand. Price will tend to rise in response to the following: (1) demand increases with no change in supply, and (2) supply decreases with no change in demand (Figures 15-5a and 15-5b). A relatively larger price will occur when supply decreases and demand increases simultaneously (Figure 15-5c).

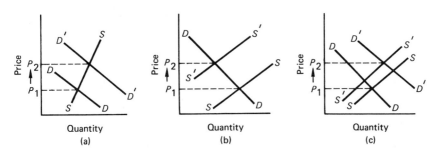

FIGURE 15-5
Price Increases Resulting from Changes in Supply
and Demand

Price will tend to fall in response to the following: (1) demand decreases with no change in supply, and (2) supply increases with no change in demand (Figures 15-6a and 15-6b). A relatively large decline in price will occur if supply increases and demand decreases simultaneously (Figure 15-6c).

If supply and demand change in the same directions in equal magnitudes, the equilibrium price will tend to remain unchanged (Figures 15-7a and 15-7b).

Price Determination in Imperfectly Competitive Markets

Monopoly. In single-firm industries, the seller will attempt to set a price that will maximize his profit. This price would be determined without regulation from the demand curve, corresponding to the quan-

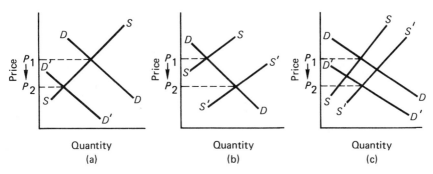

FIGURE 15-6
Price Decreases Resulting from Changes in Supply
and Demand

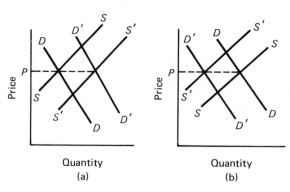

FIGURE 15-7
Price Stability with Changes in Supply and Demand

tity where marginal cost is equated with marginal revenue (Figure 15-8). Under regulation, the monopolist would probably be forced to reduce his price to P_2 in Figure 15-8, a price at which he is just able to recover full costs. Full costs would include a fair return to factor inputs. Most often, regulatory commissions allow monopolies such as the utility company to earn a return of 6 percent above explicit costs on the capital invested. The utility company is then allowed to set a price that will yield this return.

Oligopoly and monopolistic competition.   Pricing in oligopoly and monopolistically competitive markets is complicated by many factors. As a result, no attempt will be made here to translate pricing by one firm into terms of equilibrium prices similar to those in pure competition. The rigidity of price, particularly in oligopolies, has already been discussed. But how the price is established at the level used by each and all firms is another matter. Details of profit maximizing by firms is discussed in Chapter 13.

Often in oligopolistic industries, a price leader will emerge whose price policies will be followed by other firms in the industry. U.S. Steel is an example for the 25 years prior to 1962. In service industries, such as morticians and barbers, price may be more or less tacitly agreed upon and controlled through their professional associations.

Cartels, or written agreements among producers regarding share of market and price stipulation, are illegal. So are other sub rosa or written forms of collusion where it can be proved that the public is hurt from market-price agreements. Therefore, a form of tacit collusion emerges in manufacturing oligopolies, a "live and let live" policy whereby nonprice competition largely determines the share of the market each firm has. Firms strive to increase their profits via advertising to get a larger mar-

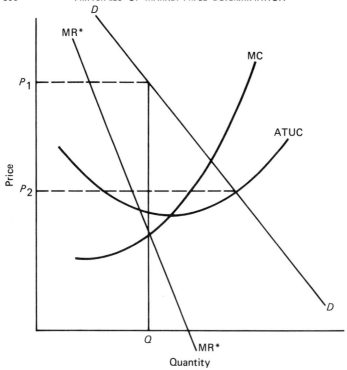

*MR is not equal to D when D is not perfectly elastic. MR will always
be at points midway between the Y axis and the D curve.

FIGURE 15-8

Pricing by Single-Firm Monopolist

ket share and to reduce unit costs through more efficient methods. The
price charged for products changes rarely and is at a level allowing the
major firms to continue production.

THE ALLOCATIVE ROLE OF PRICES

The unit price received times the number of units sold determines
the total gross revenue or return for any business. After the firm sub-
tracts all its operating costs, the amount left over is available to pay
dividends to stockholders or owners of the business. If price persists at a
low level and the firm cannot reduce its cost of production, it will
necessarily be forced to cut production and probably go out of business.
On the other hand, if price is at a high level, returns above costs, often
called profits, will be high and will encourage the firm to continue and
perhaps expand production.

Prices dictate, then, to a considerable extent, the production or output level of any good or service over time. And since resources are required to produce goods and services, it follows that prices provide the allocative mechanism in the economy that directs resources into use. Take the example of buggy whips. With the advent of the automobile, which replaced the horse-drawn buggy for transportation, consumers stopped voting for buggy whips, the price fell, buggy-whip manufacturers went broke, and resources were no longer channeled into buggy-whip production.

The price mechanism in its allocative role is a basic ingredient in a free private-enterprise system. It is a system in which no one individual, no level of government, and no other planning authority has to be conscious of effecting the "proper" resource allocation in society's interest. In our economy, profits—returns above cost—provide the incentive for individual initiative. Profits are the "carrot before the donkey" that has allowed our economy to achieve a high level of production and thus achieve a high standard of living for the American people. However, modifications of the price system, particularly in imperfectly competitive industries, was noted. In Part VII, further modifications of the price system by government action will be discussed in a policy context.

THE TIME ELEMENTS IN PRICES

Relationship of Price to Cost of Production (Pure Competition)

Day-to-day fluctuations in prices occur primarily for three reasons: (1) fluctuations in demand, (2) fluctuations in supply, and (3) experimentation in the price-discovery process. Price changes occurring for these reasons in time periods of less than one production cycle bear practically no relationship to the cost of production.

However, over a longer period of time, price tends to move toward and become equal to cost of production.[4] Why is this so? Let us assume that in any particular year, the majority of producers in a competitive industry were able to earn an excess profit—returns above what would be considered fair return for the input factors used. Such a situation is depicted in Figure 15-9a. The individual producer is selling 10 units at a price of $.80, for a total revenue of $8.00. His costs are $.65 per unit,

---

[4] This does not necessarily mean that price will eventually become equal to the cost of production with the passage of time. The tendency is always present for price to move toward the cost of production, but imperfect elements in the market may prevent it from doing so; the rigid price in oligopoly is an example. Thus, a type of "permanent disequilibrium" may occur, or new and changing market elements may continually cause "new" disequilibriums.

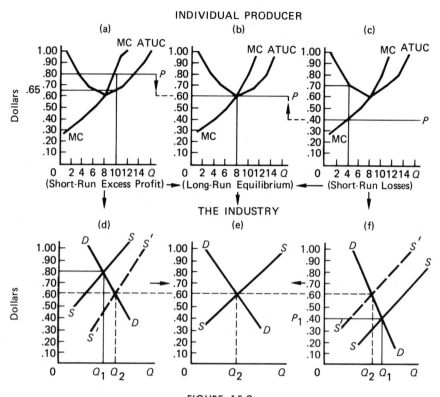

FIGURE 15-9

Movement of Price Toward Cost of Production in a
Purely Competitive Industry

or $6.50, yielding him an excess profit of $1.50. This excess profit will attract new producers to the industry the following year, generating the situation in Figure 15-9d. The increased supply will drive price downward (toward cost of production) until the individual producer has his excess profits squeezed away from him (Figure 15-9b) and until the industry equilibrium of supply and demand conditions exists as shown in Figure 15-9e.

Beginning with the opposite situation, where the individual producer is experiencing short-run losses, as in Figure 15-9c, what will happen? Again conditions will evolve to push the individual to the situation illustrated in Figure 15-9b and the industry to the situation shown in Figure 15-9e. Why? When producers experience losses, at least some will cut back or discontinue production entirely in the following year. A decrease in supply in the industry will drive price upward the following year, as indicated in Figure 15-9f. Thus, regardless of whether excess profits or losses are being incurred in the short-run time period, forces will be put in motion that will tend to generate long-run equilibrium for the individual producer and the industry, as depicted in Figures 15-9b and 15-9e respectively.

Seasonal Price Variation

Commodities whose production and marketings vary within the year experience seasonal price variation. Virtually all agricultural-commodity prices fit this pattern. Seasonality in crop production arises from the weather cycle. Livestock production is influenced by the reproduction period and seasonal changes in weather that affect pasture and other feed supplies. The magnitude of seasonal price variation is lessening, as both crop production and animal production, especially the latter, increasingly occur under partially or completely controlled environmental conditions.

The seasonal nature of production affects prices in two ways. First, perishable or semiperishable commodities that are difficult to store must move into consumption at harvest time. The increased quantity is moved to consumers only at lower prices. Then, when market receipts diminish as the commodity goes out of season, higher prices can be obtained. Examples of foods that fit this pattern well are lettuce, broccoli, oranges, strawberries, and pork and beef to a lesser extent.

Second, nonperishable commodities that can be stored tend to have their lowest price at harvest time. Then, price generally tends to rise during the remainder of the year by an amount approximately sufficient to cover storage costs. The year's production is channeled into consumption in rather evenly distributed amounts over the year.

Prices during the year are affected not only by day-to-day supply and demand conditions but also by anticipated or future supply and demand conditions. These latter fluctuations should not be considered part of seasonal price variation. Another influencing factor for some commodities is government-owned stocks and the expected way in which these supplies will be fed into market channels.

Some commodities, such as hogs, cattle, and milk, can be used for more than one purpose. When cattle receipts increase, the quantity of fresh beef sold increases and the price falls. However, part of a steer can be processed into canned meats, which can be stored for a considerable length of time. Milk can be sold fresh or manufactured into cheese, butter, and other products that are not nearly as perishable. In these instances, the seasonal price fluctuation is less than it would be if the commodity's form could not be changed to a less perishable one.

Seasonal price variations for wheat, apples, eggs, and beef cattle are illustrated in Figure 15-10. The amount of variation is the combined result of the nature of seasonal production and storability of the commodity. Wheat, for example, is all harvested within a few summer months, but because it is storable, the seasonal price variation is only about 10 percent. Slaughter of cattle is seasonally low in the spring, with corresponding higher prices.

Seasonal patterns are not completely accurate and change over time. New production and/or storage techniques will have an influence. However, an understanding of seasonal price variations is important in understanding price changes with time.

Annual Price Variations

We have discussed the general proposition that price tends to move toward cost of production, but annual price changes deserve more of our attention. Annual price fluctuations are most characteristic of crops whose year-to-year changes in production occur as acreage and yields change. Fluctuations in demand are less important in influencing annual price changes.

There seems to be little regularity in the annual variation in crop prices. Severe fluctuations in weather may result in several successive or alternating periods of large and small quantities of crops. Disregarding the influence of government programs, evidence suggests that several years of high or low prices are necessary to markedly influence crop acreages. As a result, it is variations in yields influenced by the weather and technology that account for most of the change in annual production.

Annual price variations for the periods 1910–46 and 1947–63 are given in Table 15-1. The first period included years of war and depression, which widened annual swings in all prices, including farm-product prices. The second period shows farm-price swings in a time of relative stability in the general price level. In addition, several commodities, such as cotton, tobacco, wheat, and corn, have been subjected to federal programs designed to limit price fluctuations. As a result, average yearly fluctuations are considerably less in the period 1947–63 than in 1910–46.

Individual commodity prices also fluctuate around the general farm-price level in divergent patterns. Whole-milk prices, for example, tend to move in close harmony with the farm-price level, whereas others, such as potatoes and hogs, fluctuate around the overall farm-price level in an uncertain fashion.

When the pattern of annual price changes is superimposed onto the

SEASONAL PRICE VARIATION
These Products Show Different Patterns

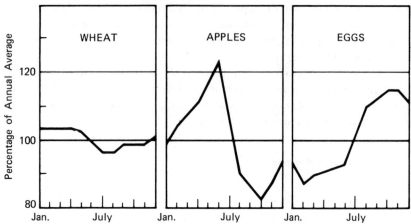

BEEF CATTLE
Farmers' Prices Usually Highest in Spring
When Slaughter is Still Seasonally Low

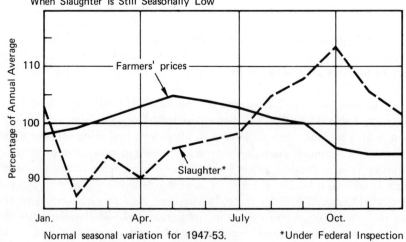

Normal seasonal variation for 1947-53.   *Under Federal Inspection

FIGURE 15-10
Seasonal Price Patterns of Selected Products,
Showing How Price Patterns Differ

TABLE 15-1

Pattern of Annual Price Variability of Selected Farm
Products, United States, 1910–46 and 1947–63

Product	Average Annual Change, Percent	
	1910–46	1947–63
Tobacco	18.2	3.0
Dairy products	10.2	5.0
Wheat	18.0	5.2
Cotton	22.1	5.7
Corn	21.0	8.4
Fruit and tree nuts	15.6	9.5
Poultry and eggs	12.2	9.8
Meat animals	15.1	10.4
Potatoes	35.2	17.3

SOURCE: U.S. Department of Agriculture, *Agricultural Statistics,* annual publication.

farm-price level, which revolves widely around the general price level, the study of prices and their movements becomes very complex. The importance of price fluctuations as they influence the farmer and agricultural policy formulation will be discussed in more detail later.

Cyclical Price Variations

In addition to their annual and seasonal price variations, some farm prices fluctuate in rather regular patterns. Livestock production and prices are a good example: When production is increasing, prices fall, and vice versa. Overall, these cycles can be explained by the decisions of managers, who tend to base future production on the cost–return relationships of the present or recent past.

For example, if cattle production is relatively low and prices are high, managers in the cattle business will look at their favorable earnings and decide to expand. Others not currently in the cattle business may decide to enter or reenter. But it takes time to realize these intentions. Heifers must be withheld from the market and bred, to increase brood-cow numbers. Time will elapse until an expanded calf crop can be raised and fattened for market. Overall, several years will elapse in the process. By that time, increasing supplies will drive prices down,

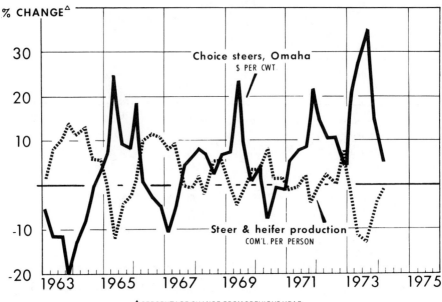

U.S. DEPARTMENT OF AGRICULTURE   NEG. ERS 2473   74 (5)   ECONOMIC RESEARCH SERVICE

FIGURE 15-11
Cattle Production and Price Cycles for a Recent
10-Year Period

and producers will see the profitability of their operations diminish.
For the same reasons as before, the cycle will reverse itself, production
will decline, and prices will increase (Figure 15-11).

There are no well-defined cycles in crop production where producers have considerably less control over production. Cycles are not
highly regular but are important in the study of price fluctuations over
time.

SUMMARY

The models of market price behavior and the kinds of reaction each
model indicates toward allocating inputs and outputs have been discussed
in a fairly general (macro) sense, outside of a particular (micro) business
firm. The dynamics of price discovery and determination, the influence
of time, types of variation in certain price movements, and applications

to farm commodity prices were also introduced. Let us now take a look at the specific adaptations open to a firm's management as goals are decided on and articulated through the various planning, organizing, production, financial, and marketing operations. A case study integrates most of the aspects mentioned and illustrates how much flexibility to make interdependent choices management really has.

PART
FIVE

16

Management—A Perspective

Many students who read this book may aspire to become managers. Management is a major productive resource in the economy and serves to coordinate the use of land, labor, and capital. Management focuses on the decision-making process, on the intelligence of men to make "right" decisions. Management combines man's mental efforts to identify, organize and classify, analyze, decide, act, and evaluate.

A good manager must be able to *observe* problems and to identify them precisely. By defining problems, he shows his awareness of the situation confronting him. He displays his knowledge about it through his ability to devise ways to cope with the problems.

Problem analysis involves identifying the exact situation causing the problem, as well as the formulation of several different ways to solve it. However, management is not content with only analysis; it must put the analysis into action. This is the decision-making function given to management. The manager must choose which of several alternative plans of action offers him the "best" solution in view of his particular goals or desires and of the resources at his disposal. Once the manager makes the decision, *action* must be taken to implement the solution. Once the action is taken, the manager becomes *responsible* for the outcome, good or bad. Finally, constant evaluation at each step of the decision-making process, both before and after the solution is put into action, helps to insure management that the "right" decision was made and offers the manager the opportunity to insert new knowledge (technology, organization, prices, etc.) into his decision-making framework.

MANAGEMENT OBJECTIVES

The essence of the private-enterprise system is the profit motive. Other business objectives may include providing good product lines and client services, staying ahead of the competition, providing for the welfare of employees, having a business growth plan, and being efficient. Some of these goals have social as well as economic orientations. A farm manager's goals are heavily influenced by family goals. The manager of a large company will have personal goals in addition to those of the business. Objectives of the company and its management need to be compatible in order for it to achieve success.

"Managing by objectives" is an oft-used phrase; it means that managers' objectives should be well understood. It implies a quantitative measurement of how well the objectives are met. In this manner, a manager can make the most of his abilities and stimulate decision making and decisive action, thereby leading to increased productivity and improved overall effectiveness.

FUNCTIONS OF MANAGEMENT

Management can be viewed as a distinct process consisting of planning, organizing, motivating, and controlling business activities to accomplish definite objectives. The process is similar whether it involves managing a farm, farm-supply, or food-processing business. The business may be small or large; it may be organized as a sole proprietorship, partnership, cooperative, or corporation.

Planning

Planning is fundamental to the management process, because it forms the basis from which all other management actions take place. Planning is oriented to the future. It implies a thorough understanding of the goals of the particular business firm involved. It requires intellectual effort, reflective thinking, foresight, and imagination. A planner must visualize the working order of a proposed pattern of activities.

Planning is a dynamic function. All plans are tentative and subject to change. A good manager will continually reassess a plan and modify it as needed. The timing aspect of planning is especially critical. There is a proper time to implement a plan—to take the action required to move it into being.

Planning describes what courses of action should be adopted and how and when they should be followed. Effective planning involves answering many questions: Why must the activity be done? Where and when will it take place? Who will do it, and how? When these questions are answered, the result is a statement of objectives, policies, and procedures that the business will follow. Necessarily, then, planning is deeply involved in policy making and its implementation.

A useful plan is simple and easy to understand. It should be geared to the needs of those who will implement it. A plan is a blueprint for action—it points a precise way to reach a predetermined goal or set of goals. The plan should be thorough and provide a visible advantage for each participant. Finally, it should be flexible, allowing for modification over time as situations change. It is not uncommon for managers to use a five-year planning horizon with periodic revisions, so that the plan is endlessly in effect and reflects a moving fixed period of time.

Scheduling gives vitality and practical meaning to planning. A schedule may be made on a basis of annual, monthly, weekly, daily, or even hourly breakdowns of the work to be accomplished. The planned-for degree of flexibility may depend on the time required to perform various tasks. New techniques such as PERT (Program Evaluation Review Techniques) are being used to aid managers in proper scheduling.

Organizing

The important question of organization is, "Where should actions take place, and who should do the work?" Organizing is breaking work down into various components, assembling tasks into operative units, placing people on proper jobs, assigning authority and responsibility so that links in the system will coordinate smoothly, and making adjustments in the system in the light of control results. It is a function of top-level management and follows the planning function closely.

Organizing is necessary for gaining effective group action. Through good organization, the manager hopes for *synergism*—a situation in which the total effort of group action is greater than the sum of the individual efforts put into it.

Before organization can be intelligently outlined, one must know the aim or set of goals to be achieved. Objectives will determine the type and number of people necessary for effective action, the time requirement, and whether a permanent structure or a temporary one is needed. In the final analysis, the objective of organizing is to achieve the business's policy goals in terms of production and profit.

Let's get specific. First, the work to be done must be divided into "packages" that are homogeneous and can be assigned to specific groups and ultimately to individuals. Persons can be assigned to work tasks based on their experience and competence. Each person should understand how his effort fits into the total picture.

Next, the work environment or physical workplace should be considered. It includes placement of machines, working materials, or people's desks so as to minimize time and effort necessary to accomplish specific tasks. Finally, there has to be a chain of responsibility and delegated authority within and between working units.

A common breakdown of activities is the one used in this book in the next three chapters. They cover production, finance, and marketing. As a business grows, this type of organization may evolve into one based on a product line or a territory.

Within a departmental structure such as production, the authority and responsibility among individuals often includes both a line and a staff basis. Line authority is easy to understand: A superior exercises direct command over a subordinate. Each person knows from whom he receives orders and to whom he reports. The person with line authority is directly responsible for the work of those below him.

Staff positions perform supporting roles. They support persons with line authority, particularly in providing top-level managers with information for decision-making. Staff people often have highly specialized knowledge and skills. Research operations are good examples of staff. From one business to another, there is no set guide as to what activities should be under line or staff authority.

Organizing is a dynamic function like planning. It is intimately involved with people and hence is a "living entity" needing constant attention. Organizations change with people and growth of businesses.

Motivating Personnel

Planning and organizing are futile activities unless people are motivated to act. "Actuating" deals entirely with people and involves effective leadership, communication, providing of incentives, and constructive criticism. Getting each employee to do his work willingly and well in an enthusiastic spirit with co-workers and his boss is the ultimate goal of this management function.

Motivating people to action is largely a matter of choosing people already predisposed to certain types of work, effectively communicating to them what they are to accomplish and how to do their job, giving them the authority to do it, and inspiring them to have confidence in their ability to succeed. In essence, it is good leadership.

There are several possible approaches one can take. Most managers rely on some type of reward system. With this approach, the manager avoids conflict with employees, tries to provide a secure atmosphere, and attempts to project a personal approach. Another perspective is that employees should receive rewards that are conditional on performance. Paying wages on piecework and giving merit raises for exceptionally good performance are techniques used. The psychological basis is that if a person takes a certain action and is rewarded, he will repeat the action. With this method, a careful basis for evaluating performance must be worked out.

Still another approach, although a more difficult one, is to try to satisfy human wants solely through the work situation. The manager attempts to integrate the entire manpower resources of his group. The basic idea is that man has many needs and works to fulfill them. By skillfully applying knowledge of human beings toward continual need satisfaction, the manager will form a highly enthusiastic group of co-operative workers. To satisfy these human wants only (or mostly) within a job setting, the worker must be aware of achieving a goal. He must receive some sort of recognition for his achievement. He must be able to grow personally toward further development of his talents. Many workers also need responsibility in order to be motivated to contribute their utmost. A good example comes from Sweden, where small teams of employees now build the entire Volvo car. No more boring production lines. The car is "theirs," and they compete with other teams. Informal leaders emerge, lines of responsibility and teamwork form, and both job satisfaction and productivity have increased significantly.

Some of the more important guides to effective personnel management include giving adequate guidance, recognizing individual differences, making people feel important, consulting them in advance as to changes to be made, being a good listener, avoiding unconstructive arguments, giving adequate guidance, and providing effective supervision. Managerial leadership is probably the most effective tool of "actuating." Managers show leadership by inspiring employees, showing them what is expected, being fair and working hard themselves, and accepting responsibility for both successes and failures. Driving employees, instilling fear, and passing the buck are examples of poor leadership. Personal characteristics of an effective leader include energy to do the job, emotional maturity, empathy, knowledge of human relations, communicative skills, teaching ability, personal motivation, and technical competence.

Controlling

The fourth function of management is controlling business activities. Are the activities of the business being performed as they were set out by the planning department? The controlling function has to do with all types of report making and record keeping. Controlling identifies what is being accomplished, evaluates it against a standard, and applies corrective mechanisms necessary to restore activities to conform to plans. Some of the more important activities that can be controlled include product quantity and/or quality, efficiency of time use, and cost. Each of these factors must be measured in some definite way. Sources of information can include personal observation, recorded statistical data, and oral or written reports. Most managers use all of them at one time or another.

There are eight major areas for which standards might be set: market standing of the enterprise, profitability, materials acquisition and usage, employee performance, capital or financial resources, productivity, physical resources, and public responsibility.

Controlling practices must be reasonable and attainable, as well as being enforceable. If they are not, the effort is costly and fruitless. Controlling is a major function of all major departments—production, finance, and marketing.

The human response to controlling is vital to its overall success. Employees must be convinced it is in their best interests. However, controlling has often led to dismissal or retraining of employees, thus causing some worker distrust. The ease and effectiveness of the controlling function is directly related to its being accepted and understood by employees. For instance, if workers feel only threatened and hostile toward management as a result of a time-and-motion study concerning production control, the results of such an effort are likely to be counterproductive.

DIFFERENCES BETWEEN FARM AND NONFARM
BUSINESS MANAGEMENT

Although the functions just discussed pertain to all managers, each person will be affected differently. Some of the differences between farm and nonfarm business management are illustrated in the following situations.

Ownership and Control of Resources

On farms and ranches, the productive resources are typically under the ownership and control of the farm family. Except in very large operations, there is no departmentalization of activities. In nonfarm business enterprises, even though there is still a large number of family businesses, most of the nation's productive resources are under a corporate business structure. In these large corporations, ownership is in the hands of stockholders, but control is in the hands of managerial executives who are separated from direct contact with them.

Source of Labor Input

As we saw in Chapter 4, the majority of farm labor comes from unpaid family members. In the nonfarm corporation, virtually all the labor and most of the management is hired. Workers' responsibility is thus mostly to some relative on the farm, and to an impersonal supervisor or board of directors in a nonfarm business.

Degree of Labor and Management Specialization

There is probably more labor specialization in nonfarm businesses than there is on farms. This is because the typical farm worker performs a much wider group of tasks than a worker in industry, who perhaps attaches the same small part to an item moving along an assembly line day after day. In addition, farming requires different tasks for different periods of the year.

Biological Processes of Production

All food-production processes on the farm are based on biological processes. Work requirements depend partly on the season, and on the particular biological needs of the crops or livestock under consideration. Farmers are at the mercy of the weather. On the other hand, in industry, many jobs can be done simultaneously in various parts of the plant regardless of weather influences, and the final product assembled along a moving line that can be shut down or speeded up.

Controlled environments for producing food products are becoming more important, however, and it is a trend for the future. Already, broilers, eggs, and vegetables are often grown under cover, using a manufacturing type of approach. An egg operation in California contains over a million hens in completely environmentally-controlled buildings. A six-story hog plant is being tested in Illinois. However, production of plants and animals can seldom be speeded up or slowed down.

Spatial Relationships

On the farm, machines are moved to where the work is conducted. In nonfarm enterprises, the work is usually moved to the machines. This difference has particular significance in the control function.

Degree of Market Control

In Chapter 15, we noted that farmers usually operate under conditions of pure competition, each farmer having little or no control over the price he might receive. Nonfarm businesses, however, are more likely to be in an oligopolistic market situation. The planning function is difficult in both instances, but more of a problem for the farm manager. He must base his production decision, at the beginning of a production cycle determined by biological processes, on anticipated prices over which he has little or no control, at harvest and for perhaps two to three years in the future.

FUNCTIONAL ORGANIZATION OF
AGRIBUSINESS FIRMS

Farm businesses are generally of a size enabling the farm operator to handle all the necessary management tasks. The operator generally decides when, what, and how much to plant; how much fertilizer to apply; and which, if any, livestock enterprises to engage in. These decisions can be grouped under the general heading of production decisions. The farm operator also decides when and where to sell his products and arranges for financing. These decisions can be grouped under the general headings of marketing and financial control.

Nonfarm agricultural business firms are frequently of such a large size that the management function cannot be adequately handled by an individual operator. This phenomenon gives rise to the need for delegation of many management functions.

A simple organizational structure, similar to organizational structures found in many agriculturally related businesses, is presented in Figure 16-1. The general manager in this type of organization does not supervise work directly or make all management decisions directly. However, he is responsible for making decisions that are basic to the entire

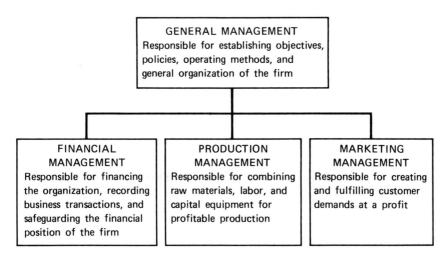

FIGURE 16-1

Functional Areas of Management Decision Making

organization. He depends upon his departmental managers to implement his decisions in their respective specialties.

Production, marketing, and financing (Figure 16-1) are the three basic functional areas involved in the total management of business firms. These three areas will be discussed in detail in the next three chapters, in an attempt to explain the nature and role of these functions in the management of agricultural business firms.

17

Production Management

Farm and off-farm business managers need to know the essentials of production management if their firms are to be profitable. The planning, organizing, motivating, and controlling aspects of management discussed in the preceding chapter will be reviewed here in reference to production. The same management aspects will be considered in following chapters for finance and marketing.

The successful management of production draws on many disciplines and scientific fields for its inputs. Operations research, psychology, industrial engineering, economics, and management science are only a few of the possible sources. It makes little difference whether one is producing a good or a service, the same principles still apply.

PRODUCTION PLANNING

There is bound to be some overlap between the planning aspects of organizing, marketing, and financing in any business. However, there are elements that are clearly separable for the overall planning function.

Planning is primarily the job of management (Chapter 16). It is a line job, even though it involves much staff work. It is the responsibility of management executives to consider short-run plans, long-run plans, growth plans, plans for new product development including research and development (R&D), and means of getting the most from both the firm's resources and external sources of information.

Traces of production management can be found as far back as 1800, but it was not until F.W. Taylor began his famous time-and-motion methods studies in the early 1900s that production management came into its own. However, the field did not really bloom until the crises imposed by World War II.

Taylor saw profound advantages stemming from the division of labor. He visualized significant productivity increases by using men in much the same manner that machines were used. He neglected to see that men might object to being treated like machines, a situation made increasingly clear by workers and unions in the postwar years.

Taylor's studies analyzed the methods of production, searching for ways to consolidate movements, place materials or machines to more advantage, allow for pertinent rest periods, and thereby increase productivity. His goal was more production from the same amount of (or less) labor. He aimed at perfecting the performance of routine tasks in terms of human engineering. His concerns were speed, capacity, and durability of the workers to fit the modes he found most efficient. It was almost entirely a physical, not psychological, analysis. There are many differences in today's business firms. Worker attitudes and desires are increasingly considered. For example, some firms allow workers to check in for a shift at their own discretion over a 10–12 hour period. As a result, absenteeism has been lowered drastically, and worker morale has been raised.

In the larger firms, management spends up to 80 percent of its time in planning functions. The planning done is consistent with the basic objectives of the business, yet it continually probes for possible modifications and ways to build complementary capabilities (Chapter 11).

Since the birth of "operations research" as a science, and the burst of computer usage and mathematical tools of analysis—including regression, linear programming, and simulation—planners can make more accurate estimates of performance under a variety of conditions than they once did. These tools enable them to extend their planning horizons in many directions within a relatively short time period. They can build models that will estimate the effects of doubling the firm's product lines, or halving them; of moving plant location, and opening foreign markets; of changing certain types of investment; and perhaps of leasing needed equipment, such as trucks, instead of owning it. You can see that the variations on the planning alternatives could be almost endless, and that the management challenge is to pick out the most relevant options for in-depth analysis.

Farmers plan, too, and some spend much money to have it done for them. Many feedlots have been computerized, with predetermined programs manipulating machinery that mixes rations, carries them to conveyor belts and the feeding bunks, and even cleans up after the animals! Many orchardists and viticulturists now use solid-state computerized irrigation systems that, at the push of a button, will irrigate, put on fertilizer or fungicides or pesticides or herbicides, and are automatically set to protect again frost or heat.

Planners use *engineering models* in conjunction with their *mathematical models*. For instance, the design of production layouts is essential to efficient product handling, whether the product is hay bales or test tubes. Two- and three-dimensional scale models are set up to help analyze any production activity. Farmers are not exempt from this process, either. When laying out a new corral, dairy milking parlor, feedlot, or vegetable-handling station, most managers make a mock-up of the proposed facility before they actually begin building.

When planning for business growth overseas, production planners must consider factors like exchange rates, tariffs, contract servicing, transportation, and personnel characteristics. What impact will these items have on both the quantity and the quality of expected production? There are many farmers who have made large investments in Australia, Mexico, Canada, and Europe, and who are influenced by them. For example, what will be the impact of a reduction in tariffs on beef and lamb, what will be the longer-run effects of the devaluation of the dollar on shipping soybeans to Europe for processing, and what if a U.S. farmer cannot own land in another country because of its land policies?

Essentially, production planning explores the same basic questions discussed in Chapter 1. It provides information for decisions about what to produce, how to produce it, and how much to produce. Plans can be made for a short time span of perhaps a year, or they can cover a five-year or longer period. How comprehensive they are will depend to a large extent on the participation by staff and line, and the ability and desire of management to delegate analytical search tasks. For example, an ad hoc planning team could explore the consequences of concentrating production on one item, or of combining enterprises for several different markets.

Planning the product line and selecting the product mix (review Chapter 13—a *what* and *how* question) can be a truly educational experience for planners themselves. One case discussion will illustrate this point. A firm manufactured all the necessary items for setting up complete poultry-processing plants anywhere. One plant was ordered from a company in Spain, and the appropriate planners and engineers were sent to set it up. However, the plant had been designed for American consumer tastes and preferences, and no one had checked on those of the Spanish people.

Think of the last time you bought chicken, and you will remember that most Americans buy primarily precut and packaged chicken. It is washed before packing, so it is usually pinkish white and wet. The production lines of the new plant in Spain were set up according to these "successful selling techniques," with killing lines, washing and chilling trays, and tables for cutting and wrapping the processed birds. There was little or no storage room. However, when the plant was about to start operation, some one discovered that on the whole, the Spanish people preferred whole, unwrapped, aged birds. They also liked the head and feet left on. Instead of a white, wet appearance, they liked their birds to be dry, with a yellow skin color. These differences necessitated a complete rethinking and rebuilding of the processing plant, including the building of storage facilities for aging the birds.

In any production process, planners must also anticipate a *continuous supply of inputs* for as long as production is anticipated. Arranging for this steady flow means that much contact work and prescheduling must be done, in order to coordinate farm producers so that their product flows come to the plant in amounts it can handle, and so that wastage is kept to a minimum. For instance, if all the carrots in one valley were harvested on the same day, perhaps the processing plant could not handle them all. Field production must be coordinated with the processing plant's plans.

Production managers must also consider, as inputs to the overall planning process, the pricing plans and sales program of their marketing people. Timing can be critical, particularly if it builds up costly inventory or demands increased storage costs.

Once a product is authorized by top management, planning must suggest such diverse things as ways to control product inventories, availability of spare parts for servicing clients, and the safety of employees. Designing a new product or product line entails a thorough search procedure. This search can involve much travel, reading, and debates about the what, where, and how questions. If a new product is decided on, it may still require additional specific research and development (such as the poultry-plant example just noted). Planners must then try to recapture these fixed (sometimes called sunk, or overhead) costs, as well as the more typical fixed and variable costs of production.

After defining the new product, or modified product, planners must relate their total business organization to its production and expected profit potential. They must reappraise the functional responsibilities that will accompany the product's entry into their old production lines. They must review the appropriate divisions of labor and responsibility relating to overall plant layout, location, receiving of input materials, assembling these materials with efficient production methods, timing of subassemblies, inspecting and checking the product by stages, finishing, and shipping or storing the product. In these situations, many planners construct a prototype engineering model of the product, paying attention to its styling, packaging characteristics, quality, and final anticipated salability.

Also, in designing a completely new production system, planners often make scale models bearing on the selection of inputs, equipment, and production processes. Through the models, they relate production designs to costs and control methods, and make sure that anticipated job designs match existing or obtainable personnel. Further, they can appraise current plant location and production facility within the plant, and compare them to some other spot that might be more advantageous and therefore more profitable.

Planning ultimately includes developing *operation process charts* which show a breakdown and analysis of each operation as it occurs in the production process, where it occurs, and who or what is involved. *Product flow charts* may also contain *activity charts* that specifically identify the men and/or machines involved at any particular point in the product's creation. Finally, planners should be able to construct a *schedule diagram,* which notes the flow of time by activity from the moment a hypothetical order is received from a client, through the parts procurement and any necessary prefabrication, their assembly into a final product, its inspection, and shipping.

Budgeting as a Tool for Decision Making

One way to test planning alternatives is to use a technique called *partial budgeting.* By budgeting out the changes in costs and revenues coincident with identifying planning objectives, one can discover the net economic results of possible changes in resource use.

Budgets put information to use. Budgets aid in projecting future firm costs based on past records and experience and help identify which costs are most likely to increase. They also help to predict expected revenue from production and aid in its scheduling and timing. Budgets help guide the farmer to choose between those farm enterprises most likely to fulfill his family's needs, and his own personal goals of income and satisfaction.

Budgeting is the mechanical vehicle for calculating maximum profit points and for looking at the probable results of many alternative actions. The concept of marginality (discussed in Chapters 10 and 11) says that managers should think in terms of additional costs and the additional returns resulting from a change in organization or production practice. It is logical, then, that there are two general sets of data that are basic to any useful budget. First, the changed physical input (with accompanying costs) associated with a particular action; and second, the changed physical production (with its value) that results from the action. In any business-resource adjustment, one may add to or reduce existing income. A typical budgeting form would follow this outline:

Additional costs: $_____
Reduced returns: $_____
  Subtotal: $_____
Reduced costs: $_____
Additional receipts: $_____
  Subtotal: $_____
    Net change in income (plus or minus) $_____

The job of identifying the changes in costs and returns resulting from a change in the business will vary with the complexity of the change. Farmers will recognize that with some changes in their farm business, certain costs will remain unchanged, while others will vary proportionately with the size of the change. Adding two sows to a large-sized hog business would probably not necessitate additional costs for taxes or building insurance or perhaps even equipment (fixed-type costs), but it would require additional costs for feed (variable-type cost) in direct proportion to the number of sows added.

On the other hand, the additional costs and returns resulting from adding a secondary enterprise, such as growing heifers for sale, may be more difficult to identify, since the additional enterprise may involve joint use of resources and entail changes in every aspect of the going farm business. The identification of the costs that will not change—that is, of those that are *fixed* as a result of a particular action—and of those that will change—the *variable* costs—constitutes a major problem in the budgeting procedure.

The key point to remember in the mechanics of testing alternatives through the budget process is that only variable or additional costs should enter the calculations (Chapter 11). Fixed costs by definition are those costs that do not change with the adjustment. Adjustments may be measured in terms of additions to and subtractions from existing total costs and returns. It is not necessary to deal with the totals themselves.

The budgeting process is rapidly becoming more sophisticated with the advent of new mathematical techniques such as linear programming and the use of computers. These new developments allow more variables to be considered at one time in budgeting problems, because of the speed at which computers can do arithmetic.

PRODUCTION ORGANIZATION

Many businessmen view their formal organizations as primary social institutions, structures that show channels of authority and responsibility. These channels note the bureaucracy, or executive hierarchy. Their purpose is to designate the decision-making process, influence management awareness, and direct employee behavior patterns. Change the organization, and the responsibility and behavior patterns will also change.

The object of an organizational chart is to focus, and thereby force, information flows needed for management decisions. It makes authority visible. One method to obtain higher visibility, and thereby anticipate higher levels of performance, is to departmentalize the firm. Separating a business into only a few components, such as planning, production, marketing, and finance, may not give the desired degree of control. It may mask the matter of who is responsible for making which decision. For that reason, it might be advisable to divide a department into smaller increments for planning and controlling purposes (Figure 17-1).

In this hypothetical situation, the XYZ Company is broken into four major divisions reporting to a president, who, in turn, reports to his board of directors. Each of the four main departments of the business are further divided. In the production department, a vice-president is in

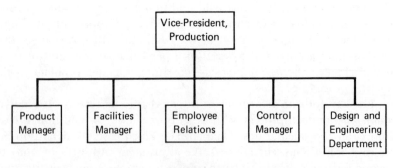

FIGURE 17-1
Organization Chart for Production Management of
XYZ Company

charge, and responsible to the company's president. The vice-president's responsibility is to see that the production lines work—that goods are produced when they are promised and sent to the people who order them. It is he who is also responsible for maintaining good relations with production workers, their union if they have one, and his foremen or supervisors.

Under the vice-president, there are five major subdepartments upon which the vice-president may call for help, and to which he can delegate authority and responsibility. The first person under the vice-president is a manager for overall physical production. It is his job to make sure the product lines are running properly, and the flows of inputs and output maintained.

Next is a facilities manager, who sees that the machinery in the lines is kept in proper working shape, the building kept to safety standards, and that everything to do mechanically with production is handled according to standard.

The person in charge of employee relations is responsible for setting up union contacts and training courses, handling grievances, and making suggestions for promotion.

The control manager is perhaps the key person in the production operation. He must keep the records determining the assignments that yield the highest total value for a specified time period, either short run or long run. It is he who decides on the degree of desired dependence on other departments, and suggests other means of complementing the capabilities of his own production department. All the cost and time records, the product flow charts, and quality scheduling are funneled through his office. This manager must be alert and interested in logical detail, yet he must also be enough of a generalist to see where his staff enter the decision process and the possible contributions they might make to the overall planning effort.

The design and engineering department can be called on by each of the other departments. This department is set up here as a servicing function, a staff effort trying to bring engineering expertise to bear on immediate and long-range problems, such as quality control, from machine repair through the design of more efficient machine layouts to new-product design and styling.

It should be stressed that there is probably no one "best" way to organize a firm's management, its divisions and departments. A firm that has plants in several regions of the country will probably have a more complex organization chart than will a firm with only one plant. There are many other reasons for variations in organization forms. The question of centralization versus decentralization of production-management decision-making is one reason for varying degrees of complexity in a firm's organizational chart. Responsibility lines will also be different if the board of directors wants to keep tight control on the purse strings and not relinquish authority to control capital expenditures. Other factors influencing organization are the degree to which a firm's management chooses to stay flexible to fit the stresses and strains put on it by changing business conditions and market opportunities; characteristics such as the degree of independence desired within management itself; the possible policies with regard to the enterprises undertaken, including new projects; and the extent to which modifications might be made as a result of control evaluations.

In a farm or small nonfarm business, production organization is usually quite simple—one man or woman is solely responsible for all the firm's commitments. In a firm with many people, few managers are allowed this autonomy.

With all the flexibility needs we have mentioned, and with all the variations in organizational possibilities we have discussed, let's review what an organizational chart does: It identifies who controls whom and what, what the flows of information are, and who is responsible for certain kinds of decisions. It shows who approves plans, establishes project priorities, and implements their production. It pinpoints the managers who participate in major cost and performance decisions, who approve buying and selling plans, and who oversee reporting activities. Responsibility for evaluating, suggesting policy modifications, and making budgeting assists is allocated to each department. The handling of customer relations, employee motivation, and new project development is also identified.

PRODUCTION MOTIVATION

Motivation of either production employees or management is a complicated task. Essentially, it is the challenge of *how to get people to participate* in a coordinated effort. Theories of organization suggest that the motivation process is really a continual testing of the responses that are associated with offering different stimuli. If responses do not come up to expectation, then it is time to offer a different stimulus.

Common kinds of stimuli include wage incentives, additional responsibility, status symbols, and noncash awards such as certificates or the 25-year watch. Almost everyone in a business firm wants to feel that he is a meaningful part of a worthwhile effort, that he has some choice in making the operation better, and that what he does or thinks counts for something. Increasing this kind of employee satisfaction is highly correlated with increasing productivity.

There was once a famous experiment directed at increasing worker productivity. The researchers first had music piped into the plant; output per person increased. Lighting was adjusted; output again rose. The plant was painted, supervisors were polite, coffee breaks were liberalized, and productivity continued to climb. Then someone had the idea of making the lighting a little less good. Output still rose. Lighting was made worse, paint chipped, and music was cut off, but output continued at a high level. The researchers' conclusion was that as long as the workers felt that someone was paying some positive attention to them, they did count for something, and as a result they put more effort into their work. However, if they observed that they were being thoroughly abused, production would decline.

Motivation can be extended to management just as it can to any other kind of employee classification. Sensitivity training, planning workshops, and other educational programs have been authorized in many firms. These programs also are a help in selecting and developing management personnel to move into the top positions.

Essentially, motivation for people to produce anything depends on the character of a particular set of initiatives, their perceived consequences, and the relation of these consequences to the personal goals and values of the individuals involved. Some people may prefer a better work environment and more rest breaks to being a supervisor. Other people might prefer to have supervisory responsibility than spend all day on a routine task. Still other people would prefer complicated jobs to simple ones. To find the stimulus that will appeal to people so that it evokes a particularly desired response is a never-ending challenge to the firm's personnel department.

PRODUCTION CONTROL

The main objective of controlling production is to see that completion occurs on time, within budget, and in full quality compliance with items or contract specifications. Control also provides a capacity to cope with product changes (some of which might be unexpected) that are brought about by R&D, competitors, or innovations in more effective cost controls. It demonstrates how to phase production and marketing policies, reduce inventories, and eliminate unprofitable items that the firm may produce without realizing they are losers.

The maintenance and control of product quality has been mentioned before. It is a professional field within itself. Established and contracted standards must be maintained. Inspection is certainly a part of quality control—and probability concepts play an important role in determining what sampling techniques are appropriate to control the predetermined quality production of a particular item. Control charts can track critical machines, people, or production processes.

It is important to note that despite agreed-on sampling procedures —random, sequential, or for various attributes—individual human judgment still remains a crucial element of product control. How bad is really bad? Did the micrometer fall on this side or that side of the point, and how important is that in terms of the specified customer? What is the sum of minor defects that add up to product rejection? Although electronic measurements, including X ray, are advances over the use of hand calipers, they nevertheless continue to demand the same elements from supervisors and inspectors—judgment in their use and in interpreting the results.

Management whose job is control must assume a delegation of authority and responsibility to make suggestions according to specified predetermined minimum standards. Control also connotes a constant evaluation process bearing on the synchronization of production, R&D, marketing, and finance.

Controllers usually establish policies under which they can operate freely throughout the company. Characteristics of these policies include the visibility of the control process; if hidden procedures are allowed, the controllers will find they are unable to get accurate information. The policies must be uniform throughout the company and not permit double standards for "special" departments. Also, the policies must be capable of modification if any kind of change is indicated. Finally, the control process should be comprehensive. In Figure 17-1, for example, the controller should have access to information from all the departments under the vice-president, and selected interdepartmental considerations.

Once the operating policies are established and the company objectives understood, what are the most effective control mechanisms? Without doubt, the most effective tool the control manager can use is the budget. It is certainly the most widely used control mechanism in business today. Profit-and-loss statements by product, product lines, or department are other control tools, but are really adaptations of using budgets for analyzing cost effectiveness and management by objectives.

Controllers can use all the quantitative methods and tools that planners use. They can computerize inventory and test it against probable orders throughout the year or season. They can apply many different kinds of probability statements to various quantity and quality control problems by means of many statistical techniques. Further, they can provide relevant suggestions to management for the maintenance and reliability of the entire business system. Even though there is usually no profit without some risk taking, the controller is there to see what he can do to minimize the risks of operation once the decision to undertake the project is made.

Because the most effective control tool concerns income and expenditures, he needs cost and revenue data. The kinds of costs he needs were covered in Chapter 12. Also, in order to cost out some of the alternatives, he will also probably need to bring future costs and revenues to present-day values, so that management can fully understand them. How to perform this function is covered in Chapter 18.

SUMMARY

Production planning, organization, motivating, and controlling have been discussed in general in the preceding pages. Every firm's management will have to decide on the most appropriate forms of each function for their own business, based on their own resources and market opportunities. Planning and control are clearly key functions of any production operation; organization and motivation perhaps play more subordinate roles.

18

Financial Management

Financial management deals with all money aspects of a business enterprise. The efficient use and control of all revenue, expenditures, capital assets, and funds are also implied. Although the control function of management is readily apparent, the finance department makes a major contribution to overall business planning as well. A business cannot grow and expand unless financial resources are available or can be marshalled for use. Proper financing is essential to entrepreneurial success. The right amount of funds must be expended for inventories, adequate loans must be arranged, sufficient fixed capital (land, buildings, machines, and equipment) must be provided, credit must be extended wisely, and the total physical volume of the business unit must be maintained at a level compatible with funds available. If a business cannot pay its obligations within a reasonable period of time, or grow when the time is ripe, it is forced to disband; thus, liquidity and financial soundness are necessary for survival.

THE ACCOUNTING SYSTEM

Financial managers accomplish their control function by interpreting information furnished through an accounting system. Additionally, certain types of records are legally required by law for reporting information pertaining to tax liabilities and employee benefits. Two types of interrelated financial statements form the basis for financial control. They are the balance sheet and the profit-and-loss statement.

Basic Financial Statements

A *balance sheet* is a picture at one point in time of the way a business is using funds and the source of those funds. A balance sheet is sometimes referred to as a *net-worth statement*. Mechanically, it is simply a listing of assets on the left-hand side of the page, and liabilities and ownership equities (net worth) on the right-hand side. The balance-sheet equation is:

$$Assets = Liabilities + Ownership\ equity$$

An *asset* is any tangible good or intangible item legally owned by the business that has a positive monetary value. Personally owned assets of the managers of the business are not included. A complete listing of assets is similar to an inventory. Assets are commonly divided into *current assets* and *fixed assets;* the difference is that current assets are readily convertible into cash and have a high liquidity, whereas fixed assets are not. Cash on hand is the best example of a current asset, and land of a fixed asset. Current assets also include accounts receivable, stored crops, prepaid expenses, and livestock ready for market. Fixed assets include land improvements, buildings, machinery, equipment, office furniture, and vehicles.

A business *liability* represents a legal obligation to pay money to another person or business entity. It is an incurred debt that is due to carrying out the business' policies. Liabilities may also be grouped as current or fixed, depending on the time until the debt must be paid. Obligations due, say, within the next 6–12 months are considered current. An unpaid utility bill that will be paid next month is an example. However, a mortgage payment on land, due to be paid several years from now, is a fixed liability. Current liabilities include accounts payable, accrued taxes payable, short-term notes, and short-term bank loans. Fixed assets include mortgages, long-term bank loans, and any other long-term indebtedness of the business, such as debentures and bonds.

Equity is an accounting term describing ownership of assets. Ownership equity, or net worth, is total assets minus total liabilities. For corporations, stock issued is listed as an ownership equity valued at its initial selling price to stockholders, along with *retained earnings,* which represent the accumulation of undistributed profits in the business. The balance-sheet equation always "balances" by definition; therefore, it is possible for net worth or retained earnings to be a negative figure if liabilities are greater than assets.

A hypothetical balance sheet for a business is shown in Table 18-1. The valuation of fixed assets when preparing the balance sheet might be handled in several ways. However, a common procedure is to value land at its initial cost when purchased by the business, even though its current market value might be substantially more. Buildings, machinery, land improvements, equipment, and breeding stock are usually valued at original cost less accumulated depreciation and notated as "net." The calculation of depreciation is discussed later in the chapter. Inventories of stored and growing crops or growing livestock are usually valued at a conservative market value.

Given the balance-sheet information in Table 18-1, the student can see that the business depicted is not a corporate type, because stock issued and retained earnings are not listed in the ownership-equities section. The owner(s) of XYZ Farm and Ranch had 52.4 percent equity in their business on January 1, 1975, the ratio of $124,600 to $238,000. In

TABLE 18-1
Balance-Sheet Illustration

XYZ Farm and Ranch
January 1, 1975

Assets		Liabilities	
Current:		Current:	
Cash in bank	$ 2,000	Accounts payable	$ 3,400
Accounts receivable	5,000	Accrued taxes	2,000
Stored grain	3,000	Bank loan	10,000
Growing livestock	25,000	Total current	$ 15,400
Total current	$ 35,000		
Fixed:			
Breeding stock	$ 30,000	Fixed:	
Land	100,000	Mortgages	$ 58,000
Buildings (net)	35,000	Bank loan	40,000
Machinery (net)	20,000	Total fixed	$98,000
Equipment (net)	8,000	Total liabilities	$113,400
Vehicles (net)	10,000	Net worth	$124,600
Total fixed	$203,000	Total liabilities	
Total assets	$238,000	and net worth	$238,000

other words, for every dollar of assets listed, they were using 52.4 cents of their own money and 47.6 cents of other people's money.

In a real sense, then, the liability and ownership-equities side of a balance sheet shows the principal sources of funds being used in the business, and the asset side shows the uses to which those funds have been put. In the XYZ Farm and Ranch example, the sources of funds were these: $124,600 from the owners; $50,000 from bankers; $58,000 from the financial institution or person holding their mortgages; $3,400 from other businessmen; and $2,000 from the federal, state, and local governments. Looking at the assets side, the farm managers were using $100,000 in land; $35,000 in buildings; $38,000 in machinery, equipment, and vehicles; $30,000 in breeding stock; $28,000 in crop and livestock inventory; and $5,000 to carry accounts receivable; and they had $2,000 in a checking account.

Businessmen should prepare balance sheets at least once each year, and preferably each quarter. It is a statement any banker or other lender will want to see when a firm is applying for credit. Another advantage is that by comparing one balance sheet with another, a manager can see the financial growth of his business. When he is considering the sale of his own business, the purchase of another business, or a merger, balance sheets are necessary and prudent statements to have during the negotiation process.

Measuring Profits and Losses

A record of the income from sales and expenses of a business, used in measuring profits and losses, is called an *income statement*. It is also referred to as a *profit-and-loss* statement. In contrast to the balance sheet, which is prepared for a specific date, the income statement represents financial activity over a period of time—usually one, three, six, or twelve months, depending on the needs of management.

Income and expenses should be accounted for on an *accrual* basis if they are to be of value for business analysis and management purposes. However, a *cash* basis of accounting is acceptable for tax purposes, and is the method most often used for personal accounting.

What is the difference? In the cash method, income is considered to be received on the day money is actually put into hand. Under the accrual method, income is considered to be received the day the item was sold, not when the money was obtained. For instance, suppose hay was sold for $2,000 on December 10, 1975, and you were immediately paid $1,000, with the remaining $1,000 to be paid a month later, on January 10, 1976. Under the cash method, the 1975 income record would show $1,000, and the 1976 income record would show $1,000. Under the accrual method, the full $2,000 would be credited to 1975. Similarly, on the expense side, suppose you pay a fire insurance premium of $250 on March 15, 1975, which gives you protection for two years, until March 15, 1977. Under a cash method of accounting, the full $250 would be charged as an expense and appear as a cost of doing business in 1975. Under the accrual method, however, $125 would be charged in 1975 and $125 in 1976. These examples make it easy to understand that the accrual method matches the appropriate expenses with the appropriate income, and is more useful to management in analyzing fixed and variable costs of production. A cash system may yield distorted information.

The format for the income statement is presented in Table 18-2.

TABLE 18-2
Income-Statement Illustration

XYZ Farm and Ranch
January 1, 1975—December 31, 1975

Sales:		
Crops	$10,000	
Livestock	45,000	
Total		$55,000
Expenses:		
Hired labor	$ 3,600	
Feed purchased	10,000	
Fertilizers and seeds	2,400	
Supplies	1,500	
Pharmaceuticals	700	
Gasoline and oil	800	
Electricity	750	
Telephone	200	
Property taxes	4,500	
Insurance	600	
Repairs	1,800	
Veterinary	1,000	
Accounting and legal	500	
Depreciation	7,000	
Total		$35,350
Net income (before interest)		$19,650
Interest expense		8,650
Net income (after interest)		$11,000

Sales can be broken down into relevant categories, depending on the business. The income from sales of assets should not be included; only the income from sale of products. For businesses like farm-supply and retail food stores, the cost of goods sold is subtracted from sales and the difference listed as "gross margin" at the top of the income statement. *Cost of goods sold* refers to the invoice cost to the retailers of goods purchased from the wholesaler or other supplier for resale. Expenses are then subtracted from gross margin to yield net income. For example:

Sales	$735,000
Cost of goods sold	600,000
Gross margin	$135,000

Expenses include both fixed and variable costs and do not necessarily represent cash leaving the business. Depreciation is a good example.

Depreciation.   Depreciation is the slow using up of a long-lived asset. A depreciation schedule is prepared for capital items that have a useful life of more than one year, and hence whose initial cost cannot be written off as a business expense in the year that they are purchased. Farm buildings, farm machinery and equipment, breeding and dairy livestock, fences and tile, orchards and vineyards, and wells are the common items for which a depreciation schedule is prepared. The discussion of costs in Chapter 12 listed depreciation as one of the fixed-type costs that have no bearing on determining the most profitable level of production.

The difficult question with regard to depreciation is how much of the initial cost of a capital item, such as a tractor, should be charged against each year's business operation over its expected life. An easy method is to charge equal dollar amounts against each year of expected life. This is called the *straight-line method*. For example, if a new tractor were purchased in January for $4,000 and its expected life was eight years, $500 of depreciation expense would be charged against the farm operation in each of the succeeding eight years. This method is more commonly used on buildings and livestock.

Since 1954, other methods that allow a more rapid write-off, or greater depreciation expense in the early life of the item, have been legal. These methods, used principally for machinery and equipment, allow the book value (original cost minus any depreciation expense taken) to more nearly approximate the market value over the life of the item. Using one common method, called the *declining-balance method,* a constant percentage of the book value is taken in arriving at any year's depreciation expense. The percentage allowed for new items is two times the straight-line rate. If used equipment is bought, only $1\frac{1}{2}$ times the straight-line rate is allowed. For example, using the tractor just mentioned, the straight-line rate is $12\frac{1}{2}$ percent (100 divided by 8). Therefore, the allowable percentage would be 25 percent, since it was purchased new. Depreciation allowed in the first year would be $1,000 (25 percent of $4,000); the second year, $750 (25 percent of $3,000); the third year, $562.50 (25 percent of $2,250); and so on. This method of faster write-off allows more depreciation expense to be taken in the early years, which tends to reduce tax liability. To encourage the purchase of capital equipment, various laws now allow for extra depreciation the first year, liberalization of the estimate of expected life, and several other considerations.

SUMMARY

The balance sheet is usually prepared as of the closing date of the period represented by the income statement. In other words, the income statement represents what transpired between two balance-sheet dates as regards income and expenses. Using XYZ Farm and Ranch as an example, the $11,000 of net income would enter a balance sheet prepared as of January 1, 1976 and increase the net-worth figure by $11,000 (or up to $135,600). The $11,000 net profit could have been used to decrease liabilities, purchase new assets, or some of both.

MEASURES OF PROFITABILITY

Return on Total Investment and Owner's Equity

Commonly used measures of business profitability are return on total investment, and return to owner's equity. In the XYZ Farm and Ranch illustration, return on total investment is 8.3 percent, computed by dividing $19,650 by $238,000 and multiplying by 100. Managers can compare this return to similar businesses and judge how well their own business has done. The return can also be compared to those from other types of investments.

Return on owner's equity for XYZ Farm and Ranch would be 8.8 percent, computed by dividing $11,000 by $124,600 and multiplying by 100. The owner-operator of XYZ Farm and Ranch may conclude that he had a fairly good year, since the 8.8 percent return is above what the same amount of money invested in the local savings and loan association would have earned. However, he has forgotten about his own labor and management input for the year. Shouldn't he charge himself something for it? The answer is yes.

The $11,000 is a return to not only his own investment (equity) but also to any unpaid family labor plus his own labor and management. Thus, if the manager of XYZ Ranch used $1,000 worth of unpaid family labor and imputed a value of $9,000 to his own labor and management input, he would have only $1,000 left as a return to his own investment in the business. This would represent a return of only 0.8 percent—($1,000 ÷ $124,600) × 100—which may not be acceptable. Looking at it another way, if he charged a 5 percent interest cost for use of his own money invested, which he could earn from it in a local savings account, he would have $3,770 left as a return to his own labor and management ($11,000 − $1,000 − [5% × $124,600]). Again, the result is not very satisfactory. Thus, the general conclusion would probably be that the XYZ Farm and Ranch was not a very successful operation from an economic point of view. However, if the manager derived $5,000 or $10,000 worth of nonmonetary satisfaction by living in the clean air of the country and viewing the scenery, he may have successfully reached his business and family goals.

To be more precise, the sales figures should be credited with the value of farm products used by the family and not sold. Note also that the $11,000 net income after interest expense is after a $7,000 expense deduction for depreciation, which is not a cash cost. Therefore, the manager would perceive a net cash income of $18,000. Finally, if the manager made new capital outlays to purchase additional assets during the year, an average investment for the year should be used, rather than beginning asset value. Likewise, if he sold off any of his assets during the year, his investment ought to be averaged downward.

Corporations. For corporations, all labor and management inputs receive wages and salaries, so that the income statement reflects all costs. Profitability measures are couched in terms of net profit to sales, net profit to total assets, and net profit to net worth before corporate income taxes. If XYZ Farm and Ranch were a corporation and $6,000 were included in costs as the manager's salary, net profit would be $5,000 instead of $11,000. Then net profit to sales would be 9.1 percent —($5,000 ÷ $55,000) × 100; net profit to total assets would be 2.1 percent—($5,000 ÷ $238,000) × 100; and net profit to net worth would be 4 percent—($5,000 ÷ $126,400) × 100. It is also customary to list these returns on the net amount left after corporate income taxes are paid.

Liquidity Measures

Liquidity is the ability of the enterprise to meet its current financial obligations or liabilities when they become due. Measures of liquidity are used to determine short-term financial strength and operating efficiency.

Current ratio. The current ratio is the relation of current assets to current liabilities. The ratio for XYZ Farm and Ranch on January 1, 1975 (from Table 18-1) was 2.27 ($35,000 ÷ $15,400). It means that there was $2.27 available to meet every $1.00 of obligations coming due in 1975.

Quick ratio. A more severe test of liquidity is the quick ratio, calculated by dividing quick assets by current liabilities. *Quick assets* are cash plus accounts receivable. For XYZ Farm and Ranch, the quick ratio is 0.45 ($7,000 ÷ $15,400). Since the ratio is less than 1, the manager will have to get money from somewhere, perhaps by selling livestock or crop inventories, to meet short-run obligations.

Inventory turnover. For retail businesses, which buy goods and resell them, the manager is interested in moving items into and out of his store as fast as possible. A can of beans sitting on a retail store's shelf for eight months takes up costly space and increases financing costs. The inventory turnover gives an indication of the number of times merchandise moves through the business in one year. It is calculated by dividing the cost of goods sold by the average inventory on hand. Average inventory is determined by adding beginning inventory to ending inventory and dividing by 2. If a retail store has an average inventory of $3 million and cost of goods sold is $6 million, its inventory turnover rate is 2, meaning that the inventory turned every 183 days (365 ÷ 2). Turnover can be calculated by department, and even by product type. All wholesale and retail business managers try to achieve as high an inventory turnover as possible, because a high rate reduces per-unit costs of operation and tends to improve net profit.

Average collection period. For businesses that extend credit, the credit manager computes an average collection period. First, annual credit sales are divided by 365 days, or the number of business workdays in the year, to determine average daily credit sales. Then, accounts receivable are divided by average daily credit sales.

Suppose average daily credit sales are $2,000 and accounts receivable are $64,000. The average collection period is 32 days ($64,000 ÷ $2,000), meaning that there are 32 days of sales outstanding in accounts receivable. This number of days is compared with the credit policy of the business. One period can be compared with another to see if credit policy is being effectively implemented.

Solvency Measures

Liquidity refers to the ability of a business to meet its cash needs for current business operations. *Solvency* refers to the firm's ability to pay the principal and interest on long-term financial obligations.

Owner's equity to total debt. The ratio of owner's equity to total debt measures the amount of net worth of the owners, compared to claims against the business by outsiders. For XYZ Farm and Ranch, the ratio is $124,600 divided by $113,400, or 1.1 (see Table 18-1). This means that for each $1.00 of liabilities outstanding on January 1, 1975, there was $1.10 of net worth. The larger this ratio, the more protection creditors have and the less risk there is that the business will be faced with lack of liquidity and insolvency.

Long-term debt to total assets. This ratio is calculated by dividing long-term debt by total assets. For XYZ Farm and Ranch, it would be 41.2 percent—($98,000 ÷ $238,000) × 100. This measure shows the percentage of the business's assets being financed by long-term debt obligations. A prudent manager will be unwilling to finance too great a part of his assets with long-term debt, as the future is uncertain and to do so might jeopardize the long-run solvency of the business. Management must thoroughly analyze the nature of its anticipated cash inflows for future years before undertaking long-term borrowing.

FINANCIAL PLANNING

Financial planning goes hand in hand with financial controlling. Planning the receipt and spending of cash, otherwise called the cash flow, is of primary importance.

The Cash-Flow Budget

The cash budget is an estimate of cash receipts and cash disbursements for a specified period of time. In the budget, cash needs are forecast and matched with expected cash income in order to determine potential credit needs and the firm's ability to stay solvent. The cash-flow budget is generally for a future planning period. For the farm and ranch manager, one year is a reasonable planning period, although for livestock enterprises, a longer period of time may be planned. A retail food store may need a monthly or weekly cash-flow plan.

The cash-flow budget is concerned only with cash coming in and cash flowing out. Thus, not only expense items are included, but also planned outlays for bank-loan and mortgage principal payments and new capital assets. The format for the cash budget is shown in Table 18-3. It is patterned after the situation of XYZ Farm and Ranch for 1975 (Tables 18-1 and 18-2). Note how the month-to-month situation changes. Note also that the manager needed extra credit funds in February, March, May, and June. In considering whether to lend him these extra

TABLE 18-3
Cash-Flow-Budget Illustration

	Jan.	Feb.	March	April	May	June	July	Aug.	Sept.	Oct.	Nov.	Dec.
Cash receipts:												
Livestock	$15,000	—	—	$10,000	—	—	$10,000	—	—	$10,000	—	—
Crops	—	—	—	—	—	$2,000	—	—	$5,000	—	$3,000	—
Total	$15,000	—	—	$10,000	—	$2,000	$10,000	—	$5,000	$10,000	$3,000	—
Disbursements:												
Hired labor	300	300	300	300	$300	300	300	$300	300	300	300	$300
Feed	500	1,000	1,000	500	1,000	1,000	500	1,000	1,000	500	1,000	1,000
Fertilizer, seeds	—	—	1,800	—	—	—	—	600	—	—	—	—
Supplies	125	125	125	125	125	125	125	125	125	125	125	125
Pharmaceuticals	200	—	—	—	—	—	200	—	—	300	—	—
Gas and oil	100	—	200	—	100	—	150	—	100	—	150	—
Electricity	80	70	60	60	60	60	60	60	60	60	60	60
Telephone	17	17	17	17	17	17	17	17	16	16	16	16
Taxes	—	—	—	—	2,000	—	—	—	—	—	2,500	—
Insurance	—	300	—	—	—	—	—	300	—	—	—	—
Repairs	150	150	150	150	150	150	150	150	150	150	150	150
Veterinary	250	—	—	250	—	—	250	—	—	250	—	—
Accounting	—	—	500	—	—	—	—	—	—	—	—	—
Interest	770	770	700	740	700	715	720	705	705	705	710	710
Mortgage principal	—	—	—	—	—	—	—	—	—	—	—	—
Bank-loan repayment	—	10,000	—	—	—	—	—	—	—	—	—	6,000
Total	$2,492	$12,732	$4,852	$2,142	$4,452	$2,367	$2,472	$3,257	$2,456	$2,406	$5,011	$8,361
Monthly cash change	$12,508	-$12,732	-$4,852	$7,858	-$4,452	-$367	$7,528	-$3,257	$2,544	$7,594	-$2,011	-$8,361
Cumulative change	$12,508	-$224	-$5,076	$2,782	-$1,670	-$2,037	$5,491	$2,234	$4,778	$12,372	$10,361	$2,000
New credit needs	—	$224	$5,076	—	$1,670	$2,037	—	—	—	—	—	—

NOTE: Assume initial cash of $2,000 and minimum cash balance of $2,000 kept throughout the year. At end of year, cash balance would be $4,000.

funds, his banker would probably have wanted to see the cash-flow budget. The cash-flow budget is widely used and necessary for sound financial planning.

Given the initial balance sheet in Table 18-1, the income statement in Table 18-2, and the cash-flow budget in Table 18-3, can you prepare the balance sheet for XYZ Farm and Ranch as of January 1, 1976? Try it.[1]

CAPITAL-FUNDS MANAGEMENT

The finance department must also plan for acquisition and liquidation of fixed assets in accordance with the company's growth plan. A capital budget can be prepared that lists proposed investment projects. In the case of XYZ Farm and Ranch as presented, no new capital acquisitions or capital liquidations were made during 1975. However, the fixed assets depreciated in book value by the $7,000 depreciation expense charged.

Sources of credit for expansion of capital assets were discussed in Chapter 5. Corporations can also consider the issue of new stock or sale of bonds to raise money for purchase of new capital assets. It is reasonable that any new capital investment proposed must be justified on the basis of the return on investment it will bring to the firm. If it brings a rate of return below the going interest rate, it is not likely to be approved by management.

Present-Value Concept

For proper assessment of the rate of return on investment in long-lived capital assets, the present-value concept must be understood.

If one were asked whether he preferred to have a dollar now or a year from now, he would probably take it now. If one were offered a dollar now or $10 a year from now, he would probably wait and pick up the $10. What about a dollar now or a $1.10 a year from now? This is more difficult. Essentially, present income is worth more than future income. In other words, one tends to discount the future. It is this discounting that generates interest rates.[2]

What is the present value of a dollar income a year from now? It

---

[1] For assets: cash up $2,000, fixed assets (buildings, machinery, equipment, and vehicles) down $7,000, total assets down $5,000. For liabilities: bank loans down $10,000, mortgages down $6,000, total liabilities down $16,000. Net worth up $11,000. Total liabilities and net worth down $5,000.

[2] Except for administrative costs and the risk costs in lending money.

depends on what value you impute to the use of your money. If it is 10 percent, the present value of one dollar is 90.9 cents. The proof is that should you invest 90.9 cents for a year at 10 percent interest, it will grow to a dollar. So this idea also helps us understand rate earned on investment. The return is the discount rate, which, when applied to earnings, equates the present value of the earnings to the investment.[3]

Let us take one example. Suppose you are making a financial decision with regard to whether to buy or lease a particular piece of equipment. Assume that you are considering a five-year period. The machine costs $1,000, has no salvage value, and will return you annual net earnings of $250 each year for the five-year period. You can rent the machine for $17 a month, which is $204 a year or a total of $1,020 for the five-year period, and this is about the same dollar outlay as buying it new. What should you do?

First, let us compute the present value of the net earnings that the purchase of the machine will give you.

Year	Net Earnings	Discount Factor at 8%	Present Value of Future Earnings
1	$250	.926	$232
2	250	.857	214
3	250	.794	198
4	250	.735	184
5	250	.684	171
		Total	$999

It is now clear that making the investment in buying the machine will surely return 8 percent, since the present value of the net earnings for the five years, using an 8 percent discount factor, totals about $1,000. Note that someone who did not utilize the present-value concept might conclude that buying the machine would return 25 percent a year ($250 ÷ $1,000).

But back to the decision of whether to buy or lease. You would buy

---

[3] The formula for computing the discount rate is $\frac{1}{(1+r)}$, where r is the rate of interest. In the example, then, the discount factor is $\frac{1}{(1+.10)}$, or $\frac{1}{1.10}$, or .909. The discount rate for the second year is $\frac{1}{(1+r)^2}$, for the third year $\frac{1}{(1+r)^3}$, and so on.

the machine if the next best alternative investment for $1,000 of equity capital returned less than 8 percent. If your $1,000 of capital were already earning you more than 8 percent, the best decision would be to rent the machine.

Note that the present-value concept also helps you to decide whether to purchase the machine in the first place. If there was an alternative investment in some other venture for the $1,000 return, you might not even buy the machine.

Capital-Replacement Decision

Another major financial decision is when to replace capital equipment. How old should a tractor be before it pays to buy a new one? How many times should the livestock escape before a new fence is built, or how many times should a fence be repaired? These types of problems constantly face any manager. Let us take one example. You have a two-year-old tractor. Its original cost was $5,400 and you have been depreciating it under the declining-balance method, taking the maximum write-off. Therefore, it now has a book value of $2,400. This assumes an original expected life of six years and no salvage value. (Check your understanding of depreciation by proving that this is correct.) Your equipment dealer will sell you a comparable new model for your old tractor plus $2,400. The list price of the new tractor is $5,600, since prices have gone up. It appears that the dealer figures your old tractor to be worth $3,200. Should you trade? How do you decide? Let us assume that it is your practice to analyze your tractor situation every two years.

The trade would involve an immediate capital outlay of $2,400. If you had enough money in your savings and loan account, you would have to sacrifice $120 a year interest to move the money capital into the form of the new tractor if the rate of interest was 5 percent. Another consideration that is difficult to calculate is whether depleting your cash would jeopardize any other aspect of the business, as the risk of failure because of finances may be increased. This is partially offset by the fact that you could probably sell the tractor and recover cash, but then this would hurt farm production and farm receipts, since a tractor is necessary to operate the business. To finance the tractor from debt capital from a bank loan, assuming that your credit rating would allow a loan of $2,400 over a two-year period, you would incur an interest cost of $192 a year at an interest rate of 8 percent.

You then figure that the new tractor will have a maintenance and repair cost of $50 for the next two years, $50 lower than if the old one were kept. Your state levies a personal property tax, and the cost of the new tractor will increase by $40 the first year and $25 the second year. You estimate that as a result of using a new tractor, the variable costs of the machine can be reduced by $30 the first year and by $20 the second.

Depreciation expense compared for the old and new tractors for the next two years would be as follows:

Old tractor: Year 3 (in terms of age), depreciation would be $\frac{1}{3}$ of $2,400, or $800. Year 4, it would be $\frac{1}{3}$ of $1,600, or $533.

New tractor: Year 1 (in terms of age), depreciation would be $\frac{1}{3}$ of $4,800 (cost basis equals book value of old tractor plus cash outlay, under present tax laws), or $1,600. Year 2, depreciation would be $\frac{1}{3}$ of $3,200, or $1,067.

The difference would be that depreciation expense would be $800 higher with the new tractor the first year, and $534 the second. If the farmer fell in the 20 percent bracket for income tax, he would save $160 of income tax the first year, and $107 the second. Remember that depreciation is a fixed cost but that this is a legitimate deductible expense in figuring income tax or farm income. These computations of added costs and savings utilize budgeting for analysis. Summarizing, then (assuming that you finance the purchase with equity capital):

Item	Added Costs from Buying New Tractor		Adding Savings from Buying New Tractor	
	1st Year	2nd Year	1st Year	2nd Year
Opportunity costs of money	$120	$120	$	$
Additional property taxes	40	25		
Lowered maintenance costs			50	50
Lowered tractor variable costs			30	20
Tax savings			160	107
Total	$160	$145	$240	$177
Total (both years)	$305		$417	

From a farm-management viewpoint alone, it appears that it is a wise decision to trade the old tractor in and get the new one. However, when the farm operator considers total family needs and goals, he may decide not to trade. Perhaps his son needs the $2,400 to go to college, or his wife needs new kitchen appliances.

FINANCIAL ORGANIZATION

Perhaps the final aspect to consider about financial management is its organization. As in the other functional areas, the farm manager is also the financial manager. A business must reach moderate size before a separate person can profitably be hired to spend full time in financial management. Typically, the specialized services of auditing, credit collections, and accounting are hired. In a business with a large dollar volume, however, the organization of the finance department might be as depicted in Figure 18-1. Reporting to the top finance executive, perhaps with the title vice-president for finance, would be a *treasurer* who is responsible for custody of cash funds, securities, insurance policies, and other valuable papers. The *controller* is responsible for the accounting functions involving record keeping and preparing financial statements. He checks budget preparations and may prepare the payroll for the treasurer's approval. The *credit manager* presses the collection of delinquent accounts receivable and assists in formulation of overall financial credit-extension policy. The *auditor* checks on the accounting and control systems in the business. Each of the persons in these positions will have staff assistants in proportion to the needs of the company.

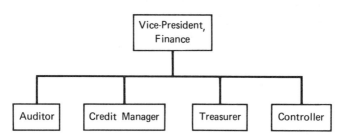

FIGURE 18-1
Organization Chart for the Finance Department

19

Marketing Management

Managing the market activities of a business firm has become increasingly important since World War II, when the major emphasis was on production and sales. As the pent-up consumers' demands built in the war years were increasingly satisfied by the mid-1950s, a different point of view emerged, phrased somewhat like this: "If this is what consumers want, can we produce it at a profit?"

Focus on the relative importance of consumer preferences was introduced in Chapter 9, which discussed food marketing. The idea advanced there was that consumers, in effect, cast votes through their purchases of food and services, and as a result act as directors of what is produced. Although there is certainly a lot of truth in the notion of "consumer sovereignty," it is equally true that the choice of foods and food services that consumers buy is influenced considerably by the marketing efforts of food-business firms.

THE MARKETING PROGRAM

All businesses that sell a product or service have marketing programs. A small farmer may not be conscious of having one, but there is always a program—planned or happenstance. The more successful a manager is, the more he will think through his marketing program and develop a *market strategy*.

Planning is the first function of management—remember? Let's apply the planning concepts we discussed to marketing. The first element of a marketing-program strategy is to select a *marketing target*. A marketing target is a particular group of consumers to whom the business wishes to sell its products. The second strategy element is selecting a *marketing mix*, or the choice of tools a business can use to effectively reach the chosen market target. This mix of tools typically includes the product or products, their price, the channel of distribution and marketplace, and promotion or advertising.

Marketing Target

In an overall sense, the marketing target for all agricultural businessmen includes the entire population, because everyone eats. In a more specific sense, however, the farm-supply businessman views his marketing target as the farmer; the farmer may view his target as a particular grain elevator, a packer-buyer, motorists who pass his roadside stand, the local market people, or his cooperative. Meat packers may view wholesalers and retailers as their targets. Only the retailer views his target as the food consumer directly.

Depending on the size of the business firm, the marketing-department manager may have a support-staff group of marketing researchers to study the choice of marketing targets for the company. From a market analysis, the manager also gets an idea of what aspects to include in the marketing mix. Typical market analyses include the number of consumers in the market area (population); population growth rate; income levels of the consumers; social characteristics of consumers; quantities of the product currently used or, if a new product, quantities used of closest substitute; consumers' views of degree of satisfaction with present product use; and share of market held by competition.

The market target is defined by a detailed analysis of potential consumers in the light of the firm's abilities and business objectives. Another outgrowth of the analysis is that management may determine that the market for a particular product consists of several submarkets. For example, the market for farm machinery would consist of submarkets for tractors, tillage implements, planters, and harvesters. These submarkets could in turn be further subdivided by size of tractor and amount of auxiliary equipment.

The particular abilities of the business are important at this stage of marketing-strategy analysis. For example, if the firm specialized in selling farm machinery, it is not likely that it would also be interested in marketing beef, because beef would probably not make good use of the firm's production facilities, engineering talent, distribution channels, and existing personnel expertise.

Marketing Mix

Consumers, or what they may be influenced to buy, are the keys to selecting a marketing strategy. Once the consumer targets are chosen, the marketing manager combines all the resources at his command to reach them. The variables that the manager can influence directly are product, price, place, and promotion.

Product planning. What product is to be produced? What will be its nature or design? What size will it be? How will it be packaged? These are all questions to be answered in product planning. Many agricultural businesses are just as involved in "new-product" development as are nonagricultural firms. Frozen peas packaged in a two-pound bag is a new product if only one-pound boxes were on the market previously.

New-product development is a major element in the marketing program of any business enterprise. Since almost all consumers in the United States already eat as much food per capita as physical limits allow, there is considerable emphasis on new products as food-industry groups vie for a portion of the "consumer's stomach." Developing a new product is not easy. Necessary stages include the idea, its development and improvement, and its evaluation. For products of all kinds, it is estimated that for every five products actually developed for mass production, only one is ever produced and distributed for target markets; and of those actually placed on the market, only about half are commercially successful.

In the food industry, new-product efforts are generally concentrated on giving the product a better appearance, improving its shelf life, improving its taste, or making it more convenient for the homemaker to prepare.

Market planning—place strategy. Another planning decision is determining the channel of distribution to be used in reaching the consumer. In Chapter 8, channels for the farm-supply industries were described briefly for various kinds of farm supplies. In Chapter 9, the institutional approach to marketing was outlined, describing the marketing functions carried on by various types of middlemen. Since farmers and ranchers sell unprocessed food to which further form utility must usually be added, their place strategy is often limited to choosing a market outlet that gives them the highest price. The manager's knowledge of how markets function and his ability to recognize a relatively high-priced market is important. Remember that most farm products are sold in a purely competitive market (Chapter 15). Depending on the food type involved, other marketing-place alternatives may include a roadside stand, local assembly-type markets, terminal markets, a food processor, or a marketing cooperative.

Location principles of economics tell us that prices will be lowest at the point of highest production concentration and will increase in magnitude by the extent of transportation cost as one moves away from the center of production. However, there is virtually no product for which there is one center of production. Asparagus, cranberries, and rice come the closest for products in the United States. It is clear, however, that fluid-milk prices are higher in New Mexico than in Wisconsin; oranges are cheaper in Florida and California than in Kansas; corn is cheaper in the Midwest than in Utah; and raw tobacco is cheaper in North Carolina than in North Dakota. Similarly, in marketing of livestock, prices for medium steers may vary between a local market two miles from your farm and a terminal market 300 miles from your farm by the cost of transporting a steer 300 miles. Imperfections in markets, where prices are in disequilibrium, occur all the time because of factors discussed in detail in Chapter 15.

The alert manager will be well informed about price variations among kinds of markets and market locations, so that he can strive to increase returns. The U.S. Department of Agriculture, the state universities, trade associations, farmer organizations, radio and television, and newspapers are all sources of help to enable the farmer to improve his marketing strategy.

For food processors or manufacturers, a singularly difficult problem is not one of selecting a market, but how to select the most rewarding marketing channel. Alternative marketing channels include going through some type of wholesaler, selling direct to the retailer, or perhaps directly contacting the consumer, as mail-order houses now do. Food processors may also sell directly to institutional establishments or to large food-service businesses.

Wholesalers usually buy and sell in larger quantities than does the typical retailer. A food wholesaler might purchase a carload of canned goods and sell to grocery stores in case lots, whereas the retailer sells in quantities as small as a single can. Wholesalers perform the important economic function of storage, imparting time and place utility of goods.

Manufacturers can use three basic types of middlemen to distribute products. They are merchant wholesalers, manufacturers' sales representatives, and agents and brokers. The merchant wholesaler purchases the merchandise and assumes all risks and costs associated with ownership.

The importance of the merchant wholesaler's activities varies with the product and the customer serviced. For example, if the product is bulky and requires regular deliveries and extensive servicing, the merchant wholesaler may be more desirable than if the product is complex, not well known, or highly technical in nature, in which case a manufacturer's sales branch or franchised dealership may result in better contracts. Sales branches may or may not carry product inventory. These branches allow the manufacturer rather direct contact with the ultimate user, which may have some advantages. Finally, agents and brokers, a third alternative, offer the advantage of eliminating the need for a sales force.

Retailing in the food industry is mostly carried out by independent and chain food stores. Direct selling to consumers is limited in scope. However, small, localized freezer-plant-type operations, which purchase carcasses for cutting up and sale, are examples of direct selling.

Pricing

Pricing is fundamental to all marketing transactions and a vital consideration for the marketing manager. To the farmer or rancher operating in a purely competitive market, there is no pricing problem per se, since he must usually accept the market price offered by the market at a given time. His managing ability, however, to understand price movements within his various marketplace alternatives is of considerable importance. Cyclical, annual, seasonal, and day-to-day price variations should be understood. Further, if his food products have unusual quality attributes or if his market surveys respond to some event like a local freeze or flood, he may be able to bargain for a price premium. Also, he may be able to exercise some control over price through the bargaining in a marketing cooperative, because of the market power that the larger quantity of product affords.

In imperfectly competitive markets, pricing policy is based on a number of considerations. If a patent is involved for a new product, management may decide to capitalize on a monopoly position by charging a relatively high price in order to recoup development costs quickly. Such a pricing policy is sometimes referred to as "skimming the market." If the business objective is to capture a relatively large share of a market quickly, management may decide on a low price, in the hopes of building sales volume fast and holding it by winning consumer loyalty. This type of price policy is called "penetration pricing."

In oligopoly (review Chapter 15), price may be fairly rigid at certain levels. Any firm attempting to capture a market share by charging a lower price will quickly meet retaliation by other competition. Therefore, firms entering these markets must charge about the same price as others and plan to compete on a nonprice basis.

Pricing-policy considerations are based heavily on costs. Over time, the price received must cover all fixed and variable costs of operation, including a fair return to management and risk costs. The degree of substitutability of the product with other products is an important consideration, and is a major factor affecting the products' price elasticity of demand. For products with a highly inelastic demand, more total revenue may be obtained by charging higher prices and selling a smaller quantity. The opposite is true for products with elastic demands.

Pricing policy in multiproduct businesses. In multiproduct off-farm agricultural businesses, pricing is complex. Some of the general considerations for this type of pricing policy have been covered, but let's look at some specifics. In the long run, all costs become variable, and managers must charge prices high enough to cover them if they are to stay in business. Price to most farm managers is not a variable that can be manipulated.

If price can be manipulated within some limited range, and if average variable costs are linear over a relatively large range of output and fixed costs must be allocated over many products, what are the pricing strategies that can be applied? Managers find that marginal analysis is an incomplete tool for developing these strategies. Instead, they find that for short-run pricing considerations, mixed-margin pricing and analyzing the contribution to overhead and profit for each item are more useful.

What is *mixed-margin* pricing? It is a strategy of pricing products in a multiproduct business, by which a different percentage markup over cost is used for each product or group of products, but each is designed so that the overall return from all products will cover total costs of the business. Food retailers serve as a good example. To achieve a 16 percent gross margin for all food items that is required to cover costs, the manager may price the grocery, meat, and produce items in several ways. If 70 percent of sales are from grocery items, 22 percent from meat, and 8 percent from produce, a manager could achieve a 16 percent gross margin by grocery, meat, and produce markups, in that order, in any of the following combinations: 14-20-22½, 16-15-22½, 15-16-25, and 14-19-30. A store can gear its advertising program to any of the three groups and create a reputation for low prices in any of the areas.

Alternatively, a particular item may be priced as a "loss leader." This is the situation in which the product's price is below its cost but the loss on that product is made up by charging a relatively higher price on other items sold. It's an attempt to attract customers to the store so they'll also buy other goods. The mixed-margin composite can be changed at any time in order to expand total sales.

To successfully use mixed-margin pricing as a strategy, managers must be aware of the contribution to overhead (fixed costs) and profit that each item contributes, particularly for short-run pricing decisions. Let's work through an example.

Suppose you operated a farm-supply business selling feed and fertilizer. Let's assume that you sell only four products: a complete feed, a concentrated feed, bag fertilizer, and bulk fertilizer. Now suppose the variable costs for handling, storage, trucking, labor, and miscellaneous expenses are $9.00 per ton regardless of product, and that you experience 0.2 percent bad-debt losses on every ton sold. Fixed costs for depreciation on buildings and vehicles, interest on investment, maintenance repairs, insurance, and taxes total $3,000 per month.

Currently, your selling price, cost of goods sold, gross margin, and sales per month are as follows:

Product	Selling Price	Cost of Goods Sold	Gross Margin	Bad-Debt Loss	Sales
		(dollars per ton)			(tons)
Complete feed	80	65	15	.16	400
Concentrated feed	100	80	20	.20	120
Bag fertilizer	75	63	12	.15	180
Bulk fertilizer	65	56	9	.13	300
					1,000

The contribution to profit and overhead (fixed costs) generated would be:

Product	Gross Margin	Total Variable Costs	Contribution to Profit and Overhead	Sales Volume	Total Amount Contributed
		(dollars per ton)		(tons)	(dollars)
Complete feed	15.00	9.16	5.84	400	2,336
Concentrated feed	20.00	9.20	10.80	120	1,296
Bulk fertilizer	12.00	9.15	2.85	180	513
Bag fertilizer	9.00	9.13	−.13	300	−39
Totals				1,000	4,106

Under current pricing policy, all but bulk fertilizer make a positive contribution to overhead and profit. Net profit per month would be the $4,106 less fixed costs of $3,000, or $1,106. With the variable costs on bulk fertilizer of $9.13 per ton and a gross margin contribution of $9.00, the manager must adjust its price upward or discontinue the sale of it, because at present it is making no contribution to fixed expenses. But what about the other three products? Do their prices need adjusting? Currently, all are making a positive contribution to overhead and profit. But if further analysis is made, we can see an important price consideration the manager should make regarding bag fertilizer. Let's follow it out and see why.

A reasonable assumption could be made that the fixed costs of $3,000 could be allocated among the products on a per-ton basis. This would result in a $3.00 fixed cost per ton of sales ($3,000 ÷ 1,000 tons). A profit analysis would then be:

Product	Gross Margin	Total Variable Costs	Contribution to Profit and Overhead	Allocated Overhead Costs	Net Profit
			(dollars per ton)		
Complete feed	15.00	9.16	5.84	3.00	2.84
Concentrated feed	20.00	9.20	10.80	3.00	7.80
Bag fertilizer	12.00	9.15	2.85	3.00	−.15
Bulk fertilizer	9.00	9.13	−.13	3.00	−3.13

Product	Volume Sold	Net-Profit Total
	(tons)	(dollars)
Complete feed	400	1,136
Concentrated feed	120	936
Bag fertilizer	180	−27
Bulk fertilizer	300	−939
Total	1,000	1,106

After consideration of fixed costs, the summary shows that a price of $75 per ton for bag fertilizer is not sufficient to cover all costs. At $75 per ton, bag fertilizer contributes to overhead but nothing to net profit. In the short run, strategy may well be to price it at $75 per ton, as it does make a net contribution to overhead of $2.85 per ton; but for the long run, the manager should ask what the effect would be of raising the price to, say, $77 per ton so that the price would cover all costs including profit. At this price, contribution to overhead would be $4.85 and contribution to profit would be $1.85 per ton. The important question is, How much would a rise in price influence sales?—or, phrased in economic terms, What is the price elasticity of demand? If price elasticity were such that sales would not drop below 106 tons per month, net profit would be no lower than at present. The manager must ask whether the price increase would bring retaliation from competitors and, if so, must determine how loyal his customers are.

Sales Promotion

Merchandising is a general term used to signify all the firm's efforts to expand sales. A key feature of a merchandising program is sales promotion through advertising.

Because of the homogeneity of a large number of raw farm products and the cost of grading products, it does not pay most individual farmers to advertise or promote their products unless there is some special situation involved. For producers who choose to specialize, or for those in close proximity to a consuming area, such as a sweet-corn or melon producer near a suburban housing development, there may be gains to revenue by incurring variable promotional costs. Producers of purebred livestock who sell for breeding purposes are another example of a farm business that can probably benefit from specialized merchandising techniques. In such cases, the product sold is a differentiated one because of breeding-line differences.

Advertising. In most nonfarm agricultural businesses, advertising is an important ingredient of the marketing mix. Advertising is the communication of ideas about a product to many people. This information can be sent simultaneously through newspapers, television, radio, magazines, posters, and leaflets. These alternative means to reach consumers are called "media." Mass-media advertising is a relatively low-cost-per-unit way of contacting consumers, but it may be less effective than personal selling. For the introduction of new products, mass-media advertising may be used to precondition the market for more direct selling efforts. At the retail-store level, displays of products and their physical arrangement or layout within the store are part of advertising.

In agriculture, products are often advertised by trade associations representing a particular food commodity. Thus, in a sense, the producer belonging to a trade association advertises his product. For instance, the

American Dairy Association buys television time to promote the consumption of milk.

The total advertising cost can be quite high for a product. For cigarettes, as an example, advertising to develop brand loyalty is the major kind of nonprice competition, and accounts for a significantly large proportion of per-pack costs.

Branding. Businesses may spend sizable amounts of merchandising money and effort to develop consumer loyalty to a brand name. This is another way to attempt to differentiate a product and make it more essential in the mind of the consumer. By this process, it becomes more price inelastic and better able to withstand competition from firms that offer market substitutes for it. To the degree that the branding effort is successful, there is more control over price, an existing share of the market maintained, or market share increased. A business may have one brand name for all its products or different brand names for different products. Having only one brand name has advantages if all the firm's products are of a consistently high quality. If not, one "bad" product may destroy consumer loyalty to all products of the company.

MARKETING ORGANIZATION

What organization setup in a business's marketing department is most conducive to implementing its marketing program? A farm manager makes most of the farm's marketing decisions. For a somewhat larger firm, salesmen may be hired who report to the general manager in the same way as do production employees or the bookkeeper. For large agricultural businesses, particularly those in farm supply and food manufacturing, a full-fledged marketing department may be organized.

The top marketing executive is of equal importance to the top production and finance executive and often has the title of vice-president for marketing, although other titles, like vice-president in charge of sales, general marketing manager, or general sales manager, may be used. The top marketing executive reports to the chief executive officer, either the president or the executive vice-president.

A marketing department might be organized in the manner shown in Figure 19-1. Reporting to the top marketing executive would be the director of marketing services, who heads a support group engaged in marketing research, sales forecasting, and product development. He may also head the advertising and sales-promotion group, which might work in a staff capacity. Under the top marketing executive in a line responsibility would be the domestic sales manager, who directs regional offices. The regional managers might have under them district managers who

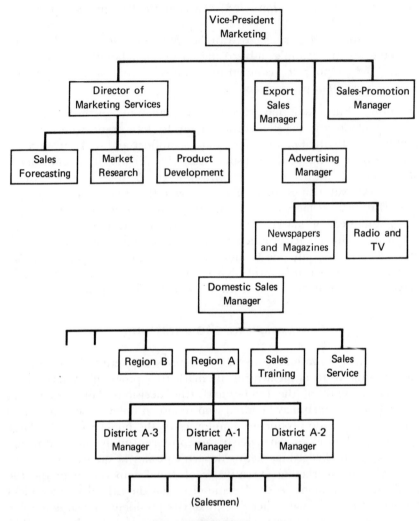

FIGURE 19-1

Partial Organizational Chart of a Marketing
Department in a Large Business Firm

supervise their field salesmen. Support staff to the sales manager could
include a sales-training and a sales-service group. The organization of
the marketing department will vary from business to business, but the
organizational elements shown are apt to be major components.

MOTIVATING

The third function of management as regards the marketing department is mostly concerned with stimulating the marketing personnel, and particularly the sales force, to achieve their particular objectives. For field salesmen, objectives may be set in terms of sales-generation goals per month, quarter, or year. Monetary rewards in form of bonuses may be awarded for sales generated above quotas. Often, field salesmen are paid commissions in addition to a minimum salary. This tactic provides the same kind of incentive that piecework bonuses do for production employees.

The sales force is often supported and provided motivation with two items. First is the development of sales-promotion materials to complement their direct sales efforts. These may include store and window displays, counter cards, bumper stickers, descriptive leaflets, discount coupons, samples, premiums, contests, and special demonstrations. The salesmen's job is to coordinate these items with their regular sales techniques.

A second kind of support effort is the holding of educational and training sessions for sales personnel. Workshops and seminars to keep salesmen updated, to teach new sales techniques, and to stimulate company *esprit de corps* among the sales force can be an effective way to motivate sales personnel if organized and handled well.

CONTROLLING MARKETING EFFORTS

The nature of marketing—its multitude of activities, dispersion of sales force, and necessity of working with buyers who are continually influenced by changing economic conditions—requires that marketing management have a sound set of controls. Constant evaluation of marketing efforts is needed. Detailed records of sales are of paramount importance so that weaknesses can be spotted immediately, whether they are geographic or by type of product. In the small family farm business or a large corporate firm, sales information as to date, amount, product, product quality, buyer and revenue received must be recorded to aid in future planning decisions. Also, standards should be developed against which sales personnel can be evaluated. One such criterion is sales per salesman, which could be further analyzed by product type or market area.

SUMMARY

Marketing, within a successful business, is of equal importance to production and finance. College graduates most commonly begin their careers as sales representatives in the marketing department of off-farm agricultural businesses. Marketing effectiveness depends to a large extent on the imagination and foresight of sales personnel. It is clearly one of the most exciting and challenging departments in any business.

Appendix to Part Five

Case problems are used extensively in the teaching of business-management principles. The following case exhibits problems that managers face in the production, marketing, and finance areas of operating a business. It is designed to help you visualize the various management functions of planning, organizing, actuating, and controlling. It is hoped that the case will help tie the material presented in the last four chapters into a more meaningful whole.

CASE PROBLEM: DELTA FISH FARMS, INC.

In late 1969, a group of ten people decided to go into the catfish-farming business. Several had read about the new business of fish farming; however, none had had any prior experience in raising fish.

After some discussion, they selected the corporate business-organization form, primarily because of its limited-liability provisions. They made application to the state corporate commissioner in November

---

Case problem prepared by Professor William D. Gorman, Department of Agricultural Economics and Agricultural Business, New Mexico State University.

1969, anticipating that their corporate charter would be received by January 1, 1970.

Their first step was to collect information on the capital investment required, operating costs, and expected returns from catfish farming. Discussions with catfish farmers, their local agricultural extension agent, and bankers led them to conclude that a 300-acre farm would be a reasonable size for a beginning enterprise. They figured that it would take approximately $500 an acre, or $150,000, to purchase the necessary land. Discussions with a local engineering firm indicated that dike construction, including water-control valves, would amount to approximately $100,000. They also figured they would need holding vats, buildings, feeding equipment, wells, seines, and other miscellaneous equipment that would amount to approximately $50,000. They estimated their total investment to be approximately $300,000 (Exhibits 1 and 2).

On the revenue side, their investigations suggested that they should be able to obtain a net operating profit of approximately $30,000 annually from operating the 300-acre farm (Exhibit 2). Research information available in publications, as well as visits with other fish farmers, indicated that it was possible to produce and harvest up to 2,000 pounds of fish per acre annually. However, they decided to use a more conservative estimate of 1,500 pounds per acre based on only 250 acres.

The two principal anticipated market outlets were "pay-lake operators" and fish processors. A pay-lake operator is a person who charges a fee to others who want to fish his lake. These lakes are generally stocked with legal-sized fish purchased from fish farmers. A processor, on the other hand, takes the fish, skins it, and either freezes it or sells it in the fresh form. Pay-lake operators had been paying from 40

EXHIBIT 1

Estimated Investment Requirements, 300-Acre
Fish Farm

Item	Cost	Annual Depreciation
Land—300 acres @ $500	$150,000	$ 0
Land improvement: Dikes	100,000	8,000
Buildings, vats	20,000	1,000
Equipment	30,000	3,000
Total	$300,000	$12,000

EXHIBIT 2
Estimated Annual Income Statement, 300-Acre
Fish Farm

Sales: (based on 250 acres water × 1,500 lbs. fish per acre, or 375,000 lbs.)

To pay-lake operators	175,000 lbs. @ .40	$70,000
To processors	200,000 lbs. @ .35	70,000
Total sales		$140,000

Expenses:

Labor	$18,000	
Management	18,000	
Feed	45,000	
Chemicals	4,000	
Depreciation	12,000	
Utilities, fuel	8,000	
Other	5,000	
Total		$110,000
Net operating profit		$30,000

to 50 cents a pound for fish, and processors had been paying from 30 to 40 cents a pound in the last few years.

Delta Fish Farms received its permit to incorporate on January 1, 1970, and immediately sold $200,000 worth of common stock. The beginning balance sheet, showing assets of $200,000 in cash and equities of $200,000 in capital stock, is shown in Exhibit 3.

All ten stockholders were placed on the board of directors; it was decided that they would meet monthly and that each board member would receive a $100 fee for participating in the monthly meetings. The group elected Dr. Jones, a local physician and stockholder, as board chairman. The local high school biology teacher, Jack Fin, was selected

EXHIBIT 3
Beginning Balance Sheet
Delta Fish Farms, Inc.
January 1, 1970

Assets:		Liabilities:	None
Cash	$200,000	Capital Stock	$200,000

as the manager and given an annual salary of $12,000. Jack was an aggressive young man but had had no previous business-management experience.

Early in January, they purchased 300 acres of land at $600 an acre. Although this was $100 an acre more than they had anticipated, the land was level and they thought it was worth the price. They paid $80,000 in cash for the land and gave the seller a mortgage of $100,000, to be paid off in annual installments, over twenty years, of $5,000 principal plus interest at 8.4 percent on the unpaid balance.

Dike construction began in February and was finished by April, at a cost of $100,000. All the necessary buildings and equipment were purchased and in place by May, with a total capital outlay of $50,000.

EXHIBIT 4
Cash Flow
Delta Fish Farms, Inc.
January 1–December 31, 1970
(in thousands of dollars)

	J	F	M	A	M	J	J	A	S	O	N	D	Total
Cash in:													
Stock sales	200	–	–	–	–	–	–	–	–	–	–	–	$200
Bank loan	–	–	–	–	100	–	–	–	–	–	–	–	100
Cash out:													
Land	80	–	–	–	–	–	–	–	–	–	–	–	80
Dikes	–	25	25	25	25	–	–	–	–	–	–	–	100
Buildings	–	–	10	–	10	–	–	–	–	–	–	–	20
Equipment	10	–	–	10	10	–	–	–	–	–	–	–	30
Mgt., admin.	2	2	2	2	2	2	2	2	2	2	2	2	24
Labor	–	–	–	–	1	1	1	1	1	1	1	1	8
Feed	–	–	–	–	–	1	–	1	1	1	–	1	5
Other	–	1	–	1	–	–	1	1	–	–	1	–	5
Brood stock	–	–	–	–	2	–	–	–	–	–	–	–	2
Fingerlings	–	–	–	–	–	20	–	–	–	–	–	–	20
Monthly total	92	28	37	38	50	24	4	5	4	4	4	4	
Cash balance	108	80	43	5	55	31	27	22	18	14	10	6	

The group purchased $2,000 worth of brood stock in April 1970, with arrangements to pay during May. Although the brood stock would be spawning in May and June, it would be approximately two years before there would be many adult fish ready for sale. Hence, the company decided to purchase $20,000 worth of 5- to 7-inch fingerlings for immediate stocking of their ponds. They anticipated that these fingerlings would be of sufficient size for sale in eight to ten months.

A monthly cash flow for the operation in 1970 is shown in Exhibit 4. By May 1970, the cash outlay had exceeded the $200,000 collected in the original stock sale. Jack Fin warned the board that the company had insufficient cash as early as February 15, but they took no action until the crisis developed. To meet the emergency cash situation, the board of directors arranged a $100,000 bank loan for one year, paying interest at 12 percent annually. However, because of the fingerling purchase paid for in June and other normal operating expenses, the cash

EXHIBIT 5
Income Statement
Delta Fish Farms, Inc.
January 1 to December 31, 1970
(in thousands of dollars)

Sales:				None
Expenses:				
Labor	$8			
Feed	4			
Management	12[a]			
Depreciation	8			
Other	5			
Total	$37[a]	0		
Administrative		12[b]		
Total				12
Net operating profit				(12)
Interest expenses: Land mortgage			8	
Bank loan			8	16
Net income (loss)			—	(28)

[a] Transferred to balance sheet as increased value of growing fish inventory.

[b] One-half of $24,000 cash outlay to production management and one-half to administrative overhead.

balance in the company deteriorated to $6,000 by the end of 1970. The income statement for the 1970 operations is shown in Exhibit 5, and the balance sheet for December 31, 1970, is shown in Exhibit 6. Since there were no sales made during the year, all direct production expenses were transferred to the balance sheet as additions to the inventory value of growing fish. However, administrative and interest expenses amounted to $28,000, which resulted in a $28,000 loss for their first year of operation.

This December 31, 1970, balance sheet indicated cash on hand of $6,000. The board of directors realized that this cash would not be sufficient to meet January 1971 commitments, since $8,000 interest on the land mortgage was due, as well as a $5,000 principal payment. They also knew that $12,000 of interest on the bank loan would be due in May. Although they had originally anticipated selling fish as early as March, it now appeared that it would be May before they had any fish of salable size. To solve their second cash crisis, the stockholders agreed to lend the company $50,000 for one year at 10 percent interest. However, several board members complained that their manager should have planned for this in advance and not allowed them to get into this posi-

EXHIBIT 6

Balance Sheet
Delta Fish Farms, Inc.
December 31, 1970
(in thousands of dollars)

Assets:		Liabilities:			
Cash on hand	6	Accrued interest:			
Fish in production	57[a]	Land mortgage	8		
Feed inventory	1	Bank loan	8	16	
Brood stock	2	Bank loan		100	
Land	180	Land mortgage		100	
Dikes, buildings, equipment:		Total liabilities			216
Original cost	150	Equities:			
Depreciation	8	Capital stock		200	
Net	142	Retained earnings		(28)	
		Total equities			172
Total assets	388	Total liabilities and equities			388

[a] Fingerlings purchased $20, plus $37 of fish in production.

tion. Jack Fin replied that he had not been able to get a decision from the board when he needed it; that by the time all ten members had agreed on something, it was too late.

Sales began in May, with a 10,000-pound order at 40 cents a pound to pay-lake operators (Exhibit 7). This was followed by 40,000 pounds sold to pay-lake operators during the month of June, with an $8,000 cash payment and $8,000 taken in accounts receivable. An additional market for which they had not planned developed in June, when they found they were able to sell 5,000 pounds directly to consumers who came out to the farm to pick up the fish. Since this was more of a spontaneous market than a planned outlet, a price of 40 cents a pound became established. In October, they sold 110,000 pounds at 30 cents a pound to a fish processor. Because of their need for cash, they would have liked to sell more, but the remaining inventory of fish averaged

EXHIBIT 7
Sales Record
Delta Fish Farms, Inc.
1971

| | | | Price | | Accounts Receivable | | |
Month	Market Outlet	Pounds Sold	per Pound	Cash Received	Taken	Col- lected	Balance
May	Pay lake	10,000	$.40	$ 4,000	$ —	$ —	$ —
June	Pay lake	40,000	.40	8,000	8,000	—	8,000
	Farm	5,000	.40	2,000	—	—	—
July	Pay lake	20,000	.40	4,000	4,000	—	12,000
	Farm	5,000	.40	2,000	—	—	—
August	Pay lake	10,000	.40	3,000	1,000	—	13,000
	Farm	5,000	.40	2,000	—	—	—
September	Pay lake	—	—	—	—	3,000	10,000
	Farm	5,000	.40	2,000	—	—	—
October	Farm	5,000	.40	2,000	—	—	—
	Processor	110,000	.30	33,000			
Yearly total	Pay lake	80,000	.40	22,000	—	—	10,000
	Farm	25,000	.40	10,000	—	—	—
	Processor	110,000	.30	33,000	—	—	—
Total		215,000		$65,000			$10,000

less than one pound in size—too small to meet the specifications of the fish processor.

Total sales for 1971 accounted for 215,000 pounds of fish. They collected $65,000 in cash and had $10,000 in accounts receivable at the year's end.

Their cash position continued to deteriorate during 1971 (Exhibit 8). They had a cash balance of $39,000 at the end of January; however, this decreased to the dangerously low level of $7,000 in May. Jack Fin's planning pleas were still ignored. In order to maintain some cash and meet their payroll, they paid only part of their feed bill during the months of May through September. They also chose not to pay the board of directors for fees and expenses for participating in board meetings starting in May. However, with the large sale to the fish processor in the month of October, they were able to pay off all back bills and have an ending cash balance of $8,000. It became apparent, however, that they would not have sufficient cash to operate for the rest of the

EXHIBIT 8
Cash Flow
Delta Fish Farms, Inc.
January 1–December 31, 1971
(in thousands of dollars)

	J	F	M	A	M	J	J	A	S	O	N	D	Total
Cash in:													
Cash on hand, 1/1	6	—	—	—	—	—	—	—	—	—	—	—	6
Fish sales	—	—	—	—	4	10	6	5	5	35	—	—	65
Stockholders' loans	50	—	—	—	—	—	—	—	—	—	—	—	50
Total	56	—	—	—	4	10	6	5	5	35	—	—	121
Cash out:													
Mgt., Admin.	2	2	2	2	1	1	1	1	1	7	1	—	21
Labor	1	1	1	2	2	2	2	2	2	3	1	1	20
Feed	—	1	1	3	2	2	3	3	2	20	—	—	37
Other	1	1	1	1	1	2	2	1	1	2	—	2	15
Interest	8	—	—	—	12	—	—	—	—	—	—	—	18
Mort. prin.	5	—	—	—	—	—	—	—	—	—	—	—	5
Total monthly	17	5	5	8	18	7	8	7	6	32	2	3	116
Cash balance	39	34	29	21	7	10	8	6	5	8	6	3	

year, or to meet early 1972 commitments, without additional debt or equity capital.

The company sustained a net loss of $46,000 during the operating year of 1971 (Exhibit 9). The manager indicated that low prices, higher-than-anticipated costs, and high interest charges were the principal reasons for the net loss. He also reiterated his anxiety over the lack of a centralized decision-making procedure. However, he also indicated that the firm had not yet reached full production but would do so during 1972.

The balance sheet of the operation as of December 31, 1971, indi-

EXHIBIT 9

Income Statement
Delta Fish Farms, Inc.
January 1–December 31, 1971
(in thousands of dollars)

Sales:			
Fish: Pay-lake operators, 80,000# @ .40		32	
Direct farm sales, 25,000# @ .40		10	
Processor sales, 110,000# @ .30		33	
		—	
			75
Expenses:			
Beginning fish inventory		57	
Management	12		
Labor	20		
Feed	40		
Depreciation	12		
Other	15	99	
	—		
Total		156	
Ending inventory		72	
		—	
Cost of goods (fish) sold			84
Gross profit on sales			(9)
Administrative expense			12
Net operating profit			(21)
Interest expense:			
Land mortgage	8		
Bank loan	12		
Stockholders' loan	5		25
	—		
Net income (loss)			(46)

cated that cash on hand was $3,000, and accounts payable and accrued interest payable in January amounted to $14,000 (Exhibit 10). The stockholders' $50,000 loan to the corporation was also due in January. It was apparent that they would be unable to pay this loan, but many of the stockholders definitely wanted the interest, amounting to $5,000, paid. They also knew that the $100,000 bank loan was coming up in May. They had been able to renew the loan the previous May, but given their current position, they were doubtful that the bank would be very interested in renewing the loan this year.

Since it was readily apparent that the life of the new company was in jeopardy, they decided it was necessary to attempt to plan next year's operation to determine cash needs before looking for alternative solutions for their financial problems. Jack Fin prepared a monthly sales forecast by types of outlets, as shown in Exhibit 11. After checking around, he decided that they could price their fish sold at the farm at 60 cents a pound without adversely affecting sales. He expected the price

EXHIBIT 10
Balance Sheet
Delta Fish Farms, Inc.
December 31, 1971
(in thousands of dollars)

Assets:			Liabilities:	
Cash on hand		3	Accounts payable:	
Fish in production		72	Feed	3
Feed inventory		1	Salaries	3
Accounts receivable		10	Accrued interest:	
Brood stock		2	Land mortgage	8
Land		180	Bank loan	8
Dikes, buildings, equipment:			Stockholders' loan	5
Original cost	150		Bank loan	100
Depreciation res.	20		Stockholders' loan	50
		130	Land mortgage	95
			Total liabilities	272
			Equities:	
			Capital stock	200
			Retained earnings	(74)
Total assets		398	Total liabilities and equities	398

EXHIBIT 11
Sales Forecast
Delta Fish Farms, Inc.
1972

Month	Market Outlet	Pounds Sold	Price per Pound	Cash Received	Accounts Receivable Taken	Col- lected	Balance
January				$5,000		$5,000	$5,000
February				5,000		5,000	0
March	Farm	5,000	.60	3,000			
April	Farm	5,000	.60	3,000			
May	Pay lake	10,000	.40	4,000			
	Farm	5,000	.60	3,000			
June	Pay lake	40,000	.40	8,000	$8,000		8,000
	Farm	5,000	.60	3,000			
July	Pay lake	20,000	.40	4,000	4,000		12,000
	Farm	5,000	.60	3,000			
August	Pay lake	10,000	.40	4,000		6,000	6,000
	Farm	5,000	.60	3,000			
September	Farm	5,000	.60	9,000		6,000	0
October	Farm	5,000	.60	3,000			
	Processor	90,000	.40	36,000			
November	Farm	5,000	.60	3,000			
	Processor	90,000	.30	27,000			
Yearly total							
	Farm	45,000	.60	27,000			
	Pay lake	80,000	.40	32,000			
	Processor	180,000		63,000			
Total		305,000		$122,000			

of 40 cents a pound to pay-lake operators to remain the same. Processors were willing to contract at 40 cents a pound for fish between two and three pounds average weight, and 30 cents a pound for fish between one and two pounds average weight. He anticipated that he could have 90,000 pounds of the larger fish and 90,000 pounds of the smaller fish available in October and November of 1972. Total expected sales were 305,000 pounds, for a total revenue of $122,000. He also decided that he would take a stronger stand on credit and did not anticipate ending the year with any accounts receivable.

EXHIBIT 12
Projected Cash Flow
Delta Fish Farms, Inc.
January 1–December 31, 1972
(in thousands of dollars)

	J	F	M	A	M	J	J	A	S	O	N	D	Total
Cash in:													
Cash on hand, 1/1	3	—	—	—	—	—	—	—	—	—	—	—	
Fish sales	—	—	3	3	7	11	7	7	3	39	30	—	110
Accts. receivable	5	5	—	—	—	—	—	6	6	—	—	—	22
Total	8	5	3	3	7	11	7	13	9	39	30	—	132
Cash out:													
Mgt., Admin.	5	2	2	2	2	2	2	2	2	2	2	2	27
Labor	1	1	1	2	2	2	2	2	2	3	1	1	20
Feed	3	1	1	3	5	6	6	6	5	5	3	1	45
Other	1	1	1	2	2	1	1	1	1	2	1	1	15
Land-mort. prin.	5	—	—	—	—	—	—	—	—	—	—	—	5
Interest, land mort.	8	—	—	—	—	—	—	—	—	—	—	—	8
Bank-loan interest	—	—	—	—	12	—	—	—	—	—	—	—	12
Bank-loan prin.	—	—	—	—	100	—	—	—	—	—	—	—	100
Interest, stock. loan	5	—	—	—	—	—	—	—	—	—	—	—	5
Prin., stock. loan	50	—	—	—	—	—	—	—	—	—	—	—	50
Total	78	5	5	9	123	11	11	11	10	12	7	5	287
Net monthly balance	−70	0	−2	−6	−116	0	−4	2	−1	27	23	−5	
Addl. funds needed	70	0	2	6	116	0	4	0	1	0	0	5	
Addl. funds needed (cumulative)	70	70	72	78	194	194	198	196	197	170	147	152	

376

Based upon these expected sales and expected expenses, a projected monthly cash flow was prepared (Exhibit 12). It was noted that they would need $70,000 in January 1972 if they paid off their stockholders' loan. It was readily apparent that they would need nearly $200,000 in additional funds to operate in 1972 if they were to pay off both the stockholders' loan and the bank loan.

The projected income statement for the 1972 operating year indicated that, for the first time, they would have a positive net operating profit, amounting to $11,000 (Exhibit 13). However, anticipated expenses, including interest on a $200,000 line of credit, would more than

EXHIBIT 13

Projected Income Statement
Delta Fish Farms, Inc.
January 1 to December 31, 1972
(in thousands of dollars)

Sales:				
Fish:	Pay-lake sales, 80,000# @ .40		32	
	Farm sales, 45,000# @ .60		27	
	Processor sales, 180,000# @ .35		63	122
Expenses:				
Beginning fish inventory			72	
Additions:	Management	12		
	Labor	20		
	Feed	42		
	Depreciation	12		
	Other	15	101	
	Total		173	
Ending inventory			74	
	Cost of goods (fish) sold			99
	Gross profit			23
	Administrative expense			12
	Net operating profit			11
Interest expense:				
	Land mortgage	7		
	Bank loan	4		
	Emergency line credit	17		28
Net income (Loss)				(17)

offset the profits from operations. The projected balance sheet for December 31, 1972, shown in Exhibit 14, indicated that they would have approximately $375,000 in assets, $266,000 in liabilities, and net value of equities of $109,000. Their assets would be primarily in fish in inventory, land, dikes, buildings, and equipment.

With these projections available, Dr. Jones called a board meeting to decide on their course of action. As usual, there was much confusion in their meeting.

EXHIBIT 14

Projected Balance Sheet
Delta Fish Farms, Inc.
December 31, 1972
(in thousands of dollars)

Assets:			*Liabilities:*		
Cash on hand		$ 0	Accrued interest:		
Fish in production		74	Land mortgage	$ 7	
Feed inventory		1	Emergency loan	17	24
Brood stock		2	Emergency loan		152
Land		180	Land mortgage		90
Dikes, buildings, equipment:			Total liabilities		266
Original cost	$150		*Equities:*		
Deprec. res.	32	118	Capital stock		200
			Retained earnings		(91)
Total assets		$375	Total liabilities and equities		$375

QUESTIONS

1. What course of action would you suggest?
2. Looking back, what mistakes do you think the company made? Classify these mistakes in terms of those associated with production, organization, marketing, and financial management.
3. Suggest some courses of action that could be taken to make this company profitable.
4. What management-organization problems developed? Did these contribute to the present financial situation of the company?

PART
SIX

20

The World Agricultural Situation

The world agricultural situation can be viewed in several ways. "Prophets of doom" look at the rapid rate of increase in the world's population and compare it to the slower rate of increase in food production. Admittedly, comparison of these two rates over the past 25 years, for many of the countries of the world, provides a dismal outlook. Looking at the situation in another way, however, considerable optimism can be generated. The productive potential of the vast unopened lands in Africa and South America, the forward strides in discovering new biological and mechanical technologies that can be applied for more intensive cultivation of existing farm lands, the improvements in communication and transportation facilities, the ability of man to influence and often control the biological environment in which agricultural production takes place—all of these factors and more constitute legitimate reasons to be hopeful. However, present rates of resource use cannot proceed indefinitely (see Chapter 3). Behavior patterns will have to change. The challenge to us all is how to change, and to what patterns.

THE OVERALL VIEW

The world food problem arises from the uneven distribution of the food currently produced—among the countries of the world, within countries, and among families whose level of income differs. On a total basis, there is enough food produced in the world to give everyone an adequate diet. But its distribution is such that 20 percent suffer from too few calories and 60 percent from too little protein. There are families with nutritionally deficient diets in every country of the world.

In the "developed economies," the major causes are not a lack of availability of food but rather an inadequate purchasing power to buy the right foods and ignorance about what constitutes a good diet. These would still remain serious problems even if the current world food supply could be distributed properly in a physical sense. Individual government efforts to subsidize food purchasing power or institute education programs can help the situation, but the difficulty experienced in getting many of the low-income families in the United States to purchase more better-quality food under existing programs points to no easy answer.

Dietary variations within countries are perhaps as wide as between countries. Using minimum diet standards developed by the Food and Agricultural Organization of the United Nations (FAO), surveys in South Asian and Latin American countries show that the poorest 25 percent of the people consume diets with caloric and protein contents that are only about three-fourths of the country average and fall far below minimum nutritional requirements. Within these low-income groups, preschool children, pregnant women, and nursing mothers are particularly susceptible to malnutrition.

World Food Needs

World population was about 4.0 billion in 1975. It is expected to grow to about 5 billion by 1985 and reach 6 to 7 billion by the turn of the century. If the world population continues to increase at 1965 rates (1.8 percent), about half again more food calories will be required in 1985 than in 1965. Even with a progressive reduction to 30 percent in fertility rates, there will be need for a 43 percent increase.

These projections of world requirements, however, mask the needs of heavily populated countries within the underdeveloped world. For example, India and Brazil at their present rate of population increase will need over 100 percent more calories in 1985 than in 1965, and Pakistan will need nearly 150 percent more.[1]

These quantity estimates portray two crucial aspects of the relation-

---

[1] Estimates taken from *The World Food Problem*, a report of the President's Science Advisory Committee, Report of the Panel on the World Food Supply, The White House, May 1967, Volume 2.

ship between population growth and food needs. First, population and food problems are centered in the already poor, diet-deficient countries, where food production is low and population growth rates are high. Second, the disproportionate need for food in the developing countries cannot be solved during the next twenty years by successful programs of family planning.[2]

The protein dimension is of equal or greater importance than the caloric dimension. There are 22 amino acids required for proper nutrition, of which eight must be ingested with food; the human body can manufacture the others. *Amounts* of protein vary among foods; the protein *quality* is based on the degree to which all the amino acids are present. Wheat, rice, and corn, which constitute staples in the diet of nearly all peoples in the underdeveloped countries, are all incomplete protein sources, since one or two of the essential amino acids are either missing or present in very small amounts. Protein requirements also vary with a person's age, weight, and rate of metabolism. FAO has estimated that world protein requirements will be 50 percent higher in 1985 than in 1965. Again, as in the case of calories, protein needs in developing countries such as India and Brazil run two to three times higher than the 50 percent world-need estimate.

Regional Needs

The Foreign Regional Analysis Division of the Economic Research Service, U.S. Department of Agriculture, prepared in 1964 a report titled *The World Food Budget 1970*, which summarizes the supply and utilization of food commodities for the countries of the world, assesses world food needs, and evaluates the problems and possibilities of closing the food gap.[3]

The report divided the world into two groups: diet-adequate[4] and diet-deficit[5] countries. The diet-deficit countries are usually poor, and food deficiencies merely reflect the low level of living in general. A diet

---

[2] Assuming 1965 rates of population increase, the world population would be 5.03 and 7.15 billion respectively for 1985 and 2000. A 30 percent reduction in fertility would reduce these figures to 4.65 and 6.00 billion. Note that the difference in the two estimates is only 385 million for 1985 but widens to 1.15 billion by the year 2000.

[3] *The World Food Budget 1970*, Foreign Agricultural Economic Report No. 19, October 1964.

[4] U.S.; Canada; Mexico; Brazil; Argentina; Uruguay; Northern, Southern, and Eastern Europe; USSR; Southern Africa; Japan; and Oceania.

[5] Central America and Caribbean; Bolivia; Chile; Colombia; Ecuador; Paraguay; Peru; Venezuela; Northern, West Central, and East Africa; West Asia; India; Pakistan; Ceylon; East Asia; Mainland China.

deficit was defined to exist when food availabilities per capita per day (calories, protein, and fat) yield a nutritional level below that representing minimum physiological requirements for normal activity and health, plus a 10–12 percent loss allowance between the retail level and consumption.

The diet-adequate countries are typically higher in total calories consumed per capita, lower in the percentage of calories ingested from high-carbohydrate foods, and higher in the percentage of calories obtained from meat, fish, eggs, fats and oils, and milk products. Diet-deficit populations get most of their calories from cereal grains, high-carbohydrate foods, and other starchy crops. (Review Table 10-1.)

RESOURCE AVAILABILITY FOR WORLD FOOD PRODUCTION

The physical agricultural potential of any land area is influenced by (1) the physical, chemical, and biological properties of the soil, (2) the annual range and seasonality of temperature, (3) the annual amount and seasonal distribution of precipitation relative to evapotranspiration, and (4) man's ability to make available additional moisture through irrigation. Whether or not that land will produce food is mostly the consequence of man's decisions. In this context, the political, social, and institutional pressures will exert the primary influences.[6]

Soil and Water

Recent estimates indicate that the area of potentially arable land is about 7.86 billion acres, or 24 percent of the ice-free area in the world. Less than half of the potentially arable land is now cultivated; this amounts to more than three times the world acreage actually harvested in the 1960s. Another 9 billion acres (28 percent of total) has potential for grazing; the rest (48 percent of total) has no agricultural potential.

In Asia and Europe, over 80 percent of the potentially arable land is cultivated, but in Africa and South America, there are many acres of land to be opened to cultivation (Table 20-1). More than half the potentially arable land lies in the tropics. Most of the currently cultivated land is in the cool temperate zones.

About 11 percent of the potentially arable land in the world needs irrigation water to grow even one crop. In the remaining 7 billion acres,

---

[6] Data in this section taken from *The World Food Problem*, pp. 407–69. Human-resource availability is omitted, as it is discussed elsewhere in the text.

TABLE 20-1

Present Population and Cultivated Land on Each Continent, Compared with Potentially Arable Land

Region	1970 Population (millions)	Land			Cultivated Land per Person (acres)	Ratio of Cultivated Land to Potentially Arable Land (percent)
		Total	Area Potentially Arable (billions of acres)	Cultivated[a]		
Africa	344	7.46	1.81	.39	1.1	22
Asia	2,057	6.76	1.55	1.28	.6	83
Australia and New Zealand	15	2.03	.38	.04	2.7	1
Europe	462	1.18	.43	.38	.8	88
North America	320	5.21	1.15	.59	1.8	51
South America	191	4.33	1.68	.19	1.0	11
USSR	243	5.52	.88	.56	2.3	64
Total	3,632	32.49	7.88	3.43	.94 (avg.)	44 (avg.)

[a] Same as FAO "Arable land and land under permanent crops." It includes land under crops, temporary fallow, temporary meadows for mowing or pasture, market and kitchen gardens, fruit trees, vines, shrubs, and rubber plantations.

SOURCE: *The World Food Problem*, report of the Panel on the World Food Supply, President's Science Advisory Committee, The White House, May 1967, Volume II, Table 7-9, p. 434; and *World Population Situation in 1970*, Department of Economic and Social Affairs, Population Studies No. 49, United Nations, New York, 1971, p. 46.

385

at least one crop could be grown without irrigation, and multiple cropping is possible over much of it. Without irrigation, multiple cropping could increase the gross cropped area (cultivated area times number of crops) to 9.8 billion acres annually. This is about three times the amount of land now cultivated and about 2 billion acres more than the total potentially arable land. If irrigation water were made available for double or triple cropping, the gross cropped area on the earth would amount to over 16 billion acres.

The rate of increase in harvested acreage has averaged nearly 4 percent since 1960 in South America, but only 1.4 percent in Asia and even less in Africa. If population increases in developing areas are to be matched by increases in food production, expenditures on water and land development must be increased to more than four times present levels. The cost of developing new land for agricultural use varies widely and is influenced by political and social conditions as well as physical and economic factors. Development costs per acre range from only a few dollars to over $1,000.

About 11 percent of the world's cultivated land was irrigated by the mid-1960s. This relatively low percentage suggests that irrigated farming plays only a small role in the world food situation. But this is not the case. When the irrigated acreage is related to the distribution of world population, it becomes apparent that a large fraction of the earth's people, mainly in diet-deficit countries, depends heavily upon irrigation for food. Diet-deficit countries with two-thirds of the world's people have less than half the arable land, but three-fourths of the irrigated land. Estimates place the total irrigated land at 500 million acres by 1975 and 750 million acres by the end of this century.

Fertilizer, Seed, Pesticides, and Machinery

Four kinds of capital inputs of major importance to increasing agricultural production are fertilizers, seeds, pesticides, and machinery.

Fertilizer. Only ten (20 percent) of the 50 million metric tons of commercial fertilizers used in 1968–69 was applied to crops growing in the developing countries.[7] To keep food production growing at a pace equal to that of population, it is estimated that fertilizer usage should increase to 34 million metric tons by 1985 and 67 million metric tons by 2000.

To achieve the needed increase in fertilizer by 1985 will require a $17 billion investment, plus an additional annual cost to farmers of $9

---

[7] Neither human nor animal wastes used for fertilizer are considered. Includes 2.5 million metric tons for mainland China. See FAO, "The State of Food and Agriculture," Rome, 1970, p. 29.

billion. There will be large increases in international trade in fertilizer and fertilizer raw materials. Because efficient potash and phosphate mining operations are large and complex, they are usually located at the source of raw materials. The suggested cost estimates do not include costs associated with facilities, roads, and railroads that might be required. Additionally, it is estimated that three skilled and five unskilled people are required for each thousand tons of plant nutrients that are provided and distributed per year, which suggests that 50,000 college graduates could be needed by 1985 in the fertilizer and associated agricultural industries.

Seeds. Improved seeds must be available and used by farmers if significant gains are to be made in crop yields. FAO has given a "seed rating" to characterize nations on their development, production, distribution, and proper use of better seeds. Using corn, rice, and wheat as indicators, the highest rating (1) was given to such countries as Japan, Taiwan, and the Netherlands. The lowest rating (4) was given to, for example, Pakistan, Iran, and Jordan. Yields for nations with a 1 rating averaged 2.3 times higher than those in the 4 category, and the top group had almost all their grain cropland planted with improved seed, as compared to less than 10 percent for the lowest group.

It has been estimated that if 50 percent of any cultivated area is planted with improved seeds instead of traditional varieties, yields can be expected to double. Even in developing areas, the private commercial firms could supply a good portion of the new seed. These estimates assume that other improved practices, such as the use of fertilizers, pesticides, and machinery, will also be used. If commercial firms supplied only 25 percent of the seed requirements of the developing free-world areas, implying a doubling of food production by the year 2000, an investment of about $305 million in seed plants would be required (70 percent in Asia and 15 percent each in Latin America and Africa), and the annual operating costs to farmers would approximate $1.6 billion.

Pesticides. Large increases in pesticides will be necessary to increase food production. Minimum losses of food from pests range from 20 to 30 percent on a worldwide basis. Viruses, bacteria, fungi, protozoa, nematodes, insects, birds, and rodents compete directly with man in consuming food; and weeds, although they do not consume food directly, compete with plants for water and soil nutrients, thus reducing crop yields.

Pests can be controlled by biological or chemical methods. The development of rust-resistant wheat varieties has also had a major impact on yields in the United States, although constant research effort is necessary, since the rust organism changes rapidly. Elimination of certain insect varieties has been accomplished by sex sterilization techniques. However, chemical agents—fertilizer, fungicides, herbicides, and fumigants—remain the chief control weapons, and their use increases rapidly as plant production is intensified. The amount of pesticides applied in Africa or India is only about 1 percent of that used in Japan, with its intensive agriculture and high yields.

In the United States, the use of herbicides is regarded as a labor-saving measure, but recent studies on rice in the Philippines indicated that when propanil (a modern selective herbicide) was applied as a weed control, a 43 percent increase in yield resulted over that from conventional hand weeding. If these favorable results can be duplicated in other areas, selective herbicides are likely to be widely adopted for rice production, even in areas having large labor supplies and low wages.

By the mid-1960s, only 120,000 metric tons of pesticides were used annually by the developing world (excluding China). To double food production, usage is expected to increase fivefold, requiring $1.2 billion in manufacturing-plant investment plus $670 million for formulation and distribution facilities.

Machinery.   In the United States, the rapid mechanization of agriculture has been construed as an attempt to make more efficient use of labor rather than to increase yields. However, recent studies have shown that the use of mechanized power influences yields favorably for several reasons: Seedbed preparation is better and more timely, it may allow double or triple cropping, seed placement is more accurate, machines allow for a uniform application of pesticides, and, finally, more timely harvesting is possible.

The basic machinery units needed include tractors, plows, disc harrows, peg harrows, grain drills, planters, distributors, cultivators, sprayers, and threshing equipment. Improved animal-drawn seeders, harrows, and cultivators would also help.

The number of tractors used in the developing world has increased 50 percent, from about 2.4 million in 1961–65 to 3.6 million in 1970. For 1961–65, this number represented 19 percent of all tractors in use in the world; in 1970, it was 23 percent.[8] It is estimated that the addition of horsepower per unit of land in developing countries has a significant effect on increasing yields up to at least 0.5 horsepower per hectare (2.5 acres). The United States has about one horsepower available per hectare, whereas Latin America has .19 and Africa only .05

The cost of agricultural machinery is surprisingly low relative to the costs of other inputs. To provide manufacturing plants to produce

---

8 Wheel and crawler tractors, estimated average of 30 horsepower each.

tractors, power tillers, power sprayers, and power harvesting and threshing requirements up to half a horsepower per hectare in Asia, Latin
America, and Africa would require about $1.8 billion. A more difficult
problem would be developing the manpower to develop, produce, and
distribute the machinery and train people in its use.

Livestock

Total livestock in the world numbers over 3.5 billion animals plus
an equal number of domesticated fowl. Although about two out of three
animals are located in the developing countries, they produce only 22–23
percent of the world's meat, milk, and eggs. This low productivity can
be attributed to a failure to utilize scientific principles of breeding, sanitation, and disease control. The quantity of animal food products produced in the developing world is sufficient to supply an average of only
nine grams of animal protein per person per day. In contrast, there are
44 grams available per person per day in the developed countries.[9]

Infrastructure

Agricultural production is aided and encouraged directly by the
amount of infrastructure, or social overhead capital, available. Roads,
communications systems, power, and educational institutions are examples. Without roads, inputs of seed and fertilizer may not be moved
to farmers, and similarly, they allow farmers to move their product to
market. Generally, the more infrastructure a country has, the lower the
probable relative cost of its food production. There is more economic
incentive to produce food.

With this brief sketch of resource availability in the world, let's
look at recent world food production.

THE RECENT RECORD OF
FOOD PRODUCTION

Excluding Communist Asia, the past twenty years has brought
steady increases in world food production. The compound annual rate
of growth was 2.7 percent in the developed countries and 3.0 percent in
the less-developed countries (Figure 20-1).[10]

---

[9] FAO *Production Yearbook*, 1971.

[10] Data in this section taken from U.S. Department of Agriculture, Economic
Research Service, *The World Agricultural Situation*, Foreign Agricultural Economic
Report #38, February 1968; and *The Wheat Situation* and *The Feed Situation*, vari-
ous issues.

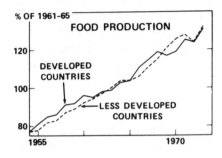

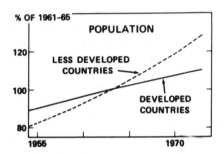

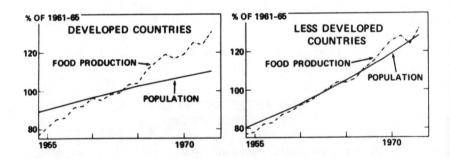

POPULATION EXCLUDES COMMUNIST ASIA

U.S. DEPARTMENT OF AGRICULTURE   NEG. ERS 426-73 A (12)   ECONOMIC RESEARCH SERVICE

FIGURE 20-1

Food Production and Population, Developed and
Less-Developed Countries

Although total food production has advanced at nearly the same rate in all parts of the world, per capita food production reveals quite a different picture. In Chapter 4, you learned that population was increasing at a much more rapid rate (2.5 percent per year or more) in the less-developed countries than in the developed group (presently below 1 percent annually). This results in per capita food production gaining ground in the developed countries but barely keeping pace in the less-developed group (Figure 20-1). The problem is compounded by the increasing proportion of the world's people in the less-developed countries —now 62 percent, compared to 56 percent twenty years ago—and the gap will continue to widen for the rest of the century (see summary in Figure 20-2). Within the less-developed group, East Asia has fared the best and Africa has shown a decrease in per capita food production since 1961 (Figure 20-3).

Grains

Cereal grains continue to play a dominant role, for direct consumption by people (review Table 10-1) and for feed to expand the livestock economics—particularly of the developed countries. World grain production in the early 1970s was about 1.2 billion metric tons, up one-fourth from the mid-1960s. In the late 1960s, the developed countries accounted for half of the world area planted to grains, and two-thirds of total production (Figure 20-4). The less-developed group between 1950 and 1970 increased their area planted to grains and yield per unit by one-third, and their production by 80 percent. Their average yields are still about one ton per hectare behind the developed countries.

Wheat. World wheat production in 1973 was about 363 million metric tons—48 percent higher than the 1960–65 average. The world's leading producers are the USSR, the United States, Canada, China, France, India, Italy, Turkey, Australia, and Argentina. Wheat is grown mostly in the temperate climate zones, and provides one of the staple foods for several developing countries, including Northern China and India. The United States and Canada account for over half of total world exports of wheat. Western Europe and Asia are major importers.

Rice. Rice rivals wheat as a food grain, being the staple food of the populous Far East. World rice production in 1973 reached 212 million metric tons, with most of the increase occurring in the traditional importing countries. Mainland China produces one-third of the world's total production, followed by India (23 percent), Pakistan, Japan, Indonesia, Thailand, Burma, Brazil, the Philippines, and the United States.

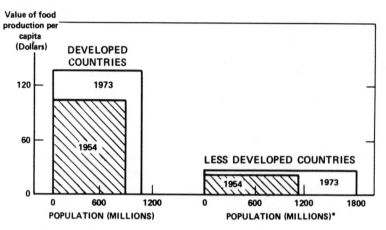

*Population excludes Communist Asia

In this chart the <u>area</u> of each rectangle, determined as the product of population (measured on the horizontal axis) times value of food production per capita (in dollars on the vertical axis), <u>represents</u> the total <u>value</u> of food production in million dollars for an indicated group of countries at a specified time. All four rectangles may be compared in height, in width, and in area. (Values computed at 1961–65 average prices.)

1. Developed countries in 1973 accounted for:

    a. Two-fifths of world population

    b. Three-fourths of world food production

    c. Three-fourths of the <u>increase</u> in world food production since 1954

    d. One-fourth of the <u>increase</u> in world population since 1954

2. From 1954 to 1973, the developed countries:

    a. Increased <u>population</u> one-fourth, reaching 1,100 million, about equal to population in the LDC's in 1954, whose populations increased 60 percent by 1973.

    b. Increased food production per capita one-third, reaching $139 per person, more than 5 times the level of the LDC's.

    c. Increased <u>total food production</u> two-thirds, to $150 billion, more than 3 times that of the LDC's.

3. In the LDC's:

    a. Food production per capita increased only 5 percent.

    b. Aggregate food production rose two-thirds by 1973, to total little more than half that of the DC's 20 years earlier.

U.S. DEPARTMENT OF AGRICULTURE   NEG. ERS 428–73 (12)   ECONOMIC RESEARCH SERVICE

FIGURE 20-2

World Population and Food Production in 1954 and 1973

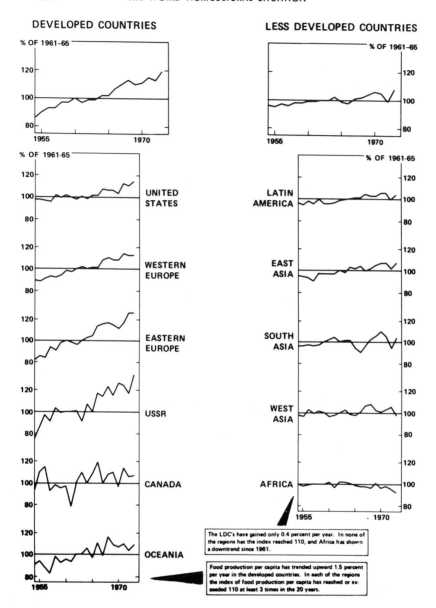

DEVELOPED COUNTRIES

LESS DEVELOPED COUNTRIES

The LDC's have gained only 0.4 percent per year. In none of the regions has the index reached 110, and Africa has shown a downtrend since 1961.

Food production per capita has trended upward 1.5 percent per year in the developed countries. In each of the regions the index of food production per capita has reached or exceeded 110 at least 3 times in the 20 years.

U.S. DEPARTMENT OF AGRICULTURE   NEG. ERS 427-73 (12)   ECONOMIC RESEARCH SERVICE

FIGURE 20-3

Per Capita Food Production in Developed and
Less-Developed Countries, 1954 to 1973

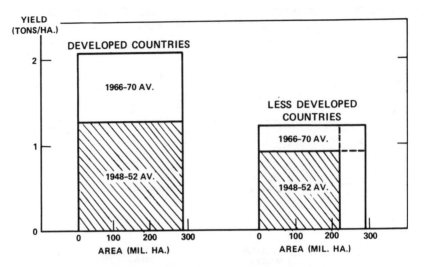

In this chart the area of each rectangle, determined as the product of the amount
of land in grains (in million hectares or the horizontal axis) times yield per hectare
(in kilograms on the vertical scale), represents the total production of grains in million
tons for an indicated group of countries at a specified time. All four rectangles may
be compared in height, in width, and in area.

1. Developed countries in 1966-70 accounted for:

    a. 50 percent of area in grains

    b. 65 percent of world grain production

    c. 61 percent of the increase in grain production over the 1948-52 average

    d. None of the increase in world grain area

2. From 1948-52 to 1966-70 the LDC's:

    a. Increased grain area 35 percent, reaching nearly 300 million hectares,
       thereby catching up with area in developed countries,
       which made no gain over this period.

    b. Increased grain yields 32 percent, to 1.2 tons per hectare,
       nearly equal to developed countries' 1948-52 yields
       which increased 63 percent by 1966-70.

    c. Increased grain production 78 percent to 356 million tons, nearly
       equal to the developed countries' 1948-52 production,
       which increased 64 percent by 1966-70.

      The increase in production in the LDC's was 156 million tons:

        45 percent from increased area
        41 percent from increased yields
        14 percent from combined effect of increased area and yields.

U.S. DEPARTMENT OF AGRICULTURE   NEG. ERS 429-73 (12)   ECONOMIC RESEARCH SERVICE

FIGURE 20-4

Area Planted, Yields, and Total Grain Production in
the World, 1948–1952 Compared with 1966–1970
for Developed and Less-Developed Countries

Leading exporters, however, are the United States, Thailand, and Burma.

Gains in rice yields have been disappointing in the rice-bowl countries of Asia, except for Japan. After extensive research in breeding desirable characteristics selected from several thousand rice varieties, the International Rice Research Institute completed the development in 1968 of a new variety that can significantly boost yields when packaged with other improved inputs.

Corn.   Corn is classified as a feed grain, but some varieties are also an important food source for many people in the underdeveloped world. The United States accounts for one-half of world corn production, which totaled 291 million metric tons in 1971. Other important producers are the USSR, Brazil, Argentina, Yugoslavia, Mexico, Romania, and South America. Western Europe is the major importing region. The United States, Argentina, South Africa, and Romania are principal exporters. In recent years, Japan has become an important importer of corn, to supply her rapidly growing livestock industry. A large part of Japan's corn imports come from Thailand, where production has grown rapidly—quadrupling since 1960.

Other grains.   Barley production was 130 million metric tons in 1971, up two-thirds over 1960. Barley is the world's second most important feed grain, and like corn, is used as a food grain throughout Asia and Africa. Principal producers are the USSR, the United States, Mainland China, France, Canada, and the United Kingdom.

Millet and sorghum are widely grown and used as feed grains except in Asia and Africa. World output of sorghum, which was stable at 34–35 million metric tons in the early 1960s, rose to 41 million metric tons in 1971. Mainland China, India, and the United States are leading producers, with the United States as the only significant exporting country.

Oat production, at 55 million metric tons in 1971, was nearly the same as in 1960. Production is limited to temperate North America, Europe, and the USSR. Rye production, at 29 million metric tons in 1971, is 15 percent lower than in 1960 and is produced principally in Soviet-bloc countries.

Oilseeds

Oilseeds (including oil-bearing tree fruits) are the source of more than half the world's supply of fats and oils. In terms of quantity harvested, soybeans, cottonseed, and peanuts are the leading oilseeds. There were record world crops of soybeans, peanuts, and sunflower seed in

1972. The United States accounts for about 75 percent of total world production of soybeans.

India is the world's leading peanut producer, with about one-third of the total. Nigeria, Senegal, the United States, Indonesia, and Brazil account for another fourth. African countries are the major exporters and European countries are large importers. About two-thirds of the peanut production is crushed for oil. Peanut oil comprises one-fifth of total world trade of edible oils and oil-beanery materials.

The economic components of cottton are lint and cottonseed. As a source of human food protein, cottonseed is limited, because a toxic agent, gossypol, is present. A new variety has been developed without the toxin. However, a great virtue of cottonseed is that it is indigenous to protein-poor tropical areas of Africa, Asia, and Latin America, and can readily be used as a feed for ruminant animals.

Other important oil-beanery crops include sunflower seed, produced mainly in the USSR; rapeseed, produced principally in India, Canada, and Mainland China; flaxseed, largely produced in Argentina, North America, India, and the USSR; olives, the traditional source of oil in the Mediterranean area; and tropical-palm products—coconuts, obtained mostly from the Far East in the form of copra, and oil-palm fruit, coming mostly from Africa as palm oil and palm kernels. Palm-oil production doubled from 1967 to 1973, with one-third of the world total accounted for by West Malaysia.

Livestock

The world has over a billion each of cattle and sheep, two-thirds of a billion pigs, about one-third billion goats, 125 million buffalo, and more than 130 million horses, mules, asses, and camels. World meat production increased 22 percent in the period 1961–65 to 1971 (Table 20-2). Beef and veal constituted about 47 percent of the total, pork about 44 percent, and mutton and lamb the remaining 9 percent. Gains in Latin America and Africa were substantially below those in other areas.

Milk production in the world gained 13 percent in a similar period. Cow milk accounts for 90 percent of the total; buffalo milk is an important food source to people in the Far East (Table 20-3). Egg production increased 32 percent in 1971 over 1961–65, showing wide gains in the Near East, the Far East, Latin America, and Africa.

SUMMARY

Growth in per capita food supplies must be accelerated above the recent record in developing countries if the problems of hunger and mal-

TABLE 20-2

Indexes of Average Meat Production from Indigenous
Animals by Geographic Regions, 1971
(1961–65 = 100)

Region	Beef and Veal	Pork	Mutton and Lamb	Total Meat Increase
World	123.8	123.2	112.2	122.4
Europe	120.4	127.3	104.9	123.3
North America	126.2	123.3	74.5	123.9
United States[a]	123.5	120.9	75.5	123.5
Latin America	113.4	129.4	113.5	116.4
Near East	126.3	237.5	116.4	121.4
Far East	121.7	151.5	109.6	131.8
Africa	112.6	151.9	124.9	118.5
Oceania	122.8	143.0	132.8	128.5

[a] Included in North America.
SOURCE: United Nations, FAO *Production Yearbook,* Vol. 25, Rome, 1971.

TABLE 20-3

Indexes of Average Milk Production and Egg Weight
by Geographic Regions, 1971 (1961–65 = 100)

Region	Cow	Goat	Sheep	Buffalo	Total Milk	Total Egg Weight
World	112.9	97.9	113.3	119.3	113.0	132.1
Europe	111.9	84.8	109.8	77.0	111.4	129.8
North America	94.4	—	—	—	94.4	111.3
United States[a]	94.4	—	—	—	94.4	110.3
Latin America	122.3	97.7	121.1	—	121.8	142.4
Near East	121.9	102.1	111.8	123.5	116.9	142.1
Far East	117.0	121.9	118.4	119.3	118.3	181.8
Africa	123.5	115.0	146.4	—	123.6	149.4
Oceania	106.1	—	—	—	106.1	128.4

[a] Included in North America.
SOURCE: United Nations, FAO *Production Yearbook,* Vol. 25, Rome, 1971.

nutrition are to be alleviated. Population reduction through programs to reduce fertility will help but will not have any major impact before 1985. Remember, even if the world takes on a zero-growth population program, before it will stabilize, the world's population will double! Time is a critical dimension in demographers' minds today.

There is less of a shortage of land resources in Africa and South America. In Asia, however, the emphasis will probably be on increasing yields on existing cultivated land from the introduction of improved seeds, fertilizer, and pesticides. Water-development projects and the introduction of mechanical power should give added impetus to the possibility of more double and triple cropping.

Despite their lack of several essential amino acids, wheat, rice, and corn will continue to be the principal food sources for most of the world's people. However, oilseeds are increasing rapidly, particularly soybeans. Present cereal-grain production levels indicate a potential to supply as much protein as that supplied from animal sources. Animal-meat supplies have great potential in places like East Africa and South America, provided that certain animal health hazards, such as ticks and tsetse flies, are effectively controlled.

Trained and educated manpower may be as much a limiting factor to realizing gains in world food production as is any physical or biological input. For example, the estimate of technical manpower needed to produce and distribute the inputs of seeds, fertilizer, pesticides, and machinery in the developing free world is 75,000 university graduates or their equivalent by 1985. Additional specially trained people will be required for research and extension education programs.

21

Increasing World Food Supplies

Although an increase in world food supplies might be considered a matter of organizing the land and water resources, adding necessary capital resources and man's labor, and teaching managers to efficiently coordinate the production processes involved, its initiation and coordination are enormously complex. Much also depends on the institutional and political aspects of the world's societies. Let's review some of the more important ideas.

In Chapter 2, the efficiencies gained in production processes by specialization were emphasized as a key to man's early economic development. This notion has not lost its significance. In Chapters 3 through 6, natural resources, people, capital, and technology were discussed regarding their role in agricultural development. In Chapter 9, the importance of an effective marketing system was portrayed. Chapter 10 discussed food consumption and pointed out that money purchasing power was a prime factor determining the economic demand level for food for that part of the population not growing their own. In Part III, the economic principles that managers can use to guide their decisions as to what, how, and how much to produce were explained. In the chapter preceding this one, world resources that contribute to food production were surveyed. In addition, the favorable effect of a country's social overhead capital (infrastructure) was pointed out. A continuing awareness of these broad-based ideas will be helpful.

THE CONCEPT OF
A "PACKAGE OF TECHNOLOGY"

How often people commenting about the world food situation make statements such as this: "What's so complicated about increasing the food supply abroad? Fertilizer on those rice paddies in Asia is what's needed. In South America, straighten out the land-reform problem and the rest will be easy. In the arid areas like Egypt, it's just a matter of getting irrigation water to the land."

All these statements certainly contain some truth and sound quite plausible to the uninformed layman. But these people miss one extremely important idea that should never be forgotten. Although the use of one improved technology will probably have some positive influence on yields, it will also generate a need for other technologies to be introduced simultaneously if yields are to continue to be significantly increased. The process continues as each new technology is introduced. Higher levels of management input are also required. Hence, it is nearly always desirable to introduce several new technologies at the same time, because of the interaction effect on yields. Adding fertilizer to the rice paddy on a Thailand farm might well cause the plant to grow much taller and add more rice kernels. But, if a strong-stemmed rice variety is not used when the larger seed head forms at the top of the longer stem, it is likely to fall over and be lost, resulting in a yield below that received from an unfertilized plot.

In the village of Tegalega in West Java, Indonesia, 57 farmers increased corn yields 600 percent by (1) using a new variety, (2) using recommended amounts and kinds of fertilizer, (3) changing the depth of planting the seeds, and (4) controlling insect pests. In most cases, only a *package* of new techniques can achieve such results.[1] Because of risk and uncertainty factors, a farmer in most developing countries needs promise of a substantial gain in yields (perhaps 40 percent or more) before he will be convinced to adopt a farming change. A cautionary factor in all countries is that sometimes a farmer's managerial capacity may be too low to effectively "put the package together." The widely publicized success of the "Green Revolution" (to be discussed later in this chapter) is the result of applying several new technologies as a package.

---

[1] A. T. Mosher, *Getting Agriculture Moving* (New York: Praeger Publishers, Inc., 1965), p. 78.

METHODS OF ATTACKING THE WORLD
FOOD PROBLEM[2]

Intensification of Plant Production

A comparison of crop yields between developing and developed countries indicates that food supplies can certainly be increased through intensification of plant production. For example, rice yields in Japan and the United States are over three times larger than in India (Table 21-1). Corn yields within the United States were nearly three times higher in 1961–63 than in 1931–35; soybean yields were up 60 percent in the same period.

TABLE 21-1

Indexes of Comparative Yields of Major Food Crops
in Selected Regions of the World, 1971
(World Average = 100)

Crop	Latin America	Africa	Asia	Europe	U.S.A.	India	Japan
Wheat	91	58	74	180	144	82	168
Corn	54	44	45	128	200	44	110
Rice	74	66	87	202	228	75	230
Potatoes	60	54	77	140	189	66	157
Sweet potatoes	105	83	116	186	132	80	229
Millet, sorghum	216	81	61	340	380	58	168
Peanuts	122	86	91	187	234	86	199

SOURCE: United Nations, FAO *Production Yearbook,* 1971.

Developing higher-yielding varieties. The development of new grain germ plasm and varieties by conventional plant-breeding techniques is one approach. The practice of hybridizing crop varieties has played a major role in increasing the quality and quantity of crops in the United States.

Adaptation of plants to specific environmental conditions—tolerance to drought, heat, light, soil salinity, and poor drainage—has received

---

[2] *The World Food Problem,* a report of the President's Science Advisory Committee, Report of the Panel on the World Food Supply, The White House, May **1967**, Volume 2.

considerable effort. Plant environments are also continually changed by the introduction of other new technologies, such as increased levels of fertilizer use and better use of irrigation water. Developing new varieties capable of absorbing improved practices is required. Such developments were the basis of the "Green Revolution."

Genetic resistance to pests, a form of biological control, is often the most economical control measure. Control of many damaging species of rust that attack cereal grains is an outstanding example, although such control measures are not usually permanent, since rust organisms rotate and attack previously resistant varieties. Genetic resistance to attacks from insects, such as the Hessian fly in winter-wheat varieties, is relatively newer, and good progress is being made. Other examples include building a resistance to aphids in alfalfa, to the European corn borer in corn, and to nematodes in lespedeza and soybeans. The breeding out or lowering of toxic agents like gossypol in cottonseed and prussic acid in Sudan grass and forage sorghum are additional improvements.

Dwarf plants can be used to increase production, since more plants can be planted per acre, utilizing sunlight more efficiently. They respond to high fertilization rates without the resultant tall growth that stimulates lodging and reduces the efficiency of mechanical harvesting. Grain sorghums, wheat, corn, and rice have received primary attention.

Grain-quality improvements have been sought in wheat, where good milling and baking properties are essential, and also in barley, where malting quality is important. Gas chromatography has expedited analyses of the fatty acids in vegetable oils. The improvement of the quality of protein will be discussed later in this chapter.

Utilization of hybrid vigor.   Few programs to increase yields by hybrid vigor have been as dramatic as that for hybrid corn. Corn is one of the few plants that produce male and female flowers separately, and the relative ease of removing the male flowers (tassels) makes it easy to hybridize. Few plants exhibit the necessary degree of self-sterility that allows cross-pollination by interplanting. Male sterility, which is transmitted from one generation to the next in the cytoplasm of the female sex cells, was discovered in onions in the 1920s and used in the production of commercial hybrids. It was later found in corn. But because commercial corn breeding depends on seed production, fertility must be restored when the hybrid is grown, or seed of nonsterile types must be blended with the hybrid seed. This difficulty has been overcome by incorporating fertility-restoring genes in the male lines to overcome the sterilizing effect of the female cytoplasm. This method of hybridization eliminates the need for costly detasseling. More recently, cytoplasmic male-sterility and genetic-restorer genes were found in grain sorghum and Sudan grass.

There is hope for hybrid wheat varieties. Germ plasm for wheat hybridization was found in the early 1960s, and intensive research efforts are under way. In plants where cytoplasmic male sterility has not been found, attempts to introduce male sterility by genetic means are being pursued. Limited success has been achieved in castor beans, spinach, and barley.

Broadening the germ-plasm base.   Improvements in crops through plant breeding are limited by the available genetic diversity. When certain desired characteristics do not appear within the germ plasm of a crop, the plant breeder must look to other sources. Alteration of germ plasm by irradiation is one source. X rays and ultraviolet rays were used earlier and, with the advent of nuclear energy, gamma rays and neutrons have brought new possibilities. Mutation can also be introduced by chemical means.

Single-gene changes are sought that will offer resistance to pests. Oats resistant to blight and rust-resistant bluegrass have been isolated. The most spectacular results, however, have been obtained by breaking the chromosomes and rearranging their fragments. Wild progenitors of domestic crops often retain desirable characteristics that are no longer present in the germ plasm of domestic species. As a result, wide crosses are sometimes helpful, although they pose other serious problems. Leaf-rust resistance was transferred to wheat from a weedy wild relative. When close linkage of the new rust-resistant gene to other undesirable characteristics posed a barrier, irradiation broke the chromosome, freeing the resistant gene from the undesirable gene.

Plant nutrition and fertilizer.   Plant-nutrition and soil-fertility research, coupled with rapid advances in fertilizer-production technology, have resulted in huge increases in fertilizer use. Sound fertilization practices, the result of plant-nutrition and soil-fertility research, when combined with other good practices of soil management and crop protection have produced phenomenal increases in yields. In the early 1940s, corn yields in the southeastern United States were not markedly different from yields in many of the developing countries in the late 1960s. However, between 1945 and 1965, average corn yields in North Carolina increased from 21 to 70 bushels per acre. Most of the fertilizer research has centered on nitrogen, phosphorus, and potash. However, more attention is being given to the micronutrients and trace minerals, such as boron, zinc, and iron.

Plant protection.   Losses to insects, diseases, and weeds take a huge toll each year all over the world. Use of agricultural chemicals for pest control has been a significant factor contributing to the takeoff in crop yields in the United States. Empirical evidence shows that increasing the intensity of plant production is associated with the need for increased use of pesticides. Pesticide usage is also closely positively correlated with fertilizer usage. The average return, measured as yield increase per dollar invested for pesticides, is usually considered to be about 5 to 1. Even though these advances have brought about many additional problems from undesirable side effects, pest control of some kind is an integral part of modern farm management.

Intensification of Animal Production

The potential for increasing animal production is huge. Although it is indisputable that human food cannot be produced as efficiently in terms of animal production as of grains, livestock thrive on many feeds, forages, wastes, by-products, and even chemicals that are not suitable for human food. Whether or not grains that man can eat are fed to animals is a matter of economics, confined largely to the developed countries, where most consumers have enough purchasing power to choose to eat more of their food in animal-product form than as cereals.

The hen and the dairy cow are the most efficient in converting protein in feed to human food products. They are followed by the broiler, the pig, and finally, the beef animal. The ruminant animal can utilize feed that cannot be used directly by man, and is indeed salvaging materials otherwise lost and making them available to humans. Also, the animal proteins that they provide humans are of much higher quality than are the plant proteins.

Use of world grazing lands. Nine billion acres (27.8 percent) of the earth's surface is suitable only for potential grazing by livestock. The productivity of these lands could be improved greatly if modern forage and range management techniques were used. Even some of the arable land produces a more valuable human-food resource through the production of high-yielding forages, alfalfa, or Sudan grass for conversion by livestock than when it is used to produce cereal grains for consumption by people.

Use of wastes and by-products. Almost every food crop or product has some usable waste or by-product associated with it. Unfortunately, most of these valuable products are lost in developing countries, where animal proteins are badly needed. Corn, wheat, rice, sorghum, sugar beets, and oats have large plant residues and mill wastes that are extremely valuable sources of energy and protein. The animal industry generates a number of salvageable products as animal feeds, including meat scraps, tankage, bone and blood meal, animal fats, and even animal manures. Oilseed by-products in meal form are also valuable animal feedstuffs.

Production of animal protein by urea. Cattle, sheep, and goats can use nonprotein nitrogen in the form of urea as a source of dietary nitrogen, because microorganisms in their rumens convert these substances to proteins. Dairy cows fed urea, ammonium salts, potato starch, cellulose, and sucrose have produced up to 9,515 pounds of milk containing 361 pounds of protein without any other source of protein.[3] A beef calf weighing 290 pounds gained an average of one pound per day until it weighed 930 pounds and produced a calf, with urea as the only protein source.[4] Where a shortage of protein feedstuffs exists in developing countries, urea may be able to make a significant contribution.

Improved animal nutrition. Inadequate nutrition is a major cause of low livestock productivity in the developing countries. Animals, like man, have nutritional requirements that vary with age, sex, and rate of growth. Livestock's needs are also determined by its production of meat, milk, and eggs, and by diseases, climate, and other stresses. Animals are highly adaptive and can survive in nearly any environment, but their usefulness to man as a food source is dependent upon their having proper nutrition.

Feed preservation and storage. Few areas of the world are endowed with the climate, soil, and rainfall to support year-round high-quality plant growth. Animal production can be intensified where improved systems of harvesting, preserving, and storing plant materials provide food for animals the year round. In the developed countries, extensive use is made of hay, silage, crop residues, and root crops that have been preserved and stored.

Animal breeding. Livestock developed in temperate climates cannot thrive under the adverse tropical and subtropical conditions prevalent in most developing countries. Thus, importing highly productive animals from the temperate zone will not suffice as a means to increase production in these areas of the world. The indigenous breeds in Asia and Africa have evolved an ability to survive the heat, parasites, exotic diseases, and the low level of nutrition available to them from native vegetation, although their ability to produce meat, milk, and eggs is relatively low. Through careful selection, animal breeders can develop new

---

[3] A. I. Viramen, "Milk Production of Cows on Protein-Free Feed," *Science,* 153 (3744) (Sept. 30, 1966), 1603–14.

[4] L. A. Moore, et al., unpublished data, U.S. Department of Agriculture, Animal Husbandry Division, Beltsville, Maryland.

strains and breeds. Some of the more successful new breeds of cattle developed in the tropics are the Santa Gertrudis, Brahman, Boran, and Nandi. Although indigenous breeds, such as the Sindi dairy cow, can be upgraded, the process is painfully slow and yields poorer results than crossbreeding programs do.

For swine and poultry, relatively more attention is being given to transplanting the whole "production package" into the developing country as a means of reinforcing animal production, rather than cross-breeding existing stock. This involves introducing the improved breed or strain along with a complete balanced diet and husbandry practices that provide protection from the adverse environmental factors, including disease. For example, commercial egg and broiler operations in the United States control the environment in which the animal lives to such an extent that they approach a manufacturing industry. In such a situation, the total "system" can be transplanted into another part of the world, provided that inputs are available and management is capable.

Animal reproduction.   Reproductive efficiency is a key item in the success of intensifying animal production. In the United States, 70 to 80 percent of healthy range cows become pregnant when inseminated with high-quality semen or mated with a fertile bull. In many areas of the world, however, reproductive rates of 40 calves per 100 cows are common. Calf mortality is also higher. The same situation exists for swine and sheep. The difference is largely due to a lack of understanding of basic principles of reproduction. Estimates are that the use of fertile sires, improvements in the management of females of breeding age in relation to the reproductive characteristics of the species, and an understanding of normal reproductive processes could double or triple present reproductive rates in some countries.

Animal disease control.   In 1962, FAO estimated that losses caused by animal diseases were 15–20 percent of total annual production in those countries having reasonably adequate veterinary services, and 30–40 percent in countries having less intensive services. Based on these conservative estimates, a 50 percent reduction in losses from animal diseases would increase the supplies of animal protein in areas of greatest need by 25 percent.[5]

Epizootic diseases capable of killing or debilitating large populations of animals are largely uncontrolled in developing countries. These include rinderpest, contagious bovine pleuropneumonia, hemorrhagic septicemia, foot-and-mouth disease, hog cholera, fowl plague, trypano-

---

[5] W. R. Pritchard, "Increasing Protein Foods through Improving Animal Health," National Academy of Science Proceedings 56 (2), August 1966, pp. 360–69.

somiasis, African swine fever, and Newcastle disease. But the greatest total loss results from the many parasitic infections and nutritional, toxic, metabolic, and organic diseases that particularly affect livestock in the developing countries. Some of the more important are brucellosis, tuberculosis, mastitis, vibrosis, lumpy skin disease, bluetongue, parasite infestations, and localized diseases such as Nairobi sheep disease. To control these diseases will probably require a worldwide plan, sponsored by some association such as the International Veterinary Congress.

With regard to priorities, foot-and-mouth disease is estimated to reduce South American cattle production 25 percent annually. Rabies kills another million head annually, and the reproductive disease of brucellosis has been recorded as having up to a 40 percent prevalence. In Africa, rinderpest has decimated cattle populations on several occasions. Contagious bovine pleuropneumonia is probably as widespread as rinderpest once was. Trypanosomiasis is endemic in nearly 5 million square miles of Africa infested with the tsetse fly. Eradication of the fly would enable Africa to stock another 125 million head of cattle, and significant progress in this direction is under way. In Asia, hemorrhagic septicemia of cattle and water buffalo destroys a million animals in some years. Hog cholera is enzootic in many parts of Asia, and its control depends on the successful distribution of vaccine. Sheep pox occurs commonly in the arid pastoral regions of Asia, causing death losses of up to 50 percent.

Increasing High-Quality Protein

So far, this chapter has dwelt primarily on increasing the *quantity* of food produced per unit of land area per unit of time. Remembering from earlier discussions that there is a quality dimension to the world food problem, let us survey ways of increasing the *quality* of food in order to alleviate malnutrition problems.

Diets of the world's peoples can be classified into (1) those high in protein calories of animal origin, (2) those high in grain calories, and (3) those low in grain calories and high in fats, sugars, or tubers. In the first group, characterized by North America, Oceania, and most of Europe, there is no acute malnutrition problem. In the second group, the protein-quality problem becomes increasingly worse as the staple food changes from wheat to rice to corn. Sensitive groups within the population, such as preschool children, suffer most. Kwashiorkor, a childhood disease caused by protein deficiency, often occurs in the rice-staple diet and is also prevalent in the corn-staple diet. People in the third group suffer most; kwashiorkor is widespread here, since the protein intake is inadequate. It has been shown that about 90 percent of a person's brain development takes place by age 4, and a protein-deficient diet that begins immediately upon weaning may cause irreparable damage to one's mental capacity.

Improving protein quality by genetic means. It has already been pointed out that cereal grains provide incomplete proteins. An exciting research area is the improvement of protein quality of cereal grains by genetic means. This is a long-range effort, but some scientific break-throughs have already been made. A superior variety of corn, containing about 65 percent more lysine, more tryptophan, and a better amino acid balance than ordinary hybrid corn, has been developed.[6] Young children fed this high-lysine corn at the rate of two grams of protein per kilogram per day retain amounts of nitrogen similar to children who are fed skim milk.[7] This finding illustrates the feasibility of attacking the protein problem in cereals by germ-plasm manipulation.

Fortification of cereal grains. Fortification of cereal grains is simply the addition of the limiting amino acid(s) or protein concentrate(s) to the grain in order to increase its nutritive value. A pertinent question is whether such a practice is really nutritionally sound. Many experiments have been conducted and others are continuing. Pioneering work at the Institute of Nutrition of Central America and Panama since 1952 has demonstrated the potential efficacy of cereal fortification with amino acids or protein concentrates, or both.[8] The conclusion has been reached that fortification will not cure protein malnutrition in children but is effective in alleviating much of the problem. In diets where calories are derived mainly from sugar or from tubers such as cassava or plantains, the problem is extremely difficult, since these diets need more protein as well as protein of a higher quality.

The exact technique of fortification depends on the grain, on the form in which it passes through central facilities (whole or in flour), and on the cost. For flours, it is possible to improve the quality of the protein by adding amino acids or protein concentrates, such as oilseed meals or fish-protein concentrate. Fortified flours must not be priced too high

---

[6] E. T. Mertz, et al., "Mutant Gene That Changes Protein Composition and Increases Lysine Content of Maize Endosperm," *Science,* 145 (3629) (July 1964), 279–80.

[7] E. T. Mertz, et al., "Growth of Rats Fed on Opaque-2 Maize," *Science,* 148 (3678) (June 25, 1965), 1741–42.

[8] N. S. Scrimshaw, et al., "Supplementation of Cereal Proteins with Amino Acids. 1. Effect of Amino Acid Supplementation of Corn-masa at High Levels of Protein Intake on the Nitrogen Retention of Young Children," *Journal of Nutrition,* 66 (4) (Dec. 10, 1958), 485–99; and R. Bressani, "Improvement of Nutritional Status in Developing Countries by Improved Food Production: Cereals," International Congress on Nutrition Proceedings, 1966.

compared to unfortified products if low-income consumers are to purchase them.

Fish-protein potential.   Only a few dozen of the 20,000–25,000 species of fish are used directly or indirectly as food by man, and the 69.4-million-metric ton harvest in 1971 is a small part of the potential. Fish protein is a high-quality protein and is important to improving the quality of the rice-staple diet of people in the Far East. Fish are efficient converters of feed into meat, and fish farming is gaining momentum. Fish-protein concentrate with a protein content of 80 percent by weight is an important means of fortifying foods.

Single-cell protein.   Single-cell protein produced by the culture of yeasts or bacteria is being given added attention as a new source of protein. It can be produced independently of existing agricultural techniques or climate. However, little impact is expected before the 1980s.

Fungi appear less desirable than bacteria or yeasts as sources of single-cell proteins, because their protein content is lower and they grow no more quickly. Amino acids of single-cell proteins seem to be comparable to other proteins, but little information is available on the digestibility of such proteins, their taste, and their salability.

Leaf protein.   A protein-containing material can be isolated by extraction techniques from leaves of plants and grasses.[9] Its composition approximates that of other plant proteins.[10] Frequently, leaf materials are wasted or, at best, fed to animals. Some leaf protein is used directly by humans, in the case of leafy green vegetables, a significant factor in high sugar-and-tuber diets.

Algae.   Although the composition of algae protein is comparable to that of other plant proteins, the major barriers are economics and palatability. Its principal contribution to human nutrition is more likely to be through its use as an animal feedstuff.

PRODUCTION INCENTIVES FOR FARMERS

Even if large quantities of fertile land, fertilizer, water, seeds, pesticides, machinery, and so on were available, no commercial food produc-

[9] M. G. Davys and N. W. Pirie, "Protein from Leaves by Bulk Extraction," *Engineering*, 90 (4923) (August 1960), 274–75; I. H. Chayen et al., "The Isolation of Leaf Components," *Journal of Science Food Agriculture*, 12(7) (July 1961), 502–12.

[10] R. F. Wilson and J. M. A. Tilley, "Amino Acid Composition of Lucerne and of Lucerne and Grass Protein Preparations," *Journal of Science Food Agriculture*, 16(4) (April 1965), 173–78.

tion would take place unless a farmer decided to use them. What gives a farmer the incentive to produce? Mostly economic profit, a desire to provide for his family, and the basic drive to survive. Fundamentally, the input–output ratio or cost–return ratio has to be favorable. Initially, the farmer is interested in producing food for his family, but as additional goods and services become available in his community for purchase, he wants to upgrade his family's level of living. To get the necessary purchasing power to educate his children, buy a radio or bicycle, and obtain medical services, the farmer must sell products worth more in the market than they cost to produce. The difference or margin between cost and return represents the farmer's *net income* for his labor and management.[11] In order for him to achieve a rising standard of living, his net income must rise.

There is an increasing amount of evidence that farmers do respond to favorable prices. The response to favorable price includes both increased acreage planted and an attempt to increase yields per unit of land.[12] In the "how-to-produce" decision, farm prices directly influence the amount of inputs used. Farmers can afford to use new inputs of fertilizer or pesticides if the value of the extra yield exceeds the cost of the extra inputs. In the 1960s, a Thai farmer, for example, had to produce five times as much rice to pay for a bag of fertilizer as did the Japanese farmer, so it is not surprising that the Japanese use much more fertilizer than do the Thais. The principal reason is that the Japanese farmer can sell his rice at a much higher price than the Thai farmer can, because in Japan, the price is subsidized by the government (held higher than equilibrium), whereas in Thailand, the government's policy of extracting taxes from exports of rice artificially holds the farm price at a low level. This suggests that price policies and taxation methods by central governments are mechanisms to thwart free market prices in either direction. Thus, government policies can and do influence production incentives through farm-product prices.[13] In addition, governments can and often do influence the price of inputs to the farmer.

Another factor affecting incentive is the share of the harvest going to the landlord if the farmer leases the land he farms. Generally, the larger the share of the harvest going to the landlord, the less incentive

---

[11] Also, it is a return to the fixed costs associated with his long-term capital investments, like buildings and machinery.

[12] Readers should be able to become more sophisticated students of economics by using new elasticity ideas, such as "elasticity" of acreage planted, "elasticity" of total supply, of market supply, etc.

[13] A compelling example in the United States was the effect of the Steagall Amendment to the Agricultural Act of 1941, which finally became effective in 1949; see Chapter 23.

the tenant has to use a new technology to increase production. This accounts for part of the efforts to encourage ownership of farms and/or change share rentals to cash rentals.

INFRASTRUCTURE AND AGRICULTURAL PRODUCTION

Infrastructure, or social overhead capital, has been mentioned briefly as influencing food production. Its relevance is discussed more fully below.

Transportation

Transportation, along with production incentives, markets, constantly changing technology, and local availability of supplies and equipment, is listed by Mosher as an essential ingredient for agricultural development to take place.[14] Without low cost and efficient transportation, the other farm essentials cannot be effectively provided. The essentials of a transport system are shown in Figure 21-1.

Agricultural production is necessarily widely dispersed over large areas of land, since food production depends ultimately on capturing solar energy. If farming is to rise above a subsistence level and become commercial, road networks are necessary to get "inputs in" to the farm and "outputs out" to commercial markets. The relationship between transportation and the ability to grow and market food can be vividly pointed out by two examples. When Friendship Highway was built in Thailand, partially used jungle land was transformed into highly productive farms along a 100-mile course. Average travel time to market was reduced from eleven hours to three. The production of sugar cane, vegetables, bananas, and other fruits more than tripled in three years, and Thailand began to export corn produced in the area to Japan.[15] In Costa Rica, before the Inter-American Highway was constructed, driving beef cattle from grazing lands to San José customarily resulted in a 40 percent weight loss, and the country had to import beef to satisfy domestic demand. With an all-weather highway, it became possible to deliver cattle by truck-trailer overnight, and Costa Rica has become self-sufficient in meat.

A transportation network complete with main highways and feeder

---

[14] A. T. Mosher, *Getting Agriculture Moving*, pp. 111–20.
[15] Wisit Kasiraksa, "Economic Effects of Friendship Highway," SEATO Graduate School of Engineering, Bangkok, 1963.

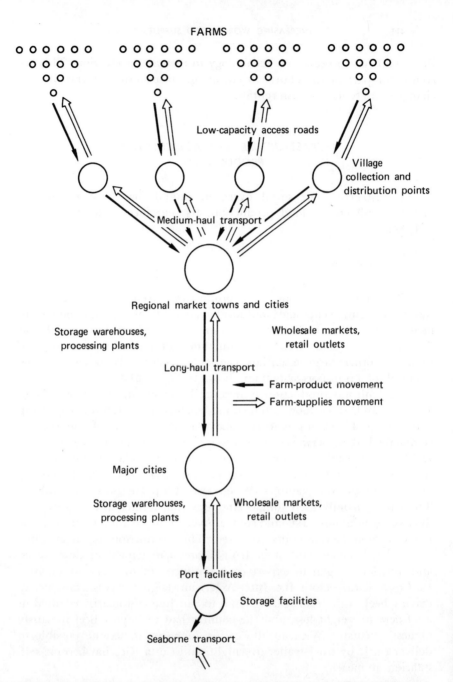

FARMS

Low-capacity access roads

Village collection and distribution points

Medium-haul transport

Regional market towns and cities

Storage warehouses, processing plants

Wholesale markets, retail outlets

Long-haul transport

◄─── Farm-product movement

⇒ Farm-supplies movement

Major cities

Storage warehouses, processing plants

Wholesale markets, retail outlets

Port facilities

Storage facilities

Seaborne transport

SOURCE: "The World Food Problem," a report of the Panel on the World Food Supply, President's Science Advisory Committee, White House, May 1967, Volume II, Figure 11-1, p. 577.

FIGURE 21-1

Essential Elements in Transportation System Serving
Agriculture

roads, besides reducing the cost of inputs, potentially increases the farmer's income by lowering marketing costs. A Philippine study showed local village price increases of 25 percent for corn one year after feeder roads were built. In addition to bringing in inputs for purchases by farmers, roads bring in manufactured goods from the city. Additionally, new services become available: The Philippine study also indicated that visits to the locality by educational and service officials increased dramatically. Rural-health doctor visits increased 580 percent, social workers' visits were up 1,000 percent, and those of agricultural credit representatives up 267 percent, for only a few illustrations.[16]

Marketing Processing and Distribution

Commercial agriculture and urbanization of the population necessitate the establishment of markets and a marketing system. Storage facilities to allow the creation of time utility, processing plans to produce form utility, and a communications system to permit rapid dissemination of market information were all discussed in Chapter 9. Both private and public investment are likely to be involved. The functions of standardization and market information are government-controlled, and the systems evolved are part of social overhead capital. Although the evolution of a complex market system is necessary for agricultural development, the rate of increase in per capita income is the primary factor in influencing market development. A farmer must have a market in which to sell his produce, or else there is no incentive to produce. Rapid growth of the urban population in many of the developing countries complicates the task of providing efficient marketing machinery to move food. For example, between 1941 and 1961, the total population of the area that is now Pakistan grew by nearly 30 percent, while the population of the cities increased by 250 percent.[17]

Research and Educational Institutions

A form of infrastructure affecting agricultural development is the country's educational institutions. They are directly responsible for upgrading the quality of the management input. They also improve the literacy rate of rural populations. When farmers learn to read, they can learn about new farm practices, as well as obtain market news and information of nonfarm job opportunities, through newspapers, pam-

---

[16] A. T. Mosher, *Getting Agriculture Moving*, p. 117.

[17] U.S. Department of Agriculture, Economic Research Service, *The World Food Budget 1970*, Foreign Agricultural Economic Report No. 19, October 1964, p. 17.

phlets, and books. The more formal education a person has, the more complete and informed his thought processes can be, contributing to management decision making.

Extension education. Informal, noncompulsory education programs for adult farmers can have a significant impact on agricultural production. Continuous learning is essential for all managers, as new technologies are constantly discovered. Extension education may take the form of group farmer meetings, method and result demonstrations, presentation of analyses for management purposes, farm tours, exhibits, and fairs. A good extension worker is one who makes the farmer aware of new ways to do things on the farm, as well as relating the nonfarm economy to the farm economy.

Experiment stations. A constantly changing technology is considered necessary for agricultural development. No country has achieved a high level of agricultural development without the establishment of objective experiment stations for agricultural research. Although good farmers do some experimenting on their own, research stations with scattered field trials in various parts of the country and access to technical experts are necessary. To be effective, research stations need to be adequately financed, organized to attack the correct problems, and equipped to continually train new personnel.

Financial Institutions

Farmers must buy improved inputs to produce more food, which increases their cash expenses prior to any returns from sale of the crop. These expenditures must be financed either out of previous saving or by borrowing. In many developing countries, money is available from local moneylenders, but interest rates tend to be so high they become restrictive. The purpose of production credit is to allow farmers to purchase improved inputs. Thus it follows that while production credit is one input, it is secondary to the actual availability of other inputs. This is the reason some economists list input availability in local areas as an essential ingredient for agricultural development and classify production credit as a development accelerator. The value of production credit in the development of U.S. agriculture is well accepted (see Chapter 5).

Other Considerations

The list we have given of indirect factors and institutions that can affect food production is by no means complete. Social clubs and farmer organizations can have an impact. Formal or informal group action by farmers to help each other in times of emergency, to build community facilities, to build local feeder roads, to build a market facility, to meet and exchange ideas on farming—these and many other considerations might be cited as necessary or accelerating development factors.

The concepts of national planning are gaining strength in nearly all developing countries, and planning for agriculture is an integral part of the total planning effort. Comprehensive planning can be helpful by providing certain incentives to food production. For example, government efforts to open and settle new lands, to improve land tenure systems, and to finance water-development projects can all contribute significantly to increased food production.

The challenge facing mankind to increase food supplies and eliminate hunger and malnutrition is real. It cannot be shrugged off. Almost all nations are attacking the problem with numerous solutions, some more effectively than others, depending on the gravity of the domestic situation, the culture, and the national political responsibility.

THE GREEN REVOLUTION

In the late 1960s, the rapid expansion of certain cereal food grains, mostly wheat and rice, in the developing world became known as the "Green Revolution."[18] It came about through major technological breakthroughs in food production. Improved seed varieties were coupled with adequate supplies of water, fertilizer, pesticides, and modern equipment in "new" packages of technology. Almost overnight, the image of farming in the developing countries changed from that of an economic backwater to that of a major potential contributor to overall development.

The new cereal grains were spread rapidly both within countries and across national boundaries. In 1968–69, it was estimated that 11.5 million acres of rice were planted to the new varieties, compared with only 2.5 million two years previously. About 80 percent of these rice plantings were in India and the Philippines. However, this acreage represented only 7 percent of the total plantings of rice in the world in 1968–69, as well as only 7 percent of the total rice area planted in India in that year.

For wheat, it was estimated that 18.2 million acres were planted to the new high-yielding varieties in 1968–69, compared with only 1.5 million acres two years previously. This acreage in high-yielding varieties represented 21 percent of total world wheat acreage, with 88 percent of

[18] There is considerable literature on this subject. Two articles of importance are Walter P. Falcon, "The Green Revolution: Generation of Problems," *American Journal of Agricultural Economics,* Vol. 52, No. 5 (December 1970), 698; and Clifton R. Wharton, Jr., "The Green Revolution: Cornucopia or Pandora's Box?" *Foreign Affairs,* Vol. 47, No. 3 (April 1969).

the new-varieties acreage concentrated in the two countries of India and Pakistan. Turkey accounted for another 10 percent.[19] The use of commercial fertilizer in the five countries where the new rice and wheat varieties were planted increased from 12 million tons in 1965–66 to 26 million tons in 1968–69.

These high-yielding varieties and the increased use of fertilizer produced average yields per acre about double those possible with most of the older, local strains. In quantitative terms, wheat production in Asia (excluding Mainland China, North Korea, and North Vietnam) during 1969 was 30 percent more than the 1960–64 average, and rice exceeded the 1963–67 average by 18 percent.[20]

These data left no doubt that great strides were being made in increasing food-grain production. Some observers of the Green Revolution believed that the race between food and population was essentially over, that the new agricultural technology constituted a cornucopia for the developing world, and that victory was in sight with regard to the "war on hunger." Others, however, saw the development as opening a Pandora's box; its very success would produce a number of new problems that might be far more subtle than those faced during the development of the new technology. Although the Green Revolution no doubt offers an unparalleled opportunity to break the chains of rural poverty in certain parts of the world, its success will depend upon how well the opportunity is handled and how alert we are to its inherent consequences. Let's examine some of them.

A closer look at the areas where the Green Revolution has been successful reveals information further substantiating the "package of technology" concept (Chapter 6). In Asia, the new wheat and rice varieties spread rapidly onto lands that had adequate and controllable water supplies. It has proven difficult to adapt varieties capable of producing high yields under the uncontrolled monsoon conditions that exist in many parts of the Far East and India. A district-by-district analysis for Pakistan and India shows clearly the high correlation between the growth in crop production from the new varieties and controlled irrigation. Moreover, fertilizer use is also highly correlated with both the previous variables. In short, the new varieties require controlled irrigation; without that control, fertilizer provides only a low return;

19 Randolph Barker, "Green Revolution," *Current Affairs Bulletin*, Vol. 45 (January 1970), 66–79; and Dana Dalrymple, "Imports and Plantings of High-Yielding Varieties of Wheat and Rice in the Less Developed Nations," U.S. Department of Agriculture, Foreign Agricultural Service, November 1969.

20 U.S. Department of Agriculture: Economic Research Service, *Rice Situation*, RS-15, March 1970; and Foreign Agricultural Service, *World Agricultural Production and Trade: Statistical Report*, January 1970.

and without new seeds and fertilizer, the possibilities for rapid increases in crop production have distinct limitations.

A second important constraint on adoption of the new wheat and rice technology has been the inadequacy of pesticide programs in most countries. Any solution to this problem must deal realistically with organizational issues and with the important social costs, including health, associated with pesticide use. With small-size holdings, it does one farmer no good to spray if his neighbors do not.

Even though the Green Revolution tended to solve an immediate food-production problem, it brought with it some second- and third-generation problems of great magnitude. For example, with the increased output of grain, the amount going into commercial markets rose dramatically. The physical marketing facilities available in India and Pakistan were simply not geared to handling this large increase in quantity. Transportation bottlenecks were often a critical problem. In West Pakistan, rail marketings of rice in 1969 completely swamped the system. Large, uncovered piles of rice accumulated at railheads, and prices to farmers fell substantially. Millers were working their equipment at capacity and running into severe inventory and working-capital constraints. It nearly required a French-style, pitchfork rebellion to obtain more railroad cars and change government policy to permit trucks to deliver rice to seaports. Similar stories on milling, grading, storage, and transport can be told for other countries.

There are also formidable second-generation problems concerning pricing and markets that have both economic and political dimensions. A number of the food-deficit countries have historically had structures of domestic prices that bore little relationship to world prices. Price-support policies are common. For instance, the per-ton price-support range for paddy rice was $93 in the Philippines, $123 in Ecuador, and $36 in Burma. For wheat, the price per ton of price supports varied from $64 in Mexico to $87 in Turkey to $101 in India.[21] Countries that experienced sharp increases in the quantity of grain to be supported as a result of the Green Revolution suddenly found themselves tying up very large sums of money. These funds delayed, perhaps even precluded, other developmental expenditures that were of higher priority and more productive to the country. (The same type of problem occurs in this country, and is one reason why the executive branch hesitates to endorse any permanent price-support legislation. If yields are good, the financial drain on limited funds available for public spending can be disproportionate.)

---

21 Lyle P. Schertz, "The Green Revolution: Production and World Trade," *Columbia Journal of World Business*, Vol. 5, No. 2 (March–April 1970), 53–59.

In addition to these marketing and price problems, the Green Revolution brings problems with regard to employment, welfare, and political and economic stability. Within given regions of the country, greater income inequality among farmers can result, creating a strain on personal and administrative relationships. These in turn, can cause political problems regarding questions of equity (income level and distribution).

Rough calculations for India and Pakistan indicate that of each $10 transferred to farmers by way of a price-support system, only about $1 goes to "small" farmers. Mechanisms to keep social and private benefits from diversion from small to large farmers are a major problem in all countries. The solution to this situation may come only through political means.

Demographers raise another issue, along Malthusian lines. They point to the fragile population–food-resource balance that existed in many countries prior to the Green Revolution, and draw attention to the fact that life for many was already at the point of malnutrition or actual starvation (see Chapters 3 and 20). They go on to suggest that unless other measures are taken in conjunction with the increased "one-shot" food production, in the not too distant future there may simply be millions more starving than there are now. Food production for one generation may inadvertently spell doom for future generations.

In summary, first, the impressive gains of the Green Revolution to date can be applied correctly to only 10 to 15 percent of Asia. Second, sudden increases in agricultural output cannot be adequately managed by existing marketing facilities; such increases will necessitate basic pricing decisions on the parts of governments. Third, although the limited technological revolution in agriculture has permitted an easing of one critical development constraint regarding the quantity of food produced, it has not provided a panacea for the society's employment and equity problems. In a very real sense, it has been a destabilizing force, by widening income disparities within and between regions.

The challenge of the future will be to forge institutions that can deal simultaneously with the demographic explosion, rapid economic growth, and equality of income distribution. A principal cause of both international conflict and internal strife is unfounded expectations. What we have in hand seems to many people to approach magic; let us hope that it does not become a source of deception. No one is suggesting that the Green Revolution as defined should be suppressed. But it does point up how the forces that promote or retard agricultural development are closely interrelated. Perhaps it is the time to place the Green Revolution in its proper long-range perspective.

PART SEVEN

PART
SEVEN

22

The Problem-Solving Approach
and Policy Formation

This chapter introduces a practical way to approach policy formulation. It suggests a method of identifying problems and issues, focusing on alternative solutions to the problems, and concentrating on effective decision making. In this context, the materials covered in Chapters 1 and 16 on management goals and processes should be reviewed.

POLICY DEFINED

A policy can be defined as a specific plan of action to attain a specified goal within a designated span of time. The plan of action may be quite vague and loosely defined, or it may be a rigid, step-by-step program procedure. The time for which the policy is operative may be an extremely short period, as in time of flood or fire emergency, or it may last many years, like the Old Age and Survivors Insurance Program (Social Security), or our national Bill of Rights, which has been a policy of this country from the beginning. In any case, policy determination and application imply a degree of control over the means necessary to achieve the specific goal.

GOALS OF POLICY MAKERS

The broad goals for which most national policy is created and initiated are relatively few. These goals are peace, economic growth, stability, security, justice, and freedom. All societies in the world today wish to have each of these goals to a certain degree. Some of the goals are contradictory; some are compatible. Let us look at them.

Peace is a national goal of our country today. But as a nation, we have not interpreted that goal to mean peace at any price. We maintain armed services to fight at designated times in a state of national emergency when our peace is in jeopardy. Perhaps peace cannot be maintained without sacrificing time, effort, money, and sometimes even lives.

The goal of *stability* poses many questions. *Economic stability* refers to the avoidance of inflation and depression or wild fluctuations in the nation's output and purchasing power of the dollar. How much stability should we have in this country? We certainly want as much economic stability as possible. Runaway inflation is disastrous because a predictable and stable purchasing power of the dollar (or any currency) is necessary for trade within the country and between countries. But how much stability can we have if we have economic growth?

In many ways, *economic growth* promotes instability and uncertainty. Growth refers to increasing the national product per capita, which gives us a higher standard of living. It is disturbing to many people to see familiar landmarks torn down and uprooted in the name of progress. Almost everyone wants to have more than he now has—more money, a better job, more time to enjoy the social and cultural advantages available in our society. But hardly anyone wants the maximum economic growth possible from our society, since it would probably entail restrictions on personal freedom in the form of increased hours of labor and reduced leisure time.

We are a country that prides itself on *freedom* of the individual. However, there are many restrictions we voluntarily impose on ourselves that curb this individual freedom. Stop signs and speed limits deny a person the freedom of driving as fast as he chooses. However, most of the social and legal restrictions we impose on our individual freedom give more freedom to individuals and groups than they take away. For example, many families can send their children to school with little worry about fast drivers because they realize that speed limits will help protect their youngsters. At the same time that we cherish the notion of individual freedom, we are also constantly creating laws and regulations that limit individual freedom, business entrepreneurship, and certain types of social activities. Economic freedom refers to the freedom to produce and to consume whatever goods and services the individual desires in the economy.

Personal *security* is a high-priority goal with most people. Fear and uncertainty of what will happen after death to one's family is a major reason why we have life insurance. Sickness, unemployment, and old age are all factors influencing security. Some people would feel secure if the status quo were kept indefinitely; others would feel more secure if there were a change of some kind. Policies designed to increase personal and family security are in evidence everywhere. Retirement programs, unemployment insurance, health insurance, and church programs are evident in almost every community.

Everyone wants some degree of *justice:* economic justice (equal pay for equal work); social justice (no discrimination against minority groups); legal justice (trial with due process of law for everyone, regardless of the accusation); and political justice (everyone who is qualified to vote can vote). Throughout this country, we have a complicated legal system dedicated to providing this justice. In fact, the founders of the nation set up the judicial branch (the Supreme Court) to act as a check and balance on the rest of government in insuring equal opportunity for justice. Economic justice also raises the questions, What is the income distribution among people that will maximize satisfactions? How much poverty can, or should, exist in a society? How much luxurious living?

Each of the goals above is essentially a statement of personal or group values. Some people want one goal more than another; some people would substitute one goal completely for another; many people have never thought about the goals at all. Since certain of the goals are contradictory, it is impossible to have an unlimited amount of all of them. The attainment of these goals is of varying degree throughout our country and among the nations of the world. Recognition of the varying attainment of these goals, based on varying degrees of personal conviction, knowledge, and values, is an essential first step in the problem-solving approach to policy issue and questions.

SOME CRITERIA OF POLICY FORMULATION

Awareness and general understanding of the pertinent issues and conflict of interest involved in a policy question are fundamental to its solution. This understanding is relative, varying from group to group and from person to person. We have earlier pointed out that education is essential to this understanding and awareness, but we have also pointed out that experience and a broad acquaintance with many people of different points of view and background are also essential. Formal schooling is no substitute for inherent shrewdness and reasoning ability; it is merely a complement and tool to bring out the natural characteristics with which a person is born.

The process of policy formulation is one that must be meaningful in terms of people's particular needs, their goals, and their resources. An effective policy must also be politically acceptable, administratively feasible, economically sound and socially acceptable, and capable of modification as conditions change. For example, in this nation, few people will vote for a new policy if its aim is to destroy the things for which this country stands. If a policy cannot be administered, it cannot even be tested by action; if a policy is not economically sound or socially acceptable, it will soon fail of its own accord or be voted down. Furthermore, if a policy is not capable of modification, a dynamic society will soon outgrow it (our Constitution is a perfect example of a political and social policy that allows change through amendment). To meet these criteria, the area for policy decisions is severely restricted (see Figure 21-1, where policy decisions may take place only in the blacked-out area), and compromise is necessary.

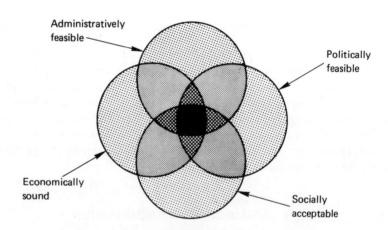

FIGURE 22-1
Illustrations of Compromise Area for Policy Making
within Social, Economic, Political, and Administrative
Constraints

THE PROBLEM-SOLVING ENVIRONMENT

Problems arise from individuals and groups for personal or collective reasons. Usually these reasons revolve around conflicts of interest. Such conflicts originate from the basic questions of what should be produced, when it should be produced, how it should be done, and who shall benefit from the production and distribution. Underlying these questions are the individual and group goals we have just discussed. One can easily see that there can be a great many answers to each of the questions above when the variety of opinions concerning the desirability and extent of a nation's goals is considered.

A problem-solving orientation to policy problems is really the application of the scientific method. This approach to policy provides a basis for selecting facts that will help in problem analysis. The approach also reduces random effort and focuses analysis on a specific problem area. For example, when a community does an economic study, there are certain defined steps through which the study proceeds, based upon the desires of the community. First, the goals of the community are defined so that everyone starts from a common ground. Second, there is an inventory of the resources available in the community, followed by an identification of the obstacles in the way of attaining the specific community goals. Finally, the study will finish by outlining plans to overcome the obstacles identified.

When one begins to use the problem-solving approach, he immediately realizes that awareness of problems and of their causes is a relative situation, depending upon his level of knowledge and training, his experience, and his intuitive analytical ability. This recognition applies equally well to groups and to nations. A student will soon find that there is no end to the problems to be solved, but that he can improve in his ability to solve them.

Decision making about policy would be much easier if one could work in a static framework, where everything is held constant and no changes are allowed. But the world does not operate that way. Decisions have to be made periodically despite the lack of certain information. This condition is simply the result of a dynamic economy. Time, money, and labor shortage put limitations upon the amount of knowledge one can gain and the depth of analysis that can be done before a decision must be made. However, despite the pressure of time, the value of the method by which problems are approached should not be overlooked. The method itself provides savings in time, because it is a logical procedure that helps to eliminate waste of time and effort.

When one deals in the area of policy, there is a good chance that there will be controversy and differences of opinion that must be reconciled before a solution can be formulated and put into action. In order to create meaningful policy and in order to stay out of meaningless arguments that waste the time of the policy makers before a decision can be made, it is helpful to remember the following: People make decisions primarily on the basis of three categories of knowledge. The first is facts. Facts are provable statements or data than can be collected, analyzed, and duplicated by anyone. The second category is statements or propositions that are taken as facts even though it is not absolutely sure whether or not they are. In either case, the statements are treated as facts in the decision-making process. When relevant facts are generalized upon, guiding principles are evolved. The third category encompasses all one's personal values, which determine his attitude toward any person or subject, such as friends, religion, business, government, or politics. One must formulate policy on meaningful facts and principles and must be aware of the values of the people who will be affected. If these considerations are ignored, the forthcoming policy will be quite limited in its duration and effectiveness.

Factors that influence the decision in one way or another include the simple economics of the solution. Does the policy pay, or does it not? Often the sheer size of the problem approached outweighs the economic considerations. For example, during a wartime emergency, troops and citizens are treated in a particular manner, with little or no mention of the cost involved. Traditions of individuals or groups within the society may also have a bearing on how certain decisions are reached. The relative strength of pressure groups and the lobbyists they employ to provide data and analysis will undoubtedly influence some people who have to choose between two or more alternative solutions. There are many other types of influences directly related to the knowledge, experience, and values of the problem solver, whether it be an individual or a group responsible for the solution, whether the problem occurs in private or in public life, or whether the problem is big or small.

At the National Level

The creation of policy at the national, and sometimes the state, level is often extremely difficult to pinpoint at the start. The "felt needs" stemming from grass-roots opinion, and the sometimes vague phrasing of issues and subjects upon which there is no majority of agreement, create an extremely loose problem-solving framework for legislators. For example, questions with which policy makers begin a study are usually those that start, "*What* shall we do about . . . ?" or "*What* should be done about . . . ?" Asking the question this way permits all alternatives to be considered, including the choice of doing nothing. Once the question is asked, the issue is framed and the alternative courses of action and their consequences can be discussed and studied. After a specific course of action has been chosen, the principal problem for national policy makers is how to state the particular policy choice in legislative language and get it voted into law.

At the State and Local Level

In contrast, policy makers working on some state issues and on almost all county or community development issues are mostly concerned with questions that begin with the words *how* or *which* or *ought*. These words imply that the basic issue has already been analyzed, that many of the *what* questions have been answered, and that a specific course of action has been decided upon. Analytic effort has been focused, and the question of what ought to be done is no longer relevant. The problem thus resolves itself into the community, and some method must be found by which that particular policy can be implemented if the community desires it.

Examples of national issues include the following: What should be done about the poverty problem in agriculture? What ought to be done about controlling floods on the Mississippi River? What ought to be done about medical aid to people over 65? Examples of state issues: How can the property tax best be administered? Which of our highways should be developed first? Examples of local issues: How can we make our municipal power plant more efficient? How can we make our schools better? What should be the level of our local tax rate?

To summarize, public policy formulation usually deals with a particular issue about which no general agreement has been reached. Local policy formulation deals primarily with how to activate more broadly defined policies at the state, county, or community level. A public policy issue can arise from the "grass roots" if enough people become concerned about a particular subject. Or a public policy issue can arise separately from local concerns.

THE PROBLEM-SOLVING APPROACH

The problem-solving approach consists of the following general steps: defining the current and historical situation from which the problem comes; defining the goal(s) to be attained; stating the problem; outlining the alternative means by which the problem could be solved and tracing the consequences of each; choosing one of these solutions and implementing it; and then, after a time, evaluating the policy to see if it needs to be modified in any way. Wise policy formulation, therefore, builds on both descriptive economics (gathering and organizing relevant facts) and on principles of economics (generalizations about economic behavior).

Throughout the problem-solving approach, the analytic frame of reference provided by tested generalizations or principles, the use of logic, experience, and intuition offers the main criteria for determining which facts are relevant to the problem at hand. As man's knowledge of the world around him increases and as he becomes more aware of the physical, social, political, and institutional relationships around him, his ability to correctly diagnose troublesome situations increases through the application of scientific methodology. Continually refined tools of analysis, more internally consistent and expanding disciplines of theory, and previous trial-and-error attempts at analysis all indicate more clearly which factors or relationships are relevant for use in analyzing a particular problem.

The Situation

When people begin to solve problems or resolve issues, they often neglect getting any facts on the subject they want to discuss. Sometimes the assumption is made that everyone already knows the facts and that there is no need to repeat them. Only a very small percentage of the time is this assumption valid. Most of the time it is necessary to establish a firm footing of fact that describes the historical situation. For instance, if the problem involves employment, data showing trends in the number and kinds of jobs in the area and in wages, population, and training facilities are highly important. Some people might know the facts about one of these areas, but it is highly unlikely that everyone will know the facts about all the items.

Goal Identification

The next step is to identify the goals to be attained. These may be individual goals or they may be goals some group or nation wants to achieve. The goals of national policy makers generally tend to be those discussed earlier (peace, stability, growth, freedom, security, and justice), and are generally either known or intuitively agreed upon. However, the goals of local policy makers will usually be very specific. For example, a town board may state a goal of creating 500 new jobs in the town within the next year. If a group is involved in determining the goals, there will probably not be unanimous agreement on them, but there will be a consensus of opinion instead. The explicit goals may include such items as increased income, increased employment, a better library, more health facilities, increased efficiency in government administration, and so on.

Problem Formulation

It is important to recognize that without a goal and without carefully defining the situation to be used as a point of departure, it is impossible to identify and solve a problem. The problem emerges when one tries to decide how to move from the present situation to the desired position or goal.

It has been said that the problem of problems is to determine the problem. Identifying the problem explicitly is an extremely difficult thing to do. What are the obstacles to formulating the problem? The biggest block is one's own value system. Sometimes our minds are made up without the facts, and often we honestly do not want to know the facts. Differences in opinion concerning the general underlying goals of peace, freedom, security, growth, stability, and justice also cloud the issue. Our own lack of knowledge about an area further limits us in our ability to formulate problems in that area.

It is perhaps easiest to view problem formulation in terms of asking a question. For example:

> *Situation:* Five hundred people are unemployed in city X. There are four old industrial plants whose managers are not anxious to hire new employees. City X is gaining population but the county is losing rural population.
> *Goal:* To create new employment in city X.
> *Problem:* How can employment be created in city X for those who want jobs?

When a question is asked, an answer is demanded. That answer is the solution to the problem. Questions focus directly on some issue about which there may be controversy and about which some policy might be formulated. By asking the question, analytical effort is brought to bear immediately on the subject at hand. Only relevant data need then be gathered, and the minds of the policy makers can be put to work.

Outlining Alternative Solutions and Their Consequences

It is a general maxim that if there is one way to solve a problem, there are usually several other ways to solve it. These alternative solutions should be outlined and the consequences of each should be noted before a final choice is made, since otherwise the best solution might be overlooked. Although each of the various alternatives suggested may well attain the desired goal, there might be severe economic hardships imposed on a particular sector of the economy by one solution, a short-run hardship by another solution, and an economic gain from a third solution. One alternative may necessitate relatively large political or social changes, whereas another may work within the existing political and social framework. A final alternative may speak for the creation of a whole new set of institutions, whereas none of the other suggested alternatives contemplated institutional change.

Some type of compromise solution will be forthcoming when people having different social, cultural, economic, and political values meet to decide an issue. There will probably be some give-and-take on all sides in order for an agreement to be reached. In policy solutions involving the problem-solving approach, it is rare that anyone is completely happy with the final decision.

It should be understood that compromise does not mean compromise of principle. Far from it. What it does suggest is that, through the democratic process and given the limitations of time, knowledge, and analytical effort, the best possible solution to a problem is reached, consistent with the total values of the people who made the decision.

Solution Implementation and Evaluation

The final steps are simply to implement the policy decision and to evaluate it. Policy implementation is more an administrative task and a technical one than it is a function of legislation. Yet policy must be implemented in order for the policy makers to see whether or not it should be modified; and if it should be changed, they must decide in what manner the changes should be effected.

In each of the following chapters, dealing with farm price and income policy, the low-income problem in agriculture, international trade, and other selected problem areas, the problem-solving approach will be applied. Using this approach is not easy for the student. But once the method is learned, it will be most helpful in solving many problems usually encountered at some time by most people.

23

Farm Price and Income Problems

The purpose of this chapter is to introduce the topic of national farm price and income programs and their influence on farm price and income levels, their stability, and their interrelationships to overall resource management. There are many books on this subject that the more interested student can pursue.[1]

THE BACKGROUND

Farm price and income policy issues have undergone considerable changes since the first farm-price legislation was introduced into Congress. The first price-support laws were based on a concept of parity between the farm and nonfarm sectors of the economy. Later, farm-price

---

[1] For example: Dale E. Hathaway, *Government and Agriculture: Public Policy in a Democratic Society* (New York: Macmillan Company, 1963); R. J. Hildreth, *Readings in Agricultural Policy* (Lincoln: University of Nebraska Press, 1968); Harold Halcrow, *Agricultural Policy in the United States* (Englewood Cliffs, N.J.: Prentice-Hall, Inc., 1953); Luther Tweeten, *Foundations of Farm Policy* (Lincoln: University of Nebraska Press, 1970); Don Paarlberg, *American Farm Policy; A Case Study of Centralized Decision-Making* (New York: John Wiley & Sons, Inc., 1964); Vernon W. Ruttan, Arley D. Waldo, and James P. Houch, *Agricultural Policy in an Affluent Society* (New York: W. W. Norton & Company, Inc., 1969).

legislation was aimed at stimulating food production for the World War II effort. During the 1950s, the main emphasis was on maintaining farm incomes and helping to ease the adjustment of the human resource out of farming. In the 1960s, the main policy thrusts were an attempt to apply voluntary supply management through acreage limitations, continued rural-development program formulation, and expanded programs of foreign trade. In the 1970s, policy makers are attempting to return farming to the market forces of supply and demand rather than maintain a dependence on government by commercial farms. Income supplements will be reduced as much as possible, while increased food production will be encouraged to keep prices relatively low for both domestic and overseas-sold foods.

Previous legislative attempts helped policy makers in the 1950s and 1960s to realize that the "farm problem" was not just the farmer's problem but was an integral part of the economic growth process of a country and concerned the entire society. During this time, Congress explicitly recognized that a majority of the farmers do not benefit from commodity-price supports, since less than half the commercial farmers produce 90 percent of the volume of products; and by 1972, only about 12 percent of the farmers produced 85 percent of our food and fiber. Price supports are geared to the farmer who has a significant volume of production, because supports are offered on a per-unit-of-output basis; a man with few tillable acres and little output will get a correspondingly lower income from supports than will a farmer with a large acreage and large volume of output. The fact that supports are offered on only part of the agricultural commodities further emphasized the concern that support prices were not solving the farmer's income problems.

Many people have suggested that there is no one farm problem, and that instead, the farm problem is composed of many relatively small problems that occur simultaneously, each in its own turn being both a cause and an effect. In any case, farm problems are interrelated and connected to the rest of the economy. And their magnitude is large, affecting all the farmers and most of the rest of society.

Policy makers have recently concentrated their legislative efforts on three major problem areas: (1) Returns to the labor of some farmers and their workers are low, particularly on small farms. (2) Price fluctuations can be severe as a result of weather, livestock-production cycles, and international developments. (3) And price instability is compounded by the excess capacity characteristic of a developed economy and a consequent chronic tendency to produce more of certain major crops than the market can readily absorb at reasonable prices. Other problems related to these three primary ones include concern about the equitable distribution of farm income within the farm sector; the misallocation of resources in farming, with resulting inefficiencies of production and loss of benefit to all of society; a lack of rapid enough adjustment of the farm population to nonfarm progress, particularly with respect to education and training; and the question of whether or not we should have stored surpluses.

The complexity of the situation confronting policy makers is better understood when one considers how a country's development binds the farm and nonfarm sectors together. The diversity of human attitudes, purposes, and values from both sectors creates a continuing conflict of interest. These conflicts are also seen within agriculture. Combined with the complexity of the problem is the declining political importance of the farm vote. What might happen to farmers as a result of the decline is not yet fully understood or appreciated. A majority of people now live in urban or suburban centers, and their problems, on the surface at least, are not rural ones.

The criteria for any farm legislation vary according to who is doing the evaluating. Urban people consider certain criteria more important than will rural people, and both these viewpoints may be in conflict with that of the highly specialized commercial farmers who produce the majority of our food and fiber. But even though opinions of the relative importance of the criteria we shall consider will vary, most of them will be considered. The fact that some sort of compromise can be worked out from the conflicts of interest in the essence of a political system that permits legislation to be created.

One criterion considered is the effect of forthcoming policy on farming and on those in farming. Will the proposed legislation improve the income situation, increase efficiency in resource use and production techniques, aid in reducing risk and uncertainty, and not distort price relationships within the agricultural sector? Another criterion is the effect of the policy on the same items in the agribusiness sector. Other criteria include the effect on government (the cost of the program and how it relates to other domestic policies), the effect on consumers (quantity, quality, and price of food), and the effect on foreign policy and world trade.

THE FARMER'S DILEMMA

Since World War II, there have been significant changes in our farm economy.[2] Technology has been adopted by farmers at an unprecedented rate. Agricultural output has increased at the rate of about

---

[2] This section draws heavily on an understanding of the historical development of farming and resource use (Parts I, II, and III) and on the tools of economic analysis (Part IV). Policy is the medium in which historical knowledge, experience, judgment, and reasoning ability are blended.

2 percent annually since 1950. Taken as a whole, per capita increases in production in the less-developed nations have been less than $\frac{1}{2}$ of 1 percent annually; in the developed nations they have been about $1\frac{1}{2}$ percent annually. Domestic demand for food, based primarily on population growth and consumer disposable-income levels, has increased at slightly less than the 2 percent rate, and has been insufficient to match our agricultural-output potential. In fact, the combined demand increases for farm commodities for domestic food, foreign demands, and industrial uses have still left the United States with an agricultural plant geared to produce and process 5 to 8 percent more farm products than could be taken off the market at reasonable prices.

Overall demand for food products is highly inelastic. Although the derived demand for farm products at the farm level tends also to be inelastic, the demand curve facing each individual farmer is almost perfectly elastic. No matter how much of a commodity any one farm sells, the same price will be received for the item. Furthermore, the only way that an individual farmer can increase his income in this situation (inelastic industry demand, elastic farm demand) is to increase his production. Thus, despite the fact that an inelastic demand for the industry (at both retail and farm levels) means less total revenue for the industry if supplies are increased, the response of individual farms to lower prices was to search for further cost-reducing technologies that were generally available. With a high proportion of committed resources, total farm output was maintained and even increased in the face of lower prices. Increased production continued to depress price, and the seemingly paradoxical situation of lower prices and increased output continued.

Because farm income is affected by both prices of farm products and the return to resources—that is, costs of production—labor moved out of farming to higher-paying nonfarm jobs. Capital in the form of new technology was substituted for labor. Technology was also adopted partly because it helped an individual farmer increase his production and partly because it tended to lower per-unit costs of output. By the adoption of technology, marginal costs of production could be lowered, and the most profitable level of output for farmers was a larger amount at a lower price. As a result, many farmers, particularly those without any alternative place to "sell" their labor, found themselves on a treadmill, running faster and faster. They had to adopt new technologies in order to hold costs down, but this also meant increasing output. Industry or total farm output increased faster than demand, bringing lower and lower farm prices (Figure 23-1). The farm cost–price squeeze was on.

Two other facets of farming aggravated the situation. Many of the farmer's resources are fixed, and when he adds more land, buildings, and equipment to his existing resources, it makes his total resource base

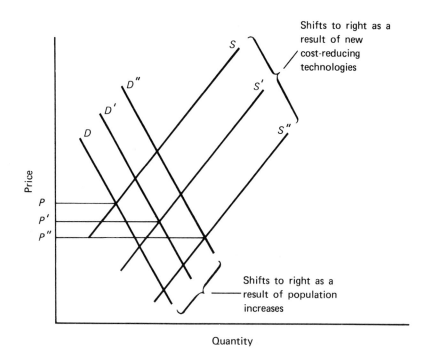

Shifts to right as a
result of new
cost-reducing
technologies

Shifts to right as a
result of population
increases

Quantity

FIGURE 23-1
Illustration of General Supply–Demand Relations in
the Farming Industry

even more fixed. It is therefore harder for him to move off the farm
profitably. Also, the substitutability of resources among enterprises within
the farm sector is relatively easy compared with moving resources outside
the farm sector. Therefore, a reduction of output of one commodity
because of continued low prices, or some production-control program,
most often results in resources being transferred to the production of
other food commodities. An attempt to solve the farm-income problems
on a partial basis, then, is not likely to succeed. The farm price and
income problem is an aggregate problem.

Although migration of people out of farming has continued at a
rapid rate since the 1940s, a rate of movement fast enough to equalize
incomes between the farm and nonfarm sectors was hampered by the
lack of nonfarm job opportunities available to farmers. In general, the
skills that the farm population had to transfer to nonfarm employment
were inadequate. This situation was particularly noticeable among the
young high school dropouts, among those men and women who chose

not to go to college or could not afford to take some form of technical training, and among many of the elderly farmers who felt compelled to give up operating small unproductive tracts of land.

All the farm-resource adjustments to declining farm income were taking place during a rapid rate of economic growth in the rest of the economy. Even the recessions experienced by the whole economy were not as deeply felt in the nonfarm sector as in the farm sector. Real non-farm income levels were rising faster than farm incomes, nonfarm population was increasing while farm population was falling, educational levels were rising more rapidly in nonfarm areas than in farming areas, and the number of nonfarm jobs was also increasing while farm job opportunities actually declined. An exception, perhaps heralding a new technology–production–demand–income era, was the period 1973–74.

At the heart of the farm problem lies the fact that the rapid adoption of new farm technology permitted output gains never before anticipated. Besides more efficient use of resources, new technologies forced changes in farm organization, in managerial techniques, in marketing structures, and in techniques of wholesale and retail food distribution. At the beginning of the 1950s, rates of increase in yields of crops per acre began to exceed the rate of increase in the population. Average crop yields increased by about one-third during this time, while the demand for food from our population only increased about one-fifth. It took less land, less labor, but more capital per farm unit to feed the population in 1974 than it did in 1950.

The farm problem of the commercial farmer can be summarized in the following way. Gross farm income depends on farm prices and on the quantity produced and sold. Farm output has continued to expand in the face of lower prices, since the individual farmer must adopt new technologies in an attempt to lower costs. Lower costs increase the level of output that is most profitable. At the same time, a higher output level will more fully utilize his fixed resources. These resources cannot easily be transferred out of farming. Farm prices fluctuate more than farm production costs. The result is that net farm income fluctuates to a much greater extent than gross farm income. Look at the following hypothetical example:

	One Year (bils.)	Following Year (bils.)	% Change
Gross income	$30	$27	−10
Production expenses	17	17	0
Net income	$13	$10	−23

A 10 percent reduction in gross income coming from lower prices can reduce net income by 23 percent if production expenses remain unchanged. The commercial farmer is vitally interested in stabilizing his income situation from year to year. However, this may or may not come about by stabilizing commodity prices.[3]

FARM-POLICY GOALS

The goals for farm policy have been the same for many years. First, there is the need to have the farm sector operate at such a level of production efficiency and profitability that our nation need never fear for lack of food and fiber, and consumers can buy food at reasonable prices. Second, there is a sincere desire on the part of legislators to have the economy operate in such a way that all the people in farming may contribute the use of all their talents and total productive powers to the benefit of all society. Third, there is the explicit desire to create legislation that will remove the instability and price risks that have traditionally characterized farm income, and at the same time raise farm incomes up to reasonable levels in comparison with the rest of the economy. These three goals, again, must complement the broad goals previously discussed, within which all of policy is constructed. In addition, there may be specific budgetary, foreign-trade, and foreign-food-aid goals that need to be considered.

WHAT ARE THE POLICY ALTERNATIVES?

Because our country is now fortunate enough to have a potential capacity for surplus of food and fiber, a key question confronting farm-policy makers is: What should be done about farm incomes and resource adjustment within farming, and between farming and other sectors in the economy? Many proposals have been advanced over the years to cure the various ills of the farmers. Essentially, there have been variations on three main policy approaches offered: (1) to expand the demand for farm products both domestically and through foreign outlets, (2) to establish programs of price supports and farm-product storage, and (3) to adjust farm production to demand through some type of resource or quota controls. Each of the three approaches would solve the farm problem as defined. However, the relative weight attached to each of the

---

[3] A stable price could actually unstabilize gross income, particularly if a farmer specializes in the production of one commodity whose output varies considerably from year to year.

methods has varied over the years. The criteria mentioned previously have been applied to the formulation of farm price and income policy, and certain proposals have been found lacking in one or more respects.

Before the principal policy alternatives are discussed, a word should be said about the permissiveness of policy alternatives. There is a constant battle about how much the farmer should be allowed to do on a voluntary basis for himself, as opposed to how much should be imposed as mandatory controls. Congress has not explicitly answered this question for all the farm products for all time. Some programs are mandatory, some are voluntary. For example, federal milk-marketing orders are under quite strict control, but participation in land-retirement programs was completely voluntary. Some of the most rigidly controlled programs affecting farm commodities have been instituted by private industry. The citrus and walnut crop associations are perhaps the best examples of commodity production and marketing control by private industry.

One of the real policy issues, derived from the questions of whether farm policy should be mandatory or should allow for voluntary participation, is to what extent the farm production or resource adjustment is actually desired. The extent of voluntary participation in any program is difficult to predict, and the program can be inefficient for this reason. On the other hand, policy makers know that if the proposal is accepted voluntarily by the farm public, it is evidently palatable to the majority of farmers from a value standpoint. Policy makers can see that mandatory controls remove the uncertainty of not knowing how much farmer participation there will be to speed its implementation. However, they can also see that proposals of this type run the risk of not being well accepted by the farmers and by the rest of society, and may have dire political implications. There have been examples of each kind of control in the past. No conclusive answer has been found on which kind of proposal is best, since this determination is up to the values of the individual or group evaluating alternative proposals. For instance, during wartime emergencies, the strict controls established in order to stimulate production may not be deemed desirable when peace has been won. Generally, a compromise position is found in most farm price and income legislation that is passed, implemented, and found effective and acceptable by the majority of farmers and farm groups, and by the rest of society. Let us now examine some of the proposals advanced in each of the three categories: demand adjustments, price-support and farm-product-storage programs, and supply adjustments.

Expanding the Demand for Farm Products

Expansion of domestic demand. The main reasons given for trying to solve the farm problem by expanding domestic demand (consuming more farm products at any given price levels) are that the nutritional level of our people will be improved, surpluses will be reduced, and more farm products will be sold in the long run. All these consumption effects will act to raise farm income at the same time that the whole of society is also benefited.

Annual per capita consumption of food in the United States for the last 50 years has been about 1,500 pounds. People in this country generally get enough to eat, but there are many people who might improve their nutritional level with a proper diet. With a relatively inelastic demand for food in general, and with everyone getting most of the food energy they need from their food, the opportunity for expanding domestic demand lies in three areas: population growth, income growth, and a change in diet from a low-value-food diet to one of higher value.

Population growth provides the agricultural sector with more stomachs to fill. An inelastic demand for food products and a fairly full and satisfied population probably mean that there is not likely to be much future expansion of demand except in terms of the addition of more people (population elasticity for food is thought to be about unitary). Income elasticity of demand for food is quite low and tends to be reduced toward zero as levels of income rise. However, as incomes go up and as more total money is spent for food, there tends to be more waste and a substitution of high-value foods for low-value foods. As consumers change their eating habits toward higher-quality foods, more farm resources are used. For example, the consumption of livestock products requires from five to ten times as many farm resources as the consumption of basic cereal products.

Effecting a change in diet probably offers the greatest hope for significant expansion of domestic consumption of farm products. This change can be helped by promotion and advertising and through various food-distribution programs. Some promotion campaigns (such as trading stamps) by commodity-group or retail food stores would be added to this total. The merits of advertising food and food products are a subject of much controversy. Results from advertising campaigns are hard to evaluate, especially over the long run. Some people evaluate promotion programs by asking the question, "What would happen if we didn't advertise?" Some food "communes" buy food in large lots at farmers' markets in order to avoid having to pay for advertising they do not want, and in order to offer their members lower food prices than other stores do.

Government-sponsored food-distribution programs have taken many turns. Federal assistance for feeding schoolchildren first became available in the early 1930s. A school milk program was authorized in the Agricultural Act of 1954. During the school year 1971–72, about 25.4 million children were included in the school lunch program, and 21 million participated in the milk programs. Other programs include distribution of food to needy people in designated communities. A food-stamp program, attempted during the 1930s, has recently been revitalized. This program attempts to provide people with low incomes and low levels of nutrition with an adequate diet. Such a program is justified on the basis that these people are then in a better position to contribute their talents and productivity to society In 1973, over 12.4 million people were on a food-stamp program.

In general, programs to expand domestic demand offer only a partial solution to the farm price–income problem. The total volume of goods affected is a minor share of the total farm output.

Expansion of foreign demand.   There are several reasons for trying to expand demand for our food products overseas. One is the simple humanitarian desire to share our farm abundance with the hungry peoples of the world. Other reasons are to promote economic development and thus to stimulate international trade for our other products, as well as our food.

Competing in world markets with other countries of the world presents problems. Some countries depend almost wholly on agricultural exports for their income, and competition by the United States in these markets can cause severe internal economic disturbances in these countries. Another facet of competition, which also has political and economic ramifications, arises with the producers of commodities within the foreign countries who raise either the same crop we are trying to export or a crop that acts as a close substitute. These farmers and their merchants are not at all happy if the United States crowds the world market with her products, which ultimately may force down the price they receive for their output.

As a result of this situation, our policy makers tried to dispose of some of our agricultural surpluses of the 1950s and 1960s through such programs as Food for Peace (Public Law 480 and others). Although some farm production may be sent overseas, many problems are encountered, which often depend for their solutions on the policies and attitudes of people within the countries to which we are trying to send our food. On the other hand, when foreign countries are willing to pay high prices for our food production, many consumers do not want to increase food exports if prices are rising in our own food stores. Stimulants to higher food prices such as inflation, poor harvests, and strikes also put pressure on policy makers not to sell abroad.

Expanding demand through new food and nonfood uses.   New uses are primarily aimed at developing new products for consumption on overseas markets. Such programs confront the challenges of foreign competition and policy conflicts just discussed.

Nonfood use of farm products takes between $3.5 and $4.5 billion worth of the gross value of production annually. Optimistic reports indicate that perhaps an additional $1.5 billion worth of products could be diverted into industrial uses if research were first stepped up accordingly. Farm products are facing severe competition with other commodities that can be substituted for them in industrial uses. For example, nearly half the market for natural fibers of cotton, wool, flax, and silk has been absorbed by synthetic fibers; about two-thirds of the shoes made today utilize leather substitutes; about two-thirds of the soap market now uses detergents instead of agricultural fats; and paint and varnish are being made with continually lessening proportions of vegetable oils.

There is little evidence to indicate that new uses for farm products will even approach solving the farm problem by themselves. Although they contribute partially to the solution, their overall contribution is not large, and many problems are encountered, especially in developing new uses for overseas markets.

Summary. Evaluation of the principal policy suggestions for getting rid of our farm surplus production through expanding demand shows that demand expansion is a slow process, geared primarily to the natural increase of population. Stomachs are limited in their capacity to absorb food, increasing incomes have little impact on food consumption, foreign trade and development and the increased use of farm products in nonfood uses offer limited hope. A policy to improve the diets of our existing population perhaps offers the most immediate favorable prospect of solution.

Farm-Product-Storage and Price-Support Programs

Crop storage. Experience with crop-storage programs has shown that they can be effective in supporting farm incomes if the storage program is big enough. However, such a program in no way removes or reduces the cause for potential overproduction and hence for low farm incomes. In certain cases, crop-storage programs have stimulated crop production when the support prices and storage payments combined to offer higher profits than might be expected with immediate sale after harvest.

Storage programs were initially set up in 1929, and later modified in 1933, to stabilize farm income. The objective was to smooth out price variations caused by production variations resulting from weather influences. However, within a very few years, the objective changed from merely stabilizing prices to "stabilizing them upward." When the storage programs were used as price-raising programs, they became less relevant to the problems of reducing an already-existing overproduction that was the cause of low farm prices and income.

One of the equity problems associated with programs having storage and nonrecourse commodity-loan provisions is that they reward the large producer proportionately more than the little producer, and are thereby somewhat self-defeating in terms of really being of much economic help to the small or low-income farmer. In the mid-1960s, for example, farmers grossing less than $5,000 farm income had realized net farm incomes of around $1,200, of which only about $200 came from agricultural programs. This same group averaged almost five times as much income from off-farm sources as from farm sources. In the early 1970s, this situation had been intensified. Such information has caused many people to question the reasons behind keeping price-support programs on the basis of helping raise the level of income for our low-income farmers.

Storage programs act as a temporary price and income support for farmers by withholding crop stocks from the market. However, studies indicate that if and when these stocks are released, they will depress farm prices about as much as they raised prices when they were taken off the market. In addition, the costs of storage must be paid.

Direct payments to farmers.   Direct payments support farm income by supplementing farm-product prices rather than by raising income through price supports. This type of program has been in effect in this country for sugar cane, mohair, and wool. Such a payment has sometimes been called a compensatory, transfer, deficiency, equalization, income, stabilization, or production payment.

Direct payments work in the following manner. Growers sell their product in regular commercial markets at free-market prices. An "intended price" is calculated on a national or "large-area" average. If the commercial market price received is less than the price intended under the program, growers then receive a direct payment from the federal government equal to the difference between the market and the intended price for each unit of the product that is sold.

Direct payments that raise prices above long-run free-market prices do not offer a solution to the problem of overproduction. In fact, if the price were raised above current support rates, production would be further encouraged. Direct payments will also not encourage an inefficient farmer to manage his resources more efficiently. However, they do have the potential of stabilizing and increasing farm income. Under the Agricultural Act of 1973, income payments were put on a deficiency basis, dependent upon a predetermined set of "target" prices.

Multiple pricing. Multiple pricing means setting two or more prices for the same commodity. Marketing orders are sometimes an example of multiple pricing. Markets to which the different prices apply may be separated on the basis of location, time, utilization, or quality. Domestic and foreign markets illustrate separation by location; fluid-milk markets utilize milk in a manner different from milk manufacturing plants; potatoes for human consumption are separated by a quality differential from potatoes for livestock consumption; and holiday consumption of certain foods illustrates time division.

The effectiveness of multiple pricing depends upon the ability of the market to maintain its price differences, to clearly identify all products, to sell most of the product in the higher-priced market, and to institute an adequate and fair method of making the payments. The principal objective of multiple pricing is to reduce the incentive for farmers to expand their production. Multiple-pricing programs require the use of the product bases, and farmers are paid higher prices for base production than for excess or overbase production. The administration of such a program is quite involved, and experience with programs of this type is too limited to determine exactly how effective they might be in curtailing increased production.

Free-market prices. Free-market prices provide perhaps the most automatic resource allocator and guide to production and consumption. However, the total social costs may be too high to institute such a policy quickly, since they may also emphasize price and income fluctuations, and lead to drastically reduced farm incomes, at least in an unspecified "short-run" period. Free-market prices for farm products mean the removal of all production controls and price supports and the offering of products for sale on both domestic and foreign markets. No restrictions on the freedom of the individual farmers or of commodity groups would be imposed. Any overall increases in production would occur in response to actual or anticipated increases in commodity prices; decreases in production would occur in response to actual or anticipated declines in prices.

The effect of free prices on farmers would probably lower net farm income by between 25 and 30 percent in the short run. How long this short run would last is not known. Undoubtedly, there would be considerable adjustment within the farm sector of people who would have to seek nonfarm employment. The magnitude of this transition has been theoretically likened to the kind of farm depression that existed during the 1930s.

The immediate effect of a free-price policy would be to intensify the price–cost squeeze in agriculture. Exactly how steep the price decline would be depends partially upon what policy might be adopted with regard to the large storage stocks of farm production now held by the government. Long-run adjustments might mean fewer farmers more closely organized, so that consumers might end up paying more for their food products than they now do. In the short run, however, consumers would benefit by paying less for their food. Undoubtedly, a return to free prices would solve any problem of overproduction in the farm economy. However, it is of considerable doubt that the cost of such a move would be worth the gain.

Production-Quota and Resource Controls

Marketing quotas. The objective of a policy establishing a marketing quota is to limit the marketing of farm products. In effect, this reduces supply (shifts the supply curve to the left or temporarily slows the advance to the right, so that it is in balance with increases in demand).

This is the way marketing quotas might work. Congress would set what it considers to be a price that would return a fair income to farmers for their food-production efforts. With these goals of price and income in mind, it would then become the task of the Department of Agriculture to establish national sales quotas designed to call forth the desired food production. Each farmer could receive his share of the national quota. His share could be determined from a historical record of production on his farm. One or more certificates would be issued to the farmer, indicating how much his share of the local market might be. Production and marketing regulations would be rigidly enforced, with many penalties on both the producer and the buyer for nonconformity. Farmers would be free to buy or sell their certificates in an effort to expand their farm business or to get out of farming altogether. Regardless of the movement or transfer of certificates within the farm sector, the limits on production would be set. Production (denoted by certificates) would tend to move to those farm managers who have the greatest efficiency of production, and into those areas that have the greatest comparative production advantage. The program would be protected from undue imports by foreign countries.

A program of this kind would probably succeed in holding farm incomes high. However, there might be some resource misallocation. Either part of the resources now used in farm production would become unemployed, or if all available agricultural resources were used, it would be in a less-efficient manner. The use of historical bases in establishing quotas would mean that the most efficient farmers would probably get the bulk of the quotas. Thus, there would probably be a mass migration out of farm production into the nonfarm sector. However, since the people who moved out under these circumstances would probably not be highly trained, the net impact on the whole economy could be more un-employment. Consumers might have to pay more for their food items, but this situation would depend ultimately upon the price levels set by Congress.

The certificates of production and marketing ability would most likely be capitalized into the farm sector quite rapidly. For this reason, the government would hesitate to withdraw its support from farming, because of the high losses that might accrue to certificate owners. This argument is similar in many respects to the reasoning that a return to free farm prices would be so painful. Further, if quotas were not im-posed on all commodities, resources within farming would shift to non-designated commodities. This would be apt to result in continued overproduction and would necessitate further extension of quotas.

Land-retirement programs. The objective under both a voluntary and a compulsory land-retirement program is to limit the amount of land on which farmers can raise crops or livestock. Under a mandatory pro-gram, a national acreage allotment would be determined from a national "need" estimate, or national marketing quota. This acreage allotment would then be allocated to individual farmers in much the same manner as a marketing quota. The program would control the land resource while it permitted the farmer to apply freely all the capital, technology, labor, and management he could and wanted to. Penalties would help enforce the law. Production rights under this program would be salable. Land withdrawn from production would be put into a compulsory con-servation reserve. Federal assistance would be provided to plant this acreage to trees, grass, and so on. The effect on farm incomes from this program would be to push them upward, but eventually the acreage al-lotments would be capitalized into the farm units, and the then-current owners would fall heir to windfall gains in much the same manner that they would under a marketing-quota system. The total amount of land under cultivation would be reduced, as would the number of farmers needed.

Under a voluntary system of land retirement, much the same total effects will take place. One of the major problems would be to make pay-ments high enough to induce voluntary retirement of the 60 to 70 mil-lion acres that will have to be withdrawn in order to reduce farm production significantly. Land could be retired voluntarily on a per-farm basis, on a per-region basis, or on the basis of quality of productive land. On a national basis, payments to withdraw the necessary land would probably average $50 to $60 per acre, and require total payments, administrative costs, and conservation payments of perhaps $3 billion annually.

If enough land is taken out of cultivation, farm production can be reduced and farm incomes increased. Land can be taken out on a compulsory basis, or enough land may be withdrawn voluntarily, provided that the payments offered are high enough to induce withdrawal.

Restricting capital and technology. Throughout Parts II and III, we discussed the increased use of almost all capital items and the rapid adoption of technology. We have also noted that the use of new technologies is at the heart of the overproduction problems of farm income. It is a natural conclusion now to consider policies that restrict the use of capital and technology.

Farm production could be cut back by restricting the use of farm credit, fertilizer, hybrid seeds, improved strains of livestock, and investment in the technical research of farm production and education. Little public support of such a program would be likely, as food prices would rise, and inefficiencies of production and distribution would be the result of a restriction of research inquiry and legislated obstacles to adoption of the resulting technology.

Programs to help farmers move out of farming. The idea of a program to help those farmers who choose to move out of farming is not a new idea. It has been suggested time and again over the last 30 years. However, how to make such a program palatable to the people involved is another question. A program to reduce the number of farmers would eventually mean that the farm income would be divided among a smaller number of people, presumably small enough so that each family left in farming would have an adequate income.

The difficulty with such a program comes after the people move off the farm. Training programs have been suggested for farmers who migrate to nonfarm jobs. However, the training that is currently available will not provide jobs for all the people who move off the farm. In addition, if increasing unemployment is evident in the nonfarm economy, brought about by many of the same reasons (increasing technology adds to structural unemployment), it becomes a question whether a low-paid farmer is better off on the farm or risking unemployment in the town or city. In terms of total cost to the nation, which combination of farm income-support programs and welfare programs can best support the possibly unemployable, recently removed farmer? Personal values cannot be overlooked in such a determination.

HOW WILL AGRICULTURE BE ORGANIZED?

Consumerism has caused many farmers and farm lobbyists to re-evaluate their approaches to farm-policy formulation. Despite its being a rather unorganized movement, and sometimes ill-informed, consumer concern has become another viable, powerful political force in farm-policy making. Combined with a continuing loss of political power in rural areas, consumerism is causing the 1970s to be a period of organizational change in agriculture.

Farmers growing rice, peanuts, tobacco, wool, and sugar are covered by permanent price-support legislation that did not expire with the Agricultural Act of 1973. However, all other producers, excepting dairies in milk market-order areas, will have severe adaptations to make. What are the alternatives open to the decision-making units of farm production and food processing? How might they link into the suppliers of farm-production inputs, and into retail-store outlets?

Some of these questions are discussed in Chapter 26 and in other sections. Pressures of increasing technology, rising labor costs and substitution of capital for labor, increased size of farm enterprise and a reduction in the number of operating commercial farms, improved management, losses of prime farmland, and more pressure on inheritance, property, and income taxes—all these factors have turned people's attention to the underlying organizational structure of farming. Many farmers and their representatives in Congress have been asking, Who will control the country's agriculture? Who will benefit, and in what ways? What will the cost be, and who will bear the burden?

There is concern over the decrease in small farms, the rise in the number of corporate farms (even though many are family units), and the impacts that these changes have made on rural communities and on the families living in them. There is concern about the possible loss of "farmer freedom" with increased integration, and with the loss of on-the-farm management decision making. Producers are bothered that processors may not buy all they used to, or that only those people with contracts will be able to sell their produce. As a result, there is a resurgence of interest in farm producer and processor cooperatives. Many view co-ops as a means of providing countervailing power in buying and selling —giving a chance to the little operations to combine forces and become big. Such a move is seen as offering economies of size and market strength. Still other people observe that "legitimate" farming is being abused by "outside capital," which is interested only in tax write-offs.

What are some of the facts about the farming picture in the 1970s? Farm corporations account for 5–7 percent of the total value of farm marketings. Also, although a decline in the open-market system has occurred, production contracts account for only about another 12–15 percent more of farm sales.

Wide differences can be seen in the marketing systems of various commodities. Less than 3 percent of feed grains, soybeans, food grains, and hogs are under contract or integration. On the other hand, all the sugar, and over 85 percent of the broilers, processing vegetables, and citrus fruits are contracted or integrated. Fluid milk is almost all contracted, and beef, eggs, and turkeys fall somewhere between the extremes.

These issues might be analyzed in many ways—in terms of production, providing of inputs, product marketings, or government intervention—but a framework of analysis dealing with organizational control might offer the most insights. This framework includes discussion of independent farmers operating on an open market, of corporation farms, of cooperative farms and markets, of a larger role for government intervention, or of some combination of these stereotyped models. Let's take them one by one.

Independent Farmer in an Open Market

The system of independent farmers in an open market closely resembles the current system. However, this familiar system cannot stay as it is. It requires (1) open-market trading or its equivalent in buying supplies or selling products, (2) farmland in units of such a size that most landholders can be the operators, (3) financing that is under the control of the farm operator, (4) half or more of the labor performed by the operator(s) or family, (5) the managerial functions performed by the farmer, and (6) technical information readily available from public and private institutions.

Farmers would like the retention of independence and community status this system offers, but aggregate incomes from farming might not be much different from what they are now. Local marketing and supply firms would have important roles to play. The loss of businesses and people from rural communities would probably be the lowest from this system. Farmers in an open market probably would ask for, and continue to get, selected services from government. On the other hand, consumers' food costs would be kept relatively low because of the proven farm-productivity record when each farmer must produce to raise his income.

If national policy were to encourage this system, the government would have to do some or all of the following: (1) guarantee open markets; (2) end volume discounts that go beyond savings in handling costs; (3) develop innovative and flexible credit practices; (4) eliminate tax advantages to high-income investors; (5) design environmental control regulations for average-sized farms—not large farms; (6) continue some form of government price and income support programs; (7) prohibit agribusiness corporations from producing farm products; and (8) place limits on land ownership by nonfarmers.

Implementation of policies to encourage this system obviously calls for policy discrimination in favor of large numbers of farmers. This system will lose some scale or technical efficiencies, but it will gain some pricing efficiencies.

A Corporate Agriculture

Farmers generally have not taken seriously the possibility that control of agriculture would shift to the corporate-type farming system. They see operating errors and argue that the corporates do not have large-scale-efficiency advantages. That may be true, but corporations in the industrial sector did not always grow because of competitive or efficiency advantages. They had long-run growth objectives and achieved success through financial, marketing, and management advantages (see Part V).

A corporate farming-system model would feature (1) a replacement of present public marketing institutions such as auctions, terminals, and market news with contracts or closely coordinated production and merchandising methods; (2) land control attained by ownership, leasing, or contracting (control need not rest with ownership); (3) financing of the agriculture division of farming corporates through sale of stocks, bonds, loans, mutual funds, and limited partnerships; (4) specialized hired farm labor to replace farm operators; (5) decision making at various levels, from corporate headquarters to division headquarters, resident farm managers, foremen, supervisors, and technical advisors; and (6) technical information from private sources, internal or external to the corporation.

As farming corporations expanded, there would probably be an erosion of open markets. Today's successful farmers and rural businessmen would be absorbed into management positions; others would gravitate to the employee payroll. Many agribusiness firms would disappear, and rural communities would either industrialize or fade away. Farm-program costs would decline sharply, but the large corporations might get other types of subsidies. Some economies of scale are possible but might be offset by rising labor costs. Food costs might not differ from those in the other systems discussed here.

A more concentrated, industrialized type of agriculture will develop compared to that existing under the present rules. To further accelerate this system, policy actions opposite to those of the open-market system could be taken. Bigger farm payments could be made. Pollution-control regulations and systems could give advantages to the bigger operators. Tax policies could encourage more nonfarm capital.

A Cooperative Marketing Organization

A cooperative-dominated agriculture could take many forms. The degree of involvement and size of operation would be much more intensive and much larger than in today's cooperative marketing structure. In this marketing system, it is assumed that cooperatives would control the first level of marketing. However, from this point on, competitive forces would prevail, and any organizational arrangement might develop. On the farm-supply side, some input markets might be integrated or contracted by the cooperative. Others might be left to operate independently.

This market organization features the managing of markets, thereby assuring access to markets. The broad approach would include (1) bargaining to influence prices and terms of trade; and/or (2) marketing products through full supply contracts, owning the processing facilities, cooperatives' processing part of the product supply and negotiating with private processors for the remainder, or joint ventures with merchandising firms.

Under the co-op system, the producer would be the financier and laborer. Land ownership would be dispersed. The cooperative would assume some production, management, and marketing decisions.

The cooperative system would restrict farmers' freedom in decision making more than the independent open-market system would, but producers' incomes from the food system would improve. Agricultural supply and marketing firms would face new competition; some would survive and others would fail, depending upon whether the particular input became integrated or contracted or the supplier operated independently. Government spending for farm programs would be reduced. Consumer food prices would be higher than in an open-market system.

If national policy were to favor the cooperative marketing system, major consolidation of cooperatives would be necessary. For example, all milk, all livestock, or other product procurement and market services in the nation might be handled by one cooperative. This would require not only legislation but a big commitment by producers to join forces (quite an assumption, given the disunity of farmers). Legislation might require mandatory cooperative membership and exercise of control by the cooperative through marketing orders, marketing boards, bargaining rules and regulations, or other devices. These privileges probably would be accompanied by closer public supervision, to assure the public interest.

More Government Intervention

Historically, government has played a big role in agriculture, through defining property rights, distributing land, controlling acreage used in production, supporting prices, providing credit, financing research, and providing technical information, market news, and other services. Under this alternative, there would be control within our representative political system only to achieve or preserve selected objectives. These might include the number and size of farm units, type of business

organization, extent of nonfarm business participation in farm production, farm income and its distribution, consumer food prices, efficiency
in food production and marketing, farm investment, and welfare of
rural communities.

The type of government control could vary, but might be similar
to something quite common in the United States—regulation of the public utilities. Various devices are used in public utilities, including (1)
regulating prices, as in electrical rates; (2) regulating marketings, as in
granting exclusive radio or TV rights; (3) controlling investment, as in
power plants; and (4) public ownership, like TVA and city water
systems.

If government were to expand its control of agriculture, one means
would be through regulating marketings—the volume, quality standards,
prices, and market access of producers. Landholding could be influenced
through capital gains and estate taxation. Production rights could be
used to control land use. Licensing of farmers and farm workers would
control their number. A new form of credit system could favor younger
farmers, perpetual debt, or other innovative devices to assist agriculture.

The effects of expanded government control over agriculture would
be dependent upon the major objective chosen. For example, if control
policies were to enhance farmer incomes, then incomes from farming
would be improved but farmers would lose some managerial freedom.
Such a policy would bring higher land prices and higher consumer food
costs. On the other hand, if a plentiful, low-cost food supply were the
major objective, then consumers could enjoy lower food prices, but tax-
payer costs probably would increase to maintain farm income at some
level. The effects on agribusinessmen and rural communities would
differ widely.

SUMMARY

Of all the policies considered in this chapter, the two dealing with
marketing quotas and land retirement (under a program of modified supports) have received the most support from Congress and the farmers
throughout the country. The adoption of the Soil Bank Program is
explicit recognition of the ability of a land-retirement program to eventually solve and set aside aspects of the farm problem. On the other
hand, increasing adoption of federal market orders for milk is explicit
recognition that quotas also have a significant part to play.

A growing blend of two organizational setups is evident in contem-
porary farming. They are independents (some under the guise of family
corporations, primarily for tax purposes and credit access) and coopera-

tives. It is likely that government farm programs of the 1970s will encourage and support this evolution.

A vital and responsive agriculture and a dynamic nonfarm economy present our country's policy makers with a continual challenge. The goals of increasing economic growth, freedom for the individual, and security for the farmer and his family present conflicts of interest that must be resolved. The task is not an easy one. But it is imperative that it be attempted and continually modified to fit the changing conditions of our times.

24

Problems in Resource Use

An increasing volume of questions relate to resource-use policy choices and their consequences. As mentioned in previous chapters, emphasis on economic growth per se is declining, although most people admit that growth within limits and under certain conditions is desirable. Analyzing resource uses and growth strategies under locally determined limits and assumed conditions throws light on the economic consequences of implementing those uses and strategies.

PROGRAMS IN RESOURCE DEVELOPMENT

This chapter will deal with several national programs of resource development, such as the Tennessee Valley Authority (TVA) and the Rural Development Program, known in the 1970s as Community Development, or the Community Resource Development Program[1] stemming

---

[1] Other major resource-development programs of importance include those of the U.S. Department of the Interior, the Army Corps of Engineers, and the Urban Renewal Administration. No attempt is made here to evaluate the alternative uses of government funds spent by the foregoing agencies, or invested in the resource-development programs discussed in this chapter. However, cost–benefit analysis is a highly challenging area for economists, and all interested students should be encouraged to explore its opportunities further.

from the Rural Development Act of 1972. Although these programs are often said to be outdated, they are increasingly pointed out in the developing nations as showcase examples of successful social and economic experimentation. There will always be a need to read history, and to draw from its successes. The forces for and processes of resource development are not that different, country to country. In the United States, we are fortunate to have had the breadth of resource base that allowed us the opportunity to develop several models of resource use. The urgency of actual physical survival has not been imposed on most of us.

Changes in resource development usually occur when a community or area is facing a relative economic decline. When things are going well for people, they have little interest in changing the situation. However, when a large concentration of people in a particular part of the country faces severe economic and social hardship, as did those living in the TVA area in the 1930s, or when most of an entire segment of the economy is affected adversely compared to the rest of the nation, as was the case in noncommercial farming during the late 1940s and early 1950s, people begin to try to develop resource-use alternatives that will reverse the situation. Other examples of resource-development programs are those put into effect because of the "Dust Bowl" of the 1930s, and urban-redevelopment pressures.

Local communities are the backbone of community-resource development in this country, as the economic-analysis case study included in this chapter will point out. County, city, and town planning commissions and boards, and local development organizations of all kinds, as well as nationwide private and public agencies, spend a great deal of time and money to achieve the development of local resources.

Passage of resource-development legislation affecting economic development implicitly recognizes two things about the economic growth process: (1) Economic growth is a process that spreads unevenly across the country. There are pockets of low income, underemployment, and unemployment within or close to areas of rapidly increasing incomes. These pockets develop because of differences in natural and physical resource endowments, the ability of the area to combine its resources into salable products, its geographic location and transportation facilities, its accessibility to markets (either where it can buy its inputs or sell its output), and the technical ability of its people to engage in production. These factors tend to operate in a fairly independent manner for most areas. (2) Legislation recognizes that although some things about an area cannot be changed, there are people within that area who may have a desire to change certain other things, and they can do so if they are provided the means.

The comparative production advantages of an area can be limited by many things. Differences in the adoption of technology, differences in transportation rates and in the costs of buying production inputs and selling output, and institutional barriers and the attitude of local people are factors which might limit the economic advantages of an area. However, inasmuch as the people can and want to change any of the factors above, they will change the rate of economic growth in the area by changing their patterns of resource use. It is very important to understand this concept, because it is the basis upon which most of our economic resource-development legislation is built. The values and capabilities of the people in the areas affected by resource development are the ultimate keys to the success of any enabling legislation.

OBJECTIVES OF RESOURCE DEVELOPMENT

The intent of most resource-development programs is to permit the local people to change the rate of local economic growth, either entirely by themselves or with the help of some public agency. In Figure 24-1, two rates of economic growth are shown; one is for an area with a poor resource base, the other for an area with a relatively rich resource base. Initially, there is a difference (a) between their rates of economic growth. This is to be expected, because of the differences in the resource base of the two areas. However, as time progresses, the difference, or the development gap between the two areas, widens (b). The purpose of a resource-development program is to lessen the gap (c), and achieve a more rapid rate of growth, as shown by the dotted line.

THE PROBLEM OF THE TENNESSEE VALLEY

Our country is not immune to the social and economic ills that result from the deterioration of a resource base, such as happened with the Tennessee Valley people forty years ago and is still occurring in many parts of rural America. Let's explore some of the programs introduced to counter these situations.

The situation facing the Tennessee Valley region in the mid-1930s was one of declining farm income and few full- or part-time nonfarm jobs of any kind. Off-farm jobs that were available paid relatively low wages. Floods were frequent throughout the Tennessee Valley, periodically destroying homes and farmsteads. And finally, nature had not been generous with the area in terms of its land and mineral resources.

The goals facing Congress in the midst of the Great Depression were to increase incomes, increase employment, and to do a better overall job of developing the country's resources. And one of the areas with

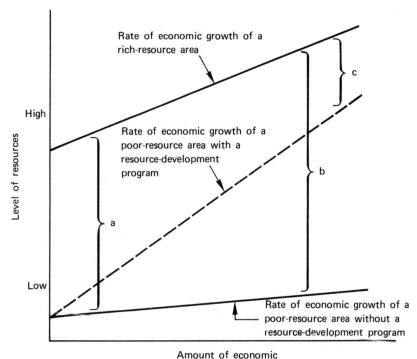

Rate of economic growth of a
rich-resource area

Rate of economic growth of a
poor-resource area with a
resource-development
program

c

b

a

High

Low

Level of resources

Rate of economic growth of a
poor-resource area without a
resource-development program

Amount of economic
development over time

FIGURE 24-1

**Comparison of Areas with Poor and with Rich
Resources, with and without a Resource-Development
Program**

the greatest problems was the Middle South. The alternative solution
Congress chose was the creation of the Tennessee Valley Authority, a
program of extensive and intensive resource development, a program of
massive changes in resource use.

The Tennessee Valley Authority

The Tennessee Valley Authority (TVA) was established by Congress in May 1933. Initially a highly controversial subject involved in
partisan politics, the authority is now supported on a solid bipartisan
basis. Its record of economic success has long since removed any "political experimentation" stigma attached to it in the minds of most people.
The TVA was founded on the assumption that the living standards of
people in a certain area can be considerably improved by the full de-

velopment of the physical resources on which they depend for a living.[2] People employed by the TVA were given broad powers for implementing effective action in flood control, navigation development, generation of electric power, land-use planning, and reforestation.

The Tennessee Valley region covers 92,000 square miles, comprising the entire state of Tennessee and parts of six other states (Mississippi, Alabama, Georgia, North Carolina, Virginia, and Kentucky). There are 201 counties in the combined wastershed–power-service Area. The watershed of the Tennessee River includes 125 counties; the TVA power-service area includes 170 counties, 76 of which are outside the watershed.[3]

The land covered by the TVA is rough, ranging from the Appalachian mountains—about 6,000 feet high—in the eastern part, to low river valleys of altitudes of only a few hundred feet. More than half the land area is forested and extremely rough, making commercialization difficult. The valley's mineral resources consist mostly of coal and of phosphate-rock deposits, from which fertilizers are made. There is an abundance of surface-water resources, but the soils in the area tend to be poor and highly susceptible to erosion.

The TVA is managed by a three-man board of directors, one of whom is elected chairman. There is also a general manager, who is in charge of all the operations of the TVA, including all its divisions and branches. Congress gave the TVA an initial loan, which is being repaid from profits from its various resource-development projects. During the summer of 1960, the board voted to sell bonds on the commercial capital market in order to finance further dam construction and power-development expansion.

One of the principal functions of the TVA is to generate electricity, which it then sells wholesale to various electric-utility companies, or retails to both private industry and public agencies such as the Atomic Energy Commission, which uses great quantities of TVA power. In cases where it markets wholesale power, the TVA retains a voice in its retail resale, to make sure that only a reasonable profit margin is received from their low-priced power. No power is sold by the TVA to private individuals or to households.

The TVA has several different divisions and branches, which handle hydropower projects, agriculture and chemical developments, area development and regional analysis, reservoirs, dams and property developments, engineering projects pertaining to resource development, refores-

---

[2] John R. P. Friedman, *The Spatial Structure of Economic Development in the Tennessee Valley*, Research Paper No. 39, Department of Geography, University of Chicago, March 1955, p. 8.

[3] *Ibid.*, pp. 6–8.

tation of the area, and recreation projects. Perhaps the most widely known TVA projects other than dam building and power generation are the manufacture of fertilizers (also munitions during World War II and the Korean War), the extensive research conducted and/or sponsored by TVA, and the educational activities conducted by its employees or consultants.

For example, within the Agriculture Division, there are four branches: the Agricultural Economics branch, which does research on a variety of subjects; the Farm Test Demonstration branch, which acts in an extension-education capacity for farmers on fertilizer application and total farm planning, including crop rotation, livestock and pasture programs, and woodlot management; the Distributor Demonstration branch, which extends research findings to distributors of fertilizer and to other farm-supply industries; and the Agronomy branch, which conducts research necessary to service and stimulate the other branches. In addition to these activities, there is much research of an agronomic-economic nature sponsored by TVA in cooperation with the experiment stations of various land-grant universities throughout the country. This research is an attempt to bring together people from many institutions who are interested in production economics and farm management—primarily response to fertilizer and the evaluation of the social and economic aspects of this increase in production. Research projects include the application of fertilizer in conditions of drought or through irrigation systems. The demand for fertilizer and the credit available for fertilizer application has been studied, as have farmers' attitudes toward fertilizer, its technology of application, and the attitudes of dealers who sell fertilizer to farms. Comparative production-cost studies and the kinds of equipment needed to farm efficiently in the area are other examples.

Perhaps the largest single fact that the TVA has proven beyond doubt about economic development is that increased urban-industrial development also helps the farmers in an area. Not only does increased industrialization offer underemployed farmers jobs at higher incomes than they could earn on the farm and provide additional markets through which farmers can market their produce, but it also provides an additional or increased source of income to the farmer. As a result, he need not be dependent solely upon the income from his farm for the purchase of all his farm inputs as well as for the necessities of his family. An increase in an area's total economic activity ultimately offers farmers more opportunity to buy more fertilizer and better equipment. Increased use of these inputs raises the farm production in the area and thereby also raises income from farming. Productivity per farm worker increases and, accordingly, the farmer is paid more. The spiral of increases in farm income and in nonfarm income results in more fertilizer and other technologies being applied to farm production. In this manner, the economic development of a large area, initially poorly endowed with natural resources, can become stimulated and encouraged.[4]

THE RURAL LOW-INCOME PROBLEM

The low-income farm situation in the United States described by the 1950 Census of Agriculture was this: In 1950, 1.5 million, or 28 percent, of farm-operator families had net cash incomes under $1,000. Over half had net cash family incomes under $2,000. These low-income farm families lived for the most part on small farms, located in areas bypassed by current technologies and by the rapid urban-industrial development that characterized most of the nation. With respect to agriculture, an important goal of Congress had been to provide better income opportunities for farm people on the farm and off the farm. The problem facing Congress was, "What ought to be done about the low-income farm families?" One solution was to establish legislation called the Rural Development Program (RDP). This program was to be administered by the Department of Agriculture through the Extension Service, but was also to rely heavily on local leadership.

The Rural Development Program (RDP)

When President Eisenhower submitted his recommendation to Congress in January 1954, he suggested that the secretary of agriculture should give special attention to the low-income problems of small farmers. As a result of this directive, the secretary, in cooperation with other agencies and departments, prepared a report that outlined the extent of the low-income problem in agriculture and made suggestions and recommendations to solve or alleviate this problem.[5]

This report was unique in several respects. First, it recognized that the solution to low-income problems in farming needed to be a long-range program and could not be quickly implemented. Second, it separated the farm price and income policy problems (discussed in Chapter 23) from the low-income problems in farming. And third, it recognized that to accomplish the desired goals of increased income for farm people, the approach taken must be comprehensive and involve the total community and all its resources.

The objectives of the RDP were to increase employment opportu-

---

[4] Publications explaining the progress of TVA can be received by writing to the Division of Public Relations, TVA, Knoxville, Tennessee.

[5] "Development of Agriculture's Human Resources: A Report on Problems of Low-Income Farmers," Report prepared for the Secretary of Agriculture, Washington, D.C., April 1955.

nities off the farm as well as to show improvement in the kind of jobs available within farming, to raise the income level of workers on farms and off farms in areas of severe underemployment, and to involve local people at all stages in drawing up their own development plans and putting them into action. Because there were many elderly people in farming who were incapacitated for one reason or another, a further objective was to extend meaningful Social Security coverage to this group.

Approaches to attain these objectives included efforts to increase the productivity of those able to remain in farming, to improve the prospects for part-time farming and full-time nonfarm jobs, to increase the number of opportunities for training of all kinds, and to strengthen health programs and health facilities. The decentralization of industry and the widespread distribution of defense contracts to some of these low-income areas was also advocated.

The RDP program was formally initiated in 1956, with less than 25 rural counties involved. By June 1960, there were 210 counties involved in 30 states and in Puerto Rico.[6] National meetings and regional conferences and workshops were held on an annual basis from the beginning of the program.

The structure through which this program was set in motion was based on "grass-roots" interest and participation. Without local effort, little could be done to bring about any effective, long-lasting change or improvement in the low-income areas. Pilot counties were set up in several states, organized to experiment with different forms of community organization and different ways of servicing these groups. It was generally intended that as the pilot counties improved themselves, other counties would learn from them and initiate their own programs of local development.

Most of the states involved in the RDP formed state committees of various kinds. These organizations kept the local committees supplied with technical information and acted as a coordinating agency in many other respects. Membership on the state committees drew from public agencies of all kinds, private industry, commercial businesses, and individuals from all walks of life who had shown an interest and an analytical ability in the problems at hand.

The membership of local community development committees—or RDP Committees, as some county groups called themselves—generally represented the county on four levels: geographically, with all townships represented; occupationally, so that a broad cross-section of business and job interest was represented; age-wise, so that both young and old people were placed on the committee; and by sex—both men and women were

6 5th Annual Report of the Secretary of Agriculture on the Rural Development Program, Washington, D.C., September 1960.

members. Group size usually ranged from about 20 to 50 people, but some county groups had more than 100 people involved. The number of people who participated in the program depended upon the judgment of the county extension agents, who had been given the responsibility for organizing the committees and prompting interest in the county's problems. In some instances, the county RDP committee was both an analytical-educational group and an action-oriented group. In other cases, the committee analyzed the situation in relation to data gathered by consultants and resource people from the universities and other institutions willing to help, and turned their findings over to legally authorized county and state groups to put them into action if they saw fit.

All the agencies in the U.S. Department of Agriculture contributed much time and effort through their field staffs. State and federal agency personnel also attended meetings whenever they were asked, to contribute technical assistance or information. Technical assistance already provided to farms by the Federal Extension Service was stepped up, and special efforts were made to direct it more toward helping the low-income farmers in areas in which they were concentrated. Some funds were also allocated through universities, for research projects that explored the adjustments necessary for farm families if they stayed in farming under more intensive management, or if they moved from farming to some nonfarm occupation.

Appropriations for the RDP were quite small compared to the price-support program and others that government sponsored nation-wide. Most of these funds were directed through existing agencies, and some were allocated to add personnel to handle RDP work either in the field or at the universities. Primarily, the funds appropriated by Congress were allocated for FHA farm-operating loans for low-income farmers. In general, these loans did not make significant contributions to farm income in low-income areas, because the size of enterprise they would permit was small and the management on these farms was often quite limited.

Low-income farm areas are found scattered all over the country. However, at the time the RDP started, the majority of the areas were located in the Southeast (north from the Gulf through the Mississippi Delta area into Arkansas and central Missouri, then east, covering nearly all the area south of the Ohio River). Other areas include the northern parts of Minnesota, Wisconsin, and Michigan, northwestern New Mexico, and parts of the Cascade and Rocky Mountain areas in Montana, Washington, and Oregon. These areas were then characterized by rather dense rural settlements with high birthrates, few nonfarm jobs, and low levels of formal education. Topography, farmer attitudes, and credit limitations also restricted the use of modern farm machinery.

Three criteria were used through the RDP areas in the nation to denote the severity of the low-income problem: (1) less than $1,000 residual farm income to operator and family, with level-of-living index below the regional average, and 25 percent or more of the commercial farms classified as "low production"; (2) level-of-living index in lowest fifth of the nation; and (3) 50 percent or more of the commercial farms classified as "low production." If all three of these criteria were met by an area, it was classified as a serious problem area. If two of the three criteria were met, the area was classified as having a substantial low-income problem, and if one of the three criteria were met, the area was said to have a moderate low-income problem. Although the farms in these low-income areas had many differences with regard to tenure, age of operator, and so on, they were also similar. They were all small farms with little capital investment. On the average, farm operators of the low-income farms had completed only seven years of school, and only one out of ten was a high school graduate. In contrast, farmers in the rest of the nation averaged 8½ years of school completed, and one out of four was a high school graduate.

Credit for success of the program was often difficult to determine fully because of the large number of agencies, organizations, and individuals working in the program. Increased farm income, increases in the number of nonfarm jobs, the attraction of new industrial plants, clean-up campaigns, and "stay-in-school" promotions could quite easily be counted and assessed. But perhaps the more basic and lasting success of the program was that the local people learned to identify their own problems and to do something about them. There were subtle changes in personal attitude that would have lasting effects but could never really be identified and put in a report for congressional budget hearings. There were increases in self-respect and self-confidence that a job could be done to improve the community, and furthermore, that the job *was* well done. In retrospect, history may tell us some day that the educational, social, and psychological benefits of the RDP program were of equal or greater benefit than the immediate increases in income.

RURAL DEVELOPMENT, 1960–74

The same situation that confronted the lawmakers at the time of the Rural Development Program legislation in 1956 still remained in 1961. The intensity of the problem had lessened somewhat, owing to the large numbers of farmers who had left farming; however, areas bypassed by urban industrial development still persisted. The goals of Congress were much the same as they had been during the creation of RDP legislation, with one major difference. This time there was some money available for the job. The law that resulted from congressional action created the Area Redevelopment Administration.

President Kennedy signed the Area Redevelopment Bill on May 1, 1961. This new law replaced the old RDP program, and authorized $394 million in loans, grants, technical aid, and other benefits over a four-year period. A total of $100 million was specifically earmarked for low-income rural areas.

The purpose of the ARA was to create persistent and lasting employment in areas of unemployment and underemployment. The intent of the law was to improve income opportunities in rural and urban areas where a large number of people operate small farms or are out of work. As in the case of the RDP, ARA work relied heavily on local initiative to find and develop new jobs.

In the late 1950s, 22 percent or over a million farm families still had money income from all sources (after farm-production expenses were paid) of less than $1,000, and one-third of the farm families were receiving under $1,500. In addition, over a million rural nonfarm families had incomes of $1,500 or less. In contrast, only 3 percent (600,000 families) of urban families were under $1,000, and only 6 percent under $1,500. These data indicate clearly that the poverty or low-income problem in the United States is predominantly in rural areas. Even if an allowance were made for higher living costs in the city, the situation would not materially be altered.

All the counties that were under the RDP program were also eligible for ARA benefits. However, the requirements for new counties to become eligible under the law had shifted from low-income criteria to specifications of unemployment. Thus, although part of the funds would go to areas counted as low-income areas under the old law, the new areas would have to qualify on the basis of unemployment. Labor-market areas were designated throughout the country, and the Department of Labor provided unemployment data to help determine eligibility. Newly designated areas had to have 6 percent or more unemployment for a specific number of months before they were considered eligible for ARA loan funds.

The $394 million authorized by Congress for ARA funds provided five broad types of assistance.[7] A $200-million loan and grant fund was established for industrial and commercial projects, including tourist facilities to be divided equally between rural and urban areas. A $100-million loan fund and $75 million in grants were set aside for the improvement of public facilities, such as water and sewage systems and

7 "Your Community and the Area Redevelopment Act," U.S. Department of Commerce, Washington, D.C., June 9, 1961.

power lines. Four and one-half million dollars were provided for grants in technical assistance to be obtained through federal, state, and private sources by all communities. These funds were available for surveys of resources and program planning. Ten million dollars were authorized for subsistence grants to workers out of jobs and small farmers while they were training for a different job or improving their skills. There were $4.5 million in grants allocated to finance retraining programs for persons qualified to use them. Also, there was an increased opportunity under the Federal Housing Act amendments to rehabilitate blighted industrial and commercial areas and to obtain urban planning aid in cities, small towns, and counties.

General administration of the program was concentrated in the Area Redevelopment Administration, a new Department of Commerce unit. Under the law, an Office of Rural Areas Development (ORAD) was set up in the Department of Agriculture to administer the Rural Areas Development (RAD) part of the program. Loan funds were distributed to both urban and rural areas. This money was called "5a" and "5b" loan money, designating whether it was used for urban or rural purposes respectively. In general, both ARA and ORAD had to approve the projects for which 5b money was lent or given in rural areas. The 5a funds were allocated solely at the ARA's discretion after consultation with various other agencies, such as the Small Business Administration.

Within the ORAD, as the organization worked itself from the federal to the state and local levels, several changes from the RDP took place. Although the work was now carried forward under the banner of the RAD, it still retained essentially the same operational philosophy as the RDP. However, there were three major differences. The RAD had more money with which to work. Also, it had the added push of a legislative edict to get something done. The third change was that the Department of Agriculture had to organize the ORAD so that the Federal Extension Service was no longer primarily in charge of the activity. Extension's job was to organize the state and local committees, but it was now at the same operating level as the Rural Electrification Administration (REA), which was given most of the responsibility in agriculture for industrialization, and as a Technical Panel, later changed to Technical Action Panel (TAP), which combined the resources of the Soil Conservation Service (SCS), Farm Home Administration (FHA), Rural Electrification Administration (REA), Forest Service (FS), Agricultural Stabilization and Conservation Service (ASCS), and Extension (FES). These organizations were to supply technical information to any and all public or private groups interested in the development of their local resources and areas.

In order to qualify for loans once the area or county was designated

eligible under ARA criteria, the county had to compile an Overall Economic Development Plan (OEDP). "The basic elements of the OEDP
include a description of the local organization that represents the area on
redevelopment matters; a background picture of the area as a place in
which to live and work; a summary of the factors basic to economic growth;
the economic potentials in light of resources, markets, and labor skills; and
a program of action for creating new employment opportunities or
otherwise reducing unemployment and underemployment. . . ."[8]

The ARA and RAD effort far surpassed that of the RDP. By
February 1, 1963, the ARA had designated 1,052 areas for redevelopment, 853 of which were rural counties.[9] These areas depended for the
major part of their initiative on local leadership. In those counties that
had previously been engaged in RDP work, the transition was smooth,
and an OEDP was generally created easily from the basic analytical
work that the county committees had done previously. In newer counties, where there was pressure to get an OEDP done quickly so that loans
could be made, the local people were often deprived of the learning opportunity of making up their own OEDP, which requires considerable
time.

During the 1960s, RAD efforts were expanded to many rural communities. More loan funds and grants were authorized for increased
development efforts in areas identified as not sharing equally in the
nation's growing wealth and income opportunities. TAP (Technical
Action Panels) committees were set up in most of the country's counties.
The purpose of TAP groups was to coordinate and stimulate growth by
offering a "package" of resource personnel and talent from which local
development committees and organizations could draw help.

By the end of the 1960s, the philosophy of rural development had
spread throughout the country. All states had some type of statewide
committee, and most counties also had committees exploring possible
changes in local resource use. Although the switch in national adminis-
trations also brought switches in the funding of many programs, the
concept of rural development was encouraged. Increased funds were
made available to the FHA for housing and water and sewer loans.
Rural America was offered an increased opportunity to boost its public-
service infrastructure.

Motivation for supplying these funds had changed slightly. The
point of view of the much more urban-oriented Congress was that if

8 U.S. Department of Commerce, ARA, "The Overall Economic Development
Program," August 1961, p. 1.
9 U.S. Department of Agriculture, ORAD, "Rural Areas Development Handbook," Agriculture Handbook No. 245, June 1963, p. 9.

rural people could be kept in rural areas, cities and metropolitan areas would not grow as rapidly, and consequently the rate of increasing costs of providing services for urban populations might slow down. Not only was rural development good for rural people, but it might cut the taxes of urban people, too.

However, in 1972–73, the money available for rural development was reduced significantly. Other program needs and limited funds caused budget reallocations. There was also an attempt to form a new Department of Community Development, which would combine programs from many existing Departments (Labor; Agriculture; Health, Education and Welfare; Commerce; and Interior). Although this suggestion has not yet been implemented, it is highly likely that it will come about in order to avoid waste and duplication of program efforts, and to make the entire rural–urban development work more effective than it now does.

In late 1973–74, funding for various titles of the Rural Development Act of 1972 was granted. Water and sewer grants were authorized; but less than $5 million were appropriated and released for research and extension programs conducted by the land-grant universities. It is clear that rhetoric is long and dollars short, as far as rural-development programs are concerned. It is equally clear that each state and county must decide what it is it wants to do in rural development; the philosophy and challenge of self-help, self-determination, and self-analysis will have to be accepted "locally" if anything is to be done in this area.

A CASE STUDY OF COUNTY RESOURCE DEVELOPMENT: CRAWFORD COUNTY, INDIANA, 1958–73

In order to provide a better understanding of resource-use patterns, Crawford County in Indiana will be used as a case study. Crawford County was last on the list of Indiana's 92 counties when ranked by almost any economic criterion. However, the county contained some of the most determined, energetic, and hard-working people in the state. These people were responsible for the remarkable success story initiated by the Crawford County Economic Development Committee.

This committee was formed in the early summer of 1958. Much previous work had been done by extension specialists in community development with the county extension agent, who had had to learn the problem-solving approach and apply it to his county's problems and resources. The overall County Extension Committee gave its approval for work in this area and thus legitimized the agent's work, which might have been considered out of bounds by the county's farmers. Coincident with training the extension agent, the work-unit conservationist of the Soil Conservation Service in the county was also briefed and was a tremendous help in getting the program on its feet. A list of people who might be placed on a development committee was drawn up with the help of the agent, the SCS man, a local farmer, and a local businessman. People from this list were invited to attend a meeting at which data were presented concerning population movements in the county, employment opportunities locally, and comparative incomes in farming and off-farm jobs both locally and in other areas of the state. The people decided that there were some problems evident from the data and voted to go ahead with another meeting to investigate the situation further. After the next meeting, they voted to engage in county developmental work on a long-run basis and forced themselves to do some significant analysis.

The size of the group at this time was approximately forty. Membership included men and women, people who worked in town and on farms, people who commuted to work outside the county, and people who had never been far away from their home county. These people had been handpicked because they were the leaders and the policy makers of Crawford County. They represented the catalyst in the county, and if any development program was to get started, these people would start it.

The group met regularly once a month. A chairman, vice-chairman, and secretary were elected. No treasurer was needed, because at the beginning there were no funds to handle. This group of officers decided on an agenda for each meeting with the help of the entire group. Outside people were asked in if they had anything to contribute to the subject currently being discussed by the committee.

Extension specialists from Purdue University were used, but their role was primarily one of group maintenance and stimulation; they made no decisions for the group. The group acted independently of any university, state, or federal agency or program. Their decisions were entirely of their own making, and the priority of problems they discussed was entirely of their own choosing. The role this development committee played in the county was one of objective, impartial fact-finding and analysis. No other group in the history of the county had ever done this type of thing before, and as a result, this group achieved a great respect and performed a service to the people in the county that no organization had offered. The people on the committee were there willingly because they were interested and had a stake in the future of the county, and any problems they considered important were taken up. There were no "right" or "wrong" things to be done, nor was there any particular value structure giving rise to any priority of problems other than that of the local committee.

The situation in Crawford County, Indiana, was typical of other counties in southern Indiana. The county had a population of about 8,400 in 1959 and had undergone continued out-migration of population for almost fifty years previously. The main source of employment and income was farming; there were only about 250 jobs in manufacturing in the entire county. Incomes from nonfarm employment were the lowest in the state at the time, and income per farm was also low.

When they were faced with this situation, one of the first things the people wanted to do was attract new industry. This would help employment, increase incomes, allow people to move off the farm to higher-paying jobs, and improve the tax base to provide better public facilities of all kinds. Someone on the committee had read a recent article stating that new industry needs to know the number, age, skill level, and health of its potential employees before it will seriously consider moving into an area. With these conditions in mind, the people decided that they wanted to survey the county population. With the help of specialists from the Indiana State Board of Health and from Purdue University, a questionnaire was devised that could fit individual and family information on 26 subjects all on one piece of paper. More than 300 persons carried this questionnaire throughout the county and obtained detailed information on 94 percent of the people living in Crawford County. This took only three weeks and was done without charge to the local people involved. The state board of health said it had established a national record for a volunteer organization in terms of population coverage, depth of questioning, and survey time elapsed. This effort is indicative of the interest and effort put out by the local people—a national record established by people who were materially from the poorest county in the state!

The information they obtained from the survey was analyzed, written up, and then printed by a local printer in the county, a woman intensely interested in getting factual information out to her readers. The uses to which this newly acquired information was put were many. First of all, it outlined the health picture of the county's inhabitants. Because there was no full-time doctor in the county, this information was used to try to attract one. Special effort was made to begin a class for exceptional children in the county and for those who suffered from defective speech, hearing, or eyesight, epilepsy, or rheumatic fever. The state Department of Public Instruction was helpful in this endeavor.

The information was also used to compile labor-force statistics into a brochure for industrial promotion. A new school was being considered in one township, because many of the people had heard about the population explosion and thought they would need new facilities.

When the survey showed that almost half the population was 65 years or older in that township, plans for the new school died a natural death. The survey also provided information useful in tax calculations, because of certain county and state deductions made for age and health considerations.

Another project that the county group helped with was procuring an area forester for their county and two adjacent counties. He was needed to help do a better job of marketing the timber and to help with tree cultivation and woodlot management.

Working with the concept of an area approach, the group soon realized that there were some things that were better handled by cooperative action from several counties. Accordingly, they were instrumental in forming first a three-county group and later a four-county group. This area group met to discuss common problems of road building and maintenance, education, recreation, industrialization, and health. From this group of four counties sprang an action group called the Lincoln Hills, an organization dedicated to the promotion of the recreation industry in the area.

Southern Indiana has much scenery that has not been fully exploited. The Lincoln Hills group formed a Riverboat Festival and staged square dances and barbecues, to attract tourists into the area. Once the tourists were there, each country was free to try to attract them to their specific tourist attraction—historic spots, scenery, caves, and rivers. The group printed attractive brochures outlining trips that might be made through the four counties, and each county also provided a map or brochure that presented more detailed excursion routes.

There are many other things, large and small, that the Crawford County committee investigated and helped to implement. The material presented is merely representative of the things that local people can do when they are provided with relevant facts for analysis and with resource personnel to help with the technical aspects of the problems.

In order to qualify for consideration of ARA loan funds, the Crawford County Committee developed one of the first OEDP's submitted from Indiana. This OEDP was compiled almost wholly from existing reports developed from analysis done previously by the committee, the resource people it had requested, and various subcommittees, the resource people it had requested, and various subcommittees. The OEDP report was readily accepted by both state and federal officials connected with the ARA-RAD program.

During the late 1960s and early 1970s, although the county committee stopped meeting regularly, many projects on which they helped had changed the area's resource base significantly. A new stretch of interstate highway had been opened, allowing easier access to out-of-county job centers. The state had purchased a cave in the county, and was actively pursuing attraction of tourists. A dam had been built, and the resulting lake added another recreational attraction. And finally, a medical clinic had been opened in the county seat, where no doctor had worked for many years. Even though some of these projects might have been implemented in the area anyway, none of them would have gone ahead as quickly, and some of them not ever, if the county committee had not existed.

In 1973, a group of extension personnel who had been intimately involved in rural development for up to twenty years in the area surrounding Crawford County reiterated that local goal setting, involvement and development of local leadership, access to university resource personnel, "making haste slowly," imagination, and the willingness to discuss new ideas about the community were keys to helping people find a consensus of group direction.

AN EXAMPLE OF ECONOMIC ANALYSIS
FOR RESOURCE-PLANNING POLICY

Input–output analysis, long used by national planners, is being used by economists in California Cooperative Extension to help local governments in making resource-planning decisions. Money flows between the private and public sectors are examined in detail.

A project begun in 1965 helps answer such questions as, "What is agriculture worth to a county's economy?" or "What is the economic impact of a more intensive land use?" From the initial inquiries, other issues related to resource use, taxation, and employment can evolve. Analyses have been used in a variety of ways to estimate the economic results of past or anticipated changes in county resource use.

The basic tool of these analyses is an input–output model that uses a combination of economic data from local sources and information synthesized from other studies.[10] The model can be updated at any time, and new economic information can be introduced as it becomes available. One of the project's educational goals is to train local government staff to use this model on their own, calling on university economists for help in making refinements and adaptations, and suggesting related studies. In all instances, the prime purpose is to prepare information and analysis on pertinent resource-use issues faced by county officials and planners.

---

[10] George E. Goldman was primarily responsible for the statistical techniques of data synthesis for use in the I-O model.

As an aid to decision making, input–output offers descriptive analysis to people interested in estimating the economic consequences of proposed resource-use changes before a decision has to be made. For example, they can look at the probable economic consequences of different land uses, such as zoning a specific parcel of land in an agricultural preserve, using the same land as a mobile-home park, or using it for an industrial park. To be even more specific, an input–output model indicates the changes that each sector of an economy will experience as a result of land-use shifts.

There are limitations to the use of the model. Although it gives fairly reliable estimates of economic relationships and multiplier effects, it does not give answers to questions about what should be done or what ought to be done. It cannot answer the question, "What is balanced growth?" nor can it by itself suggest least-cost ways for county government to provide services. Public officials and interested citizens must still make their own value judgments.

Other studies that can be used as part of the input–output analysis include benefit–cost studies, studies describing selected economic characteristics of the population—such as distribution of income and spending habits—and studies incorporating other analytical techniques, including simulation and linear programming.

California county extension staffs worked closely with university-based economists in developing the information necessary for the model. County officials also contributed much time and information, as did local businessmen. Involving local leaders early in the study served to build a broad understanding of interrelationships in their local economy. In this process, participants learned to use the model in evaluating local resource-use alternatives, and the economists involved gained greater insights into what the people in the counties thought was important.

Have these studies been useful to decision makers? Yes. For example, after a severe spring frost in the Napa Valley a year ago, estimates of the initial economic loss to the county from the reduction in grape crush were given to county officials within a few minutes after the physical-damage estimates were received. This information was used in making an application for disaster-area relief.

In another instance, people were able to make comparisons of the economic effects resulting from putting in an industrial park, encouraging a junior college to open, and losing their county-state hospital. These examples illustrate the trade-off between private- and public-sector investment. For instance, for similar sums of money, schools that have 80–90 percent of their budget going for salaries and wages generate more economic activity within the commercial part of the economy than does an industrial plant with only 25–35 percent of its total expenditures accounted for by salaries and wages. On the other hand, the school does not add to the tax base of the community, while an industrial plant does.

Another study estimated the economic loss to the county from zoning that encouraged several mobile-home parks to be built on the county border. As a result of the suggested park location, shopping facilities in another county were more accessible to park residents than were the same type of facilities in their own county. Thus, while the county was paying for the cost of schools, fire, health, welfare, and public protection for park residents, most of the economic activity generated by the park residents' purchases was lost to the adjoining county.

When economic growth was regarded as the prime desirable goal, resource-planning decisions seemed less difficult. However, with an increasing number of questions being asked about the consequences of economic growth and the financing of local government, there is also an increasing demand for economic information concerning the effects of different growth and nongrowth strategies. Input–output analysis assists in meeting this demand. In the future, increased population, increased pressure on land, and increased concern for the quality of life will generate even greater demands for more objective means of comparing resource-policy alternatives. Therefore, it is expected that planners and county and city officials will increasingly use more sophisticated quantitative tools of analysis as aids in their decision-making process.

25

World Trade of Agricultural Products

WHY NATIONS TRADE

In the earlier chapters on the development of economic life, the importance of specialization of production and trade were emphasized as the basic contributors to the economic well-being of a country. In the chapter on production principles, the law of comparative advantage was formally stated, and an example illustrated how two countries with differing physical efficiencies of production could benefit from trade. The fundamental reason, then, for maintaining and expanding foreign trade is to increase the economic strength and welfare of farmers and other citizens. In addition, foreign trade provides jobs in export industries, and these workers' purchases of goods and services in turn provide jobs for others. Through trade, a nation obtains the goods it imports with less effort and in greater volume by producing and exchanging export goods rather than by attempting to produce all the goods it needs by itself.

AGRICULTURAL TRADE AND ECONOMIC DEVELOPMENT

Size of Agricultural Exports Relative to Total Exports

Ratios of trade to national income are strikingly similar for both developing and developed economies. However, agricultural exports constitute a larger part of total export earnings in the developing countries. For example, data developed by Tolley and Gwyer indicated that only 7 out of 23 developed countries derive more than 10 percent of national income from agricultural exports. In contrast, 16 out of 24 developing countries derived over 10 percent of national income from agricultural exports, which in most cases was over 80 percent of total exports.[1] In addition, most developing economies relied on but one or two products for most of their export earnings. For example, 85 percent of Ghana's total exports was in cacao.

There are many and diverse views on the relation of trade to long-term economic development. If the law of comparative advantage is thought to be at the core, a national policy of specializing in agriculture would seem to benefit both trade and development if there is a comparative advantage in agricultural commodities. Clearly, Ghana has such a comparative advantage in cacao. Some view economic development as a process of diversification around some staple export base—for many countries, an agriculturally produced commodity. The proponents state that with the expansion of the export industry, increases in domestic production of inputs used by that industry, processing of the export commodity, and subsequent production of consumer goods for the people employed in the export industry will "kick off" a satisfactory growth rate for the economy. But the difficulty of this idea seems limited in looking at the developing economies of today. Again, Ghana has been exporting cacao for a long time, and the alleged expansionary effects have not taken hold. Why?

More modern proponents of comparative advantage point to indirect gains from trade. Haberler puts forward the idea that trade may transmit experience and ideas, change attitudes, encourage competition, and open up channels for capital inflows, as well as provide the means

---

[1] G. S. Tolley and C. D. Gwyer, "International Trade in Agricultural Products in Relation to Economic Development," in *Agricultural Development and Economic Growth*, eds. H. F. Southworth and B. F. Johnson (Ithaca, N.Y.: Cornell University Press, 1967), pp. 404–6.

to import capital goods for development.[2] For example, in the 1960s, Thailand discovered a comparative advantage in producing corn for the Japanese market. In exchange, Thailand imported considerable capital equipment in the form of power machinery and transportation vehicles.

There are also diverse views on whether governments should try to achieve balanced growth between the agricultural sector and the industrial sector and within sectors, or whether unbalanced growth will actually spur a faster development rate. Hirschman stresses extreme concentration of investment in particular industries with deliberate neglect of others.[3] The argument goes that leading sectors (those where investment is concentrated) will provide the impetus to growth through forward and backward linkages; that is, by inducing attempts to supply the inputs for those sectors through domestic production and to utilize the outputs of the sectors in new activities. In this regard, the agricultural export industry can be a leading sector, inducing investment in agricultural processing industries (forward linkage) and investment in fertilizer, seed, pesticide, and agricultural-machinery industries (backward linkage). Writers on balanced growth implicitly reject a role for the agricultural export industry by prescribing public planning for investment among industries in accordance with income elasticities of demand. Thus there is not unanimity of opinion as to the nature and importance of the role played by trade of food commodities in agricultural and overall economic development, but clearly agricultural-commodity exports are vital to some of the world's economies, like New Zealand and Denmark. The rest of this chapter will focus on agricultural trade of the United States.

IMPORTANCE OF EXPORTS TO U.S. FARMERS

Selling farm products in the world markets is a big and highly competitive business.[4] World agricultural-trade volume advanced to record highs in the 1960s, with the United States contributing about 20 percent of the total. Although U.S. agriculture depends more on exports than does the rest of the economy, the share of total exports from the

---

[2] G. Haberler, "An Assessment of the Current Relevance of the Theory of Comparative Advantage to Agricultural Production and Trade," *International Journal of Agrarian Affairs,* Vol. 4 (May 1964), 130–49.

[3] A. O. Hirschman, *The Strategy of Economic Development* (New Haven: Yale University Press, 1958).

[4] Data in this section from *Foreign Agricultural Trade,* monthly publication of U.S. Department of Agriculture, Economic Research Service.

United States accounted for by agricultural products has fallen considerably, from 80 percent during 1865–80. The share declined to a low of 9 percent between 1940 and 1941 but rose again to 25 percent by 1960. During the 1960s, it was relatively stable. In value terms, agricultural exports averaged below $1 billion in the 1930s but climbed to a record high of $17.6 billion in 1973 (Table 25-1).

The United States is a major contributor in world trade. Of the soybeans entering world trade in 1973, 90 percent were grown in the United States; of feed grains, 60 percent; of wheat, 40 percent; of tobacco, 33 percent; and of cotton and rice, 25 percent. The product of one out of every four harvested acres was exported in 1973. Over $2 billion worth was sold to Japan alone. The United States sells agricultural products to 160 different countries, but fifteen of them take about three-fourths of the total. After twenty years of trade isolation, the United States sold $207 million worth of products to China in 1973. Grains and grain products accounted for half the total, and cotton, soybean oil, and cattle hides most of the rest.

TABLE 25-1
Value of Agricultural and Total Foreign Trade,
Selected Years, 1929–1973

Year[a]	Domestic Exports		Imports	
	Agricultural (million $)	Agricultural as % of total	Agricultural (million $)	Agricultural as % of total
1929–30	1,496	32	1,900	49
1932–33	590	42	614	53
1935–36	766	32	1,141	52
1938–39	683	24	999	48
1941–42	1,032	16	1,503	49
1944–45	2,191	17	1,729	44
1947–48	3,503	25	2,826	45
1950–51	3,411	27	5,147	48
1952–54	2,936	19	4,176	40
1956–57	4,728	23	3,800	30
1960–65	5,645	25	3,975	23
1965–69	6,331	13	4,602	11
1970–73	10,502	14	6,611	9

[a] Fiscal years beginning July 1 through 1960–65; calendar years, 1965–73.
SOURCE: U.S. Department of Agriculture, Economic Research Service, *Foreign Agricultural Trade*, January 1963 and February 1974.

In the 1930s, cotton and tobacco comprised 60 percent of all agricultural exports, but in 1970–73 they made up only 11 percent. Tobacco was the principal export crop of colonial agriculture but fell below cotton in relative importance after the Civil War. Oilseeds, primarily soybeans, now comprise one-fourth of total agricultural exports, with feed grains and wheat and flour each contributing another one-sixth (Table 25-2). As a percentage of the value of farm sales, however, rice leads, with over 60 percent exported (Figure 25-1).

Agricultural exports have exceeded the value of agricultural imports since the mid-1950s. Complementary-product imports such as coffee, crude rubber, cocoa beans, bananas, carpet wool, tea, and spice make up 35–40 percent of total agricultural imports on a value basis. Coffee alone accounts for over half the complementary products' import value. Imports from Latin American countries account for the largest percentage of the total, followed by Asia, Europe, and Africa.

Since 1963, agriculture has been making a net contribution to the balance of payments (Figure 25-2). With the prospect of continuing higher prices for major exported items in conjunction with increased

TABLE 25-2
U.S. Exports: Percentage of Contribution to Total Agricultural Exports by Commodity Groups, Fiscal-Year Averages

	1955–59	1960–64	1965–69	1970–73
	(percent of total agricultural export value)			
Animals and products	16.0	12.7	11.2	10.8
Cotton, excl. linters	17.9	13.9	6.7	5.7
Wheat and flour	18.6	23.2	17.9	18.5
Feed grains[a]	9.8	12.9	16.7	16.9
Milled rice	2.8	3.0	4.7	3.6
Oilseeds[b]	11.4	13.7	19.8	25.8
Fruits and vegetables	9.0	8.1	7.7	6.4
Tobacco[c]	9.0	7.5	7.7	5.7
Other	5.5	5.0	7.6	6.6
Total	100.0	100.0	100.0	100.0

[a] Excluding products.
[b] Including products.
[c] Unmanufactured.

SOURCE: U.S. Department of Agriculture, Economic Research Service, *Foreign Agricultural Trade*, various issues.

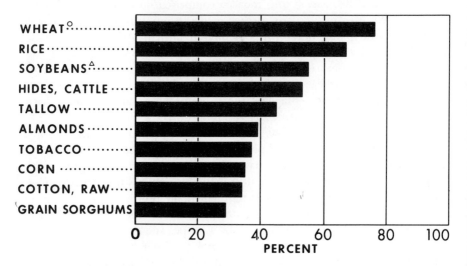

U.S. DEPARTMENT OF AGRICULTURE   NEG. ERS 5339 - 73 (8)   ECONOMIC RESEARCH SERVICE

FIGURE 25-1
Leading United States Exports as a Percentage of
Farm Sales, 1973

world demand, the dollar devaluation, and increased opportunities to
trade with communist countries, including China, it is expected that
agriculture will continue to make a net contribution to the balance
of payments throughout the 1970s.

IS FOREIGN TRADE POLICY A PROBLEM?

Commercial farmers have almost always enjoyed a liberal amount
of export-market sales. The United States was a debtor nation up to
World War I, but farm exports played an important role in helping to
pay our debts. During the 1920s, however, the shift of the United States
from a debtor to a creditor nation was not reflected in our trade policies.
At the same time that the decline in foreign demand for food received
the blame for depressed farm prices following World War I, tariffs were
continually increased. This action to restrict imports in the face of a

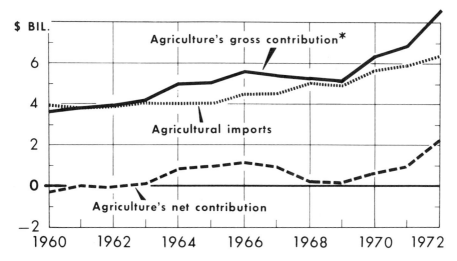

*SUM OF DOLLAR RETURNS FROM COMMERCIAL EXPORTS, DOLLAR REPAYMENTS ON CREDITS, AND LOCAL CURRENCIES (ACQUIRED FROM THE SALE OF FARM PRODUCTS UNDER GOVERNMENT PROGRAMS) USED BY U.S. AGENCIES ABROAD IN LIEU OF DOLLARS.

U.S. DEPARTMENT OF AGRICULTURE   NEG. ERS 5919-73 (8)   ECONOMIC RESEARCH SERVICE

FIGURE 25-2
Agriculture's Contribution to the U.S. Balance of
Payments, 1960–1972

continued need for exports of agricultural surpluses was a self-defeating trade policy. Foreign trade was hampered further during the depression years of the 1930s, when a wave of economic nationalism spurred efforts in many countries to increase self-sufficiency.

The scene shifted abruptly in the 1940s, when World War II created concern about possible food scarcities to meet the war efforts. Through the lend-lease program, the United States supplied friendly nations with a considerable volume of food and war materials without much concern over how payment was to be made. As a result, trade barriers lost much of their significance. Farmers responded quickly as prices increased, by speeding the shift to mechanization and adapting improved technology. When European agriculture recovered after World War II, the volume of farm exports fell, and the United States again found itself with surpluses of farm commodities. The Korean War interrupted this situation temporarily, but by 1952, stockpiles were again accumulating under the price-support-program incentives. Stocks were generally depleted during the late 1960s and were minimal in the early 1970s.

Exports Are Not Automatic

There are several misconceptions about foreign trade. One is that the foreign market is a bottomless pit, ready to gobble up anything and everything that we may want to throw into it. Much of this illusion was built up during the two world wars, when we exported considerable quantities of food to friendly allies. But these were artificial demands for food from the United States, in that they represented physiological needs rather than economic demand. They did not represent true purchasing power on the part of the importing countries, and so these foreign outlets evaporated quickly at the end of both wars.

A second misconception is that millions of people are starving in the world. Although it is true that some two-thirds of the world's people have less-than-adequate nutrition, most are not starving.

A third misconception is that if we cannot sell our food surpluses, we can give them away. Paradoxically, in some underdeveloped areas, selling food is actually easier and cheaper than giving it away. Although each country has some sort of distributive or marketing machinery through which food can flow, many of them lack distributive facilities and organizations through which donated food can be channeled to the needy. Food donations also have to be supervised carefully or other problems can arise. For example, it is often difficult to keep the food out of the black markets that exist in nearly all the countries of the world. Food donations on a short-term basis can cause serious problems if when they stop, the people receiving the food have geared their economic, social, and political decisions to be dependent on the donations. Feeding refugees may cause problems if, as a result, their diets are raised above those in the host country. These are just a few of the considerations that must be recognized. The problem of exporting food for commercial sale or of giving it away is more complex than meets the eye. Because the food needs are great in the world, the doors of export are not automatically swung wide open.

What About Imports?

Now let us turn to the other side of the trade coin and talk about imports. Trade is basically an exchange of goods and services. There is no international money as such, and if the United States is to export and get paid, payment must ultimately be in the form of imports of goods and services. The fact that trade is really an exchange of goods and services shows that a trade policy that holds a tight rein on imports by means of tariffs and other barriers also limits the ability of other countries to buy from us, and thus limits the amount of goods we can export. This is the inconsistency that was noted particularly in the foreign-trade policy of the United States during the 1920s. But what are the problems that imports bring to us?

Fear is an important obstacle to imports. Some countries look to the productivity of the American industrial giant and fear that they cannot compete successfully in our markets. And so they do not try. Americans also fear that bringing larger volumes of goods into this country at prices competitive with American goods will be harmful, and those who produce similar commodities here are vociferous about foreign competition. Cheaper labor abroad is often cited as the major factor that puts American producers at a competitive disadvantage. These charges are true to a certain extent. The law of comparative advantage does not dictate precise geographical areas where the most efficient production can take place. It also takes time for various regions to discover the items for which they have a clear comparative advantage in production.

But for the majority of products, the fear of low-wage competition is not well grounded. Look within the United States itself. Wage rates have consistently been much higher in the industrial areas of the Northeast than in the South. Yet the people in the North did not find that their incomes were lowered by trading with the South. The evidence actually indicates that trade was mutually beneficial. Those in the low-income areas have been able to upgrade their incomes and become better customers. In addition, there is evidence that the highest wages are paid not by protected industries, but by the efficient industry that operates free from trade barriers. Labor at a dollar a day may not be cheap labor. The real basis for comparison of labor costs should be the wage cost per unit of output, not wage rate per day or hour. However, if another country subsidizes exports in order to obtain dollars, this situation does present unfair competition for American producers. Countries discovering the products in which they have a comparative advantage will not need to resort to these tactics, which also tend to hurt international relations. We shall discover later that the United States has used this tactic.

Another argument for import restrictions is that they protect infant industries. Protecting a new industry from foreign competition until it becomes strong will enable it to become stronger faster, and this is desirable for the industry concerned. Often, however, protection is continued because the industry lobbyists maintain that vested interests will be severely harmed if the trade tariff is removed.

Many people argue that the United States should be self-sufficient, in order to lessen the intensity of problems in times of war or other national emergencies. These people feel that import restrictions would encourage diversification of enterprises and thus contribute to self-sufficiency. This is a valid contention, especially with regard to certain strategic materials. But the long-run result of this action could be a more inefficient use of our resources, leading to a lower standard of living for us and for the countries with which we might trade. In addition, as the chapter on natural resources pointed out, the United States is virtually wholly dependent on other countries for such raw materials as tin. Although economic policy might tell us that free trade is good for us, domestic political considerations and international relations between noncommunist and certain communist countries may well tell us not to trade.

In order to assure any success from farm price-support programs, it is necessary to put import restrictions on the commodities under the program. If this were not done, the commodity would flow into the United States, seeking the artificially high prices. This would further complicate the problem of surpluses. A vivid illustration was the necessity to restrict potato imports from Canada under the potato price-support program several years ago in order to protect the government and citizens from even greater losses than were incurred. These are some of the arguments favoring restrictions on the importation of goods from foreign countries.

Objectives of Trade Policy

The objectives of trade policy and the uses to which it may be put might be listed as follows:

1. To increase the economic strength and well-being of the American people
2. To foster international relations that will enhance our opportunity to remain a free and independent nation
3. To aid underprivileged people for humanitarian reasons

WHAT ARE THE ALTERNATIVES?

Self-Sufficiency

One alternative is to become completely self-sufficient and shun participation in foreign trade. This would certainly be an extreme policy; no country and very few politicians would advocate such a position. In fact, for most countries, self-sufficiency is not a real alternative. Even the Iron and Bamboo Curtains permit trade penetrations. Complete self-sufficiency would eventually bring a lower standard of living for the people. In order to produce some of the products for which the country was not adapted, a high cost of production and a correspondingly inefficient use of resources would be required. National resources would tend to be depleted at a faster rate, and if the country was lacking strategic materials necessary to produce military goods to protect itself, it would be an easy target for an aggressor.

Complete Free-Trade Policy

At the other extreme, a country choosing to adopt a completely free-trade policy would eliminate all import quotas, exchange controls, and tariffs. But even such countries as England and the Netherlands, which once maintained a nearly free-trade policy, now impose tariffs and import controls on many products. A completely free-trade policy would generate severe competition for markets if all countries adopted it. And for one country to pursue such a policy while others did not would put a severe strain on certain sectors of the country's economy.

Middle-of-the-Road Policy

Between the two policy extremes just discussed, trade policies could emphasize various degrees of self-sufficiency or free trade. Robinson has outlined two of these intermediate policies, one of which he labels "protection" and the other "modified free trade."[5]

Protection. By "protection" is meant a trade policy that would maintain relatively high tariffs and import controls on selected commodities competing directly with commodities produced in the home country. A lower tariff with little or no control would be imposed on items not competing with home producers. Protection measures increase the share of a nation's resources devoted to producing the protected commodity. Protection, then, is an effort to increase the output level of an industry by restricting the trading opportunities that exist by guarding against competition from more efficient producers in other countries.

Tariffs are the most common form of trade barrier to keep goods from being imported into the country to compete with home producers. A *tariff* is a form of tax, similar in nature to a sales tax, which an im-

---

[5] Kenneth L. Robinson, "Alternative Trade Policies," in *Increasing Understanding of Public Problems and Policies* (Chicago: Farm Foundation, 1952), p. 36.

porter must pay in order to bring foreign-produced goods into the United States. A tariff may be a fixed amount on a particular item, such as 50 cents a bushel or pound; such a tariff is often referred to as a "specific customs duty." Another kind of tariff, based on a percentage of the value or price of the item, is referred to as an "ad valorem customs duty."

An import *quota* is even more of a restrictive barrier than is a tariff. Quotas limit imports to specific quantities. If the quota is zero, it is in effect an embargo. It means that none of the items may be imported into this country. An embargo is sometimes used to protect against the importation of plant and animal diseases. The *import license* by a government is another device to restrict trading. This device requires an importer to acquire a license before he can bring goods into the country.

Also, our federal government is prohibited by law from buying foreign materials, or commodities manufactured from foreign materials, unless these materials are not available in the United States or unless the prices of corresponding domestic items are priced unreasonably— meaning considerably more expensive (perhaps 25 percent). These are all examples of means that can be used to afford a high degree of protection if this is the wish of those making trade policy.

For the past century, and particularly up to 1934, the United States followed basically a trade policy of protection. Following World War I, protectionist sentiment was particularly strong in Congress, and tariff increases were passed in 1922 and again in 1930. The high point in import restrictions was reached in 1930, when Congress passed the Smoot-Hawley Tariff Act, calling for very high tariffs on many products.

Since 1934, our high-tariff policy has been essentially reversed, but other kinds of barriers have been introduced. Quantitative restrictions and licensing requirements have been imposed on a number of agricultural commodities in recent years. Tariff quotas have been applied to such products as cattle, butter, potatoes, sugar, and wheat. Import-licensing provisions have been used to restrict imports of fats and oils, rice, and peanuts. And with the passage of farm price-support legislation in the 1930s and 1940s, the federal government is authorized to impose restrictions on the entry of practically any product whenever import quantities tend to interfere with farm price-support operations.

What are the consequences of a protectionist trade policy? An almost immediate result of a high tariff wall is retaliation by other countries, by restricting U.S. exports to their countries. (Following the Smoot-Hawley Tariff Act in 1930, some 25 countries retaliated within less than two years.) This makes it difficult for the United States to sell its typewriters, fountain pens, electrical appliances, wheat, corn, rice, and many other products that are highly dependent on export sales. A loss of foreign demand would mean price-depressing surpluses of tobacco, wheat, and cotton, and consequently an increase in the level of unemployment in the United States.

A reduction in the volume of imports would have very serious effects on the economies of countries such as Canada, England, Brazil, and Germany, which need foreign trade in order to stay strong economically. Since these countries are our allies, a highly protectionist policy would tend to weaken them. This, then, might necessitate additional foreign aid from us if we felt it was desirable to keep them strong in order to repel the inroads of communism.

Although an increase in tariffs would certainly benefit certain types of domestic producers—wool and sugar are two good examples—these benefits would come at the expense of consumers, who would have to pay higher prices for the protected products. And we might just have to do without such products as fine woolens, china, and pottery.

A highly protectionist policy keeps the law of comparative advantage from working, and as a result, countries are forced to forego the economic growth and prosperity that could otherwise be achieved by efficient use of resources in their most profitable production. This means a reduction in the amount of goods available. It also means higher prices and a lower standard of living.

Modified free trade. Modified free trade involves a policy by which tariffs are low, little import licensing exists, and few if any market quotas are applied. Such a trade policy would most certainly increase the amount of foreign-made goods that would come into the United States. This would tend to increase the number of dollars that foreign countries would have with which to buy American goods. With extra dollars, they could purchase more of our goods. A freer trade policy would mean that the law of comparative advantage would be able to work more effectively on an international basis, tending to make better use of the world's resources. Each country would be compelled to discover those products in which it had a comparative advantage. To the extent that a freer trade policy would increase the strength of our allies, it could reduce the burden of our foreign-aid program.

Certainly free trade would make the going difficult for some American firms. Whether these firms would be forced out of business completely would depend on their ability to adjust to the new situation. Shifting their production to a new line of products is one possibility. Government training and retraining programs help the workers put out of jobs by foreign competition to make an employment adjustment to other firms. In terms of the effect of a free-trade policy on agriculture,

Gale Johnson concluded that it would have little or no net direct influence on the number of job opportunities in farming. It was his judgment that the job losses in sugar, wool, sheep (strongly protected products), and beef, butter, cheese, fats, and oils (mildly protected commodities), would be about offset by proportionate gains in cotton, tobacco, corn, and hogs.[6] Johnson is quick to point out, however, that the many variables in the situation make it extremely difficult to assess the impact of a freer trade policy.

A LOOK AT THE AGRICULTURAL TRADE PROGRAMS OF THE UNITED STATES

Reciprocal Trade Agreements

The first move to implement a freer international-trade policy following the high degree of protectionism of the 1920s was the passage of the Trade Agreements Act of 1934. By this act, the United States pledged its efforts to work for a basic policy of freer trade between nations. The act gave the President the power to negotiate tariff reductions commodity by commodity, down to 50 percent of 1934 levels. In 1945, another 50 percent reduction was authorized for rates, effective January 1, 1945. As a result, total duties collected as a percentage of imports fell from 24.4 percent in 1934 to 12.2 percent by 1953.

A clause in the Reciprocal Trade Agreements legislation, known as the "peril-point concept," prevented trade commitments that would be seriously injurious to domestic industries. Under this provision, the industry involved had the right to be heard by the Tariff Commission and the commission had to turn its findings over to the President before he could act to reduce tariffs, and then not below the "peril point." In addition, the "most-favored-nation" principle was embodied. This means that a tariff reduction in a trade agreement with one country will be extended to all other friendly countries.

Prior to World War II, all trade agreements were primarily between two countries—bilateral in nature. *Bilateral* means one country negotiating with one other country, as contrasted to *multilateral,* meaning negotiation among several countries. After extensive negotiations in 1947, 21 major trading countries provisionally adopted a General Agreement on Tariffs and Trade (GATT). By 1962, 39 countries were participating in GATT. These countries had a combined trade accounting

---

[6] D. Gale Johnson, *Trade and Agriculture* (New York: John Wiley & Sons, Inc., 1950), p. 52.

for 80 percent of the world total. All the participating countries espoused the most-favored-nation principle, and tariff schedules on some 60,000 items had been negotiated. In effect, agreements made by GATT are multilateral in nature—a less time-consuming and more efficient way to negotiate trade agreements than by bilateral means. GATT now serves as the mechanism by which the United States implements the majority of its trade policies regarding the level of tariffs.

Trade Expansion Act of 1962

The Trade Expansion Act of 1962 espouses a liberal trade policy similar to the Reciprocal Trade Agreements Act of 1934. It provides general authority to reduce existing tariffs by 50 percent and to negotiate with the Common Market to reduce still further or eliminate tariffs on those categories of products for which the United States and the Common Market together account for 80 percent of world trade. (The Common Market, more formally the European Economic Community, includes Great Britain, Ireland, Denmark, Germany, France, Italy, the Netherlands, Belgium, and Luxembourg.) It provides for tariff reductions by categories, rather than the item-by-item approach that was mandatory under former legislation. Where existing rates are 5 percent or less, the new act would permit those products to move to the free list (zero tariffs). Provided that the Common Market takes similar action, the act also permits the elimination of duties on tropical products not produced in significant quantities in the United States. This would tend to help countries in Latin America, Africa, and Asia.

Food-For-Peace Programs

One of the objectives of our foreign-trade policy is to safeguard and strengthen the community of trading nations in the West, to provide a strong bulwark against the threat of communism. With the ability of the American farmer to produce food in amounts greater than our domestic needs plus what can be sold in world markets, the question of using food to fight against communism in some way is logically raised. The question seems particularly appropriate in the light of the fact that two-thirds of the world's people are malnourished. The motivation for helping underdeveloped countries is partly humanitarian in origin, partly for defense against communism, and partly economic. We hope that once the less-developed nations get on their feet, they will be able to purchase some of our products, which will strengthen our economy. What role can food products play, or what role should they play, in this assistance?

The elements of economic development and the process of growth have already been discussed in detail. In the case of capital, let us see how food might serve to increase the rate of capital formation in a less-developed country.

To the extent that people who are undernourished are not able to do physical work, food donations could increase the adequacy of their diet and give them the physical strength to engage in road building and other projects. To the extent that people who are undernourished are necessarily preoccupied with getting enough food to eat, food donations could relieve their worry and allow them to use their minds in formal programs of education. It is difficult to be interested in studying agriculture, history, or chemistry in school when you are hungry. To the extent that donated food would increase the health of the populace, it would again aid in increasing the returns from their work efforts. These are a few possibilities; but let us not forget Malthus. In some areas of the world, it appears that his theory is still correct: Following an increase in the means of subsistence will be an increase in the death rate from starvation. So a country that starts to donate food is compelled to continue until the people have the ability to maintain themselves, which may be a long time. The logical conclusion would seem to be, however, that food can play a role in the development of human and physical capital in a less-developed country and could certainly supplement other forms of technical assistance. For the relatively wealthy 20 percent of the world's people to carry a subsistence program that maintains a minimal consumption level for the other 80 percent would seem to be an impossible task. As a result, subsistence aid has been used only to supplement other developmental aid aimed at increasing a country's ability to increase its own productivity.

Public Law 480.   Passed initially in 1954 as a surplus-disposal program, Public Law 480 is by far the most important piece of legislation currently dealing with federal programs of food disposal. The "Food-for-Peace" program developed out of Public Law 480. Originally, it was designed to dispose of short-term food surpluses, but by 1959 it had been given a much broader framework.

The major activity falls under Title I of the act, which permits the sale of food products for local currencies. For example, India can buy wheat and cotton and pay for them in rupees rather than in dollars. Since the rupees cannot be used in the United States, they are left in India to be used for various purposes. Some are used to pay the costs of our government expenses in that country, such as the maintainance of our foreign embassy. Some are lent back to the government (India), which uses them for economic development projects. Other uses include lending the money to private U.S. firms in the recipient country to produce products for that country or to finance exhibits and trade fairs designed to promote farm products of the United States. Any money remaining is merely retained in the United States' "rupee checking account," available for future claims. Thus, to a large extent, sales made under Title I can be viewed largely as donations. Such sales were discontinued at the end of 1971.

Title II and Title III of P.L. 480 provide for donations, either direct to governments for local distribution or to voluntary agencies (church groups, CARE, or U.N. children's fund), for distribution to needy people in schools or orphanages, or through food packages. Title II has been used primarily to provide food to foreign countries faced with famine arising from natural disasters, such as earthquakes and floods, and for use in feeding schoolchildren, refugees, and other groups. This program is principally motivated by humanitarian values and is not intended to be a major contributor to the country's development. In 1972–73, Title II exports were $379 million.

Barter exports fell under Title III. These exports involved the exchange of surplus U.S. farm commodities for strategic or other materials needed by the U.S. government, or for materials that could be used in U.S. foreign aid programs. Wheat, cotton, and feed grains were the major commodities exported for barter. In the fiscal years 1949 through 1961, surpluses exported under barter contracts totaled $1.4 billion in value. Barter exports were discontinued in the late 1960s.

Title IV of P.L. 480, approved in 1959, provides for the use of surplus farm commodities in assisting economic development in friendly nations. Commodities may be delivered over periods of up to ten years. The credit period may extend up to twenty years; principal and interest are repayable in dollars. These exports, comprising about half of government-assisted exports, were $521 million in 1971.

In summary, parts of P.L. 480 exports are little different from commercial sales, where dollars are earned with which goods and services can be purchased. A large part, however, comprises donations or what amounts to the same thing. It is often difficult to tell whether exports are under subsistence aid or developmental aid. Much depends on how the products are used in the recipient country and on how the country in turn uses the loan that can result from the sales.

Private Trade Activities

An increasing awareness of the importance of foreign markets to American agriculture has prompted private trade and agricultural groups to direct more attention and resources to maintaining and developing these markets. The interest is reflected in better regulation of export-commodity quality control, salesmanship, catering to foreign-market preferences, market surveys and analyses, and improved public relations with foreign trade and agricultural groups. Trade associations representing nearly every agricultural commodity have participated, and their efforts have been closely coordinated with those of the federal government. For example, under international trade-fair activities, the Foreign Agricultural Service organizes and manages exhibits, provides space, furnishes supplies and equipment, and pays travel and administrative costs. Private-industry groups participate by supplying exhibit ideas and materials and technical personnel to man exhibits, and carrying out other promotional activities in connection with the displays. This is just one of several programs in which government and private industry work together to promote food sales abroad.

Conflict between Price–Income Legislation and Trade Policy

The effect of price-support legislation is to raise domestic prices above the going world prices. Therefore, if American exporters had to buy commodities at the artificially high domestic prices, they would be at a severe disadvantage in competing for sales in world markets. As a result, it has been the general policy of the United States to use export subsidies to maintain exports of agricultural products when the domestic market prices are above world prices. Export subsidies are the payments made to exporters to compensate for the difference between the two prices.

In 1971–72, payments totaled $237 million, but they will fall substantially for the 1970s, given the favorable outlook. For example, $75 million was paid to wheat exporters in 1971–72, but payments were completely suspended in September 1972 as a result of the higher world price.

This procedure may seem harmless and easy to administer, but it creates several problems. For example, on a commodity like wheat, of which the United States contributes a significant amount to total world trade, the world price eventually becomes heavily dependent on the export-subsidy rate. This leads Canada and other wheat-exporting countries to the view that the U.S. policy of export subsidies makes for unfair competition, since the international market price is not the one at which the wheat producer is willing to sell. In this situation, it would be possible for wheat to be sold at less than its cost of production.

Cotton is another example. To make our price-support program work and still sell cotton in international markets, export subsidies were paid on both cotton in raw form and finished cotton goods. The result was that foreign mills could buy raw cotton, process it, and ship it back to the United States at prices well below those incurred by domestic cotton processors. In the case of cotton, not only did we experience animosity from other countries exporting raw cotton by depressing the world price, but we put our own processors at a severe disadvantage. It is clear that many complications can arise when a workable foreign-trade policy is sought. The principal difficulty for the United States in recent years has been the extreme complexity in trying to move toward a freer trade policy and maintain domestic price-support programs at the same time. These two policy programs are simply of a contradictory nature.

Many countries face the same dilemma. Any government program that involves the stabilization and maintenance of domestic farm prices to aid home producers will result in a difference between domestic and world prices for the commodity involved. A major exception has been in England, where farmer income was supported by direct subsidies and domestic prices were kept at world prices. The inconsistency between agricultural price and income policy and international policy also disrupts the economic law of comparative advantage and thus reduces the efficiency by which resources are put to use in the world.

Are International Commodity Agreements a Possibility?

The main objective of international commodity agreements is to provide an orderly marketing method through which patterns of production and trade can best be adjusted to the requirements of world demand over time. If prices are to be stabilized, reasonable terms of trade secured, and world production and consumption brought into balance, commodity agreements need to include provisions for coordination with the national policies of the countries concerned.

Since the end of World War II, international agreements have been concluded for wheat, sugar, coffee, tin, and olive oil. Most have been plagued with difficulties, and only the wheat and tin agreements had operative provisions between exporting and importing nations that had much impact on world trade.

To the extent that prices negotiated under international commodity agreements are higher than what the "true" level of a free world price would be, the agreement gives rise to problems similar to those that price-support legislation creates. In order to maintain prices above levels that would clear world markets, someone must take the job of handling surplus accumulation or supervise a production-control program. Therefore, to be successful, it would seem that an international agreement should be set up so that it would not allow prices to rise above the prevailing market and that some agreement be reached in allocating reasonable market shares and production rights to countries.

A second type of commodity agreement consists of the institution of an *international buffer stock* to stabilize price through obligations to buy whenever the world price falls below a certain minimum and to sell when the price rises above a certain maximum. This plan was attempted under the International Tin Agreement, but has not been very successful. A third type of agreement is the *export restriction agreement,* which provides for limitation of exports insofar as is necessary to secure some degree of price stability. Clearly, this could be successful only if nearly all the exporting countries could be brought into the agreement. It was originally incorporated in the International Sugar Act of 1953, which was reasonably successful for three years before the Suez crisis. With further difficulties caused by the trade disruptions by the more recent United States–Cuba situation and the inability of participating governments to agree on the distribution of quotas, the agreement became inoperative in January 1962.

REGIONAL TRADE GROUPS

The rise of various trade groups throughout the world since the late 1950s has complicated our agricultural-export transactions. Today, most of our best customers belong to such regional economic groups.

Of the trade groups, the European Economic Community (EEC)—the Common Market—is the most important to the United States. The original member countries were Belgium, France, West Germany, Italy, Luxembourg, and the Netherlands. For years, this group of countries has been a major market for U.S. agricultural exports. It took about 23 percent of U.S. commercial sales for dollars in 1970–71, and we in turn got about 6 percent of our agricultural imports from the Common Market countries. In fiscal 1971, our favorable agricultural trade balance with the EEC was $1.3 billion.

The EEC was established by the Treaty of Rome, which became effective on January 1, 1958. This treaty provided for full economic unity of member countries by July 1, 1968. Through the elimination of internal trade barriers and the establishment of a single external tariff, other countries are finding it harder to sell to EEC countries.

Agricultural exporters to the EEC will doubtless find their difficulties increasing as the EEC takes more rigorous measures to support and protect its members' agriculture. Variable levies protect the EEC farmer from much import price competition. They are, in effect, simply the difference between the domestic price and that at which the exporter offers his product when it comes into the country. The exporter lowers his price; the levy rises. In addition, proceeds from the levies are used to subsidize exports, thus creating increased competition in third-country markets. In 1969, the EEC had agricultural exports equal to about 3 billion U.S. dollars. To reach that total, the EEC spent about $1 billion in export subsidies.

Preferential trading arrangements that the EEC is making one at a time with other countries are also potentially troublesome to U.S. agricultural-product exporters. EEC countries now trade preferentially with associate members Greece and Turkey and with a number of African countries.

Great Britain, Ireland, and Denmark are relatively new members of the EEC. Norway voted to remain independent. In Great Britain's case, the protective levels of tariffs and price support are generally lower than those of the EEC. Therefore, looking ahead in the 1970s, the United States must bargain in between these two levels.

Many other trade groups have been formed throughout the world since the EEC was established. The three with which the United States does the most business are the European Free Trade Association (United Kingdom, Denmark, Switzerland, Sweden, Norway, Austria, and Portugal); the Latin American Free Trade Association (Mexico, Colombia, Ecuador, Peru, Chile, Brazil, Paraguay, Uruguay, Argentina, Bolivia, and Venezuela); and the Central American Common Market (Guatemala, El Salvador, Honduras, Nicaragua, and Costa Rica).

SUMMARY

The basic trend of policy in our trade relations for the last three decades has been to work toward a free and open world-trading system. The Reciprocal Trade Agreements Act, the General Agreement on Tariffs and Trade (GATT), and the Trade Expansion Act of 1962 have been the main instruments of this trade policy.

The Reciprocal Trade Agreements Act provided for reductions in tariffs or other trade barriers. A major principle of the legislation was the "most-favored-nation" clause, which provided that any reduction of a tariff by the United States for one nation would be accorded to all other friendly nations.

GATT is essentially a "fair-play" code of conduct in international trade. The basic premise is that we give countries access to our market in exchange for our exporters' right to sell in their markets, or vice versa.

The Trade Expansion Act provided the authority to negotiate

the reduction of tariffs and other trade barriers, and to deal with increased competition from imports.

The domestic economic situation in 1971 caused a move away from the free-trade policy goal by putting a temporary 10 percent surcharge tax on all imports. Although it was justified on short-run economic grounds, it is difficult to forecast the amount of retaliation this move will cause among the nations from which we buy farm products.

Our challenges in trade policy lie in three major directions:

Our commercial relations with developed nations of the world, including trade blocs

Our policies concerning trade problems of the less-developed countries of the free world

Our trade policies with Eastern Europe, the USSR, China, and other communist countries

Developed Nations

To continue to expand trade in the world's commercial markets, we must gear our production and marketing to meet the specifications of foreign customers. Our export-sales efforts might include improvement in credit arrangements, claims adjustment, warehousing in foreign countries, specification selling, advertising, product promotion, exclusive handling arrangements, servicing merchandisers, and other strategies.

Less-Developed Countries

The economic condition of people in less-developed free-world countries is one of the great problems and opportunities of our time. Their progress is important to the United States and other developed countries not only for humanitarian and political reasons, but also because their rapid economic growth would improve the prosperity of the world as a whole. Policies toward less-developed countries include economic aid, technical assistance, and the development of commercial trade.

East-West Trade

Emotions run high on the controversial topic of East-West trade. It should be clear what kind of trade and what countries might be under consideration. All trade with North Korea and North Vietnam is currently prohibited. Trade with the countries of Eastern Europe, including the USSR, is limited to peaceful or nonstrategic goods. Trade in strategic items and items of military significance would continue to be prohibited under this alternative.

Trade between the United States and Eastern Europe has been erratic from year to year and appears to be on the rise in the 1970s. The main farm products exported to these nations have been corn, cotton, wheat, soybean meal, sorghum, tobacco, and hides and skins. Agricultural imports were primarily from Poland and Yugoslavia, and the main products were pork and tobacco. Trade with China has begun again in a small way. Clearly, the 1970s will continue to be vital years with regard to U.S. agricultural exports.

26

Persisting Problems
in Agriculture

Throughout the history of agriculture and the sector's continual adjustment to economic, social, institutional, and political pressures, one can find a series of persisting questions. Certain issues keep reappearing, and each new generation must find its own answers to them. It is particularly noteworthy that although these questions involve essentially the same basic issues through time, the answers offered by the policy makers at each stage may change radically. For example, answers to the question, "How should agriculture best be encouraged to contribute to a growing economy?" range from a policy of free prices with no production controls or price supports to a fully planned economy in which agriculture is integrated into a broad scheme of centralized social and economic planning.

Solutions to persisting questions may last for a few years or many years, depending upon the pressures to which they are subjected, including the changing values of the people involved. Some of these continuing questions are discussed below. No attempt has been made to rank the questions; each group of analysts must establish its own priorities.

EXPANDING TECHNOLOGY AND THE
FAMILY FARM

For generations, the family farm has been the epitome of individual proprietorship operating as a small business in our private-enterprise economy. There is constant concern that the family farm will be gobbled up by the huge corporations prevalent in the modern-day business world. We have seen that the average size of the commercial family farm is growing, as the substitution of capital for labor and the adoption of new biological and managerial technologies allow one farm operator and his family to handle more resources (Chapter 7). We have also noted that more than half the land farmed is cultivated by part-owners rather than full owners. What will changing technology and capital requirements call forth in the future?

The question of how expanding technology influences the organization of the farm business has been a particularly pertinent and important one for the last 200 years. Will it eventually eliminate the family farm? Will the size of the economic unit in farm production grow indefinitely, outstripping the financial resources that most families can muster or manage? Will it mean a change in the transfer of ownership from one generation to another? Will it mean that the farm will be operated with a large percentage of hired labor, and will all farm labor be unionized?

Indigenous to the sociopolitical mind of the typical family-farm operator of colonial times was the idea that proprietors deserve the right to make all the decisions with regard to the procedures for operating their business enterprises, and that the individual manager and his family alone are responsible for the economic security of the entire household. In colonial times, any government intervention was deemed undesirable, as it would tend to impinge on the freedom and responsibility of the family as a producing unit. Individual thrift and industry took the form of accumulating land and capital and called for extraordinary effort in many cases. To come to old age without having sufficient security was considered a reflection of a misspent life and habitual distaste for the work ethic.

Expanding technology has necessitated a reshuffling and rethinking of the ethics once held dear in the concept of the family farm. Even in the mid-twentieth century, the farm business unit could usually operate economically with one man and his family providing both the labor and the management. The farming industry, which is now capable of using all kinds of machines, results in recombining the managerial and labor inputs in many ways. As farm boys left the farms, became the captains of industry (McCormicks, Deerings, Armours, etc.), and helped reshape older rural value judgments, sociopolitical attitudes were modified. By the mid-twentieth century, with farmers eligible under Social Security and with burdensome surpluses at hand, opinions that farming was first a way of life and second a business have been reversed in the minds of many farm operators, particularly those with college training. The great American dream may still be underlaid with the spirit of the work ethic, but with great advances in technology, the sentiment of maintaining small, inefficient farm units gives way to the institution that will perform with superior efficiency in carrying out its functions of feeding the nation. This institution may or may not continue to be the family farm, particularly since the definition of a family farm is so nebulous. Farms managed by families and supplying their own labor range from a few acres to many thousand acres, from intensive operations to extensive operations, and with many variations in resource-use needs. The term is more viable as a political concept than as an economic reality. Perhaps the sacred family-farm cow will die an evolutionary death.

A study by the Agriculture Department's Economic Research Service on the extent to which corporation farming has made inroads into family farming was reported in 1969. It indicated that about two-thirds of the existing corporate farms were still family operations. However, it also showed a concentration of production and resource control on corporate farms: This group numbered only about one-half of 1 percent of all commercial farms, but it accounted for 8–10 percent of total farm output and 4–5 percent of the nation's land farmed.

Will advances in technology expand the economic size of a farm unit beyond the ability of a family to supply the majority of the labor and management?

Much of the answer to the question depends on whether future technology is labor-saving or capital-saving. To date, most of it has been labor-saving, in the form of new machines and equipment. If the farmer is able to utilize seasonal labor in peak periods of need, and if farm operations continue to become more routinized as they are in some kinds of production, such as eggs and broilers, the farm operator and his family will be able to handle the work load and still operate an efficient economic unit for some time. The trend for market-agencies closer to the consumer, such as the processor, to deal directly with the farm producer will also aid the situation, as the farmer can get more help in moving the product off his farm, and the scheduling of marketing can be arranged in advance.

Will the advance in technology expand farm investment beyond the ability of the farm family to acquire enough capital to give them major control of the business?

The fact that capital needs are continually increasing per farm and per farm worker does not necessarily mean that a farm family cannot continue to operate and control larger and larger units. The proportion of total farms operated by full owners (owners who farm only the land they own) was 50.5 percent in 1940, 57.1 percent in 1950, and 62.5 percent in 1969. These data offer no evidence that family farms are declining in relative importance.

The share of managers using part-ownership as a means to enlarge farm units without increasing their land-capital requirements is increasing. In 1940, only 10 percent of the farms were owned by part-owners, but by 1969 this changed to almost 25 percent. A part-owner is defined as one who farms his own land and rents additional land from others. This increase came at the expense of tenant-operated farms, which decreased from 39 to less than 13 percent of the total in the same period. Thus, renting instead of buying additional land is a real alternative for farmers with limited finances. Any money available may be better spent in the purchase of machinery and equipment, livestock, or other items.

Many people support the view that the future of the family farm is not threatened by the expanding farm-size requirements of the most complete mechanization conceivable. They point to the high degree of mechanization and specialization found on the wheat farms of the Great Plains, and suggest that no economies of scale are achieved through expanding such farms beyond the point where a family can do most of the work. Larger-than-family farms are least frequent in types of farming such as cash grain, where operations are highly mechanized, and they are most frequent in types such as vegetable production, where operations are least mechanized.

Is technological advance in the agribusiness sector of agriculture likely to change the marketing, which would spell doom for the family farm?

The increasing importance of the food-marketing system, in which a blend of production, processing, and marketing efforts are required to bring cheap, high-quality food to consumers, has been discussed (Chapter 9). For some products—eggs, perhaps broilers, and some fresh vegetables—market channels from farm to retail store are becoming shorter. However, for most products, market channels are becoming more complex. Integration, with its accompanying nonresident management features, plus the impersonal selling techniques employed by supermarkets and shopping centers are inevitably pushing the food producer farther and farther away from the consumer. Increased amounts of food processing, handling, and packaging support this widening gap by identifying farm food products more with raw materials in a production line than directly consumable food items. Although these processes lead to greater marketing efficiencies, they also add to the loss of identity of an individual farm unit.

What of technology and the organization of agriculture in a maturing economy?

During 1973–74, we finally understood that our nation had shifted from being a raw-materials-surplus nation to one deficit in certain strategic resources. The Arab-bloc countries, by limiting their exports of oil and also raising the price of crude, showed the world how dependent we had become on their energy sources. Not only were many farmers caught in a higher-level cost–price squeeze, but some small operations found access limited to fertilizer and other materials, such as repair parts. Even though farm-level prices hit new highs, so did the prices of many of their inputs. Large operations were often given priority on customer lists over small operations as the shortages derived from resource scarcities hit the nation.

With a relative slowing down of the economy added to the shortages of input resources, many farmers found that they also had inflation to fight. On the bright side for farmers was the fact that overseas markets were increasingly attractive. The successive dollar devaluations had made our farm production more easily accessible to consumers and firms abroad. A new perspective began to emerge in many firms, related to the technology of market organization: how to better organize for sales in both high domestic and foreign markets.

BARGAINING POWER IN AGRICULTURE

If the feed supplier or the processor makes the management decisions, the farmer becomes a hired employee doing largely routine tasks in a factory-type operation. To the extent that integration of producing and marketing agencies yields organizational economies, the family farm will tend to be eliminated. If the farmer is in a position where he does not have to bargain away his managerial prerogatives, fear of losing the family farm is lessened. This leads us to another problem area, that of bargaining power in agriculture.

The economic issue underlying the question of bargaining power is how the total income of agriculture will be divided among the owners of the factors of production and those in the food system—between the producer and the ultimate consumer. Each individual and business firm, or group of individuals or firms, is interested in increasing its share, and increasing its share of bargaining power in the market is one move toward this goal. In Chapters 13 and 15, we noted the difficulty that an individual farm producer experiences when approaching the market. In most cases, the individual producer has no influence on market price. As a consequence, the best he can do is to stay informed so no one can take advantage of his lack of knowledge about what the market price is.

Over the years, a principal weapon of the farmer to improve his bargaining power was the cooperative, a legal business entity whereby a group of individuals could collectively pool their efforts to bargain more effectively. Purchasing cooperatives are designed to pool purchasing power so that items can be purchased at lower cost. Marketing cooperatives attempt to increase the returns to the individual members by enabling them to bargain more effectively in selling a commodity. Service cooperatives attempt to increase the individual's return by providing services that would not be available if only one party were involved, and by improving existing services. Bargaining cooperatives are designed specifically to improve the price at which a commodity can be sold to the next market agency; dairy bargaining cooperatives are a good example. Organized efforts through trade associations are another example of collective action to improve bargaining power.

Improved bargaining power may be achieved in several ways. One is to favorably influence the terms of trade in day-to-day operations. This would require that the individual or group improve its ability to operate as a buyer and/or seller in the market. The first requisite would be to stay completely informed on market conditions. Another would be that the buyer and/or seller would also be a technical specialist with regard to the commodity involved, so that the correct quality of the product could be judged and proper mechandising methods could be employed. These approaches articulate most of the collective-bargaining concepts developed by nonfarm labor unions and management.

The most frequently mentioned mechanism for improving bargaining power is to withhold supplies from the market. For perishable agricultural commodities, this procedure is difficult both for an individual and for a group. Although limited "test" livestock-withholding actions by the National Farmers Organization (NFO) in the early 1960s were unsuccessful for several reasons, the milk holding action of 1967 was more organized and effective. The milk action held large amounts of milk off the market for about two weeks, during which time the production and prices of manufactured dairy products were more affected than those of fluid milk. Similar actions have been tried through early 1973.

Some groups, such as the cranberry and walnut growers, may simply reduce the quantity of the product put on the market and enhance the price enough so that greater total returns are realized through price increases. To do this requires the allocation of market shares among the producers of the group, which is by no means an easy task. This method is restricted to products for which the market demand price is inelastic and where production is geographically localized so that effective control can be exercised over a major portion of the crop. It may also be effective for commodities such as fluid milk; transport of milk over long distances is costly, the boundaries of milk markets are defined, and federal and state milk-marketing orders have exerted an attitudinal and operational influence. Market orders, which were discussed in Chapter 9, are partially of this nature. The difference is that market orders stipulate conditions as to how the quantity produced will move through market channels in an orderly fashion. The objective is more one of stabilizing commodity prices and resulting incomes, rather than of actually restricting production so as to increase price by reducing the total quantity on the market.

Another means of obtaining more market power has been called the "expanded" view. This includes the manipulation of other variables in the market, such as product development, grades, and quality standards, market information, market area and composition, technology, and government regulations that affect the trading environment. Any influence exerted on these variables would probably require group action of some kind. Expanded activity by trade associations appears to be a good possibility. The larger agribusiness firms are able to carry on their own research and development in the area of product technology.

Product differentiation is another monopoly element that affords a chance to improve bargaining power. The individual farm producer is virtually helpless in differentiating his product, except as he attempts to produce for a highly specialized quality market. Research and development programs are necessary to get new products, and although the agricultural experiment stations carry on some product technology research, the majority is done by the large agribusiness firms.

There are three possible sources of gains from activities that are generally associated with bargaining efforts: (1) through greater efficiency or increased productivity in purchasing and marketing activities; (2) from an outside group, such as consumers, from other marketing agencies, or from society in general; and (3) from the opponent in the bargaining transaction. Thus, collective bargaining can create wealth for farmers from: (1) capturing excess profits of processing and distribution firms, (2) forcing elimination of waste in parts of the input–output marketing system, (3) contributing marketing services, and (4) extracting monopoly profits indirectly from consumers through higher retail food prices or some other means. The last source certainly offers the greatest hope of monetary gains for farmers.[1]

Gains from greater efficiencies may yield a mutual benefit to both buyer and seller. Any individual or group effort to improve product quality, develop better grades and standards, facilitate more rapid movement of the product, or develop a mutually beneficial contractual agreement can result in gains to both parties. However, gains in efficiency may not necessarily spread to both buyer and seller if through market imperfections the gain can be held for some time by one party.

Gains from government may come through lobbyists who influence legislators to vote for changes that will improve the trading environment. Gains from consumers may come from effective sales promotion and advertising or from multiple pricing. Gains from these sources may also be mutually advantageous to both buyers and sellers.

To make gains directly from the agency with which an individual or group buys or sells a product requires some condition giving extraordinary market power or coercive ability. Here a real conflict of interests is involved. Such a situation might exist if, for example, the producers in a certain area were the only ones whose product exhibited a particularly desirable characteristic needed by a certain processor. By banding together, the producers might be able to bargain for a higher price.

The methods employed by any group in improving their bargaining power will depend to a large extent on the market structure of the industry and the way the firms conduct themselves (previously discussed in Chapter 15). The purely competitive nature of the farming industry prohibits individual producers from exercising any market influence. There are just too many firms, and no individual firm produces enough of the total market supply. In the agribusiness industries, the situation is different. In attempting to build market power, a group will try to reduce firm numbers. It may also try to become the price leader in the industry and differentiate its product to reduce the number of substitutes for it and also to raise barriers of entry to the industry. Market shares may be increased by nonprice competition. Building market power is probably more difficult than challenging the market power of existing competitors through sales promotion, new product variations, and price competition, which may be possible through introducing new efficiencies, particularly if the industry's performance is poor.

---

[1] See J. D. Shaffer, "Collective Bargaining for Farmers," in *Increasing Understanding of Public Problems and Policies* (Farm Foundation, 1968), pp. 109–21. Also, "Farm Program and Farm Bargaining," Hearings before the Committee on Agriculture and Forestry, U.S. Senate, April 1968.

It seems clear that bargaining will increase in the future as more prearranged marketing occurs in the form of agreements between producers and market agencies. To exercise a large degree of bargaining power will require effective control over a major portion of the supply, which is difficult for nearly all agricultural products. Gains from increased efficiencies and outside agencies, such as the government and consumers, are easier than gains from one's opponents in a transaction. Cooperatives may have a resurgence in importance, since the individual member can identify his business entity and importance more than if he were just a member of a trade association or large corporation. Organizational economies stemming from integration and other contractual arrangements will change market structure and have an influence on the bargaining position of the parties involved. The issue of how to cut the income pie is one that will certainly persist for all time.

In Chapter 23, we discussed alternate forms in which agriculture might be organized and controlled. The question of commodity pricing will increasingly hinge on who controls the resources and what economic and social goals the controllers have. When farming tends toward the perfectly competitive model, farmers are price takers, for the most part, and all consumers benefit from the resulting relatively low food prices, which come about from the economically rational supply responses of producers.

However, in both the corporate and cooperative models, a greater degree of resource control is attained. A greater concentration of market power is demanded. Higher farm income may be achieved at the expense of retail food prices, assuming a relatively free market. Thus, farm income may increase to the owners and controllers of land—producers in the case of crops, and stockholders in the case of corporations—whereas all consumers must share increased food costs. In the government-controlled model, farm incomes may rise to some predetermined level based on a series of target prices, direct income payments, and other indirect subsidies. The cost of this program would probably come out of increased income taxes from individuals, industry, and commerce.

The economic trade-offs evident in the different resource ownership and control models for farmers and all consumers should play an important role in deciding what sort of an agriculture we want, particularly as the trend away from free markets accelerates. A free-market system, in which prices and production move in response to each other, works only if there is appreciable elasticity to both supply and demand. When rigidity of elasticity sets in through market concentration or institutional regulations, the market system fails. Questions that will persist in all models discussed are: How much is fair farm (producer) income? and, What should be the relative price of food at the retail level?

WHAT IS ENOUGH REGULATION?

The complexity of the food business is growing each day. No longer is it simply sweat and soil that produces our food, but pesticides, additives, antibiotics, and all sorts of chemical phenomena used to increase production, to improve and preserve our products. The two extreme goals within which compromise is necessary are complete protection for the consumer and maximum freedom for businesses to operate. Regulation is a costly business to administer.

Two of the regulatory agencies that are constantly under fire are the federal Food and Drug Administration (FDA) plus its various inspection divisions, and the Interstate Commerce Commission (ICC). Thousands of decisions are required each year, and one party in each case often feels that he was treated unfairly. The validity of labels and advertising, the chemicals in food additives, and administration of grades and standards are just a few of the regulatory activities.

The wheels of regulation often grind slowly. One example will suffice: Armour and Company submitted informally to the FDA an enzyme used in the making of cheese. After certain tests were conducted by the Wisconsin Alumni Research Foundation from 1955 to 1958, the FDA was satisfied that the additive was not harmful to use, but it was not until March 1962 that clearance was finally given to use it.[2] Does this constitute too little, about enough, or too much protection for the consumer?

Freight-rate regulation is another difficult matter. The rates that are set can influence the location of production for commodities, the location of the processing of the product, and many other aspects pertinent to the marketing process. It is virtually impossible for regulatory-agency personnel to keep up with needed changes, as technology continually brings about market disequilibriums and changes in the comparative advantages in production for various areas of the nation. Therefore, what usually takes place is that the firm or industry group that feels it is being treated unfairly asks for public hearings before the regulatory commission. These hearings take time and mean considerable lags in making needed adjustments to facilitate a relatively free-enterprise economy.

Another difficult area is retail food pricing and the availability of

---

2 W. W. Prince, "The Role of Agribusiness in our Food and Fiber Industry—A Ten-Year Estimate," Symposium Proceedings, National Study on Agribusiness Education (Purdue University, September 1962).

certain food items in low-income or ghetto areas. Retail food stores in these areas tend to be relatively higher-cost, lower-profit operations than in most white-collar suburbs, owing to such items as higher rates of pilferage, wider use of credit, and higher insurance rates. Being small stores, they must often buy older merchandise than other stores do, and because of their low-income customers, the stores often do not carry many of the higher-priced or delicatessen food items. Higher costs suggest higher prices in order to maintain a set rate of profit, even if it is not very high. However, such a pricing policy means that the poor pay more for a narrower choice of food items than do more well-to-do families. What kind of pricing policy is equitable, considering the social costs involved as well as the entrepreneur's costs?

There are many other aspects and kinds of regulation. Some examples, such as market orders and production-control legislation, are discussed in detail in other chapters. One thing seems certain. As production and marketing of food products become more and more complex, and as the adoption of new technology continues at a rapid pace, the regulation job increases at an equal or greater rate of complexity. Depending on what position a person finds himself in—consumer, businessman, or politician—there will always be instances to which he can point and no doubt have a legitimate complaint.

ARE PROPERTY TAXES ON FARM LAND TOO HIGH?

Another persisting question is that of how much the land should be taxed and how much owners or controllers of this resource should pay. Property taxes are one of the oldest kinds of taxes. The amount of land a man owned was generally assumed to be indicative of his income and therefore his ability to pay taxes. Local government units have depended upon property taxes for a major share of their operating funds almost since the first taxes were levied. Although taxes on real property have always been of concern to those who impose them and to those who paid taxes, the recent trend in many areas for property taxes to rise faster than incomes has intensified the public's interest. Although taxes are a fixed cost in farm production and therefore do not directly influence the most profitable level of farm output, these "fixed" costs have risen significantly, tending to reduce profits. For example, average taxes per acre of farm real estate in the United States rose from 69 cents in 1950 to $2.79 in 1972 (a 304 percent increase).[3] However, average taxes per $100

---

[3] U.S. Department of Agriculture, *Agricultural Statistics 1972*, pp. 574–76.

of valuation on those same lands rose 17 percent over this period, from $1.00 to $1.17. Average per-acre taxes in 1970 ranged from a high of $7.65 in the Pacific region to a low of 66 cents in the Mountain region. New Jersey had the highest 1970 average per-acre farmland tax, $20.78; and New Mexico had the lowest, 20 cents. Taxes levied on farm real estate provided on estimated $2.5 billion in 1970, compared to $742 million in 1950 and $461 million in 1932.

A large percentage of property taxes have traditionally gone for financing local schools. With increased population, especially in the rural nonfarm classification, the number of pupils to be educated in local schools in rural areas has risen quite sharply in recent years, even though rural farm population is declining. School consolidations, the merging of entire school districts, and rising per-pupil costs have all helped raise the property tax rates.

Land falls into a special category for tax purposes, since the tax cannot be easily shifted to someone other than the owners of the property. The landowner can never escape the tax by moving his land to some other spot. For this reason, one of the most common complaints concerning land taxes is that there is not a fair tax assessment made on the land. As long as farm property taxes are low, it does not much matter if the properties are assessed on an unequal basis. However, when property taxes get to be a large expense to the farm business, there is considerable concern by the individual farmer that he does not pay more than his fair share. The farmer is concerned that there be an equalization of tax assessment within his own assessing district, and he is further concerned that there be equalization between districts. For example, if the assessment is to be 30 percent of the estimated market value of the property, the farmer wants all properties to be assessed at that rate; he also wants the adjoining districts assessed at that rate, because of possible school mergers that may join two districts.

A good tax has the following characteristics, which should be present in the property tax: (1) *Stability*—the tax should not be affected by fluctuations in the level of income, rate of assessment, or method of tax collection. (2) *Predictability*—the tax should provide revenue that can be counted upon by officials of local government and for which a budget can be written. (3) *Adequacy*—the tax should provide funds that are adequate to finance the project for which they are raised. (4) *Balance*—the tax should be complementary to other sources of taxes. (5) *Efficiency*—the tax must be easy to administer and collect. (6) *Popularity*—in order to survive, the tax must be popular enough with the people so that it is not rejected completely.

PLANNING AND ZONING

There is a natural desire to protect against the risk and uncertainty associated with a dynamic society. Change is as certain as death and taxes; however, what it will bring is uncertain. A question asked by people through the ages is how much planning there should be to provide security but not take away too much freedom. There are many types of planning to be considered: economic, social, political, and institutional. Also, the many voiced concerns about the conservation of natural resources for reasons of food production and protection of the environment will be increasingly evident in the resource-use planning process.

One type of planning considers regulations concerning the use of land. In the United States, most of the land-use planning is done in the public interest (from the viewpoint of public health, safety, convenience, and welfare) and protects individual freedom while promoting security through the "due process" clause in the state and federal constitutions. The public interest is made up of a total of many individual freedoms and interests. Limiting the freedom of one or of a few individuals often increases the freedom of many more. For example, limiting a person's freedom to drive at any speed in town increases the freedom of others to walk or drive safely. Limiting the freedom of one person to use land as he wishes may increase the freedom of others to enjoy their land. The real problem in a growing society is to gain the most freedoms by limiting as few as possible.

A common objection of many farmers and other people living in rural areas is that they prefer not to have planning and zoning regulations because they feel that their individual freedoms would be restricted. "I don't want someone telling me what to do and the way I have to build my cattleshed!" might be a typical objection. However, without planning of some kind for land use in the future, any kind of land use may occur—one that may actually restrict other freedoms, including the right to sell property. Lower land values may be expected from certain unrestricted uses of land. An unsupervised dump or junkyard placed across from a beautiful farmstead will undoubtedly be an eyesore for the whole community. On the other hand, if these enterprises are carried on under the supervision of zoning regulations and periodic inspections with appropriate rodent-control provisions, they will not be unsightly or restrict conditions of sale. A lowering of property value usually brings a lowering of tax revenues, and eventually a decline in the kind and quality of public services financed by local property taxes.

As applied to land, most planning of land use utilizes the democratic process. The people involved assume a self-imposed regulation that they consider to be in their best public interests. The planning issue is discussed at open meetings to which the public may come. A vote is taken on the proposed plan, and opportunity for appeal exists for whichever side is unsatisfied. Appeal also exists for those who are adversely affected by the land-use planning. In planning, the people take on a managerial role, which can be voted out or changed when the will of the majority will legally permit changes. Land-use planning is almost never a dictated instrument.

Planning and zoning are quite different. Planning refers to the blueprint that the citizens of a city, county, area, or metropolitan board decide they want. They decide what land they want to be used for residences and farms, which sites should be used or saved for industry and commercial enterprises, and where the parks, schools, and roads should go. There is no edict that tells people what specific things ought to be included in the plan. Each planning commission decides for itself what it wants to present to the public for a vote. Sometimes this process has been called an inefficient way to consider land use. Sometimes it is. But most of the time, it accomplishes what needs to be done so that the people who live in the area derive greater benefits than those that existed under the previous land-use system. In addition, the local people have adopted the land-use plan themselves because they value it as a better use of their land resources.

Zoning is a legal instrument by which the plan is put into effect. Zoning describes regulations that affect the future use of land. Existing uses of land cannot be changed unless by certain special procedures, or unless the use can be declared a nuisance. Zoning regulations set out the minimum-size lot on which one can build a house; they specify whether an enclosed sewerage system must be used or whether septic-tank systems are permitted, whether city water or well water may be used, whether livestock may be housed on the property, how close to the road a building may be constructed, or whether the land can be used for farm, residential, commercial, or industrial use. In most cases, the zoning regulations are simply created to carry out the planning blueprint.

In some areas, subdivision ordinances accompany zoning ordinances. These include building codes, which prescribe the things that have to be done if one builds a house or a commercial building. Sometimes these ordinances also include such items as restrictions concerning the disposal of trash and the amount of floor space a house is required to have.

The jurisdiction of planning and zoning regulations is generally spelled out by state legislation. Usage of planning and zoning depends upon the experience, knowledge, and understanding of the local people involved. This situation means that there certainly will be some arbitrary planning and zoning, depending on the will and ability of those authorized to develop the regulations.

Planning and zoning are a cost to the community, so they must be evaluated just like any public investment. A planning commission operates within a budget provided by the relevant legislative body, which may be a county council, city board, or state legislature. Money is appropriated for specific operations, such as personnel, office expenses, and professional services like mapping and surveying. Usually the costs are higher at the start because of all the technical services required in developing the new plans.

Evaluating planning and zoning regulations is sometimes difficult, especially when a plan is first proposed and efforts are made to motivate general understanding. Much misunderstanding is likely at this point, because planning takes effect over time and in the beginning must deal with intangible rather than tangible things. Another cause for misunderstanding is the fact that although planning and zoning are good examples of the economizing process, they are really nonmarket allocations of resources. In other words, they do not rely on the market-price mechanism to determine building and placing of schools, hospitals, and roads. Although market prices are considered in these endeavors, particularly once the decision about the land use is made, they are not generally a great influence in determining whether or not there will be a park or a museum.

Land-use regulations can be either explicit laws or simply rules adhered to and followed through custom and tradition. Sometimes the simple preference of the majority involved determines what is to be planned, including the jurisdiction involved, how the plan should be presented, who will administer the planning, and when the job is expected to begin and end.

PROPERTY RIGHTS

As a society grows more sophisticated, it also develops an awareness of an increasing number of dimensions in what has been called the "bundle of rights" associated with land and property. For example, before the advent of the airplane, there was little concern about air rights over America and its cities; and until space began to get cluttered with satellites, there was little concern about space litter.

This growing awareness is closely associated with conflicts of interest about the rights that the public should have in private property, and that a private individual should have in public property. For example, when an individual citizen wants to subdivide his land and encourage families to live there whose children will need a new school to be built, causing correspondingly higher taxes for all his neighbors, what should be the rights of the public? What should be the rights of John Doe, citizen, with respect to using a national or state park when that facility is already overused and overcrowded?

There are unresolved issues revolving around farmers and increasing numbers of urban people who view open farmlands as their recreational playgrounds, and county governments who have to provide public services for the "outsiders." Subdividers joust with proponents of open space and the environmentalists. Each group's argument has some merit. The point is that we must reach a decision about how much merit each case has, and make a decision that may have to change with developing pressures of a maturing society.

Perhaps the major reason why there is difficulty with decisions regarding property in this country is that we have been raised with the idea that if a citizen owns something, it is his to do with as he sees fit. Increasingly, there are instances where the public at large has to bear the financial burden for these actions, either because of some type of waste-management treatment that is needed, or because of the derived demands for public services from the people who are involved. Who will bear these increased costs? Who will benefit from these public expenditures? The fairness of these decisions is cause for continual debate.

NONMARKET ALLOCATIONS OF RESOURCES AND THE NEED FOR INCREASED PUBLIC UNDERSTANDING

Increasingly, society has influenced the allocation of money expenditures and revenues, as well as physical resources, on the basis of criteria quite different from those associated with traditional market-price, productivity, supply, and demand factors. For example, "the public" has initiated space-research programs, defense expenditures, pollution and poverty programs, water and sewer grants, and other investment in social capital within a structure expressly excluding individual market considerations. Increasingly, resources are being allocated more on the basis of institutional arrangements and identifications than according to active markets in the resource fields. These nonmarket allocations are usually of a public or quasi-public nature and often involve an international as well as a domestic posture.

Agricultural policy as it has evolved in this country is not synonymous with commodity programs, and food and fiber production and marketing. It is much more. A limited perspective is the main reason why more people must more fully comprehend the breadth and scope of agriculture if the nation is to continue to construct and negotiate better policies relating the farm and nonfarm sectors. The structural, foreign, regulatory, developmental, facilitating, and educational elements of agricultural policy are bridges to a continually better-nourished country and world economy. We cannot allow ourselves the luxury or arrogance of being nearsighted.

SUMMARY

Many topics were discussed in the preceding chapters that could easily have been mentioned here. What the role of agriculture should be in a political economy, what is a "best" resource-use mix for a society, how much economic growth is desirable, and what the "proper" sharing is of private and public interests, market and nonmarket, among a population—all these could be included.

The issues that confronted landowners and farmers during the reign of the pharaohs in Egypt still confront today's landowners and farmers. The only differences between those times and our own is that the social perspective and burden of power and control have changed. These changes necessitate different answers by the different generations. Certain topics will continue to haunt our society and will constantly call forth new analytical efforts on the part of policy makers.

Index

513

Bargaining power, 500
Birthrate, 78
Black Death, 31
Brand name, 361
Brazil, 25, 382
Break-even point, 259
Britain, 29
Broiler, 125
Bundle of rights, 510
Business taxes, 171

C

California Cooperative Extension, 470
California Environmental Quality Act, 50
Capital:
  accumulation, 99
  control, 99
  credit, 99
  debt, 92
  definition of, 91, 92
  depreciation, 93
  equity, 92
  evaluating, 93
  factor of production, 92
  investment, 98
  private, 92
  social, 92, 389
  technology, 99
Capper-Volstead Act, 195
Cartels, 302
Cash-flow:
  budget, 345
  monthly, 369
Census, 74
  of agriculture, 132, 459
Ceteris paribus, 15
Chicago:
  Board of Trade, 161
  Union Stockyards, 161
Chile, 51
China, 25, 476
Chromosomes, 403
Coal, 66, 68–69
Collectional economy, 27
Collusion, 302
Commercial banks, 101
Commodity Credit Corporation, 101
Common Market, 21, 487
Communications, 18, 115, 119
Community goals, 425
Community Resource Development Programs, 453

Comparative advantage, 232, 265, 481
Competition:
  imperfect, 356
  monopolistic, 288, 293, 302
  monopoly, 291, 301, 356
  oligopoly, 288, 294, 302, 356
  price, 296
  pure, 288, 289, 304, 356
Competitive relationship, 267
Complementary relationship, 267
Consumer:
  behavior, 272
  disposable income, 282
  prices, 190
  tastes and preferences, 283
Control of farming, 448
Cooperative Extension Service, 157
Cooperatives, 22, 155, 158, 180, 193
  bargaining, 195, 501
  market organization, 449, 501
  purchasing, 501
  service, 501
Corporate farming, 108, 449
  profits, 171
Corporations, 22, 155, 343, 449
Costs:
  average fixed, 244
  average total unit, 243
  average variable, 244
  externalities, 48
  fixed, 242, 329
  marginal, 243, 252
  mirror image, 245
  per-unit, 242
  total, 243
    fixed, 244
    variable, 244
  variable, 329
Cotton gin, 123
Countries:
  developing, 382
  diet-adequate, 383
  diet-deficit, 383
  underdeveloped, 74, 100
Crawford County, Indiana, 466
Cropland, 53
Crop storage programs, 441
Current ratio, 344

D

Death rate, 74, 79
Decision making, 222, 328, 425